Personal Productivity with Information Technology

Gordon B. Davis

J. David Naumann

The McGraw-Hill Companies, Inc.

New York St. Louis San Francisco Auckland Bogotá
Caracas Lisbon London Madrid Mexico City Milan Montreal
New Delhi San Juan Singapore Sydney Tokyo Toronto

McGraw·Hill

A Division of The McGraw·Hill Companies

Personal Productivity with Information Technology

This book is printed on acid-free paper.

1 2 3 4 5 6 7 8 9 0 FGR FGR 9 0 0 9 8 7

ISBN 0-07-015916-5

This book was set in Galliard.
The sponsoring editor was Rhonda Sands.
The associate editor was Courtney Attwood.
The editorial assistant was Kyle Thomes.
The production supervisor was Natalie Durbin.
The copyeditor was Durthy A. Washington.
Illustrations were done by Rolin Graphics, Inc.
The text designer was Dan Maio.
The cover designer was Juan Vargas.
The compositor was Graphics West, Inc.
Quebecor Printing Fairfield, Inc. was printer and binder.

Library of Congress Card Catalog No. 96-78928

http://www.mhcollege.com

Contents

3 Analyzing Individual Knowledge Work 73

4 Analyzing Collaboration and Work Management Requirements 103

PART 2 Data and Software Management for Knowledge Work Productivity   134

7 Accessing Organizational Data 203

8 Accessing External Data 237

PART 3 Designing and Implementing Productivity Enhancements 266

9 Selecting an Approach to Computer Solutions 269

10 Developing a Simple Program 305

11 Designing and Implementing a User Interface 341

12 Developing Solutions Using Database Software 373

13 Evaluating, Refining, and Integrating Applications 403

PART 4 Information Technology Infrastructures 432

14 Anticipating Core Information Technology 435

Preface

◇ ◇ ◇ ◇ ◇ ◇ ◇ ◇

This text originated as a response to a persistent question by students: "What course should I take to be more effective in using computers in my work?" These students had learned the fundamentals of personal computer software and had perhaps taken an introductory course on computing or information systems, but they wanted to know more. Unfortunately, the courses available to them were oriented toward specialists. These students did not want to become computer scientists, programmers, or information systems analysts; they just wanted to be more productive in using information technology. This text was developed to meet that need.

Personal Productivity with Information Technology is designed to be used in a wide variety of college or university courses. It is geared toward students majoring in areas such as business, liberal arts, social science, sciences, and engineering. The theme of productivity in using information technology is common to all. Consequently, the text could be used in any of the following courses:

1. *An information systems course.* The text fits the specifications for course IS97.2 of the Information Systems Curriculum Model developed as a joint effort by the Association for Computing Machinery, the Association of Information Technology Professionals (formerly Data Processing Management Association) and the Association for Information Systems. The IS97.2 course was designed for undergraduates; however, a similar course can be designed for MBA students without significant prior computing experience who desire a concentration in Information Systems.

2. *A business course.* Business students indicate that they want more education in how to use information technology. The elementary exposure they receive to microcomputer software through a general

course in information systems does not satisfy their needs. This course addresses these needs directly.

3. *A general service course.* Most graduates of universities (including students in fields such as economics, social sciences, behavioral sciences, and humanities) will seek positions oriented to knowledge work. These students will need conceptual and practical knowledge in how to be more effective in using information technology. A course on personal productivity with information technology provides important preparation for such positions. For those already employed, this book can be the basis for professional development study, either individually or in formal courses.

The course using the text may be a first or second course in a sequence (assuming students have had an opportunity to become acquainted with microcomputer software packages). For business students, the other course (assumed to be a broad introduction to computers and information systems in organizations) can either precede or follow the course using this text. For non-business students, this may be the principal course beyond an introduction to microcomputer use. It develops the skills and abilities needed to learn and effectively use the specialized applications of their field.

The course may be a valuable addition to the sequence of courses for information systems specialists, as it provides the future specialist with insight into individual systems and how they can be built and supported. Design, support, and management of individual systems is part of the mission of the information management function. The course also provides a simplified introduction to the principles and procedures of information systems analysis and design. Since it follows a process that is similar to the development of large systems, the small systems development approach can be extended in later courses. With this approach the student is able to grasp the entire systems development process; subsequent coursework can amplify the process by adding the concepts and procedures needed to develop large systems that have multiple users.

The text has been developed in courses in the Carlson School of Management. Colleagues in other schools of management, computer science, and social sciences have provided encouragement and ideas. We acknowledge the following reviewers for their helpful suggestions: John Day, Ohio University; David L. Feinstein, University of South Alabama; Len Fertuck, University of Toronto; Dr. John Gorgone, Bentley College; M.H. Jenkins, University of Baltimore; Ruth C. King, University of Pittsburgh; William D. Nance, San Jose State University; Douglas Vogel, University of Arizona. Janice DeGross, Executive Assistant, gave invaluable assistance in the development process for the text. Durthy A.

Washington, copyeditor, provided invaluable input on matters of style, organization, and presentation.

This is a first attempt at developing an innovative course. Consequently, issues concerning coverage, content, and pedagogy will be resolved as the text is used. We invite your comments.

Students: How to Use This Text

Information technology is as fundamental to modern knowledge work as reading, writing, and arithmetic. Although technology changes rapidly, its basic concepts and principles do not change. In developing this text, the authors had two basic assumptions:

1. Human capabilities can be extended and enhanced by the use of information technology. Therefore, by taking advantage of information technology tools, humans can perform work more efficiently and effectively.

2. Everyone, not just those who work in technical fields, should be able to use technology for more productive work.

Recently, there has been a fundamental shift in society from manual and clerical work to knowledge work: human mental work performed to generate useful information. Performing this work requires knowledge workers with the ability to obtain information and use it to design and carry out analytical and information processing activities. (Examples of knowledge workers include analysts, managers, accountants, programmers, physicians, teachers, lawyers, and researchers.) Many of the critical activities in knowledge work can be performed more productively with information technology.

Most graduates of colleges and universities will be knowledge workers all of their lives. A course on personal productivity with information technology provides important preparation for them. For those who are already employed as knowledge workers, this book can be the basis for professional development study, either individually or in formal courses.

Students invariably differ in their knowledge and expertise of computing. While some have substantial background and experience, others have had only modest exposure to personal computer hardware and software. This text can be very useful to both types of students:

◆ Those without significant background in information technology will learn new ways to use technology to enhance their productivity. They will receive broad exposure to various methods and a range of exercises for applying information technology to their work.

◆ Those with significant experience in computing will learn a new way of thinking about the use of information technology. Many students with experience still have "holes" in their knowledge and experience relative to knowledge work, which are filled in by the text. The text will also help them achieve a completeness in their mental model of how to be more productive with information technology.

The text does not depend upon a depth of computing knowledge. However, it does assume that the reader has had introductory exposure to personal computers and commonly used personal computer software such as word processing, spreadsheets, and electronic mail. Students who wish to strengthen or assess their understanding of core information technology before proceeding too far in the text may read Chapter 14 (Core Information Technology) early rather than leaving it as a later topic.

The text combines a discussion of concepts and methods with practical exercises. The concepts and methods are designed for long-lasting knowledge; the practical exercises are designed to achieve an ability to apply the knowledge. Details of current technology are de-emphasized except as needed to illustrate concepts and support exercises.

The text is divided into four parts.

◆ Part 1 (Chapters 1 through 4) stresses an understanding of productivity and the role of information management in productivity. It introduces the analysis of individual tasks and activities in knowledge work and surveys the analysis of requirements for collaborative work and knowledge work management.

◆ Part 2 (Chapters 5 through 8) focuses on data and communication required to do knowledge work and the concepts and tools needed to acquire and manage data.

◆ Part 3 (Chapters 9 through 13) explains how to modify and enhance information technology tools to support productive work. It includes information on prototyping, customizing packages, and designing and programming simple applications.

◆ Part 4 (Chapters 14 through 16) addresses two primary issues: (1) defining and developing an appropriate individual information technology infrastructure, and (2) relating to the formal organizational information systems function.

The text places important responsibilities on the student. Because the material is designed to build formal knowledge about productivity in knowledge work by using information technology, the explanations emphasize concepts, principles, software functionality, and software functions. The text does not focus on teaching any single software package.

However, given basic concepts applicable to a variety of software packages, it is relatively simple for a student to map concepts, functionality, and functions to the features in a specific package. In other words, if the text discusses the concept of reuse and the related functionality of software templates, it is easy to locate the template feature in a specific software package and use it in an exercise. This means a student must learn to use the tutorial and Help features of different software packages.

Student differences in prior experience with software packages can be used to increase both individual and group learning. Those who already know a software feature will gain added insight as they explain it to those who have not used it before. Prior knowledge can also allow a student to explore features in more depth, taking advantage of the concepts and principles of the text to enrich the discovery process.

The authors welcome student feedback.

Gordon B. Davis   gdavis@csom.umn.edu
J. David Naumann   dnaumann@csom.umn.edu
Carlson School of Management
University of Minnesota
Minneapolis, Minnesota 55455

December 1996

Personal Productivity
with Information Technology

Productivity in Knowledge Work

◇ ◇ ◇ ◇ ◇ ◇ ◇ ◇ ◇ ◇ ◇ ◇ ◇ ◇

Part 1 (Chapter 1 through 4) provides definitions and concepts that focus on how to achieve improvements in knowledge work productivity. It establishes the need for various levels of information management, describes how individual and group information systems fit into the organizational information management system, and defines the requirements for systems that support knowledge work. It also provides the conceptual and system background for Parts 2 through 4, focuses on the requirements, design, and development of "small systems" for individual and group activity, and presents simple processes that can be applied by a broad range of users. Chapter exercises help make the concepts presented concrete by enabling readers to apply them to knowledge work situations and to develop expertise in analyzing user system requirements.

Chapter 1, Knowledge Work, Knowledge Workers, and Productivity This chapter explains the nature of knowledge work and how it employs data, information, knowl-

edge, and mental models. It defines the concept of productivity in knowledge work and describes the impact of elements such as concentration, attention, and automatic processing on work productivity. It also explains the impact of information technology on work productivity and describes how technology can be used to expand and conserve knowledge work resources and compensate for limitations on human information processing. The chapter concludes with a discussion of various methods that can be used to improve productivity through efficiency in knowledge work processes and procedures, such as reducing time and effort, reusing processes and procedures, eliminating process redundancy and delay, and minimizing errors and bias.

Chapter 2, Knowledge Workers and Information Management This chapter provides a comprehensive example of how a knowledge worker can apply information technology to improve productivity. It explains individual responsibilities in knowledge work systems in both individual and collaborative work and explores the differences

among individual systems, systems supporting collaborative work, and organization-wide information management systems. The chapter introduces the use of standard and custom templates in improving knowledge work efficiency. It explains individual responsibilities in knowledge work systems, such as using personal information management infrastructures to support work, using personal systems to systematize and structure work, accessing knowledge work information, and managing individual knowledge work. It also explains the need for organizational and individual information management systems in terms of infrastructures, architectures, processes, and functions, and compares the system development risks involved in organizational versus individual information management processes.

Chapter 3, Analyzing Individual Knowledge Work

This chapter begins the process of defining information and information management requirements by identifying individual work tasks and activities. This chapter shows readers how to analyze tasks and assign relative importance to activities that provide the basis for decisions about acquiring software packages and making personal investments in learning how to use them. It defines four types of knowledge work activities (acquiring knowledge, designing, making decisions, and communicating) and four types of supplementary activities (creating input data, formatting documents and output data, filing and retrieving documents and data, and receiving and distributing information). The chapter concludes with a detailed description and examples of task/activity analysis.

Chapter 4, Analyzing Collaboration and Work Management Requirements

This chapter extends the process of defining requirements to collaborative work and knowledge work management. It explains the need for coordinating and managing group processes and describes the unique requirements associated with the management of knowledge work. It also identifies numerous factors underlying requirements for knowledge work management and describes various methods and software for maintaining work motivation, setting priorities, scheduling, switching tasks, and establishing and maintaining readiness to work. The chapter concludes with guidelines for analyzing support requirements for knowledge work management.

The definitions, concepts, and requirements processes presented in Part 1 relate to the nature and design of systems that support knowledge work. The remainder of the text explains data and software management for knowledge work productivity, describes the processes for designing and implementing productivity enhancements with information technology, surveys core information technologies, and explores issues in building an information technology infrastructure.

CHAPTER 1

Knowledge Work, Knowledge Workers, and Productivity

After completing this chapter, you should be able to:

- Give examples of knowledge work activities and supplemental activities.
- Define the six elements of knowledge work.
- Give examples of knowledge workers.
- Differentiate among knowledge, data, and information.
- Explain the differences among the four types of knowledge.
- Explain the concept of mental models.
- Explain concentration and attention.
- Describe the impact of information technology on knowledge work.
- Describe the three factors that impact knowledge work productivity.

- Explain the impact of motivation, automatic processing, and attentional resources on task performance.
- Describe some of the limitations on human information processing.
- Describe the four key factors that impact knowledge work productivity.
- Describe some of the key factors that impact efficiency of knowledge work processes and procedures.
- Describe the three types of investments required for improved knowledge work productivity.

KEY TERMS AND CONCEPTS

This chapter introduces the following key terms and concepts, listed in the order in which they appear:

knowledge work	concentration	process
knowledge worker	information technology	procedure
information	productivity	redundancy
data	motivation	error
knowledge	expertise	bias
mental model	information processing	
attention	creativity	

Productivity varies significantly among individuals performing knowledge work. Individuals who learn how to be more productive increase their value to an organization and enhance their career potential. Improved productivity in knowledge work requires effective and efficient use of information technology. This chapter explains concepts, principles, and methods for improving productivity through information technology.

Productivity in knowledge work is important to both university students and career professionals. The issue of knowledge work productivity is also important for management, as Peter Drucker, a well-known management scholar, points out:

> To make knowledge work more productive will be the great management task of this century, just as to make manual work productive was the great management task of the last century.
> —*The Age of Discontinuity*, 1978 ◊

> The primary resource in post-capitalist society will be knowledge, and the leading special groups will be "knowledge workers."
> —*Post Capitalist Society*, 1993 ◊

Knowledge Work

◆ ◆

Knowledge work is human mental work performed to generate useful information. In doing it, knowledge workers access data, use knowledge, employ mental models, and apply significant concentration and attention.

The definition of knowledge work emphasizes both results (generating useful information) and processes. Another way to understand knowledge work is through the activities that accomplish knowledge work tasks. Activities such as the following differentiate knowledge workers from production and clerical workers:

◊ Scanning a broad range of information sources
◊ Monitoring specific information sources
◊ Searching for information
◊ Modeling objects or processes
◊ Planning activities and resource use
◊ Organizing responsibilities and events
◊ Scheduling activities and resource use
◊ Authoring knowledge work outputs
◊ Performing evaluations
◊ Formulating problem definitions
◊ Analyzing alternatives
◊ Choosing among alternatives
◊ Formulating plans for action
◊ Presenting the results of an analysis

◊ Persuading others to adopt a plan

◊ Motivating a behavior change

Several characteristics common to these activities tie to the definition of knowledge work. The expected result or output is useful information. Knowledge workers performing the activities access data and employ knowledge that they have or can personally obtain. Knowledge workers develop and follow a mental model in the process and in forming the outputs. Knowledge work requires active mental involvement. It cannot be done automatically.

Knowledge workers must perform some clerical work to support their knowledge work activities. These supplemental activities may include:

◊ Keyboarding (typing text or entering data)

◊ Formatting working documents and outputs

◊ Filing

◊ Starting up or shutting down computers

◊ Entering database queries

◊ Retrieving filed information

◊ Organizing files

◊ Opening mail

◊ Distributing outputs

◊ Backing up stored data

Knowledge work can be described in terms of type of work, objectives, and four dominant process characteristics: accessing data, using knowledge, employing mental models, and applying concentration and attention (see Figure 1-1). These elements are defined as follows:

◊ *Type of work.* Knowledge work involves human information processing. It is cognitive rather than physical work.

◊ *Objective.* The objective of knowledge work is to generate useful information such as analyses, evaluations, instructions, programs, plans, assurances, reasoning, or arguments.

◊ *Process characteristics.*

  ◆ *Accessing data.* Most knowledge work tasks involve acquisition of data, either by direct data capture procedures or by retrieving from stored data.

  ◆ *Using knowledge.* Knowledge workers employ knowledge to perform task activities. They either have the required knowledge (internal) or know where and how to find it (external).

  ◆ *Employing mental models.* Knowledge workers employ mental models of the processes to be followed and the outputs to be produced.

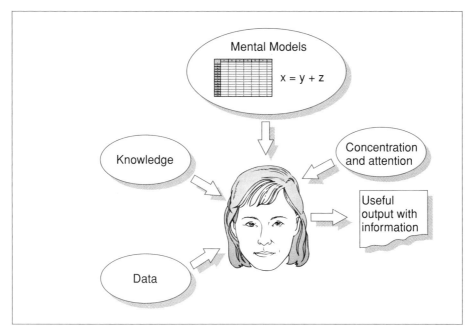

FIGURE I-I   *Knowledge work*

◆ *Applying significant concentration and attention.* Knowledge work is not effortless; it requires mental or cognitive effort and significant concentration and attention.

These six elements will be explained further in the remainder of this chapter. They differentiate knowledge work from production work that involves physical labor to produce physical output. They also differentiate knowledge work from clerical work, which is dominated by organization rules and processing procedures (rather than individual mental models) and requires less personal knowledge, concentration, and attention.

Knowledge Workers

Examples of **knowledge workers** include financial analysts, systems analysts, managers, accountants, and lawyers. They are valued for their knowledge and expertise. Although there are exceptions, knowledge workers tend to be in professional positions that require a university education as well as creative, innovative, and problem-solving skills.

Based on education and experience, knowledge workers are expected to have the personal knowledge and skills required to perform the activities of knowledge work. They are expected to know the domain (such as law, medicine, accounting) in which they work, plus the processes and procedures for performing the work. Although an organization may provide some procedures for knowledge workers to follow, they are expected to be able to apply generally accepted procedures and to develop processes and procedures appropriate to the specific organization and its situation. They are expected to be able to employ appropriate computer software and electronics communications.

Examples

An accountant is expected to understand generally accepted accounting concepts, rules, and procedures. Although the company may have some standard reports and practices, much of the work to be performed will depend on formal knowledge the accountant has obtained through education and experience. The accountant is expected to know about and locate sources of information when required for knowledge work tasks. ◆

An information systems analyst is expected to understand concepts, principles, and practices relative to the analysis, design, and implementation of information system applications. The organization may supply a development methodology and related tools, but the analyst is expected to have the formal knowledge required to apply methodologies and tools. When additional data or information is needed to design and implement an application, the analyst is expected to know how to locate, access, and use it. ◆

To perform the activities commonly associated with knowledge work tasks, knowledge workers should have a working knowledge of several software packages. These include a word processing program, plus six other packages (disregarding packages with multiple purposes): (1) a spreadsheet processor, (2) electronic mail and Internets, (3) presentation graphics, (4) statistics, (5) a database package for structured data, and (6) a database package for unstructured, text data.

Data and Information in Knowledge Work

◆ ◆

Knowledge work involves both data and information. The terms are often used interchangeably because one person's data may be another's information. However, it is possible to make a distinction between them.

Information is the output from knowledge work. It provides the recipient with some understanding, insight, conclusion, decision, confirmation, or recommendation. The information may be a report, an analysis, data organized in a meaningful output, a verbal response, a graph, picture, or video. Information has value only if it is valuable to the recipient.

Data consists of representations of events, people, resources, or conditions. The representation can be in a variety of forms, such as numbers, codes, words, text, graphs, or pictures. Data is the raw material used to produce information. Data becomes information when processed into a form that is meaningful to the recipient.

Since the output of knowledge work is information, information concepts and the benefits associated with information will be described in more detail. Data will be described further in Part 2.

Information Concepts and Definitions

Information is defined as data that produces one of the following results:

1. *It builds or adds to representations.* For example, a sales representative reports a sale. The data builds a representation of the sale. Availability and shipping date data add to the representation of the sale. Observations of customer behavior can be used to build a model representing customer response.

2. *It corrects or confirms previous information.* For example, a quarterly financial report may correct prior information on performance or may confirm the prior information based on partial data.

3. *It has surprise value* (it tells something the receiver did not know or could not predict). For example, an analysis of profitability for different products may yield a surprise relative to "most profitable" and "least profitable."

4. *It reduces uncertainty.* For example, given uncertainty about future performance of job applicants, data about college grades (if correlated with performance) will reduce the uncertainty.

5. *It changes the probabilities of expected outcomes.* For example, probabilities of making a sale to a customer who walks into the salesroom may be 1 in 20. Knowing that the customer has purchased from the company before may change the probabilities to 1 in 5 and therefore affect action to be taken. (See Figure 1-2.)

Data items associated with any of these five outcomes are understood to be information. The information has value, and individuals and organizations are willing to expend resources to obtain it. It has real or perceived benefit in connection with current or prospective actions or decisions. The relationship of data to information is that of raw material to finished product. Information that results from one knowledge worker's activity may be the raw material for another's.

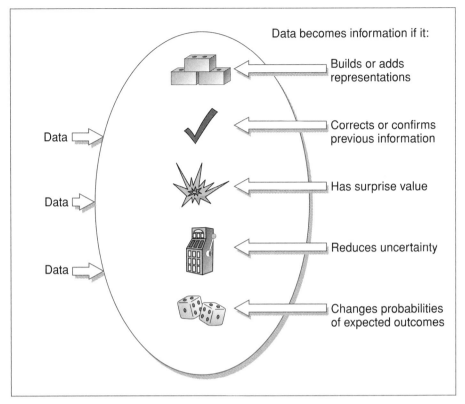

FIGURE 1-2 *Data and information*

Example

The details of customer sales by a sales representative are meaningful information to the sales representative, but they are data to the marketing executive and must be processed and summarized in order to be meaningful. ◆

A characteristic common to both information and data is that they can be used many times in a variety of different ways. Depending on the situation, information may gain or lose value when shared or widely distributed. In some cases, information may gain value through broad acceptance and use. In other cases, information is most valuable when it can be limited to one individual or to a small group.

Examples

Production data may be used in a variety of reports. The multiple use does not diminish its value. ◆

When financial reports are made broadly available to the stock market, the information is reflected in the price of the stock and, therefore, has no value to an individual investor. If only one investor had access to the financial reports, the information might have very high value in making market transactions.   ◆

Benefits of Information

Creating information or adding to existing information is one of the most important ways knowledge workers add value to an organization. Information benefits an organization if it is used in:

◊   Aligning organizational objectives

◊   Coordinating activities

◊   Building and maintaining the mental models of organizational participants

◊   Building databases for future use

◊   Building expertise in organizational members

◊   Designing organizational processes and procedures

◊   Directing and controlling processes

◊   Formulating problems

◊   Analyzing alternatives

◊   Making decisions

◊   Motivating organizational activities

The value of information communicated in an organization is increased if the sender formulates the content so that it:

◊   accurately communicates the factual content,

◊   conveys the desired meaning, and

◊   motivates human action in the desired way.

The impact of adding valuable information is illustrated by examples for decision making, setting the context for action, and building expertise.

Examples

Information is valuable in decision making. In decision making, a decision maker will select among alternatives on the basis of information at hand. New information clearly adds value if it results in a different decision with improved outcomes. New information that does not change the decision but increases the confidence of decision makers can also be valuable in organizational processes.   ◆

Information is valuable in setting the context for action. Models of the enterprise and its environment are employed in management and operations. These models exist within the minds of managers and operations personnel and are reflected in budgets, plans, and other documents. In order to incorporate current conditions and future expectations, the models must be updated by information. Reports, analyses, and communications result in changes in the model or reinforcement of the existing models. Changes in the models will influence the identification of problems and opportunities faced by the enterprise. ◆

Information is important in building expertise. The value of information utilized in a decision cannot be separated from the knowledge of the decision maker. In other words, much of the information that individuals accumulate and store (or internalize) is not earmarked for any particular decision or problem. Success in locating and solving problems depends largely on a decision maker's ability to draw on background and experience for analogies, similar situations, problem solutions, and models. ◆

Knowledge in Knowledge Work

◆ ◆ ◆ ◆ ◆ ◆ ◆ ◆ ◆ ◆ ◆ ◆ ◆ ◆ ◆ ◆ ◆ ◆ ◆ ◆

Knowledge is high-level, value-added information. Knowledge is not well defined because it is a compound construct consisting of multiple dimensions. One way to view knowledge is as sets of data items and information organized and processed to convey understanding, experience, accumulated learning, and expertise as they apply to a given problem or activity. When a set of data items about an organizational event is processed to extract critical implications and reflect experience and expertise, the result provides the recipient with high-value organizational knowledge. Knowledge allows a person to work more effectively, be more efficient in use of time and data, and make better decisions. As described in Chapter 3, building and maintaining knowledge is an important class of knowledge work tasks.

The knowledge and expertise that knowledge workers bring to activities for accomplishing a task have a significant impact on selection and use. This knowledge consists of four types: formal (declarative) knowledge, procedural knowledge, meta knowledge, and impressionistic knowledge (see Figure 1-3).

1. *Formal (declarative) knowledge.* General knowledge of problem solving and definitions, general principles, concepts, and procedures related to a domain of work. It is the type of knowledge that is structured and communicated by textbooks and courses. This knowledge is important in skill development because it provides a starting point and foundation for learning procedural knowledge. Formal or declarative knowledge of methods of problem solving is applicable to broad classes of problems. General problem-solving knowledge is often knowledge of processes that

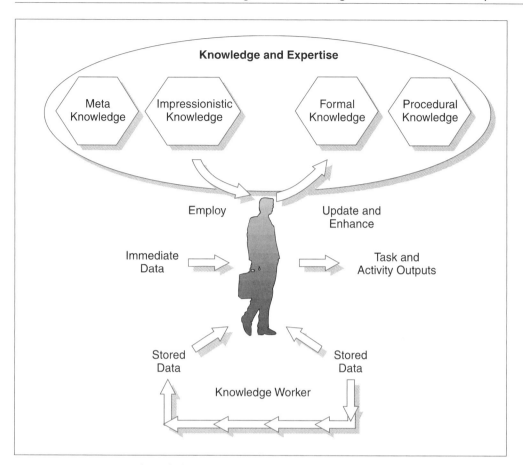

FIGURE 1-3   *Use of knowledge, expertise, and data*

help organize and transform data. This knowledge can aid in retrieving data to be included in specific problem solving, although it often lacks the focus provided by more specific procedural knowledge. Formal problem-solving knowledge sometimes provides a basis for creativity because seemingly unrelated knowledge is searched for analogies and insights. When these are found, new creative solutions may result.

2. *Procedural knowledge.* Knowledge about how to do something. Procedural knowledge is more informal and not as easily communicated by lecture or textbook. It is the ability to make effective and efficient use of the most appropriate tools and techniques available. It tends to be associated with a specific domain of work—tasks or activities. Depending upon the knowledge work task, procedural knowledge may be as simple as using a word processor or as complex as designing an integer programming solution. There is a connection between declarative knowledge and procedural

knowledge. When declarative knowledge is used to solve a specific problem, the solution procedure becomes part of the problem solver's procedural or informal knowledge.

3. *Meta knowledge.* Knowledge about knowledge. Meta knowledge concerns knowing how knowledge and expertise are organized and how to locate and access the knowledge. It is knowing what you know and don't know. It controls the application of other knowledge because it includes how individuals structure their problem solving environment, manage knowledge work, decide to employ tools, and seek advice. Meta knowledge is developed by education, experience, and reflection. The most valuable expert will have well developed meta knowledge. In terms of data, meta knowledge includes knowledge about the data environment—the location and means of access to relevant data.

4. *Impressionistic knowledge.* Although impressionistic knowledge is hidden in the sense that it is not formal and well structured, it represents the sum total of experience. It helps a knowledge worker arrive at impressions without systematic consideration of formal problem solving. It is "creative expertise" or "intuition."

The development of expertise by knowledge workers involves solving progressively more demanding and varied problems by applying formal/declarative knowledge. This leads to the development of informal/procedural knowledge. The process is guided by the application of meta knowledge. Selection of problems and goals is associated with impressionistic knowledge.

The implications of the different types of expertise relative to data requirements are that a knowledge worker needs all four types of knowledge and, therefore, must acquire and process data associated with all four knowledge types. Knowledge workers should build a good knowledge base with formal/declarative knowledge and this knowledge base should be increased by formal or informal education. Knowledge workers should seek to obtain specific training and experience and to apply general knowledge in specific problem-solving situations in order to build up a procedural knowledge base. They should pay attention to data that will help build meta knowledge and impressionistic knowledge.

Experts typically develop problem-solving skills within specific domains such as accounting, finance, or marketing or even narrower domains such as accounting for acquisitions and mergers. Their expertise involves heuristics (rules of thumb) that allow them to quickly work through large quantities of data to focus on the critical variables. One difference between an expert and a novice is the ability of an expert to focus quickly on critical issues, while the novice tends to be less focused. Domain experts can more easily and accurately specify data requirements than novices.

Mental Models

◆ ◆ ◆ ◆ ◆ ◆ ◆ ◆ ◆ ◆ ◆ ◆ ◆ ◆ ◆ ◆ ◆ ◆ ◆

Mental models are deeply ingrained assumptions, generalizations, or even pictures or images that influence how we understand the world and how we take action.
—Peter M. Senge, *The Fifth Discipline*, Doubleday, New York, 1990, p. 8 ◊

Senge uses mental models in a broad context and identifies them as one of the five disciplines that build organizational learning. (The other four are systems thinking, personal mastery, building shared vision, and team learning.) In the context of individual knowledge work processes, **mental models** are the mental representation of methods, processes, and procedures individuals employ to obtain data and process it to produce information outputs. An illustration of a simple mental model is a set of steps that an analyst has in memory that describe how to search a company database to locate and analyze data. The mental model might include a representation of methods to apply in producing an explanation to accompany a report. A more complex mental model might include representations of a process of looking for clues or patterns of performance that indicate serious problems. It might also contain analytical procedures to determine if the initial indicators were correct and to formulate recommendations.

Mental models are part of the expertise and procedural knowledge of individuals. The models are built through education, training, and experience. An individual's mental models might include mental pointers to external sources such as reference books, experts, and databases that complement what the individual knows. Rich mental models distinguish experts in a problem area from novices. They directly contribute to knowledge work productivity. For instance, in trying to resolve a complex problem, a novice will engage in a difficult, lengthy, and exhaustive search for a solution, while the expert will make use of a heuristic process in a mental model to arrive rapidly at a satisfactory solution.

Concentration, Attention, and Automatic Processing

◆ ◆ ◆ ◆ ◆ ◆ ◆ ◆ ◆ ◆ ◆ ◆ ◆ ◆ ◆ ◆ ◆ ◆ ◆

Attention and concentration are related concepts. **Attention**, in knowledge work, is focusing one's mind on a task. **Concentration** is centering time and effort on a task and eliminating distractions. A knowledge worker may apply different levels of concentration and attention in performing the activities for a task. Knowledge work activities tend to require significant concentration and attention. Some tasks and activities require extended periods of high concentration and attention. Examples are planning and creating overall mental structures to guide detailed work. Creating the outline for a report is the overall structure that guides the preparation of individual sections. Other knowledge work activities can be done in short bursts of attention. For example, reviewing a section of text in a report, an analysis, or a graph may often be done in a fraction of the time required to prepare the material for review. Often, well-formulated documentation supporting a recommended decision that took extended, concentrated effort to prepare may be reviewed in a short decision session.

Humans have limited cognitive resources, so they can concentrate on and attend to only a limited number of activities. The opposite of concentration and attention is automatic processing. Some activities are almost automatic and require little concentration or attention; others require full mental concentration and attention. In knowledge work, it is sometimes possible to work on more than one activity at the same time if one of the activities is mainly automatic.

Information Technology

◆ ◆

Information technology includes both computer and communication technologies. The term is broadly applied to computer hardware, computer software, input and output devices, visual display devices, communication networks, and communication hardware and software. It includes a wide variety of applications for information processing and communication.

The use of information technology in knowledge work is pervasive. It complements the mental and clerical capabilities of humans and enhances the performance of most knowledge work activities. Information technology is the relevant technology for improved productivity in knowledge work because the inputs are data and information, the processes involve communication as well as accessing and processing data, and the outputs are information. Productivity may be improved by the use of information technology that supports communication, data acquisition, processing, and output of information. In addition, information technology can support processes for managing knowledge work, building and maintaining knowledge, accessing knowledge, and using mental models. Information technology enables improved productivity in knowledge work, but it does not happen automatically simply by applying it. Results are most likely to be achieved when information technology is combined with processes and procedures that take advantage of the technology capabilities and functions.

Knowledge Work Productivity

◆ ◆ ◆ ◆ ◆ ◆ ◆ ◆ ◆ ◆ ◆ ◆ ◆ ◆ ◆ ◆ ◆ ◆

Productivity in knowledge work is a major concern of management. Examples of solutions proposed to improve productivity are re-engineering of work processes, reduced staffing, increased training, increased individual empowerment in work activities, and organization redesign. Information technology is a part of all of these solutions. This section will focus on how information technology affects the productivity of knowledge work.

Productivity is a simple concept when applied to the same physical products. **Productivity** consists of the resources required to produce one unit of a product.

Example

Farming productivity can be expressed as the human labor, capital, fertilizer, and other raw materials to produce a bushel of grain. If there are improvements in one or more of these factors, there will be an increase in productivity. The measurement of productivity centers on efficiency: the resources to produce a specified output.   ◆

It is difficult to measure productivity in knowledge work (see Figure 1-4). Traditional productivity measures are inadequate. Are two analyses worth twice as much as one? Is a twenty-page report twice the worth of a ten-page report? At what point is the marginal value of more knowledge work activity less than its marginal cost? Cost may not be as important as quality or usefulness of results.

Knowledge workers add value to an organization when they accomplish information-producing processes and procedures that must be performed in order for the work of the organization to be done. In evaluating the cost of the work and value to the organization, cost is lowest when the results are produced with the lowest expenditure of time and energy while value is highest when the output meets the needs of the organization. A fit with organization needs is most likely if the output reflects use of relevant data, knowledge, expertise, and creativity.

There are three major sources of change in knowledge work productivity: expansion and conservation of knowledge work resources, work effectiveness, and work efficiency. The first affects the availability of time and energy for

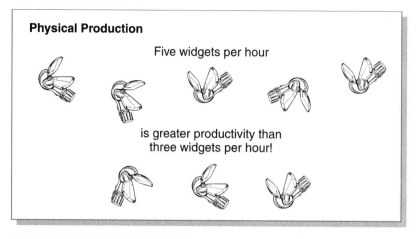

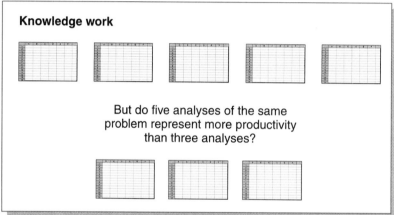

FIGURE 1-4 *Productivity comparison: physical production and knowledge work production*

knowledge work, the second affects the value of the output, and the third affects the cost of performing work activities to produce outputs (see Figure 1-5). All three change factors are affected by information technology. They are discussed in more detail in the following sections.

1. *Expansion and conservation of knowledge work resources.* A characteristic of knowledge work is that total time available may be fixed but the available mental and physical energy that can be applied to the work is affected by motivation, scheduling, automatic processing, and compensating for limitations on human information processing.

2. *Work effectiveness.* Work effectiveness is the quality and usefulness of the knowledge work outputs. It is measured or evaluated in terms of organization needs. Improving effectiveness may involve expertise and creativity,

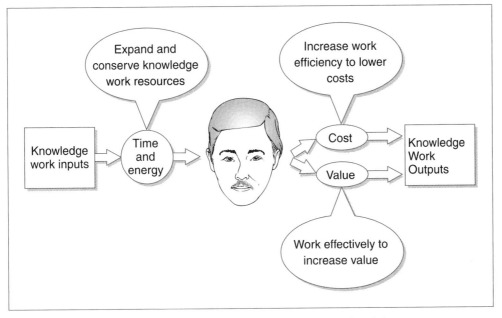

FIGURE I-5   *Three sources of change in knowledge work productivity*

increasing extent or intensity of the knowledge work processes, more complete and timely results, and use of methods not possible without computers.

3. *Work efficiency.* Work efficiency is a measure of resources expended—such as time, effort, equipment, or supplies—for a specified output. Efficiency can be improved by saving time and effort for processes and procedures, spending less time to design the work (reuse of processes and procedures), eliminating redundancy and delay, and minimizing input and process errors (because corrections add significant cost).

Improving Productivity by Expanding and Conserving Knowledge Work Resources

◆   ◆   ◆   ◆   ◆   ◆   ◆   ◆   ◆   ◆   ◆   ◆   ◆   ◆   ◆   ◆   ◆   ◆   ◆

Knowledge work time available is limited since there are only so many work hours. The amount of attention that knowledge workers can apply to tasks is also limited, so it is a scarce resource. However, the level of effort and energy used to apply to knowledge work can be increased or decreased by the level of motivation. Productivity is improved by knowledge work management and work design. These elements expand knowledge work energy through improved motivation. They also conserve scarce knowledge work resources by scheduling and communication, conserve scarce attentional resources by automatic processing, and compensate for limitations on human information processing.

Expanding Knowledge Work Mental Energy Through Improved Motivation

Motivation in knowledge work consists of motives and incentives that move a person to apply mental and physical energy to perform knowledge work and achieve intended results. High motivation tends to increase individual commitment to quality performance. High motivation also tends to energize people and increase the cognitive resources that are applied to the activities being performed. Bored or unmotivated persons tend to reduce the attention, concentration, and energy devoted to a task. In other words, increased motivation increases both the willingness and ability of individuals and groups to perform work. While some sources of motivation are not under the control of individual knowledge workers, three ways to increase work motivation are task design with feedback, task design with frequent completions, and effective scheduling. Information technology is relevant to motivation because of its use in activities, its effect on job design, and its use in scheduling of work.

1. *Task design with feedback.* Motivation is affected by the task to be performed. It is increased by meaningful, complete tasks. Individual control over the execution of the task improves motivation. Goals and standards for the task and frequent, meaningful feedback are also effective in motivation.

2. *Task design with frequent completion.* Individuals tend to be motivated by task completion. In other words, completing a task, however small, provides positive feedback and motivation. This suggests that an individual should break down large tasks into smaller tasks, each task taking a fairly short time (perhaps no more than one week). Each small task has a well-defined deliverable. An example of this approach to individual motivation is the practice of breaking computer program development into small modules that can be completed in a short period of time (such as a week).

3. *Effective scheduling.* Motivation may be enhanced by the way in which work is scheduled. Since an individual probably has a mixture of difficult cognitive work and relatively simple clerical work (rest work), scheduling difficult cognitive work at times of highest energy will result in more achievement of deliverables and increased motivation from the completion. The rest work is scheduled during times when motivation is low or during periods of rest following hard cognitive work.

Conserving Scarce Knowledge Work Resources by Scheduling and Communication

Scheduling work may be done implicitly without any formal scheduling tools such as scheduling software, or it may be done explicitly with manual forms or software. Although there appear to be significant differences among individuals in their ability to effectively do implicit scheduling of work activities, explicit scheduling tends to provide better performance. Without explicit scheduling, the most important work is not done first, work requiring periods of concentration is interrupted, and the most productive times for intensive work may be used for activities requiring little concentrated attention. One of the problems with intuitive scheduling is that the schedule may be overly influenced by interruptions and demands for immediate action. Also, well-structured, easily completed activities are often given priority in an intuitive schedule (structured activities drive out unstructured). Good scheduling processes will conserve knowledge work resources and apply them to the most important problems.

Knowledge workers tend to have high flexibility in scheduling their activities, so their ability to allocate and schedule efforts may explain much of the performance differences among individuals. Given the need to allocate time to activities, schedule activities, and set limits on certain activities, planning and scheduling are a cognitive bargain. In other words, the time spent on planning and scheduling is more than offset by improved performance.

In scheduling activities, knowledge workers need periods of rest after hard cognitive work. Workers involved in physical production with heavy physical exertion have scheduled periods of inactivity and rest. Knowledge workers tend to rest from periods of heavy cognitive exertion not by inactivity, but by performing activities with low cognitive exertion (rest work). For example, opening the mail, reading the electronic mail, and answering telephone messages tend to require low cognitive exertion. Scheduling for optimal results will, therefore, intermix heavy cognitive exertion with cognitive rest work.

Another factor in scheduling activities is based on the observed phenomenon of a daily cycle of energy and alertness. High-value knowledge work activities should, therefore, be scheduled for times of the day when energy and alertness are highest, and clerical and cognitive rest work scheduled for low-alertness periods.

One of the characteristics of knowledge work is that many activities do not have well-specified limits. They are expandable. For example, how many analyses are required to decide on a plant location? There is no practical limit to the number of analyses. Achieving productivity includes scheduling stopping rules or limits on the extent or duration of knowledge work activities.

Stopping rules to limit analysis can be explicitly developed during planning and scheduling or applied intuitively by the mental model of the knowledge worker. Information technology is important to scheduling because of the use of scheduling software.

Communication to obtain data, discuss issues, obtain approvals, distribute results, or coordinate with collaborators consumes significant knowledge work time and effort. Time and effort can be conserved by improved communication facilities provided by information technology. The technology reduces both the effort to communicate and response delays.

Conserving Scarce Attentional Resources by Automatic Processing

Humans are limited in their ability to pay attention and concentrate on activities. In other words, humans have limited attentional resources. Although high motivation may induce some increase in attentional resources, and poor motivation may reduce the availability of attention, there are still limits. Information technology supports automatic processing, both by automation of activities with computers and by providing opportunities for automating sequences of activities in using computers.

Attentional resources are significant in managing knowledge work because these limited cognitive resources are needed for all non-routine activities. Attentional resources may be conserved by making activities automatic or substantially automatic. Activities become automatic by being routinized as standard procedures or processes. Learning by repeating established sequences of operations allows them to be performed automatically.

Examples

Driving an automobile requires the full attention of a new driver; it is substantially automatic for an experienced driver who has routinized most behaviors. ◆

During the learning period for new software, the knowledge worker must cope with two tasks: using the features and functions of the new software and performing the required task. Performing two simultaneous tasks requiring attention results in significantly reduced performance. Only when the commonly used functions of the software become automatic through repeated use can high levels of performance be achieved. ◆

In addition to making activities automatic, attentional resources are conserved by **expertise**. Expertise improves use of attentional resources because experts tend to be more selective in the search and retrieval of information (they focus on the important data and usually have more automatic processing behavior).

Example

Executing certain software commands is cognitively difficult and requires full attention for a novice; the same commands are substantially automatic for an experienced user. ◆

It is difficult to do automatic processing of certain activities. Planning requires significant attentional resources because the nature of these activities is a high level of uncertainty and complexity. Uncertainty is increased because of the numbers of possible combinations of events that must be considered.

Compensating for Limitations on Human Information Processing

Humans are limited in their ability to do **information processing**. There are capacity limits for short-term memory, access limits to long-term memory, input limits to human processing, and bias in human information processing. Design of work and information technology may be used to compensate for these limitations.

Human short-term memory is used to hold information needed immediately or shortly for human information processing. Limits are expressed in terms of "chunks" of information, such as a digit, a character, a picture, or a thought. The limits are thought to be seven plus or minus two chunks (or even lower). Although a computer cannot be used in place of human short-term memory, any external memory aid such as a pad of paper or notes on a computer word processor can be used to support short-term memory.

Long-term memory is limited by the time it takes to access and retrieve that which a human has stored in memory. Computers can support long-term memory by search mechanisms to find and retrieve data in computer files.

Input limits are constraints on the ability of a human receiver to accept data. Humans can become overloaded with information. Information overload can be detrimental because it consumes attentional resources and increases complexity. Mechanisms to manage information overload include use of models that identify important data, statistics that summarize data, and expertise. Other methods include stopping rules and information distribution limits.

The concept of "need to know" may be applied to information overload. "Need to know" does not preclude information that may not be needed directly, but provides a context for tasks that may need to be performed. "Need to know" suggests that some information can be confined to those who can act upon it.

Example

It is technically possible for the chief executive officer to be made aware of every defect in each product produced. However, individual defect knowledge is information overload. The individual details can only be acted upon by line management close to the problem; the individual details, therefore, can be hidden from the higher-level executive. The higher-level executive can receive summarized data in a report that reduces overload; if the problem needs to be investigated in detail, the details can be made available. ◆

Knowledge workers must be aware of possible bias in information sources, analysis, and interpretation. For example, humans tend to be biased by recency of data. Events that have happened recently have a greater weight.

Example

A retail store has had an average of one complaint a month. In one month, there are three complaints. An intuitive analysis might conclude that there are serious problems, but a statistical analysis demonstrates that a single month with three complaints is likely to be a random event. ◆

Humans are not good as intuitive statisticians; they tend to interpret small samples incorrectly. A knowledge worker will often employ familiar analyses rather than seek out more powerful, more effective methods. There is often a bias against considering alternatives, so individuals and groups often fail to search and analyze adequately or to consider an adequate set of alternatives. In knowledge work, compensating for recency and small sample bias usually is based on performing explicit analysis with software. This helps surface the bias. Such software makes available a variety of methods and provides guidance to help select the most appropriate method.

Improving Productivity Through More Effective Knowledge Work

◆ ◆

Effective knowledge work improves the outcomes of knowledge work activities and the accomplishment of knowledge work tasks. It enhances the value of the outcomes. It is not a question of performing activities with fewer resources, but of performing them more productively. Effectiveness is achieved in knowledge work by performing with expertise and creativity, more extensive and intensive work, more complete and timely work, and work not feasible without computers.

Expertise and Creativity

Knowledge work activities are highest in value when they reflect expertise and **creativity**. Expertise is likely to reduce the time to perform an activity and improve the quality of the result. Experts are generally more efficient than novices in the use of data, analysis, decision making, and similar activities. Creativity is associated with processes that promote innovative thinking and alternative solutions. Knowledge work activities may differ in value (for a given situation). In one case, finding the data may add the highest value; in another situation, interpreting the data may be the most important and valuable. This suggests that each knowledge worker does a mixture of activities with differing values. Effectiveness is highest if the most important activities are performed with expertise and creativity and other activities are performed only to the extent necessary.

More Extensive and Intensive Knowledge Work

Extensive refers to the breadth of data used and alternatives considered. *Intensive* defines the depth of investigation or analysis. To illustrate the difference, assume a knowledge worker can, in a defined time period, manually analyze two possible alternatives in support of a decision. Assume also that the same analyst, working with spreadsheet software, can in the same period analyze ten alternatives. The knowledge work has been more extensive in considering alternatives. If the analysis of alternatives has more depth by applying different methods, the analysis is more intensive. The knowledge work improves by considering more alternatives and employing a variety of methods of analysis and presentations. In most cases, the use of computer software allows more extensive and intensive analysis without an increase in time over manual methods.

More Complete and Timely Knowledge Work

If work is divided into small parts, work on any part may be excellent but incomplete if that part did not take into account the work being done elsewhere. The same incompleteness may occur if work is done without information important to the activity.

Examples

If the work of analyzing a company being considered for a merger is divided among four analysts evaluating financial, marketing, manufacturing, and personnel functions, and there is no communication among them, the individual analyses may overlook important clues for investigation. ◆

A person dealing with a customer complaint may make poor judgments if information is lacking on how valuable the customer is to the company, such as prior purchases and future potential. ◆

The time to complete knowledge work is often quite long, especially if many people are involved in various parts of the work. The results of knowledge work tend to be more valuable if the cycle time to complete them can be significantly reduced. Redesign of tasks including heavy use of information technology has led to more effective knowledge work based on providing more complete information and reducing cycle time by supporting parallel processing, more communication, and greater worker empowerment with information.

Example

An insurance company must do an underwriting analysis before making a decision to issue a policy. Following a traditional cycle of activities involving movement of documents from person to person may require many days. The delay is detrimental to sales efforts. A redesign of the process to allow parallel work and to automate some activities reduces the cycle time to an average of 24 hours. ◆

Work Activities Not Feasible Without Computers

Effectiveness by more extensive and intensive work, more complete processes, and more timely completion can be achieved without information technology, although the cost may be high. Some work activities, for practical purposes, cannot be performed by adding more workers or work time. The effectiveness represented by these activities cannot be achieved without using computers. Sophisticated analyses, simulations, extensive data searches and retrieval require computational processes that are not feasible without computers.

Examples

Alternative budgets to explore viability of a new venture depend on numerous assumptions relating to factors such as price, sales, returns, and cost of capital. By using a spreadsheet and "what if" analysis, large numbers of combinations may be explored to select three scenarios to present to the executive making the decision. ◆

A mail order company believes its customers have patterns of purchases that, if known, could be used by those taking orders to reinforce related purchase decisions. To analyze tens of thousands of sales to find such patterns is not feasible without computers and databases of past sales. ◆

Improving Productivity Through Efficiency in Knowledge Work Processes and Procedures

◆ ◆

Since improved productivity through efficiency is achieved by using fewer resources for the same processing or analysis, efficiency objectives center on reducing the time and effort required to formulate a recommendation, prepare a report, or obtain and analyze data. The four most significant ways to achieve efficiency are reducing the time and effort to execute activities, reducing the time to design work by reusing processes and procedures, eliminating process redundancy and delay, and minimizing errors in inputs and processes. Information technology can be applied to each of these. Efficiency achieved with information technology is easily measured if the form and content of outputs such as recommendations, reports, or analyses do not change with the use of technology. However, in knowledge work, increased capabilities for factors such as data access, analysis, and formatting, lead to a change in output, so efficiency is not easily separated from effectiveness.

Reducing Time and Effort

Productivity can be achieved by redesigning work, using information technology that reduces time and effort, or a combination of the two. Knowledge work processes and procedures can be redesigned to reduce the time and effort to accomplish tasks. Actions and activities can be eliminated or simplified. Many features of information technology reduce the time and effort required to accomplish tasks.

◊xamples

Entering the text at a computer keyboard for a memorandum or report using word processing software requires less time and effort than manually writing or using a typewriter. Spell checking reduces the time to proofread a text. ◆

Creating a bar chart on a computer requires less time and effort (and results in fewer errors) than drawing it manually. ◆

Maintaining a computer file of contacts with names, addresses, and telephone numbers requires less effort than maintaining a manual file. ◆

Searching a customer order file via computer can be done automatically once the search criteria have been specified. ◆

Communicating with electronic mail can reduce time and effort to send queries and instructions, obtain data, and coordinate work. ◆

Reusing Processes and Procedures

Completing a task typically involves two parts: creating a work design and performing the operations in the work design. The work design usually includes both processes and procedures. A **process** is a sequence of actions to accomplish a desired result. For example, a process for problem solving might be described as actions to collect problem symptoms, diagnose the problem, model alternative solutions, and select a preferred solution. A **procedure** is a set of steps to conduct an action. For example, an organization may have a standard procedure for the action of selecting among candidates for a position. Creating a work design of processes, procedures, and format of outputs may take more time than executing the operations. For example, formulating the structure of a report (the framework of the report and the flow of logic to be developed) may take as much time as writing the report. Design resources use attentional resources. They require the application of creativity and design logic. Reusing past designs for processes and procedures can significantly improve productivity. Reuse can reduce the time and mental effort required to design them, reduce communication costs, increase automatic processing, and reduce training and learning costs.

Reusable processes and procedures are a form of memory for both an individual and an organization. The reusable procedure is "recalled" from the memory of an individual or from stored representations such as forms, procedure manuals, instructions, and computer programs. Computer programs are a stored representation of a reusable procedure.

Using reusable processes and procedures reduces the need for communicating with others. Those who supply data understand data needs through forms and instructions. Those who use the results of analysis understand the analytical procedures if the results are presented in a consistent manner. Only if a user of an analysis does not understand how the results were obtained will there be a need for additional communication.

Reusable procedures can usually result in more use of automatic processing, but they must be learned and used often enough to achieve it. Reusable procedures mean that new procedures (such as new software) result in costs associated with the loss of automatic processing of some existing processes and learning new ones.

Significant learning costs are also involved, both in initial training and in learning to perform procedures well enough to benefit from automatic processing. A reusable procedure reduces training costs because the structure of the task and operation are well defined.

Reusable procedures involve risk. To reduce cognitive effort associated with exceptions, people may apply standard procedures even when they are not appropriate.

Example

A credit card company may use a procedure for granting credit based on scoring certain attributes. As a result, an obviously credit-worthy person may be rejected because credit reviewers may find it requires too much effort to process exceptions to the procedure. ◆

Another risk with reusable procedures is that they can become obsolete or inefficient due to changing conditions. The re-engineering movement reflects the existence of processes and procedures that have become obsolete or inefficient.

Example

An existing procedure for handling claims for damaged merchandise may have delays and authorization limits that were appropriate when first implemented, but do not take advantage of improved availability of information in databases. ◆

Eliminating Process Redundancy and Delay

Redundancy is defined as operations and data that are unnecessary because they duplicate other operations or stored data. For example, an individual analyzing organization data may re-enter the data. This is a redundant operation because the data already exist in the organization's data storage. In some cases, there may be good reasons for redundancy. Redundant operations may be a method of achieving error control and redundant components may reduce operating costs.

Examples

An individual making a deposit at the bank fills out a deposit slip with a total. The bank rechecks the total during the operations to enter the deposit and process the checks. The redundant checking of the total costs very little and provides a check against depositor errors. ◆

Remote sites may be provided with a redundant copy of a database in order to reduce communication costs and delays. ◆

In general, processing delays should be eliminated. They are frequently caused by communication delays such as mail transit times or synchronization delays in which the work of one person must be coordinated and synchronized with that of another. When processes are initiated by the movement of documents, delays may be introduced by the waiting line of documents at each processing station. Studies of business processes involving sequential movement of documents through several processing stations suggest that most of the elapsed time is due to the documents waiting for processing and not the processing itself. Similar delays can result from waiting for data that must come from another person. Processes are often held up by incomplete information.

Example

An order may be delayed in processing because of an incomplete customer address that must be supplied by someone outside the order fulfillment function. ◆

One of the major benefits of computer and communications technology is the elimination of redundancy by allowing many users to access a single database. The technology can be used to eliminate or reduce communication delays. It can allow an individual to directly search for data rather than relying on another person who must fit the request into a schedule. Processes involving sequential movement of documents through a series of work stations may be altered to store the documents on computers and allow parallel processing. Incomplete information may often be obtained by the person who notices the omission rather than by returning the transaction to another person.

Minimizing Errors and Bias

Input and process errors reduce efficiency because error detection and correction require significant resources. For example, correcting an error in a transaction or analysis often takes from two to ten times as much time as processing or analyzing the original transaction. Errors are typically more troublesome than bias. **Errors** are incorrect data or analyses. **Bias** refers to the systematic exclusion of certain data or systematic failure to consider alternative explanations. A person who receives a biased analysis may be able to adjust or compensate for the bias; but an individual who receives a report or analysis based on incorrect data may not be able to resolve the matter as easily.

Procedure design for error minimization includes operations to detect data errors in input or in stored data provided by others. Controls detect incomplete data items, incomplete sets of data, or errors in capturing or entering data items.

Example

An identification number for a customer, employee, or supplier is critical to the transaction, but errors are easily made in entering the code. An effective method for detecting a code input error is to include a check digit in the identification code. If an input error occurs, it will be immediately detected by validating the input code with its check digit. A second or alternative check is to display the name associated with the input code so that the data entry clerk can visually confirm that the entity is correct. ◆

Information technology can be applied very effectively to minimize errors, but expertise is also important. Over time, experts develop a mental model that allows them to detect errors by comparing the actual data with a mental model of what the data should be. Experts may also be influenced by the context associated with the data. For example, expert knowledge that a company being analyzed is in financial difficulty provides a different context for financial statement analysis than that of a stable, successful company.

Investing in Knowledge Work Productivity Improvement

◆ ◆

Achieving improved productivity generally requires some form of investment. The investment may be information technology, such as a computer, applications or communications software, or custom programs or packages. There must also be investment in design of knowledge work processes and procedures and a significant investment in learning to use the hardware, software, and work methods. There is investment in initial learning to use the systems and investment in learning to a level in which many processes and procedures are automatic.

The productivity gains from expanding and conserving knowledge work energy, being more effective, and being more efficient may come in the form of a large number of small savings. Large savings may come from many instances of time savings and many instances of small increments of cognitive resources preserved by good scheduling or automatic processing. There is an analogy with industrial engineering of manufacturing processes. Large savings in manufacturing work were achieved by redesign of work motions and placing materials to reduce many small wasted motions.

The investment required for improved knowledge work productivity can be divided into three major categories:

1. Information technology infrastructures.
   a. Organization-wide technology infrastructure. Organization computers and communication and networking facilities plus organization systems, organization databases, and support personnel.
   b. Information technology systems supporting individuals and collaboration among individuals.
2. Processes, procedures, and methods for performing knowledge work activities.
   a. Application software, both packages and custom programs.
   b. Explicit design or redesign of knowledge work processes and procedures including data access methods.
   c. Knowledge work management processes and procedures and software to support them.
3. Investment in initial training plus practice and learning to achieve appropriate expertise, useful level of automatic processing, and added procedural knowledge.
   a. Knowledge worker training and learning time for hardware, software, work processes, and database access in order to achieve entry-level competence.

b. Learning in order to achieve a useful level of expertise and automatic processing for often-used features and functions in hardware and software, often-used processes, and often-accessed databases.

c. Relearning when there is a change or upgrade for hardware, software, or work methods.

d. Ongoing development of added procedural knowledge and expertise.

There is a tendency to concentrate on the investment cost for technology configurations and infrastructures and cost of software and custom programs. There is less recognition of the cost of designing or redesigning knowledge work processes and procedures. The costs of training, learning, relearning, and knowledge development tend to be underestimated or ignored. The latter costs can easily exceed the technology and software costs.

In many cases, decisions must be made as to how much to invest in initial training and learning to achieve expertise for a specific software package or to learn the individual features and functions of software. The training and learning investment is up-front; the savings may come in a stream of very small savings in time and effort and enhanced effectiveness. The up-front investment usually cannot be justified for a one-time use of the feature or function, so the analysis must consider value from the stream of small savings or effectiveness improvements.

Summary

◊ ◊ ◊ ◊ ◊ ◊ ◊ ◊ ◊ ◊ ◊ ◊ ◊ ◊ ◊ ◊ ◊ ◊ ◊ ◊

◊ Knowledge work is human mental work performed to generate useful information. It involves four primary activities: (1) accessing data, (2) using knowledge, (3) employing mental models, and (4) applying significant concentration and attention.

◊ There are two key characteristics of knowledge work: mental models, and concentration and attention.

◊ Mental models are mental representations of methods, processes, and procedures used in knowledge work. Knowledge workers build mental models and employ them in designing and analyzing work processes, formulating recommendations, and making decisions.

◊ Concentration and attention are scarce cognitive resources. Managing these resources is central to knowledge work management.

◊ Knowledge is high-level, value-added information. It may be viewed as sets of data items and information organized and processed to convey understanding, experience, accumulated learning, and expertise, as they apply to a given problem or activity. Knowledge can be grouped into four primary categories: (1) formal, (2) procedural, (3) meta, and (4) impressionistic.

◆ Data is the raw material of knowledge work. Information is the desired output.

◆ Information can be presented in a variety of forms such as reports, analyses, graphs, pictures, or video. Information has value to the user if it produces one or more of the following results: (1) It adds to or builds a mental model; (2) It corrects or confirms previous information; (3) It has surprise value; (4) It reduces uncertainty; or (5) It changes probabilities of expected outcomes.

◆ Productivity improvement comes from three sources: expansion and conservation of knowledge work resources, more effective work, and more efficient work.

◆ Managing and designing work to expand and conserve knowledge work resources involves four key functions: (1) improving motivation, (2) designing work schedules, (3) automatic processing, and (4) compensating for human limitations in information processing.

◆ More *effective* knowledge work can result from creativity and expertise, more extensive and intensive work, more complete and timely work, and activities not feasible without computers.

◆ More *efficient* knowledge work can reduce the time and effort required for knowledge work activities, eliminate redundancy and delay, and minimize input and process errors.

◆ Productivity improvements in knowledge work require up-front investment to achieve a stream of small increments in efficiency and small changes in effectiveness of outputs.

◆ Three types of investments can enhance knowledge work: (1) investments in information technology infrastructures; (2) investments in processes, procedures, and methods for performing knowledge work activities; and (3) investments in initial training, plus practice and learning.

EXERCISES

1. Using the examples in the chapter, make a list of knowledge work activities that you perform. Describe each with one or two sentences. List supplementary clerical activities you must perform and describe each with one or two sentences.

2. Describe how you add value to the organization through the processes and procedures that you perform as a knowledge worker. Give examples of how you add value through your knowledge of how to obtain and use data.

3. Think of software functions or features you employ frequently (with a spreadsheet processor or word processor). For each, explain your use in terms of conservation of your cognitive resources.
   a. Do you think about the keystrokes or do them automatically? If you do them automatically, how long did it take to achieve this automatic behavior?
   b. If you upgraded to a new version or changed to a new package, did you lose productivity while you learned the new package? Explain.

4. Think of a short knowledge work project you recently performed. Then respond to each question:
   a. Was there a deadline? If you had been given more time, could you have used it? Would you have expanded your work activities to fill the time available? Think about your answer in terms of scheduling knowledge work and placing limits on time and effort expended.
   b. Could you have improved your performance if you had devoted more time to planning the work? Would there have been a "cognitive bargain" in this case? Explain.

5. The time it takes to get something done is the cycle time (such as the time required to process an order, deliver a product, or process an employment application). Explain how information technology can be employed to reduce cycle time for knowledge work tasks.

6. Evaluate two tasks that you perform, have performed, or expect to perform. Describe how productivity with these tasks has been or can be improved. Note the sources of improvement. Specifically analyze in terms of expanding and conserving cognitive resources, improving productivity by more *effective* work, and improving productivity by more *efficient* work.

7. The chapter indicates knowledge workers should have a working knowledge of a basic set of software packages. These include a word processing program, plus six other packages (disregarding packages with multiple purposes): (1) a spreadsheet processor, (2) electronic mail and Internets, (3) presentation graphics, (4) statistics, (5) a database package for structured data, and (6) a database package for unstructured, text data. Describe the productivity implications in your use of these packages.

8. To analyze investment costs and benefits, review the costs and expected benefits of a recently acquired software package or custom application.

Explain the learning time and effort to achieve useful automatic processing. Comment on benefits that you expected and whether or not they have been received.

9. Parkinson's Law states that work expands to fill the time available. Explain this in terms of conserving scarce knowledge work resources by scheduling.

10. *External Data Exercise:* Do Exercise 1 in Chapter 8. (Chapter 8 focuses on accessing external data on the Internet. The External Data Exercises included in Chapter 1-7 are designed to prepare you for more difficult exercises presented in Chapter 8.)

Knowledge Workers and Information Management

◇　◇　◇　◇　◇　◇　◇　◇　◇

OBJECTIVES

After completing this chapter, you should be able to:

◆ Provide a concrete explanation of how productivity gains are achieved by a knowledge worker.

◆ Explain the template feature found in many software packages.

◆ Define the responsibility of an individual for personal knowledge work systems.

◆ Compare and contrast the need for both organizational and individual information systems.

◆ Compare and contrast the processes for organizational and individual information management.

KEY TERMS AND CONCEPTS

This chapter introduces the following key terms and concepts, listed in the order in which they appear:

information management system

individual information management system

organizational information management system

template

standard template

custom template

information infrastructure

application infrastructure

application architecture

information management function

application development

system development life cycle

This chapter extends the conceptual discussion of productivity presented in Chapter 1 and describes how information technology produces productivity gains for knowledge workers. It explains how specific software functions and features can produce productivity gains and describes the use of templates in improving knowledge work efficiency.

Every organization has an **information management system**. An information management system consists of the processes, procedures, and technologies for communications and information processing. Communications includes obtaining and providing data and coordinating collaborative work with persons internal and external to the organization. Information processing includes recording and storing data likely to be needed at a later time, locating and retrieving internally stored data and data from external sources, and applying processing methods to produce meaningful results. It also includes the planning, building, and maintaining of computer and communications hardware, software, and databases to support these processes and procedures. Why should an individual have a system? Doesn't the organizational system provide all necessary resources and management? The answer is that the organizational system provides *some* information management resources for knowledge workers, but individual knowledge workers are expected to manage much of the information technology they use and to build and operate their own information management systems.

Both organizational and individual information management systems have processes, procedures, and technologies for communications and information processing. They differ significantly in scope. The organizational information management system must support diverse needs by a large number of persons in a number of different organization functions in locations that may be geographically dispersed. It supports the transaction processing and other fundamental systems of an organization. By comparison, an individual information management system is small; it is limited in scope to individual requirements not provided by the organizational system. These individual requirements include processes, procedures, and data for analysis, decision making, and similar knowledge work activities.

An important difference between an **individual information management system** and an **organizational information management system** is the development process. Individual systems are designed and built with processes for "development in the small," and organizational systems are built with processes for "development in the large." Although "development in the small" has many similarities to "development in the large," many activities are eliminated or done much more simply in the small. This chapter outlines the analysis and development of information management systems for knowledge workers and describes methods for "development in the small."

Why should a person study methods for "development in the small"? The most important reason is that it provides an individual who is not an information systems specialist with knowledge for planning, building, and maintaining an individual system. The objective is to improve personal productivity by more effective use of information technology. Another reason is that understanding individual systems provides people who are not information systems specialists with knowledge and insight for participating in projects for larger, more complex organizational systems. It also provides information systems specialists with the knowledge required to advise and assist individuals with personal systems. In a sequence of learning, understanding "development in the small" provides a foundation for study of "development in the large."

Applying Information Technology to Knowledge Work Productivity

◆ ◆

Chapter 1 described three major ways to improve knowledge work productivity: (1) designing and managing work to expand and conserve knowledge work resources; (2) performing work more effectively; and (3) performing work more efficiently. Each of these three methods contributes to improved knowledge work productivity. In the analysis of this chapter, these three methods are termed knowledge work design/management, effectiveness, and efficiency.

The first section of this chapter describes a knowledge work position involving both managerial and analytical tasks and examines a sample of knowledge work activities to illustrate how information technology is employed to improve individual and group productivity.

Description of a Knowledge Work Position

The role of internal audit manager for a large, multinational company will be used to illustrate a knowledge work position because it entails a variety of tasks, such as managing, reporting, supervising, auditing, collaborating, and directing individual analytical and writing activities. The manager supervises a small staff of internal auditors located at headquarters and in subsidiaries in Canada and Venezuela. She schedules both her work and the work of the audit staff. The audit staff performs audits using programs that detail the work for each audit. She also receives special assignments that do not fall within the scope of the normal audit programs. A significant portion of internal audit work is outsourced to a firm of certified public accountants, and the manager is responsible for assigning and reviewing their work. She reports directly to the financial vice president and to the Audit Committee of the Board of Directors. Following is a list of her knowledge work tasks and activities. (A sample of these tasks and activities will be used to illustrate productivity improvement methods.)

◆ Recruit, train, supervise, and evaluate progress of internal audits

◆ Write formal performance reviews of external audit firm doing internal audit work

◆ Schedule personal work

◆ Review work of internal staff and outside firm

◆ Maintain audit programs and policies

◆ Maintain company audit and control policies and procedures

◆ Conduct on-site review of audit results with management and selected personnel

◇ Review audit work papers and audit reports and assist in revising the reports before submitting them to management, audited units, and the Audit Committee

◇ Submit audit reports to management and to audited units with recommendations for improvements in procedures

◇ Prepare audit summaries and recommendations for the Audit Committee of the Board of Directors

◇ Analyze topics assigned by management and the Audit Committee

◇ Prepare travel expense reports

◇ Review and approve staff expense reports

◇ Prepare budget plans and reports

◇ Invest in training to maintain and increase both formal and procedural knowledge

◇ Manage communications with company personnel at remote locations. Since she is the only person from the executive office that many of the remote personnel have met, she receives numerous inquiries for information on matters such as company policies, plans, and executive changes.

◇ Manage files including contact database for company personnel, external audit firm personnel, and professional contacts

The manager has a laptop computer that fits into a docking station on her desk. It is connected to a company server. She is connected to a commercial network for external databases and Internet access. Part of the company is on an internal e-mail system, but many locations use commercial networks and e-mail services. Her facilities include direct fax transmission from her computer. She takes the laptop computer when out of the office. Her software includes a word processor, spreadsheet processor, database package, scheduling package, time sheet package, presentation graphics package, communications package (including e-mail, fax, external databases, and Internet), and personal information manager. She makes extensive use of templates for analyses and reports. Templates provide predefined formats, calculations, and content. They will be explained more fully later in the chapter. The computer has significantly increased her personal productivity and the productivity of her staff.

Examples of Productivity Improvement with Information Technology

The computer is pervasive in the activities of the audit manager. Table 2-1 lists selected knowledge work tasks, and illustrates the impact of the computer on knowledge work productivity.

Table 2-1	Impact of Computer on Knowledge Work Productivity
Productivity Source	*Task: Schedule Own Work and Audit Work*
Efficiency—less time and effort. More effective—more complete and timely.	Use scheduling software to do scheduling.
Efficiency—less time and effort; fewer errors.	Use time management software to track time use by self and staff.
Efficiency—less time and effort, reuse of data, and less redundancy.	Prepare summaries and reports using word processing and spreadsheet processor. Transfer data from scheduling and time management package.
Productivity Source	*Task: Maintain audit programs, audit policies, and company audit and control policies and procedures*
Efficiency—less time since no need to distribute and make individual files.	Use software to maintain all of the information on servers and intranet networks. Auditors and others download from the network.
Efficiency—less time to update and fewer errors in accessing latest version.	All programs and policy information are updated on the server. Everyone has same access to same version of policies and procedures.
Productivity Source	*On-site review of audit and audit results with management and personnel within scope of audit*
Efficiency—less effort to communicate. Also more effective.	Use intranet to make available personal background information and picture before visit in person.
Efficiency—less time and effort to locate. No need for multiple filings.	Audit report is stored on company server and on local diskettes. Past audit reports are available on company server and intranet for locations not on company network.

In addition to the productivity achieved in the preceding tasks, the audit manager uses the following features:

◊ Personal information manager (PIM) software package used for functions such as scheduling meetings on calendar with audit staff and maintaining "To Do" lists

Table 2-1 *(continued)*	
Productivity Source	*Prepare Personal Travel Expense Reports, Review Audit Staff Reports, and Prepare Department Travel Report*
Efficiency—reuse of template, less time and effort to prepare, and fewer errors.	Use travel expense report spreadsheet template for preparing personal reports.
Efficiency—less time because of standard form and less need to check for errors because of spreadsheet template.	Staff submit electronic travel expense report form. Approve electronic version.
Efficiency—reuse of template, less time and effort to prepare summary, and reuse of data already entered in report templates.	Use copy feature to capture data from submitted template forms for use in preparing summary report (using summary template).
Productivity Source	*Review, Edit and Revise Audit Reports*
Efficiency—reduce time and effort to transmit, reduce errors and redundancy by use of comment feature to place notes and comments in text.	Review audit report prepared with report template and submitted as computer file. Add comments using comment feature of word processor. Return report electronically to auditor who prepared it. Report is reviewed by preparer. After review discussion, some comments are converted to report text and others are removed.
Efficiency—reduce time and effort. Effective because not feasible manually.	If there is a need to compare current version of report with a past version, a document compare feature of word processor is used.
Efficiency—reduces time to design output and to check for errors.	Final report, based on document template, is checked for spelling and grammar before transmittal and electronic storage. Spelling includes checking proper spelling of all names and use of Spanish alphabetic characters such as Ñ.
Efficiency—reduces time to prepare memorandum and to find and enter names. Effective because template is complete.	Transmittal memorandum is prepared using special audit report transmittal document template. Names, titles, and company addresses are pasted from address book file of audit manager.

Table 2-1 *(continued)*	
Productivity Sources	*Special Assignments for Analysis and Evaluations*
Effective because much of the analysis is not feasible or intensity is not feasible without use of software. Efficiency—linking of spreadsheet data to report summaries reduces re-entry and transcription errors.	Quantitative, analytical reports make significant use of spreadsheets. Report summaries are linked to spreadsheets in appendices.
Effective because of completeness and creativity of information search and retrieval. Much of the search would not be feasible without computers and communications. Efficiency—Reduces time and effort, allows reuse of search processes, and downloading reduces transcription and re-entry errors.	Use Internet to access repositories of reports to government agencies, financial news services, and various external databases. Some reports require use of comparative data on competitors, both financial and news reports. The reports may also include news reports of business climate, etc. Information is downloaded, so it is in electronic form to cut and paste into reports.
Efficient because time and effort and errors are reduced by using presentation software templates and linking overhead content to report content. Effective because presentation software supports creative presentation of content by modifying standard templates.	Presentations to management, Audit Committee, or Board of Directors are prepared with presentation software with pasting and linking of data from report into overheads. If report is updated, the overheads will be updated also.

◊ Macro to insert file name and date in document footers

◊ E-mail for correspondence

◊ Hypertext links in online reports and Web pages. (Hypertext links are highlighted terms; when activated by a mouse action, a related section of the report or Web page is displayed. Hypertext and Web page will be explained further in Chapter 8.)

◊ Graphics capabilities of spreadsheet packages

◊ Extensive use of templates for both documents and spreadsheets. (Many of these uses were described in Table 2-1.)

Improving Efficiency with Information Technology: Templates

◆ ◆

One of the most effective ways to improve knowledge work efficiency is by using the templates available in various software programs. A **template** defines the layout, format, and features of a knowledge work form or output. For example, a word processing template defines the format for document elements such as margins, tab settings, and headings. It may also indicate the layout and placement of graphics. A spreadsheet template creates a spreadsheet for elements such as headings, formulas, and styles. A database template defines an input form or report layout. The templates for document, spreadsheet, and database forms may include specialized toolbars, menu bars, and keyboards for use with the template.

Templates offer a simple but very useful approach to efficiency improvement with information technology. They have been selected as the first technology feature to introduce for three reasons:

1. *Templates are applicable to common tasks and activities.* They fit well with word processing packages and spreadsheets, the two most commonly used software packages. They can also be used with database packages.

2. *Templates apply the productivity concept of reuse.*

3. *Templates illustrate the concept of investment and stream of benefits.* The learning investment required for an individual to use templates is small. The benefit with each use of a template is very small. However, the benefit to investment relationship is favorable, since a relatively low number of uses of a template are sufficient to "pay back" the investment required to prepare it.

Application software packages such as word processors, spreadsheets, and database packages offer two ways to use templates:

1. *Standard templates.* These are general purpose and fit a variety of users. Standard templates are included with software packages. In addition, organizations may furnish a set of standard templates to employees. Standard templates are accessed by opening a new file and selecting from the list of templates provided by the software package. Figure 2-1 lists some examples of standard templates provided with word processing and spreadsheet packages.

2. *Facilities for preparing custom templates.* Custom templates are designed for individual or small group use. They are tailored to unique requirements.

Word Processor	Spreadsheet Processor
Business letters	Travel expense report
Fax cover sheets	Time card
Memos	Invoice
Resumes	Loan analysis
Calendars	Insurance coverage report
Reports	Gantt chart
Academic papers	

FIGURE 2-1 *Typical standard templates provided with word processing and spreadsheet packages*

The process of preparing a custom template is simple. A template is developed on a blank spreadsheet or document that is designated as a template. All of the constant parts of the spreadsheet or document are placed on it. If an existing spreadsheet or document has the layout or form desired, the variable data may be erased, leaving only the constant parts and format for use as a template. The result is stored as a template with a template name. The custom template is accessed by opening a new file and selecting from the list of custom templates maintained by the software package.

Both standard and custom templates may be modified by users to create new templates.

Templates provide improved efficiency in knowledge work. The predefined format reduces time and effort to enter repeated data. The template represents a reuse of an input form or output format with savings in design and layout. Errors and omissions are reduced. The template enforces completeness. A consistent format reduces the reading and comprehension effort for users, since the format is the same for each report. The user does not need to spend time figuring out the layout and location of data. The investment in building a template may produce a more effective format.

Using Standard Templates

Standard templates are feasible because many document and spreadsheet analyses follow a fairly standard format. For example, a memorandum heading will typically include standard elements, a business letter follows a generally accepted pattern, and calendars are well-defined. Figure 2-2 illustrates a standard spreadsheet template for a Statement of Personal Net Worth. There is a generally accepted format for such a statement which includes standard labels for

Enter Your Name Here

Statement of Personal Net Worth
08/22

Assets
Current Assets
  Cash in Bank
  Cash in Savings
  Marketable Securities
  Certificate of Deposit
  Other Current Assets   _____
Total Current Assets

Long-term Assets
  Real Property
  Automobile
  IRA
  401K (vested portion)
  Household Furnishings
  Jewelry
  Collectibles
  Business or Partnership Interests
  Other Long-term Assets   _____
Total Long-term Assets   _____

Total Assets   ▬▬▬▬▬▬▬

Liabilities
Current Liabilities
  Monthly Bills
  Credit Cards—Total Balances
  Taxes Payable
  Other Current Liabilities   _____
Total Current Liabilities

Long-term Liabilities
  Mortgage—1st
  Mortgage—2nd or Equity Line
  Car Loan
  Other Long-term Liabilities   _____
Total Long-term Liabilities   _____

Total Liabilities   ▬▬▬▬▬▬▬

Net Worth   ▬▬▬▬▬▬▬

FIGURE 2-2   *Template for Statement of Personal Net Worth (from Corel Quattro Pro)*

line items. Standard templates may increase knowledge worker productivity for both those using the templates to produce analyses and reports and those reading them. Producing spreadsheets and documents takes less time because the customary format for the output is provided, generally accepted content is specified, and accepted formulas for computations, subtotals, and totals are included. Productivity is also increased for those who read and comprehend analyses and reports produced with standard templates because they are provided with outputs that follow customary formats. Such customary formats are found in accounting, finance, and other functions.

Standard templates can be customized. For example, a person using the standard template in Figure 2-2 may create a custom template by modifying this template. For example, the user may not have Certificates of Deposit, therefore, she may want to replace that line item with Money Market Funds. The line item for automobiles may be replaced with separate lines for each of two cars. Instead of a general heading, the user may insert a specific heading that includes a name, address, and telephone number. The modified template can then be saved under a new name as a custom template. Periodically, up-to-date Statements of Personal Net Worth can be prepared using the custom format. The savings from a template are still realized with the customized version, but the output is more effective because it is more complete.

An organization may provide customized templates to assist employees in preparing standard forms and reports. For example, the traditional approach to preparing travel expense reports is a time consuming and error-prone activity. A spreadsheet travel expense form template (see Figure 2-3) reduces time and effort because the consistent form reduces the time required to figure out how to fill in the expense report. And since computations are done automatically by the spreadsheet functions—instead of manually with calculators or separate spreadsheet programs—it eliminates duplicate, redundant work and reduces errors. An organization may create a custom travel expense report or customize a standard template with its company name and logo, and add row and column headings, as desired. When an organization supplies a custom travel expense report to an employee, the employee may customize the form further by adding name, department, and other personal information to the template.

Standard templates may be used as prototypes in developing custom templates. In other words, the standard template is shown as an example of a possible report or analysis format. This initial prototype output helps users identify their requirements. They can identify what they want to change in the prototype more easily than laying out the template without any concrete idea of a result. A company might use this approach to develop a custom template of the travel expense report shown in Figure 2-3.

Expense Report

Employee Name: _____   Travel Dates: _____

Department: _____   Purchase of Travel: _____

	Monday	Tuesday	Wednesday	Thursday	Friday	Saturday	Sunday	**Totals**
Transportation								
Airfare								
Parking & Tolls								
Taxis								
Auto Rental								
Gas								
Total								
Lodging								
Hotels								
Meals								
Breakfast								
Lunch								
Dinner								
Total								
Other								
List								
List								
List								
Total								
Mileage								
Actual Miles								
Rate per Mile								
Total								
Entertainment								
1.Explain Below								
2.								
3.								
Total								
Summary								

Entertainment Detail		Cash Advances	
1		Charged to Company	
2			
3		**Due Employee**	

Authorized by _____   Date _____

FIGURE 2-3   *Template for Travel Expense Report (from Corel Quattro Pro)*

Examples

Some word processing packages have a variety of templates for resume preparation. One of them has three formats: traditional, cosmopolitan, and contemporary. A person preparing a resume may prototype using the three formats and formulate a unique solution taking into account the differences. ◆

A word processing package has four templates for a business card: contemporary, cosmopolitan, elegant, and traditional. These can be used to explore alternative layouts, formats, types, etc. ◆

Standard templates may help users prepare academic papers, newsletters, reports, and other documents. The templates typically provide options that reduce the time required to design the layout and select style elements such as headings and point sizes for various fonts. Templates can also be used to insert codes to identify the levels of headings. When the document is complete, a table of contents can be automatically generated from the coded headings. This significantly reduces the time and effort required to prepare a table of contents and minimizes errors that could be introduced by re-entering this information. Also, when the document is revised or updated, the table of contents can be regenerated with little extra effort.

The use of style features to establish levels of headings, code them, and produce tables of contents can also improve the effectiveness of report writing. Since the table of contents is essentially an outline of the report, it allows writers to examine the report structure for completeness and flow of logic. This process supports the application of expertise and creativity in building effective communication into the report.

Templates can also be used to generate an index. Users simply mark the terms to be included in the index as they work through the document. The index can then be automatically generated by the program.

Developing and Using Custom Templates

A **custom template** is suggested for knowledge work productivity whenever a document, spreadsheet, or database input form is reused, but the layout and at least some parts remain constant. Custom templates can reduce variability in the format and contents of the outputs and reduce the time and effort required to prepare standard documents. Custom templates are useful for specialized, repeated reports, analyses that are revised and updated periodically, and certain memoranda or other communication requiring specified language and data.

Example

A high technology company wants all new employees to agree on terms of non-disclosure of company technology and on the rules governing the time frames during which an employee is restricted from working for a competing firm. It is important that other unique employment conditions and terms are included in the offer letter. A custom template for an offer of employment letter ensures completeness (all terms are considered when writing the letter, even if some are not applicable).   ◆

The simple memorandum template shown in Figure 2-4 was created using a word processor (Corel WordPerfect 7.0).

The following steps for WordPerfect illustrate how to build templates in most word processors.

1. Select "New" from the file menu.

2. Select "Options" and "New Template" from the pop-up menus.

3. The memorandum template was created by setting margins, selecting fonts and bold, entering the constant data for the memo writer and leaving the "To" and "Re" lines open to be filled in. A date code was placed in the position for the date. The code accepts the current date when the memorandum is written. Alternatively, the date could be entered manually, but the date code makes it automatic. A separator line was placed as a graphic before the text area for the memo.

4. To add interest and identification (more effectiveness in communication) a graphic was added to the memorandum heading. A quick art graphic was selected from a list of graphic objects stored by the office suite being used. This was placed on the memorandum template, sized, and positioned.

5. The template was "saved as" a template. The pop-up box asked for a template name and where it should be stored. There were several groups of templates where it could be stored or it could be stored in the main list (to reduce access time).

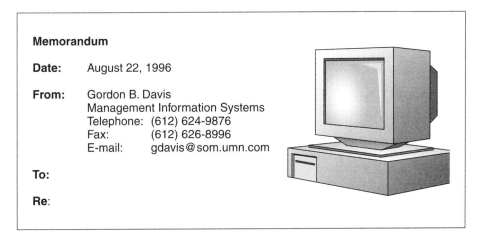

FIGURE 2-4   *Custom template with graphic*

To use this custom memorandum template in WordPerfect 7.0 for a new document, select "New" under the "File" menu. The list of templates is part of the pop-up box. The selected template is displayed ready for use.

Individual Responsibilities in Knowledge Work Systems

♦　♦　♦　♦　♦　♦　♦　♦　♦　♦　♦　♦　♦　♦　♦　♦　♦　♦

Knowledge work processes and information access involve systems. These systems may be provided by the organization, acquired from outside vendors, or developed by the individual. The individual has primary responsibility for four fundamental system design and management issues in achieving personal productivity:

1. *Personal information management infrastructures.* The design, implementation, and management of a personal information infrastructure.
2. *Personal knowledge work systems.* The design, implementation, and management of personal systems to systematize and structure knowledge work.
3. *Information access.* Access to relevant information from internal and external sources.
4. *Work management.* The management of knowledge work activities in order to perform tasks effectively and efficiently.

In physical production work or clerical work, the organization usually assumes responsibility for designing, developing, and managing information infrastructure, work systems, and information access. The management of such work is the responsibility of supervisory personnel and is implemented by scheduling systems and assigning tasks. In contrast, although the organization may provide some systems to support knowledge work, the individual knowledge worker has major responsibility for personal infrastructure, systems, information access, and work management. In each of these individual system responsibilities, information technology is a vital component in the systems and their operation.

Using Personal Information Management Infrastructures to Support Work

Information system infrastructures will be described further in the section on infrastructures for the organizational system. Every knowledge worker has personal information management infrastructures. Typically, this includes personal computer hardware, software, and communication facilities, personal files and databases, and personal applications that support work. The infrastructures may be poorly structured and chaotic, or they may be well designed and orderly. If chaotic and poorly structured, the information infrastructures do not provide adequate support and may even require extra effort to use. If orderly and well structured, they provide support for productivity. The components of the individual information management infrastructures will be described more fully later in this chapter.

Using Personal Systems to Systematize and Structure Work

The second individual knowledge worker responsibility relates to structuring and systematizing task activities. Structuring work processes and outputs is an important part of task accomplishment. Productivity is improved if the knowledge worker can draw upon personal systems that at least partially structure and systematize tasks.

Information technology is a vital part of individual knowledge work processes. Consistent with the objective of conserving and managing cognitive resources, knowledge work processes should be designed with a division of labor that recognizes the comparative abilities and advantages of humans and information technology. Repeatable processes and procedures are, to the extent possible, incorporated in computer software. This reduces the cognitive effort of designing new procedures or processes each time the activity is performed.

Information technology can be employed to reduce redundancy and delays in work processes. Communication may be improved and communication delays reduced. Information may be shared to allow parallel processing by more than one individual.

Another important effect of information technology on processes is error reduction. Various tests to validate data can be performed automatically and at low cost.

Examples

A standard format for a report incorporated in report software eliminates the design activity of deciding on the format and the clerical activity of placing the data in the format. Recipients of the report do not have to expend cognitive energy on understanding the report format; the standard format reduces the need to communicate about the format and recipients can concentrate on comprehension. ◆

Assume that logging on to an external database involves multiple steps including dialing, entering the user name and password, and selecting a database. If the steps are always carried out in the same sequence, a software procedure can be established to automate them. A single keystroke or mouse action can then be used to initiate the sequence without error. Meanwhile, the knowledge worker can perform other work. ◆

Accessing Information for Knowledge Work

Accessing information is an important part of knowledge work. The individual brings expertise to work, based on education, training, and experience. This expertise includes knowing where to find information. The information sources may be files, records, reference data, and personal contacts. Being able to locate data easily and efficiently is therefore a vital part of being a productive knowledge worker. Information technology is important in maintaining individual databases, accessing organizational data, and accessing data stored in external databases.

Managing Individual Knowledge Work

Managing knowledge work is a personal responsibility. Extreme differences in knowledge worker productivity suggest significant differences in how well this is done. Some knowledge workers may apply methods intuitively, but many do not approach the effective management of knowledge work as an important responsibility. The industrial engineering movement demonstrated that there were major differences between production work that was designed and managed compared to unplanned, unmanaged work. It is likely that there are more productivity gains available through effective management of knowledge work than were achieved by improved management of production work. The following examples illustrate knowledge work behavior that results in loss of productivity.

Examples

A knowledge worker engages in more analysis on a problem than can be justified. There seem to be no appropriate stopping rules for the analysis. ◆

A knowledge worker performs the least important tasks during the times of the day when attentional resources are at their peak. More important activities are not given priority. The least important tasks take priority because they are well structured and generally short (such as opening the mail and returning phone calls). ◆

A knowledge worker gives precedence to less important short jobs over longer, more important jobs. ◆

A knowledge worker has a variety of tasks that are active at the same time. There are frequent interruptions and much time is spent switching between tasks. Productivity is reduced by the switching time. ◆

The four individual responsibilities in knowledge work systems (personal infrastructures, personal knowledge work systems, personal information access, and personal work management) occur within the context of an organization and its information systems. The division of responsibility for systems supporting individuals and organization systems varies across organizations and within the same organization. However, the distinction between individual and corporate systems is found in all organizations.

The Need for an Organizational Information System

◆ ◆ ◆ ◆ ◆ ◆ ◆ ◆ ◆ ◆ ◆ ◆ ◆ ◆ ◆ ◆ ◆ ◆ ◆ ◆

An individual may have an information system, but this does not eliminate the need for an information system for the organization. In fact, the heavy use of information technology by individual knowledge workers increases the need for coordination, standardization, common systems, and organization-wide cooperation. In other words, individuals may build and operate their own systems, but they must fit these into the context of a larger organizational system (see Figure 2-5). The larger system is built and maintained by information systems specialists. This section explains the major uses for the organizational system and describes its technical components and major processes.

The Role of Information in the Organization

This is the information age, and information technology plays a vital role in virtually all organizations in three major areas: It is used in products and services, business processes, and knowledge work.

1. *Products and services.* Information technology may be embedded in products and services. Because of information technology, the variety of products and services can be increased and they can be individualized.

2. *Business processes.* Processes to acquire, build, and deliver goods and services and account for resources require information. Information processing is at the heart of reengineering of processes to reduce cycle time and improve performance.

3. *Knowledge work.* A major part of organizational work involves tasks such as analyzing, designing, scheduling, controlling, and managing. As explained, people doing this work are knowledge workers. They use information extensively—knowledge they bring with them from education or experience, knowledge of where to get information, and knowledge of

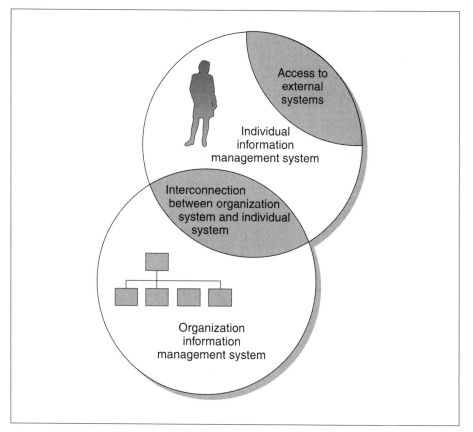

FIGURE 2-5 *Relationship of organization information management system and individual system*

how to access information within the organization. Knowledge workers make use of the organization's information system and also manage their own system.

Effective and creative use of information resources can have a significant effect on the competitiveness of an organization. Therefore, applications of information technology may be used in strategic initiatives or to respond to competition.

A characteristic of organizational processes is the need to access information provided by or being used by others. Processing of information can cross departments or other internal organizational boundaries. It can also cross external organizational boundaries through inter-organizational systems with suppliers and customers. This transfer of information across internal and external boundaries is especially true of information associated with products or services and business processes. The need to coordinate and manage systems that cross functional and organizational boundaries is a major reason for using an organizational system for information management.

Infrastructures and Architectures of Organizational Information Systems

In an economy, there must be infrastructures such as roads, bridges, and communications systems before there can be economic development with factories, warehouses, and shopping centers. These general purpose enabling facilities are termed infrastructure. The concept of infrastructures is applicable to information systems because information technology structures and data resources are needed before applications are possible. Information infrastructures are multi-purpose. They are used by many applications and by many different organizational functions and activities. Therefore, an **information infrastructure** is established to meet a variety of needs. It represents capabilities needed by applications. The infrastructure changes as needs change, but the difficulty of frequent changes suggests that an up-to-date infrastructure should support both current applications and applications expected to be in place in the near future. An architecture is the way the different components of a system fit together. In other words, an infrastructure has an architecture that describes its parts and how they fit together.

At the organizational level, there are four infrastructures (see Figure 2-6). Together these comprise the overall system for the organization:

1. *Information technology infrastructure.* A technical architecture for the hardware, software, and communication facilities.

2. *Data resources infrastructure.* A data architecture for corporate databases and other external data resources that explains how they are related and where they are located.

3. *Core applications infrastructure.* Core applications support the fundamental processes for an organization. These applications provide the basis for additional specialized applications that use data provided by the basic **application infrastructure** or are connected to the core systems. Examples of core systems are order entry, inventory and production management, billing, and payroll. An **application architecture** describes the structure of applications and how they relate to corporate processes and strategies.

4. *Core information system personnel infrastructure.* Specialists in information technology provide an infrastructure of individual expertise in building, maintaining, and operating information systems.

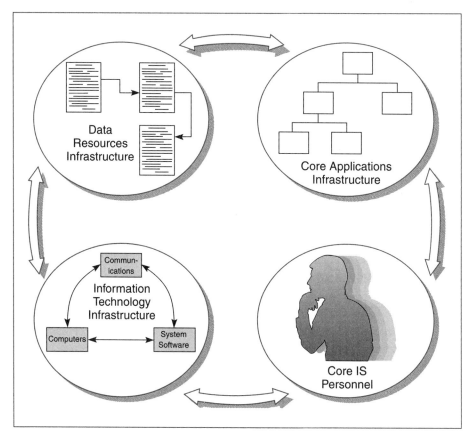

FIGURE 2-6 *Information management infrastructures for the organization*

Organizational Information Management Processes

There are five major processes used to provide and manage information and information resources at the organization level:

1. Planning the system for the organization including technical and organizational components

2. Developing, implementing, and maintaining the technology, data, and personnel infrastructures

3. Developing and implementing applications for the core applications infrastructure

4. Operating and maintaining the organizational system and its applications

5. Providing support for individual and departmental systems including assistance in planning so they can fit the organizational system standards. Also provided are technical advice, installation support, and training.

In performing these processes, the information system function employs personnel with skills in technology assessment, infrastructure design, application development, operations, and technical support for individuals.

Organizational Information Management Functions

The need for an **information management function** is the same as for any other business function such as accounting, finance, production, marketing, or human resources. These functions exist in organizations because many organizational activities benefit from use of specialist skills in performing them. Other semi-specialized activities benefit from procedures and standards developed by specialists to guide non-specialists in doing the work.

Although many of the activities associated with each business function are performed by non-specialists, there are activities that are specialized and therefore are performed most efficiently and effectively by persons trained and skilled in the tasks. This is seen in a function such as finance. Negotiating loans with banks and other lenders is a specialized skill, so a finance function is formed to provide that expertise. Likewise, designing information system infrastructures, developing core corporate applications, operating centralized computer facilities, and establishing standards are activities requiring specialized information systems education and experience.

There is also a need for an organizational function with specialists to provide the procedures and standards within which non-specialists may perform activities related to that function. This is observed in other organizational functions. For example, many non-accountants prepare budgets, record transactions, and perform analyses. However, there would be chaos if people in the organization established their own chart of accounts to describe transactions and made their own rules for reporting them. The non-accountant personnel follow the standards and procedures established by the accounting specialists in the accounting function. Likewise, in information processing there is a need for standards and procedures governing activities such as accessing databases, using applications, and transferring data among applications and users.

The Need for Individual Information Management Systems

◆ ◆ ◆ ◆ ◆ ◆ ◆ ◆ ◆ ◆ ◆ ◆ ◆ ◆ ◆ ◆ ◆ ◆

The previous section explained the need for organizational information management systems. This section addresses the need for individual or group systems.

Effective knowledge work management requires both types of systems. The organizational system developed and operated by the information management function is necessary for core systems and standards, and for coordinating other activities spanning organizational boundaries. Individual systems are needed to help individuals manage their personal information resources.

The Role of Individual Systems

One role of individual systems is to support work performed by individuals or small groups that does not fit into an organization's system architecture or is not done frequently enough to justify an organizational system. A second, related role is to support specialized, individual knowledge work in which personal knowledge and skill are applied to unique data access and processing tasks.

In considering the first role of individual systems, it is useful to classify work processes in three categories:

1. Routine or non-routine

2. Performed frequently or infrequently

3. Performed by individual workers or small groups

Figure 2-7 illustrates the dimensions of routine/non-routine and performed frequently/infrequently; these two dimensions are important in evaluating the need for formal organizational systems.

A process that is routine and performed frequently by many different workers is generally treated as an organization process to be supported by a system developed by the information systems group. The analysis and design effort can be justified by improved performance over a large number of activities.

	Performed	
	Frequently	**Infrequently**
Routine	**Routine frequently** *Example*: Check and adjust daily schedule production	**Routine infrequently** *Example*: Prepare quarterly tax withholding statement
Non-routine	**Non-routine frequently** *Example*: Diagnose and classify a product defect report	**Non-routine infrequently** *Example*: Evaluate a proposed acquisition

FIGURE 2-7 *Two dimensions of individual work processes with examples*

The system that results may have other benefits, such as training and performance evaluation. The system provides the person performing the process with all instructions, data, and processing needed. Performance is expected to be highest by those who follow the system procedures.

At the other extreme, a non-routine process performed infrequently by one person does not lend itself to a formal system project. Such processes tend to be performed by persons with education and experience that allow them to create a process meeting the unique conditions as needed. The person doing the work must identify information needed, formulate procedures, design outputs, and execute the procedures. Such systems are developed by individuals for their own use.

Between the two extremes are many variations. There are processes that can benefit from formal systems analysis and organizational procedures, and there are processes that are not sufficiently routine or frequent to justify an organizational system. The latter must rely on individuals or groups with similar expertise to develop procedures as needed. Such procedures may be reused by the individual or group, but their development still depends on users. A significant portion of knowledge work depends on individuals being able to create such processes and procedures.

The second role of individual systems is to support tasks in which performance is dominated by individual knowledge worker expertise. The individual knowledge worker identifies the analysis to be applied, the information needed, and the organization of the output. The knowledge worker also identifies the methods to be applied and the information technology to be used.

Infrastructures and Architectures of Individual Information Systems

Individuals need an information management infrastructure similar to the one used by the organization. However, there is no need for an information systems personnel infrastructure because the system will be built and managed by the individual (perhaps with assistance from the organizational personnel) (see Figure 2-8). Therefore, the individual system will have three infrastructures:

1. *Individual information technology infrastructure.* A technical architecture for the hardware, software, and communication facilities to be used by the individual. It can include access to the organization's technical infrastructure.

2. *Individual data resources infrastructure.* An individual data architecture of the databases maintained by the individual and databases—both internal and external—accessed by the individual. The data architecture describes data resources and explains how they are related and where they are located.

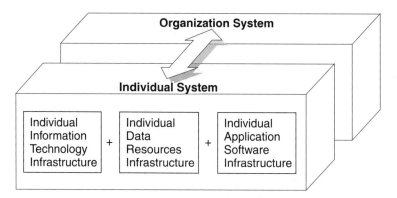

FIGURE 2-8 *Information infrastructures for an individual*

3. *Individual application software infrastructure.* Software applications required for individual work. These applications may have been provided by the organization, developed by the individual, or acquired as packaged software. Individual application software architecture describes the structure of packages and custom applications and explains how they relate to individual work and task performance.

Individual Information Management Processes

Individual information management processes are simpler than those required for the organizational system. Information management at the individual level consists of four primary processes:

1. Planning the individual technical system
2. Implementing and maintaining the individual technology and data infrastructures
3. Acquiring and using software packages or developing and implementing individual, custom applications
4. Operating and maintaining the individual system and its applications

One source of assistance in individual information management processes comes from the information system technical support function. The activities cited may be performed by an individual without external help, but personnel in the organization information management function frequently provide advice or technical assistance on system standards, software, and other technical problems.

A second source of assistance comes from within a department or group. There are often colleagues who have developed a high level of information technology expertise focused only on the technology as it is applied within the group. Some may have hardware expertise; others, specialized skill in a variety of applications software. Such "peer experts" are a source of assistance to their colleagues.

Management of individual information infrastructures and corporate support have important cost implications. The cost of an individual system includes the computer hardware, software, technical and administrative support, and time costs of user training and user system development. The cost of the hardware may be as little as one-third to one-sixth of the total cost of the system and its support.

Relationship of Small System and Large System Planning and Development Processes

◆ ◆

Although this chapter emphasizes processes for the development and management of small individual systems, it is important to understand the relationship between small system and large system processes in terms of system planning, application development processes, and development risks.

Comparing Information System Planning Processes

The planning process for the organizational system and individual systems differs in scope and complexity. Organizational system planning must identify the information needs of the entire organization, define core systems that cross internal organizational boundaries, identify interorganizational systems that interconnect the organization with suppliers and customers, identify systems that have competitive and strategic implications, and define and model data needs. The result is a plan for the technical infrastructure, a plan for the data infrastructure of centralized and distributed databases, a plan for application architecture, a schedule of development, a personnel plan, and a budget. The planning process involves numerous participants and generally results in a significant planning document.

By comparison, the planning process for an individual system involves the individual and perhaps one or more colleagues and input from an information systems specialist. System requirements are generally defined by the individual, although input from colleagues and technical specialists may be sought. Planning for systems that cross organizational boundaries involves recognition and use of such systems, as provided by the organization. Planning for individual databases and database access is much simpler and involves less complex data modeling methods than at the organizational level. Technology planning is simplified. The implementation schedule for an individual is very basic. The budget is simple in concept and scope. The plan may involve a few pages and be somewhat informal except for the detailed plans for technology and the budget. There are likely to be few predefined planning forms or reports.

Comparing Application Development Processes

Application development "in the large" involves a process in which system developers are separate from system users. The professional information analyst provides two dimensions to a project: (1) a formal process that typically follows a system development life cycle and (2) a formal on-going maintenance and improvement process. A **system development life cycle** defines the activities to be performed in developing an information system application, provides guidelines on how the activities are to be performed, and details both intermediate and final deliverables such as analyses, reports, plans, and software. Although there are a number of different life cycles, the general approach of all methods incorporates the following five phases:

1. *Feasibility study.* Defines the scope of a project, sketches alternative solution possibilities, and assesses the technical, operational, economic, and schedule feasibility of the proposal. The feasibility study provides a basis for managerial decision making in selecting projects to be approved and allocating resources.

2. *Requirements determination.* Involves fact gathering by the analysis team. Requirements are studied by analyzing documents, other similar systems, and interviewing users, managers, and others who have a stake in the new system. Completion of this phase results in a requirements document or specification.

3. *Design.* Involves formulating one or more designs that will meet designated requirements. Designs may be developed on paper, or prototypes of key elements of the proposed design may be created to elicit user comments and further evaluation. This enables users to evaluate the effectiveness of proposed designs. The result of the design phase may be the identification of a software package that meets specified needs, or an assessment of the changes necessary to use a software package.

4. *Implementation.* Involves software development or tailoring of a software package, software testing, and documentation production.

5. *Installation.* Involves installing new equipment, developing training courses, providing employee training, preparing necessary files, testing operational procedures, and starting system operation.

A second important aspect of the work of information analysts is responsibility for on-going monitoring and continuing improvement of information systems. Systems must be maintained after they are implemented because system users, the work to be accomplished, and the environment of the organization change. Systems that do not evolve soon become obsolete and extinct. Analysts respond to problem and modification requests. They evaluate the costs and benefits of suggested changes and prioritize and implement modifications and enhancements. System maintenance is a continuing activity that may lead to a new development project if there is need for major changes.

The development process for an individual system can be much simpler (see Figure 2-9). Little or no communication is involved. The individual does not need to formulate questions, describe possibilities, or explain complex concepts and models to someone else. Essentially all the information required to understand the system resides in the *individual*. The benefits of an outside observer and analyst are lost, but there is a gain in simplicity. There is no need to wait for formal authorization and project scheduling to analyze requirements and make improvements. The individual can monitor changes in requirements and directly modify individual processes.

Comparing System Development Risks

Although communication difficulties are eliminated by having a single user-developer for a small system, there are risks associated with the lack of an

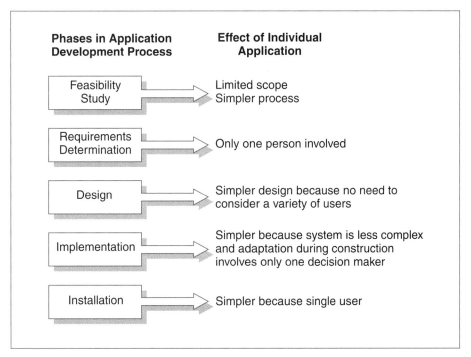

FIGURE 2-9   *Effect of individual application on development process*

objective analyst (see Figure 2-10). In large system development, users are required to interact with an analyst who questions their specifications and suggests alternatives to their system design proposals. The presence of an independent person in the requirements process increases communication problems but may reduce the chances for requirements errors often revealed through the rigorous questioning and documentation associated with the systems analysis. The analyst must obtain the requirements from users and state them in an unambiguous way so that they can be the basis for system specifications. This eliciting and documentation process can reduce ambiguities and cause users to think more clearly about requirements. Users are prompted by the analyst-user dialogue to question their requirements and consider new and innovative possibilities.

The analyst/user relationship reduces the risk of applying inappropriate methods. Users may have obsolete knowledge and be unaware of new, improved methods. Without an interaction with another person who can question why a system design is proposed, the possibilities of solving the wrong problem are increased. A user-developer may do poor problem analysis and create a system that solves the wrong problem. A user and analyst together

Issue	Effect of Separate Developer Expert	Effect of User as Developer
Application Requirements and Specification	Adds communication difficulties Increases requirements clarity because of interaction Improves documentation	Reduces outside communication Reduces outside interaction
Selection of methods to use in application	Increases base of knowledge for selection of method	Method selection constrained by user knowledge and bias
Testing	Developer has testing knowledge	User lacks testing expertise (but knows how to detect errors in work system)
Robustness of application (resistance to errors and failures)	Developer has expertise in developing robust systems	User may be able to compensate for lack of robustness (but applications may not be usable by others)

FIGURE 2-10 *Risks introduced by eliminating the independent analyst from the system development process*

may make the same error, but their dialogue during development is more likely to detect the problem.

Adequate testing is a difficult task. Familiarity with the data and the application in use makes it easier for a user-developer to spot errors in software use, but this advantage may be offset by lack of expertise in testing systems.

A mark of application system quality is robustness. A system is robust if it resists failure due to incorrect or incomplete data, user errors, and output use errors. A system is made robust by built-in instructions, clear input forms, detection and correction logic for a wide variety of errors, and output labels and formats that make outputs clear and resistant to errors in interpretation and use. Good professional developers spend significant time making applications robust for a variety of users. User-developers have less need for robustness because they understand the application and have the expertise to avoid input and output use errors. However, infrequent use causes the user-developer to forget some of the system failings of a non-robust system. Use by a colleague may also be dangerous because non-robust systems typically lack adequate documentation.

Summary

◆ ◆ ◆ ◆ ◆ ◆ ◆ ◆ ◆ ◆ ◆ ◆ ◆ ◆ ◆ ◆ ◆ ◆ ◆ ◆

◆ Knowledge work productivity is enhanced by a knowledge worker's use of information technology. The improvements focus on efficiency and effectiveness.

◆ Templates are a simple but very useful feature of many software packages. Learning how to use the template feature requires minimal investments in cost and effort, and enables users to realize small savings with each use. Standard templates are provided with a package. Custom templates are prepared by a user. Both standard templates and custom templates can be tailored to meet specific task requirements.

◆ Knowledge work processes and information access require the use of both organizational and individual management systems. An individual is responsible for the design and management of personal information management infrastructures, personal process systems to systematize and structure work, personal systems to access relevant information, and personal work management systems.

◊ The individual information management systems fit within the context of an organizational system for the entire organization. The context of the organizational system is important in understanding and using individual systems. Information is used in an organization in products and services, business processes, and knowledge work. The organizational information management system has infrastructures for technology, data resources, applications, and information system personnel. The organizational information management processes include planning, developing and maintaining infrastructures, developing and implementing applications, operating the system, and providing planning and technical support for the systems of individuals and departments.

◊ In the context of work systems, the need for an individual information management system is based on the fact that many work processes are not routine, not performed frequently, and may be performed by individuals or small groups. The individual system supports these work processes; it also supports knowledge work tasks where individual expertise dominates in the selection, design, and use of methods and data.

◊ Organizational and individual information management systems can be compared on three dimensions: planning, application development, and system development risks. Organizational information management typically includes a formal planning process that involves numerous participants and results in a formal, written plan with a schedule and budget for implementation. Individual system planning is more informal, involves fewer people, and results in less documentation.

◊ The application development process for organizational systems follows a formal application development methodology with well-specified methods. The process of individual systems follows a simplified "development in the small" approach. Knowledge of small system development can be useful to those who specialize in information systems because analysis, design, and development in small, individual systems provides an excellent starting point for learning basic concepts that are extended in building organizational systems.

EXERCISES

1. Investigate the template features available with your word processing package.

    a. Find the list of standard document templates provided with the package. Select two for use. Print the results.

    b. Use the custom document template facilities to develop a personalized template for a memo. Include a graphic that communicates something about you. Save the template. Use the template and print the results prior to adding any text.

2. Investigate the template features available with your spreadsheet processing package.

    a. Find the list of standard spreadsheet templates provided with the package. Select two for use. Print the results.

    b. Use the custom spreadsheet template facilities to develop a personalized template for an application that is of interest to you, such as a personal financial analysis or an analysis of courses, credits, grades, and grade points.

3. Make a list of classes of documents and spreadsheets you prepare that might be amenable to productivity improvement with the use of document or spreadsheet templates. Estimate the savings in time and effort for each potential template (per use and per year over likely uses). For each template, indicate whether completeness of output might be enhanced by the use of a template.

4. Explore advanced features of templates for both documents and spreadsheets. Learn how to add styles, macros, automatic text entries, toolbar buttons, customized menus, and shortcut key settings. For example, try inserting a standard distribution list to a template for a business memo. The distribution list can be selected from a menu that is stored with the menu template. The menu appears along with the template.

5. Miscommunication between users and an analysts can result in a system that does not meet user requirements. In personal applications, communication concerning system requirements is with oneself. How can one miscommunicate with oneself in determining personal application requirements? How can you overcome or compensate for such miscommunication?

6. If you developed an application for your use, why would anyone else want to use it? What problems might result if someone else used your application? What extra effort might be required before your application was used by a colleague in your department? What additional effort might be required if your application were to be used by an unknown user with whom you will not have contact?

7. A peer expert is an individual in a department or workgroup who has better than average computer skills. Others in the group will consult the

peer expert instead of calling a help line. Are you a peer expert or do you use a peer expert? Describe some incidents that illustrate your role as a peer expert or a user of peer expertise. Describe any situations in which peer expertise was insufficient.

8. An organizational system places constraints on individual systems. Some of these are very useful; others are constraining. For your organization, list those organizational system constraints (such as standards, approved software, version control, and limits to access) and explain their value to the organization and their value or cost to individual systems.

9. *External Data Exercise:* Do Exercise 2 in Chapter 8. (Chapter 8 focuses on accessing external data on the Internet. The External Data Exercises included in Chapters 1-7 are designed to prepare you for the more difficult exercises presented in Chapter 8.)

Analyzing Individual Knowledge Work

◊   ◊   ◊   ◊   ◊   ◊   ◊   ◊

OBJECTIVES

After completing this chapter, you should be able to:

◆ Explain the three major kinds of knowledge work tasks: job-specific, knowledge-building and maintenance, and work management.

◆ Explain the four major groups of knowledge work activities and the 14 activities in the groups.

◆ Explain a simple, systematic approach to analyzing individual knowledge work tasks and activities.

◆ Explain how analysis relates to the selection and use of packaged software.

KEY TERMS AND CONCEPTS

This chapter introduces the following key terms and concepts, listed in the order in which they appear:

job-specific task
work-management task
quantitative analysis
qualitative analysis
input data
output data

interrupt-driven task
calendar-driven task
workload-driven task
internal data sources
external data sources
requirements analysis

task/activity analysis
task effort profile
activity profile index
importance index

As explained in Chapter 2, a knowledge worker generally has two information management systems available for use: (1) a formal, organizational system that processes transactions, prepares reports, and provides access to organizational transactions and status data, and (2) a personal information system. The design, development, and management of the organizational system is the responsibility of the information system function. Although the organization may provide some design and management assistance, the design and management of a personal knowledge work system is an individual responsibility.

The design, development, and management of a personal information system are important issues for an individual because the information system used in work has a significant impact on productivity. It affects both effectiveness in achieving work objectives and efficiency in using time and energy. Having a well-designed information system is, therefore, an important personal objective.

The first step in designing and developing a personal information system is to analyze one's knowledge work in terms of tasks to be accomplished and the activities required to perform them. This information can then be used to establish the need for various software packages which will provide the general software functionality for work.

Knowledge Work Tasks

◆ ◆ ◆ ◆ ◆ ◆ ◆ ◆ ◆ ◆ ◆ ◆ ◆ ◆ ◆ ◆ ◆ ◆ ◆ ◆

The information system requirements for knowledge workers are based on their work activities. A knowledge worker has **job-specific tasks** assigned by the organization. These tasks contribute directly to the objectives of the organization. In addition to job-specific tasks, a knowledge worker must also accomplish tasks that build and maintain knowledge and tasks that manage knowledge work (see Figure 3-1).

Job-specific Tasks

Every job-specific knowledge work task is associated with an organizational objective that has some desired outcome. The task may be short or long, repetitive or ad hoc, standardized or novel. The task may be an individual assignment or it may involve working with a team, a group, or a task force. Examples of job-specific tasks include:

◊ Preparing a budget

◊ Analyzing a budget in terms of estimated and actual expenses

◊ Planning and scheduling a project

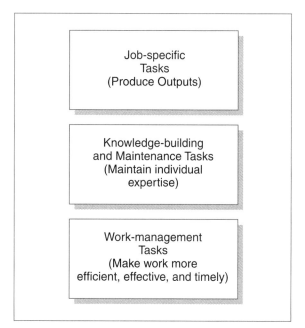

FIGURE 3-1   *Three types of knowledge work tasks*

◊ Researching a business opportunity and preparing a proposal

◊ Conducting an employee evaluation

◊ Preparing an action plan

◊ Preparing a presentation or lecture

◊ Persuading others about plans and actions

Knowledge-building and Maintenance Tasks

Knowledge workers bring personal knowledge to their jobs, obtained by formal schooling and work experience. But to maintain their effectiveness on the job, they must maintain their knowledge and expertise. Knowledge-building and maintenance tasks may be very job specific, or they may be more general and provide a context in which work is performed. Some examples of tasks associated with building and maintaining knowledge are:

◊ Scanning professional literature

◊ Attending professional meetings

◊ Learning about new technology

◊ Learning features of new software

◊ Building and maintaining a network of contacts

Work-management Tasks

When knowledge workers engage in tasks directed toward organizational objectives, they must usually plan the set of activities required to produce the desired outcomes. In some cases, as in recurring knowledge work tasks, the required activities and their sequencing are clear. In other cases, planning and sequencing activities may require considerable, ongoing effort.

Knowledge workers are often involved in several overlapping tasks during a given time period. Part of the **work-management task** for each knowledge worker is to allocate effort appropriately among tasks that compete for time and attention. Overall scheduling is a work-management task.

In order to carry out knowledge work tasks, knowledge workers acquire, use, and maintain various resources in their work environment. These resources, which provide a productive work environment for specific tasks, include:

◊ Reference sources and facilities to acquire reference information

◊ Manual and computer files that relate to current and anticipated activities

◊ Software applications

A productive work environment requires setup, operation, maintenance, and protection of information infrastructure, files, and applications. Tasks include daily startup, loading software and creating access methods such as icons, loading new releases and upgrades of software, and protection activities such as access security, virus detection and removal, and backup.

The protection activity of access security applies to equipment, data, and application outputs such as spreadsheets or documents. Access security measures may involve physical protection mechanisms such as locks on equipment and locked cabinets for storage of diskettes and operating documents. There may be access security codes applied to applications and files. For example, a financial analyst using a spreadsheet processor may protect worksheets from being opened (and reviewed) unless the user provides a password. The worksheet may be write protected, preventing certain cells from being altered unless the user has the proper password.

Viruses are small, unauthorized programs that are introduced into a computer system by diskettes containing the programs or by some programs received over electronic mail or attached to files received electronically. Viruses range from those that merely display playful messages to those that destroy programs, data, and operating system functions. The measures to protect against viruses will be discussed in more detail later in the text. As part of the protection activities of work management, a knowledge work system should have software that detects viruses and removes them before they can infect the system. The software can be set to check all files for viruses.

Another important protection activity is backup. Although clearly vital, backup is often neglected. Many applications, such as word processors, have commands that perform automatic backup while documents are being created. However, this is insufficient for protecting against the failure or destruction of hardware. Protection against this possibility requires backup onto another computer or backup on removable media such as diskettes, backup tape, or some other permanent mechanism. Backup of all stored data can be very time consuming and require significant storage. Selective backup and compression are two methods to reduce backup time and backup storage requirements. Backup software packages apply selective backup by identifying changes so that only changes made since the last backup need to be copied. Compression methods reduce storage requirements by recoding the data using methods explained in Chapter 14.

Knowledge Work Activities

◆ ◆ ◆ ◆ ◆ ◆ ◆ ◆ ◆ ◆ ◆ ◆ ◆ ◆ ◆ ◆ ◆ ◆ ◆ ◆

Every task requires a set of activities that must be organized and sequenced. Most tasks can be characterized by one or a few predominant knowledge work activities. These activities apply to all types of tasks. For the purpose of managing knowledge work, 14 knowledge work activities have been classified into four major groups: (1) acquiring knowledge, (2) designing, (3) making decisions, and (4) communicating (see Figure 3-2). These activities may be part of an individual project or may be integrated into collaborative work with colleagues or teams.

Classifying activities is useful in understanding a knowledge worker's tasks. It also helps establish a relationship between activities and software functions.

Acquiring Knowledge

A major characteristic of knowledge work is the expectation that the knowledge worker either has the knowledge required for the task or is able to acquire it. Three activities are employed in acquiring knowledge: scan, monitor, and search.

1. *Scan.* Scanning is an awareness activity. The knowledge worker pays attention to various media and sources to identify and obtain information for knowledge work tasks. For example, scanning may be associated with a job-specific task or with a knowledge-building and maintenance task. Scanning can identify new information sources.

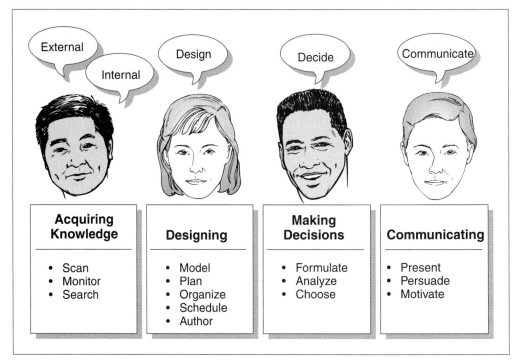

FIGURE 3-2 *Four types of knowledge work activities*

2. *Monitor.* Monitoring—reviewing sources expected to contain relevant information—tends to be a more specific activity than scanning. For example, a manager may monitor assigned activities by reviewing regular reports, but scan other documents (such as complaints) to increase awareness and identify problems that might not be found in the structured report.

3. *Search.* Searching is a very specific acquisition activity. The knowledge objective is defined and the knowledge worker must decide where to search and how to find the appropriate information. The search activity is characterized by known information objectives and unknown sources.

Designing

Design activities are part of most knowledge work tasks. Design may involve design of an output or process. There are five activities within the design category: model, plan, organize, schedule, and author.

1. *Model.* A model is an abstraction of a physical object or a process. It can be a visualization, a diagram or chart, or a mathematical or program representation. Many products of knowledge work require that models be constructed either as an output or to guide the knowledge work task. At some level, almost all design involves representation and modeling.

2. *Plan.* Planning involves generating alternatives. Selected options must be sequenced and resource implications analyzed. Planning helps knowledge workers identify a set of tasks that must be accomplished in a particular order.

3. *Organize.* Organizing involves identifying and arranging the resources necessary to complete a plan and defining responsibilities.

4. *Schedule.* Scheduling associates planned activities with available resources. The schedule specifies when each activity is to begin and when it should be completed. It identifies the person or organization responsible for each.

5. *Author.* Authoring is creating an output in the form of a document, presentation, procedure, or program. Documents can be created in various formats, such as reports, analyses, memoranda, or minutes. Almost every knowledge work output involves some authoring. The result of authoring can include text, graphics, multimedia presentations, flowcharts, or programs.

Making Decisions

There are three activities in making decisions: formulate, analyze, and choose. These activities often involve integration into the work of others.

1. *Formulate.* Formulating involves defining a problem correctly and completely. It includes recognizing symptoms that suggest a problem and distinguishing between real and apparent problems.

2. *Analyze.* Analyzing involves enumerating and evaluating alternatives. The analysis may be both quantitative and qualitative. For example, a return on investment is a **quantitative analysis**; an evaluation of effect of employee motivation is **qualitative**.

3. *Choose.* Choosing involves selecting from alternatives according to some criteria. There may be a single criterion (such as rate of return) or multiple criteria (such as those related to financial, motivational, social, or political elements).

Communicating

Communicating involves three activities: present, persuade, and motivate. They may be individual or part of collaborative or team activities.

1. *Present.* Presenting involves delivering and transferring information. Delivery can take a variety of forms. These include printed reports, electronic messages, files sent to others, multimedia computer presentations, and oral presentations.

2. *Persuade.* Persuading involves changing the beliefs of others. It may include presenting information organized with arguments and lines of reasoning to persuade the receiver.

3. *Motivate.* Motivating means energizing others to action. Although it may include both presenting and persuading communication, additional elements are often included. For example, sales data may be provided at a meeting and arguments presented as to the cause of a decline in sales; these are followed by a presentation that interprets the data and motivates the listeners to corrective action.

Supplementary Activities

◆ ◆

Knowledge work activities (of acquiring, designing, deciding, and communicating) involve some supplemental clerical activities. The distinction between supplemental clerical activities and knowledge work activities rests primarily on intellectual content and expertise requirements. Knowledge work activities tend to be dependent on knowledge and expertise, whereas clerical activities are associated with the physical operations associated with knowledge work.

The major types of activities supplemental to knowledge work are input, formatting, filing and retrieving, and receiving and distributing information (see Figure 3-3). Although some of these activities may be assigned to clerical support staff, many are performed by knowledge workers themselves, both because they are interleaved with knowledge work activities and difficult to separate, and because the high ratio of knowledge work activities to supplemental clerical work means that a knowledge worker may not be able to keep a clerical assistant profitably employed.

Creating Input Data

The keyboard is the primary method of creating **input data** for knowledge workers, but other technology may be employed. Voice input, touch panels, mouse pointing, dictation, optical character recognition (OCR), and voice mail are examples of input technology. Keyboard entry of numeric data in spreadsheets and text in authoring and e-mail tend to dominate the clerical activities of knowledge work. The term "typing" is often used to describe keyboarding of text. Useful clerical skills for knowledge workers are touch typing for entry of text data and touch entry of numeric data using a numeric keypad.

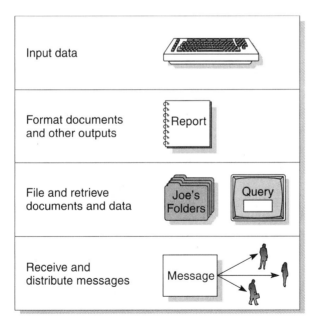

FIGURE 3-3   *Supplementary activities for knowledge work*

This allows the keying to be done without looking at the keyboard. Tutorial programs are available for those who need to develop these skills.

Formatting Documents and Output Data

Establishing the layout and format of **output data** such as spreadsheets or reports may involve significant knowledge and expertise, but frequently the layout and formatting follow easily from the problem and employ established routines and customs. Standard layouts can be stored for use in reports and memoranda.

When the format of a report is important to its acceptance and readability, the design may be thought of as knowledge work. This point illustrates the fact that the boundary between knowledge work and clerical work can at times be fuzzy. Editing a report to improve readability and comprehension generally involves knowledge work skills. Figure 3-4 illustrates the impact of format changes on readability and impact.

Filing and Retrieving Documents and Data

Maintaining data in paper document or electronic form is a major clerical activity. Documents or data must be classified before they can be filed or stored. The classification may involve judgment and expertise, but the subsequent clerical operations of filing or data entry are routine. Most manual document filing systems involve file folders based on a single descriptor. This is very constraining for information retrieval. Supplementary electronic indices may use a more complex set of descriptors to identify document file folders.

Retrieving data from electronic files or databases involves defining search criteria (a knowledge work activity) and entering retrieval commands (a clerical activity). The same concepts apply to external databases maintained outside the organization. The conceptual formulation of search strategy, descriptors, and databases to access is a knowledge work activity; the entry of descriptors and search commands is clerical in nature, but a vital supplement to the knowledge work activities.

Receiving and Distributing Information

There are numerous clerical activities associated with receiving and distributing information. Mail must be opened and sorted into types of response required. E-mail systems must be opened and messages read. Telephone messages or voice mail messages must be received.

In distributing information, letters must be addressed and mailed, faxes entered, e-mail opened and messages entered and sent, and voice messages delivered either personally or through voice mail.

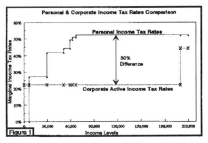

FIGURE 3-4a   *"Before" version of a newsletter*

Source: David Brickley and Dan Miller, "Publishing and Presentation Makeover." *PC World*, March 1994, pp. 238-239. Reprinted with permission of PC World Communications, Inc.

Knowledge Work Task Attributes

◆ ◆

Knowledge workers engage in tasks that are directed toward organizational objectives. Each knowledge work task consists of a set of activities that the

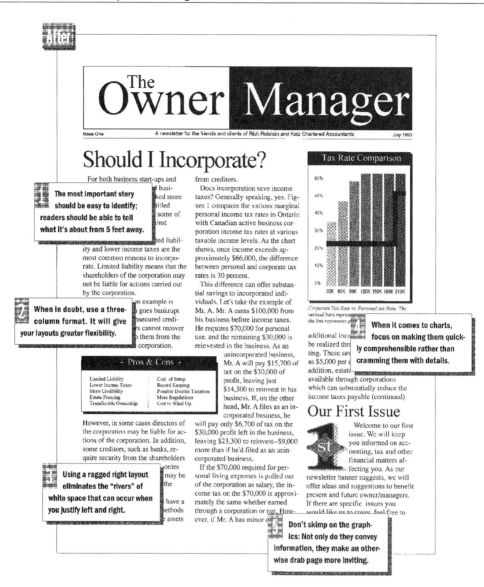

FIGURE 3-4b *"After" version of a newsletter, reformatted for impact and readability*

Source: David Brickley and Dan Miller, "Publishing and Presentation Makeover." *PC World,* March 1994, pp. 238-239. Reprinted with permission of PC World Communications, Inc.

knowledge worker must perform. In many tasks, one or a few activities dominate. Each knowledge work task has attributes in addition to the set of activities that must be performed (see Figure 3-5). The three major attributes are locus of responsibility, timing, and data requirements.

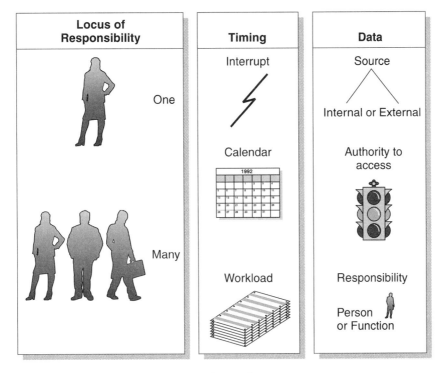

FIGURE 3-5   *Knowledge work task attributes*

Locus of Responsibility

A task may be the responsibility of one individual, a group of individuals within a department or workgroup, or a task force that crosses organizational boundaries. The locus attribute affects how a task is organized and managed.

A task that is the responsibility of one individual has low coordination requirements. The individual may need to get information from others, but the use of the information does not require further interaction. Scheduling of task activities is within the time constraints of one person.

When the locus of responsibility is within the organizational boundaries of a department or workgroup, the members tend to be reasonably homogeneous relative to areas of common knowledge, similarity of working methods, and work relationships. Coordination and management are facilitated by homogeneity, proximity, and shared access to data.

Locus of responsibility can cross boundaries of departments (a crossfunctional team) or organizational boundaries (an inter-company team). The teams are less homogeneous than intra-department teams. In such situations, the communication and management requirements are increased because of the physical distance of members and because of different backgrounds, work methods, and work cultures.

Timing

Not all tasks have the same timing characteristics. Timing can be divided into interrupt-driven, calendar-driven, or workload-driven tasks. These characteristics are important in managing activities for a single task and for a mix of tasks. A single task such as preparing an analysis for a potential investment has due dates for the analysis and each of the activities required to produce it. A person may have a mix of tasks; for example, a financial analyst may work concurrently on an analysis for a proposed investment, negotiations to make a purchase of an investment, and financing for an agreed-upon investment. When timing characteristics are combined in a task mix, issues of concurrency and task switching become important. Concurrency is the occurrence of active work on more than one task in the same time period. Task switching is moving attention from one task to another when more than one is being worked on concurrently. These will be examined further in Chapter 4.

Interrupt-driven tasks are initiated by some event or a demand that must be satisfied. Interrupts are random rather than well-specified as to timing. An interrupt may have an external source (such as a customer complaint). An interrupt may also have an internal source (such as errors detected in a process being monitored).

Calendar-driven tasks are initiated by a date, such as the first of the month or the end of the year. Calendar-driven tasks are usually deadline oriented, since the completion date is known in advance.

Workload-driven tasks are initiated when a certain level of need for the task is established. For example, a knowledge worker charged with investigating customer service complaints may handle these only when a certain number of complaints have accumulated. Another example is updating a database of personal contacts important to one's work. This is typically done when a batch of updates has accumulated.

The timing considerations that determine when a task will be initiated also affect work when more than one task is active concurrently. Most knowledge workers have more than one active task. They are limited in their ability to concentrate on more than one task activity at a time. However, some task activities are relatively automatic and have low concentration requirements. They can be performed at the same time as another task activity requiring higher concentration. For example, a knowledge worker authoring a text can compose (an authoring activity) and type (a clerical activity) at the same time if typing has been learned well enough to be automatic.

Task switching is used to change attention from one activity to another and between active tasks. For example, an auditor making data collection plans has to refocus her attention when an important phone call is received. The problems in concurrent tasks will be examined further in Chapter 4.

Data Requirements

Data requirements will be covered in Chapter 5. The important attributes relative to knowledge work activities are source, authority, and responsibility. These affect the nature of the work performed by a knowledge worker.

An important distinction concerns internal versus external data sources. **Internal data sources** such as organizational files tend to be more accessible and the person accessing the data can obtain personal knowledge of its quality. **External data sources** such as government data or reference data may require extra effort to access and data quality may be uncertain or difficult to determine.

Authority refers to authorization to access data. The highest level of access authority is to read and write (alter). "Read only" authority allows access but no alteration of the stored data. For example, an individual may have authority only to read the general ledger, but may both read and write records for a project.

Even though many users access a data source, maintenance responsibility is usually assigned to one person or function. There are well-defined procedures for maintaining data. This usually includes responsibility for error control in the data and for updating the data. Organizational databases tend to be tightly controlled. Department and workgroup databases have control appropriate to the type of data and type of use. Data maintained by individuals is their responsibility.

Systematic Approach to Analyzing Individual Requirements

Knowledge work is characterized by complex tasks and complex relationships among tasks. Knowledge work is not well understood. There are few established methods for improving the effectiveness and efficiency of knowledge workers. Even though knowledge work differs significantly from manual, production, and clerical work, there is evidence that knowledge work processes can be improved significantly. The desired results of systematic **requirements analysis** are changes that lead to improvements in the environment, tools, and processes of the individual knowledge worker.

Why should individual knowledge workers perform a requirements analysis? Although many knowledge workers may be engaged in the same or similar tasks and activities, the *mix* of tasks and activities tends to be different for each knowledge worker. This is because individuals are often at different levels of knowledge, or at different stages in their professional development, from their peers. This observation implies that it is appropriate to consider requirements analysis for each individual knowledge worker. It also means the methods used must be simple and effective. The analysis should be simple enough to be repeated when job requirements change.

Knowledge workers have resources and tools to support their activities. Organizations invest significant sums in computing equipment and other tools to support knowledge work. Far too often, however, tools are allocated based on their availability, or on "whatever is current," rather than on an understanding of need. A systematic analysis of needs helps determine the level of resources and their allocation.

A systematic approach is useful because most knowledge workers have not had training or experience in analyzing their own work and work processes. They often think of their work as having so much variety and complexity that it is impossible to think about it in a systematic way. A simple systematic requirements analysis helps overcome this misconception. Knowledge work cannot be reduced to routine work, but an analysis will lead to improved information environments and process and productivity improvements.

The process for identifying requirements for a system to support knowledge work involves three analyses:

1. *Task/activity analysis.* This analysis, covered in this chapter, summarizes the tasks performed, the mix of activities for each task, the proportion of time required for each task, and the relative importance of the different knowledge work activities. The emphasis is on the individual.

2. *Concurrency and collaborative work requirements.* The concepts underlying these requirements are explained in Chapter 4 along with simple methods for defining and documenting them. Concurrency requirements arise from the fact that knowledge workers must often work on more than one task at a time. Collaborative work requirements arise from tasks that involve collaboration with one or more persons. Both concurrent and collaborative work requirements involve task scheduling.

3. *Data and communication requirements.* These requirements (Chapter 5) identify sources of data and need for communications. They are the basis for designing information access and communications capabilities.

Task/Activity Analysis

◆ ◆

Task/activity analysis consists of four steps: (1) defining tasks, (2) developing a task effort profile, (3) defining activities and assigning importance, and (4) creating an activity profile.

Defining Tasks

The first step in the Task/Activity analysis is to name and briefly describe each job-specific task. In this analysis, tasks represent the kinds of work performed rather than small individual assignments. For example, a task is "interview prospective employees" rather than the assignment to "interview candidates for accounts receivable clerk" and "analyze cause of cost overruns" rather than "analyze Delta project overruns." If the knowledge work of an individual involves numerous job-specific tasks, focus on the "top ten" and possibly use one more category for "other tasks."

After identifying job-specific tasks, identify knowledge-building and maintenance tasks and knowledge work management tasks. These should also be broad tasks rather than individual assignments. For example, a knowledge-building and maintenance task is "build skills in using analytical software" rather than "learn to use graphing feature of spreadsheet." A knowledge work management task is "keep software packages up to date" rather than "install new word processor." There are usually fewer knowledge-building and maintenance tasks than job-specific tasks (although that might not be correct for some knowledge workers). This separation highlights the importance of each type of task. Figure 3-6 is a worksheet to use to record information about individual tasks and activities. Entering the worksheet data into a spreadsheet software package will make it easier to compute the data and create a graph of results. The result at this stage is a list of the majority of the tasks performed by a knowledge worker.

Developing a Task Effort Profile

The final step of task identification involves estimating the proportion of effort applied to each task. Since activities occur with different frequencies (some may be performed only once per year, for example), base proportions on annual workload. The Task/Activity form in Figure 3-6 has a column labeled "percent effort." Divide 100 percent among all of the tasks listed. Make sure the total is 100 percent. Be sure to include all the tasks identified. This column is the "task effort profile."

A **task effort profile** is a best estimate of how an individual spends time. It is useful in designing an information systems infrastructure and knowledge work processes and suggests the relative importance of types of software packages and applications software.

Defining and Rating Activities

Every knowledge worker task involves a variety of activities. Most tasks, however, consist of one or a few dominant activities. In this step, characterize each task by its most significant activities. The Task/Activity form in Figure 3-6 has

Name _____

Date _____

Knowledge Worker
Task/Activity Matrix

Assign a number from 1 (least) to 10 (most) important for the 3 to 5 most significant activities of each task

	Percent effort	Knowledge Work Activities																
		Acquire			Design					Decide			Communicate			Supplemental		
																	Clerical	
Activities / **Tasks**		Scan	Monitor	Search	Model	Plan	Organize	Schedule	Author	Formulate	Analyze	Choose	Present	Persuade	Motivate	Input data	Format	File/ retrieve	Receive/ distribute
Job Specific																		
Knowledge Building & Maintaining																		
Knowledge Work Management																		
Activity Effort and Importance Index	Sum of (task percent effort × activity importance rating) × 10	100%																

FIGURE 3-6 *Task/Activity matrix used to record and analyze knowledge work tasks and activities*

a column for each of the activities described in this chapter. Consider each task separately and identify its dominant activities. Focus on the dominant ones by limiting the entries to a maximum of three to five activities per task.

Within each task, rate the importance of the dominant activities. Use a scale of 1 to 10, where 10 reflects the highest level of importance for an activity and 1 the lowest level of importance. Choose rating numbers that reflect perceptions of the relative importance of activities within tasks. Note that the rating is the importance of each activity to the task, rather than the proportion of time spent on it. Perceptions of the importance of the dominant activities is recorded in this part of the analysis.

Computing Activity Profile Indexes

To compute an **activity profile index**, multiply each activity importance rating by the task effort percentage for the task in which the activity occurs. Compute for each activity column the sum of the products of task effort percentage times activity importance. Insert this total at the bottom of each activity column. The result is a number for each activity that indexes the overall importance of that activity to an individual's work. The numbers do not have any intrinsic meaning; they are neither hours nor priorities. They are activity **importance indexes**.

A simple bar graph turns the activity profile indexes into a useful report to show the activities that are dominant across all individual tasks. If the activity profile indexes were prepared with a spreadsheet processor, the bar graph facilities of the package can be used to produce a graph with little extra effort.

Interpreting the Activity Profile

The activity profile provides a basis for analyzing software needs. It is useful in the design of a knowledge work environment and support structures. The activity profile focuses on activities instead of tasks because software capabilities are designed to support activities. There may be task-oriented software for some tasks, but for most tasks the software used is generalized for the activities to be performed. In other words, the activities provide a general basis for selecting software. For example, authoring as an activity is supported by word processing software.

Task/activity analysis identifies the activities that should be supported by the information system software. Without specifying the details of important features, the activities suggest the need for both generalized and specialized software packages that provide the required function. The list in Figure 3-7 suggests the type of generalized software functionality that should be considered for each activity. The results of an individual generalized software package analysis is a list of the generalized software packages needed.

General Activity to be Supported	Generalized Software Package
Acquire	
Scan	Communications, word processor or text database
Monitor	Communications, note taking, and perhaps text database
Search	Communications

Design	
Model	Mathematical modeling, flowcharting, drawing or sketching
Plan	Spreadsheet, project management, financial modeling
Organize	Spreadsheet, word processor, personal information management (PIM)
Schedule	Personal information management, project management, spreadsheet
Author	Word processing with add-ons such as speller, grammar checker, outliner

Decide	
Formulate	Mathematical modeling, spreadsheet, outliner
Analyze	Spreadsheet, math modeling, statistical analysis
Choose	Spreadsheet, math modeling

Communicate	
Present	Presentation, graphics and charting, color, multimedia
Persuade	Presentation, graphics, word processing
Motivate	Presentation, demonstration, PIM

Supplemental	
Input data	Word processing, optical character recognition (OCR), forms and work flow
Format	Word processing, desktop publishing, drawing and sketching
File and retrieve	Database, file and directory management, file and text search
Receive and distribute	Mail list management, file and text search, e-mail

FIGURE 3-7 *Examples of generalized software packages*

Generalized software packages provide broad support for activities, but may not meet specific needs of some tasks. There are many specialized packages designed for knowledge work tasks or classes of tasks. Following are some examples of specialized software packages.

◇ *Document management.* An individual needs to input graphs, pictures, and documents not currently available on computer media. In addition to scanning hardware, specialized software is needed to control the scanner and store and catalog the results in usable collections.

◇ *Stock portfolio tracking.* An individual may need to keep track of a portfolio of stocks, and could use spreadsheet software, a generalized software capability. However, specialized software for tracking investments is available. Such software may be easier to use and provides more capabilities. To illustrate the extended, specialized capabilities available, one portfolio management package automatically retrieves daily stock prices by modem.

◇ *Tax preparation.* Tax returns could be prepared using spreadsheets or word processors, but there are specialized tax packages that support data input and output and computations and rules to simplify this task.

◇ *Professional practice billing.* Doing the billing for a small professional practice could use generalized software. However, specialized practice management software packages are available for many professions.

Analysis involves examining each task and its activities to identify needs that are not met or are poorly met by generalized packages. Known specialized packages are then listed. If no specialized packages are known but there is a reasonable expectation that a specialized package exists, the requirement should be listed for later search. The result of the analysis is a list of needs and known specialized software packages (or notes to search for specialized packages likely to be available).

Needs that cannot be met by generalized packages or specialized packages may require the design and construction of custom software. A list of tasks or task activities that may profit from custom software is sufficient at this time. The design of custom software will be covered in Part 3.

The task activity profile can also be used to evaluate the relative effort devoted to job-specific versus knowledge-building and maintenance and knowledge work management tools. This evaluation should be based on the type of work. For example, some knowledge work jobs require very large commitments to building and updating knowledge; others require less. The analysis should address the question of whether the allocation allows existing expertise to be maintained and new expertise to be built. Since individual ability to add value to the organization is highly dependent on expertise, too low a level of individual investment in maintaining and building expertise may be detrimental to both the individual and the organization.

Examples of Task/Activity Analyses

◆ ◆ ◆ ◆ ◆ ◆ ◆ ◆ ◆ ◆ ◆ ◆ ◆ ◆ ◆ ◆ ◆ ◆ ◆ ◆

Two examples of task/activity analyses illustrate the concept and procedures. The examples also illustrate an important consideration in performing such an analysis. This consideration is that the procedure must be simple enough so that it may be repeated when changes in task assignments suggest the current analysis is no longer applicable.

Task/Activity Analysis for a Professor

Figure 3-8 is the completed Task/Activity form for a professor. The five most significant job-specific tasks are listed. They take 65 percent of his time. Five knowledge-building and maintenance tasks take 25 percent. This allocation of 25 percent reflects the vital need of a professor to keep up to date in order to teach and research effectively. Two knowledge work maintenance tasks take the remaining 10 percent. The analysis adds up to 100 percent by ignoring small or relatively unimportant tasks. The idea is to focus on the tasks and activities that take the most effort and time.

The most important activities for each task are given a ranking from 1 to 10. For each activity, the importance rankings in the column are multiplied by the percent of effort for the task. These products are then summed. The sum for the columns represents the index of relative importance of the activity. In the example, authoring—with an importance index of 52—is by far the most important activity. The next most important activity is the design activity of modeling with an index of 33.5. Modeling for creating instructional materials and writing for papers and book chapters consists of visualizing a structure and flow of ideas and logic. The third most important knowledge work activity is the communication activity of presentation. The importance index suggests the relative importance of the activities and indicates how support resources should be allocated.

The most important activities in the example are author, model, and present. An information management system supporting the faculty member should therefore have very good software support for authoring, modeling, and presentation. On the other hand, support for decision making would not receive much use from this knowledge worker.

The same type of analysis is performed with the supplemental activities. The importance index for the supplemental activities can also be valuable in assessing the type of software support required.

The results of task/activity analysis can be presented as a bar chart. Since the analysis is based upon estimates and judgments, the index numbers themselves

Name _____   Date _____

Knowledge Worker Task/Activity Matrix

Assign a number from 1 (least) to 10 (most) important for the 3 to 5 most significant activities of each task

Activities / Tasks	Percent effort	Acquire			Design					Decide			Communicate			Supplemental			
																Input data	Clerical		Receive/ distribute
		Scan	Monitor	Search	Model	Plan	Organize	Schedule	Author	Formulate	Analyze	Choose	Present	Persuade	Motivate		Format	File/ retrieve	
Job Specific																			
Prepare courses	10%				8			3	2			1					1		
Prepare & deliver class sessions	35%								10				8	5	2		1		
Write papers	5%			3	5				10							1			
Write textbook chapters	10%				8	5			10						2		1	1	
Serve on committees	5%				5									3	2			1	1
Knowledge Building & Maintaining																			
Track PC Hdwr & Sftwr developments	5%	5	6		3													3	1
Track SA&D progress	5%	4	6	5														1	1
Learn a language	5%																		
Keep current on Internet, Email, Usenet, Web	5%	6	7		6		3						4			2			3
Keep up with Telecomm education	5%	5	7		4														2
Knowledge Work Management																			
Organize computer stuff	5%				8	2					4	3		5					1
Organize workload	5%					5		4		1	2	3							1
Activity Effort and Importance Index — Sum of (task percent effort × activity importance rating) × 10	100%	10	13	4	33.5	8.5	1.5	5	52	0.5	3	4	30	21.5	10	1.5	5.5	3.5	5

FIGURE 3-8   *Knowledge work task/activity matrix for a professor*

have no intrinsic meaning. The bar chart is an appropriate way to visualize the relative importance of activities. A bar chart for the faculty example is shown in Figure 3-9.

Task/Activity Analysis for a Knowledge Work Manager

Figure 3-10 is a Task/Activity Analysis for a knowledge work manager. The bar chart in Figure 3-11 illustrates the importance indexes for the manager. The position is that of supervisor of a group of professional and non-degreed technical knowledge workers. Their jobs are to process text of laws and rules from various legislative and administrative bodies to produce legal research databases on CD-ROM. The staff must test the results and make corrections. There are three to six projects active at a time with file sizes ranging from less than a million up to a billion characters. The manager's six activities with the highest importance indexes are monitor, persuade, analyze, choose, plan, and schedule.

A short discussion of three of these (monitor, analyze, and choose) illustrates the task/activity analysis. Monitoring activities are associated with both job-specific and knowledge building/maintenance activities. The job-specific tasks involve monitoring employee progress on projects. This includes checking monthly and weekly schedules, status reports, and progress reports.

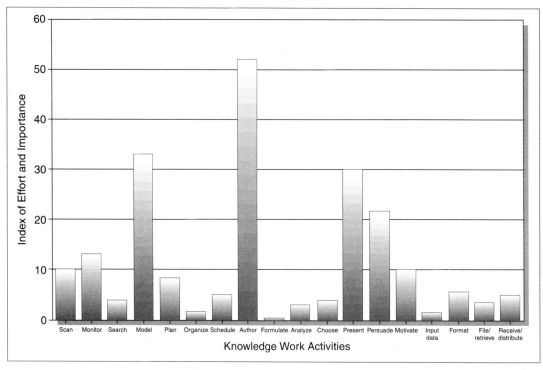

FIGURE 3-9 *Bar chart presentation of importance indexes for a professor*

Knowledge Worker
Task/Activity Matrix

Name J. R. E.   Date October 3, 1995

Assign a number from 1 (least) to 10 (most) important for the 3 to 5 most significant activities of each task

Tasks	Percent effort	Acquire			Design				Author	Decide			Communicate			Supplemental — Clerical			
		Scan	Monitor	Search	Model	Plan	Organize	Schedule		Formulate	Analyze	Choose	Present	Persuade	Motivate	Input data	Format	File/retrieve	Receive/distribute
Job Specific																			
Scheduling & monitoring employees' project progress	20%		5			7		9			7	8				5			
Supervisory administrative tasks (interviewing, salary review, etc)	10%		7				9		6					8		5			
Employee feedback, development and training	15%		6			4				7				8	8				
Intra/interdepartmental status meetings	10%	5					7						5						
Verbal status reporting for managers	5%			4									6	7					
Written status reporting for managers	5%			4									6	9			5		
Receiving & responding to voice & electronic messages	8%			3							5	8	6						7
Sorting through in-pan; reading routing & filing relevant memos	5%										7	4							7
Analyzing & reporting departmental labor resource allocation	5%			6			6		8		9						6	8	
Knowledge Building & Maintaining																			
Daily clipping from electronic newspapers & trade journals	5%		8	6															
Informal interaction with other supervisors & managers	5%		9							6									
Exploring word processing and spreadsheet macros	2%			7	7					4									
Knowledge Work Management																			
Planning of work to be done during the day/week	3%					8		8				4				2			
Organizing, saving & forwarding e-mail files	2%					7												8	
Activity Effort and Importance Index — Sum of (task percent effort × activity importance rating) × 10	100%	5	34.5	13.8	1.4	23.8	19	20.4	10	14.3	26	25.6	15.8	28	12	15.6	5.5	6.6	9.1

FIGURE 3-10   *Knowledge work task/activity matrix for a knowledge work manager*

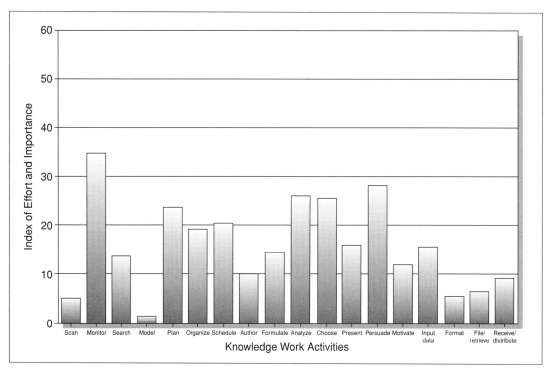

FIGURE 3-11 *Bar chart presentation of importance indexes for a knowledge work manager*

Schedule information is maintained in an on-line database that produces spreadsheet schedules. A custom software development project is under way to build a project-monitoring database that will link to data from other departments, enable updating by multiple users, and provide improved reporting capabilities. Significant time is required to monitor problems with staff activities. No information technology is used for this. An important monitoring activity by this manager is checking major news databases to keep up with news reports of what the company and its competitors are doing. Over 200 newspapers and more than 1,000 journals can be searched with the information search tools available to this manager.

Analyzing activities involves reviewing schedules and assignments. The analysis requires data on prior assignments, performance on similar projects, and status of current assignments. The analysis must be performed by person and by project. There must be an overall analysis of assignments and department workload. The manager uses spreadsheets to do this analysis and produce reports to address specific problems.

Choosing activities follows from the results of analysis. Decisions must be made relative to project assignments and project implementation. Many decisions involve managers in other departments. No cooperative work systems are in place in this manager's department, but managers in the organization are beginning to consider the feasibility of adding group decision and other cooperative work tools.

Summary

◊ ◊ ◊ ◊ ◊ ◊ ◊ ◊ ◊ ◊ ◊ ◊ ◊ ◊ ◊ ◊ ◊ ◊ ◊

◊ Creating a task/activity analysis is a systematic way to analyze individual information requirements. In a task/activity analysis tasks can be classified into three categories: (1) job-specific, (2) knowledge-building and maintenance, and (3) work-management. Activities are classified as either knowledge work or supplementary. Knowledge work activities can be grouped into four categories: (1) acquiring knowledge, (2) designing, (3) making decisions, and (4) communicating. Supplementary activities can also be classified into four categories: (1) creating input, (2) formatting, (3) filing and retrieving documents and data, and (4) receiving and distributing information.

◊ Knowledge work task attributes affect the design of individual information systems. The three major task attributes are locus of responsibility, timing, and data requirements. Locus of responsibility can refer to an individual, a workgroup, or a task force. The locus of responsibility has a direct effect on task communication, coordination, and management. Timing refers to the three ways tasks are initiated: (1) interrupt driven (by some event or demand), (2) calendar driven, and (3) workload driven. The three data attributes are source, authority to access, and responsibility.

◊ Creating a task/activity analysis involves identifying key tasks, computing the percent of time required for each task, and rating the importance of the major activities associated with each task. The results are summarized as an importance index for each activity. The same analysis is performed for both knowledge work and supplementary activities. The insight gained from the analysis can be very useful. The task/activity analysis is simple enough to be repeated whenever an individual's work activities change.

EXERCISES

1. Identify your tasks as a student using the Task/Activity matrix in Figure 3-6. Then:
   a. Estimate your task effort profile and rate the importance of your activities for each task.
   b. Compute your activity profile.

    c. Prepare a graph of the activity importance indexes.

    d. Write a paragraph for each of your three most dominant activities. In each paragraph, describe the work that the activity represents, and discuss the ways you use or can use information technology to support that work. Interpret the results in terms of need for generalized or specialized software packages.

2. Identify the tasks in your current position or in the position you expect to hold when you graduate using the Task/Activity form. Then:

    a. Estimate your task effort profile and rate the importance of your activities for each task. Compute your activity profile.

    b. Prepare a graph of the activity importance indexes.

    c. Write a paragraph for each of your three most dominant activities. In each paragraph, describe the work that the activity represents and discuss the ways you use or can use information technology to support that work. Interpret the results in terms of need for generalized or specialized software packages.

3. Estimate your relative natural or intuitive ability to do planning and scheduling by estimating your fit with the following (on a scale of 1 to 5, with 1 being "never" and 5 being "usually").

    a. When you are asked to do some task, you consistently underestimate the time it will take you.

    b. When you are asked to do some task in the future, you intuitively accept because you believe you can do it.

    c. You rather consistently over-commit your time.

    d. You consistently find that your most important activities are not given priority.

Write a paragraph suggesting how you will compensate for the deficiencies identified.

4. The following exercises relate to Chapter 8 on external access. However, in order to have time to build experience in external access, start now with some basic external access exercises. Read short excerpts from Chapter 8 as necessary.

    a. Do a file transfer using FTP (File Transfer Protocol). A useful file transfer is to obtain a form for the task/activity analysis. The form (a spreadsheet) must have been prepared and stored in a file on a computer that can be accessed by students. The spreadsheet form reduces the effort to do the analysis. (Refer to the brief description of FTP in Chapter 8.)

    b. Do a library catalog access. Many community and university libraries have catalogues on-line. Access an online catalogue and see if the library has a copy of the following:

    (1) *The Jungle* by Upton Sinclair

    (2) *The Fifth Discipline* by Peter Senge

    (3) *The Design of Everyday Things* by Don Norman

    Get the complete reference and the call number.

c. Sign on to a list server. List servers are used to distribute information to groups of people. List servers take several forms. (Refer to Chapter 8 for a short description). Your instructor may provide information on a list server. If not, use the following:

    (1) Sign on to Edupage, a summary of news items on information technology. The service is provided by Educom, a consortium of leading colleges and universities. The summary server is provided three times each week. Sign on by sending a message to:

        listproc@educom.unc.edu

        In the body of the message, enter the following:

        subscribe edupage your-name

    (2) When you wish to cancel your participation, send a message to the same address, but with the message:

        unsubscribe edupage.

5. *External Data Exercise:* Do Exercise 3 in Chapter 8. (Chapter 8 focuses on accessing external data on the Internet. The External Data Exercises included in Chapters 1-7 are designed to prepare you for the more difficult exercises presented in Chapter 8.)

Analyzing Collaboration and Work Management Requirements

4

◊   ◊   ◊   ◊   ◊   ◊   ◊   ◊   ◊

OBJECTIVES

After completing this chapter, you should be able to:

◆ Describe the pros and cons of collaborative work.

◆ Describe three new activities created as a result of working collaboratively.

◆ Describe the impact of communications costs, coordination costs, and motivation on the four types of collaboration (same time and place; same time, different place; different time, same place; different time and place).

◆ Explain the use of the following workgroup technologies: communications networks and software, scheduling and coordination software, shared access software, concurrent work software, collaboration software, collaborative authoring software, and group meeting software.

◆ Describe the differences between electronic meetings and conventional "face-to-face" meetings.

◆ Explain how software systems can be used to support productivity in collaborative knowledge work.

◆ Explain the impact of cognitive and time limits, interruptions, task switching, and motivation on knowledge work productivity.

◆ Describe the functions of Personal Information Management (PIM) software (such as calendars, notepads, card files, and clocks) and their role in enhancing knowledge work productivity.

◆ Prepare worksheets for analyzing collaborative work requirements and knowledge work management software.

KEY TERMS AND CONCEPTS

This chapter introduces the following key terms and concepts, listed in the order in which they appear:

collaborative work
shared-access software
concurrent work
version control software
simultaneous access software

simultaneous authoring tools
electronic meeting systems
Group Decision Support
  Systems (GDSS)
task switching

work management software
scheduling software
Personal Information
  Management (PIM)
  software

This chapter continues the analysis of requirements for knowledge work. It consists of two parts. The first part extends concepts of knowledge work to include new and altered requirements for collaborative work by teams and project groups. The second part describes the unique requirements and support needed to manage knowledge work. There are productivity concepts for both collaborative work and knowledge work management. Information technology is important in achieving productivity gains in both these areas.

Knowledge work that involves collaborative work by two or more individuals in a group or team requires unique information system support. Information sharing or exchange and process division introduce new or altered activities that require new or altered software functions. This chapter explains the nature of collaborative work and describes the software functions supporting collaborative or cooperative work. It also explains how to use a worksheet to record and analyze collaborative work requirements, emphasizing requirements that can be met, partly or completely, by software functions.

Information technology support for knowledge work management also has unique requirements that apply to both resource and task management and to individual activity management. Work management includes the management of information technology resources available to an individual or group, plus the management of knowledge work resources such as time and attention. The latter is vital because knowledge work is characterized by limited time, scarce cognitive resources (such as attention and concentration), interruptions, waiting for inputs from others, multiple tasks, and switching among tasks. Failure to manage cognitive resources and manage interruptions, waiting, and switching can reduce productivity. This chapter describes concepts and methods for managing work and dealing with possible productivity losses. It explains how information technology can be used to improve work management productivity. It also describes how a worksheet can be used to document the relative importance of work management software functions.

Collaborative Work Requirements

◆ ◆ ◆ ◆ ◆ ◆ ◆ ◆ ◆ ◆ ◆ ◆ ◆ ◆ ◆ ◆ ◆ ◆ ◆ ◆

A primary function of organizations is to coordinate the work of individuals. Many interesting or difficult tasks are too large for one individual, and many tasks require knowledge and expertise not possessed by a single worker. Instead of requiring each individual to perform all tasks and activities, the organization provides for specialization and division of labor. The work product of an individual is rarely independent of the work of others; there is interdependence. Interdependence and variety of specializations requires coordination and collaboration. Collaboration may be informal or formal. It may be manifest in individual contacts and communication as well as in groups. Examples of organizational groups are teams, committees, task groups, and workgroups. Group members may do all or part of their work at the same time and in the same place. Individual activities that are part of group work may also be separated in time or space, or both.

Collaboration involves linking the work activities of two or more people who contribute to a work product. It involves assigning tasks and subtasks and scheduling interactions. Sharing information, coordinating and scheduling activities, correlating work products, and managing progress require numerous forms of communication.

An organizational group is formed with an objective or purpose. Benefits are expected to result from the group structure through sharing expertise, having a variety of viewpoints or perspectives, coordinating activities, increasing communications, and developing shared understanding of goals and objectives. A group can accomplish more in a given time than an individual. However, there are significant incremental costs associated with group work. These include costs of coordination, delays from group development (training, building common understanding, sharing expertise), and interpersonal communication. The cost is justified since some tasks cannot be completed by a single individual and because of the competitive need for rapid completion of large projects. Information technology provides opportunities for significantly reducing coordination and communication costs and increasing effectiveness.

Collaborative work in various types of groups is so pervasive in organizations that a major organizational productivity issue is how to make groups operate more effectively. Collaborative activities are an important part of the workload for a typical knowledge worker. This chapter focuses on the use of information technology for more effective and efficient collaborative work (workgroup computing), an important issue for organizations.

Example

A 1995 survey cited in *Datamation* reported that 19% of the respondent companies had workgroup computing in place and 28% were planning adoption within two years. Large companies were more than twice as likely as small firms to have installed workgroup computing. (*Datamation*, 41:11, 15 June 1995, pp. 34-38.) ◆

New Activities for Collaborative Work

Chapter 3 defined four categories of knowledge work activities:

1. Acquire information (scan, monitor, and search for information)
2. Design solutions (model, plan, organize, schedule, and author)
3. Decide among alternatives (formulate, analyze, and choose)
4. Communicate results (present, persuade, and motivate)

The chapter also described supplemental or clerical functions such as data input, formatting, filing and retrieving, and receiving and distributing.

Each of these four categories of knowledge work and the associated clerical activities can be performed as a cooperative activity by more than one individual (a group). Two or more persons may work together to acquire information, design solutions, decide among alternatives, and communicate results. In other words, individual knowledge work activities also apply to group activities. The activities may be the same, but divided among a group, or the activities may be altered by collaborative work. In addition to changes in activities due to collaborative work, group activities also require new activities (see Figure 4-1).

New activities are often required to:

◊   Coordinate and schedule the work of the group

◊   Share information among group members

◊   Integrate work

These new activities have a common characteristic: they add new information and communication requirements not present in individual work.

A significant new activity necessitated by collaborative work is scheduling activities to accomplish a task. When more than one person is involved, work activities can be performed either sequentially or concurrently. In either case, work must be divided and work products compiled into the final product. When work is done sequentially, group members divide the work and the results of one person's work are passed to others in the group for adding work

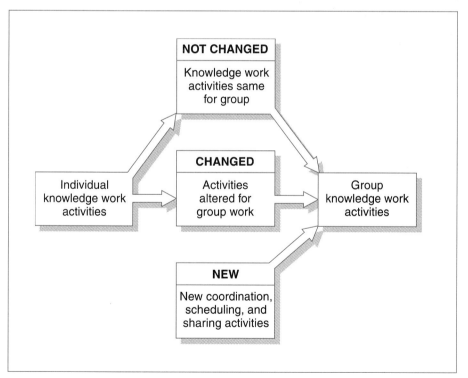

FIGURE 4-1   *Relationship between individual and group knowledge work activities*

products or reviewing and commenting on the work done so far. The sequential method requires time for documents and comments to circulate from one person to the next.

When a project is divided among group members and each person does his or her part concurrently, significant project planning is needed. The separate project parts should be clearly delineated. There should be clear standards governing the parts that interconnect. When coordination issues or potential outcome conflicts arise, there should be communication and conflict resolution methods. An example is frequent coordination meetings which can add significant time to a project.

In most collaborative work, some activities may be assigned to individuals and require little coordination, but others such as decision making require close coordination. The activities that require close collaboration among group members may be separated by either space or time, or both. Figure 4-2 illustrates collaborative activities that are separated by combinations of distance and time.

The four types of collaboration are:

1. *Same time and place.* Face-to-face communication is enriched by multi-sensory perceptions. Visual and auditory cues, body language, and the ability to share views of data and work products maximize communication. However, face-to-face communication requires the simultaneous physical presence of each participant. Coordination costs are highest for this form of collaboration.

2. *Same time, different place.* A conference call typifies this form of collaboration. Workers separated by distance can communicate orally and, with suitable technology, may be able to share partial views of the work product. Video conferencing can provide some of the visual richness of the

Space		
Time	Same time, same place technology: meeting room	Same time, different place technology: electronically connected meeting rooms
	Different time, same place technology: meeting room with stored results	Different time, different place technology: electronic connections with stored results

FIGURE 4-2 *Separation of work group activities by time and/or space and type of enabling technology*

face-to-face meeting. Coordination costs are quite high, and sharing views of the work product adds to the coordination costs.

3. *Different time, same place.* This form of collaboration is represented by a bulletin board and other forms of stored results in a shared space. Other examples are logs and journals maintained by shift workers. Communication is usually limited to stored results in this relatively rare form of collaboration. Coordination costs are affected by how many people are involved in each meeting.

4. *Different time and place.* Collaboration across time and space is exemplified by electronic mail, notes, and internal Web pages. Communication is performed by sharing and viewing various work notes and work products. This form of collaboration has the virtue of relatively low coordination costs because communication does not need to be synchronized. Motivation toward this type of asynchronous, distributed collaboration is quite high because of the geographic dispersion of organizations across time zones and the increasing need for rapid product delivery.

The coordination of collaboration across either time or space is difficult because each individual in the workgroup has a personal work schedule that affects the scheduling of group activities. Each individual in a group has non-group assignments. Group members also have personal activities that impact the group schedule, such as business travel, training, vacation, lost time due to accident or sickness, and personal time off. The net result is an increasing level of scheduling effort and difficulty as the number of group members increases.

Example

If ten people are to be scheduled to attend a one-hour group meeting, it is necessary to find a suitable open time slot in all ten schedules. A sequential process of checking each schedule until a time is available can require several rounds and take significant time. One alternative is to schedule the next meeting as the final agenda item of the current meeting. A second alternative is to use information technology in the form of electronic calendars. A built-in software function can examine the calendars and suggest times that fit the constraints. This requires much less clerical time to arrange, but has other costs because complete and current calendars must be maintained electronically for each group member. ◆

The second new activity in collaborative work activity is sharing information. In order to work effectively together, members of the group need background information on the project and the group members. They need progress reports, problem reports, and process descriptions. When assignments are completed, they need to know. The traditional approach is to distribute paper copies of various reports and memoranda, although this procedure involves significant delay, especially when participants are separated by space. It also involves a cost to coordinate and share information.

Example

Estimate the proportion of a workday required for communication. A person working alone has no team communication costs. Assume that each person in a team requires 20 minutes of coordination and scheduling time with each other person on the team. A 10-member team requires three hours of time on the part of each individual (9×20 minutes) for coordination and scheduling. As teams become larger, there may be subdivisions of the team structure to reduce coordination, but in general, the costs of coordination and scheduling rise with team size. ◆

The third new collaborative work is integration. When work is divided among members of a group, the individual contributions to the work product must be integrated into the whole. Reviewing and revising work-in-process requires understanding, communication, and feedback. Work to be reviewed is often queued in individual in-baskets. Consequently, questions and tentative modifications that require interaction must often wait for the availability of both parties. Information technology can help minimize the delay and facilitate rapid interactive communication without requiring the simultaneous attention of both parties.

Activities Altered by Collaborative Work

Many knowledge work activities are altered when they are carried out by members of a workgroup instead of by an individual. These changes occur due to several factors: interpersonal dependencies, increased coordination, multiple information inputs, and a more complex decision process.

◆ *Interpersonal dependencies.* An individual working alone is not dependent on the work of others. There is no need to wait for the work of a group member to be completed or for a group meeting to be scheduled.

◆ *Increased coordination.* When persons work individually, a task can be completed with a minimum of coordination with others. When people work as part of a group, the coordination effort is altered: many actions cannot be begun or completed until they have been checked and reviewed with others. For example, an individual developing a computer application can make a decision about the scope of a program module without checking with others. When the program is a group effort, the module cannot be changed without making sure the proposed changes do not adversely impact other modules.

◆ *Multiple information inputs.* With group work, there may be as many sources of input as there are group members, and the process of accomplishing an activity must take into account all of these often conflicting inputs. Multiple inputs are frequently designed to assemble information and knowledge not available to one person. The results of multiple inputs can be beneficial, but may have undesirable consequences as well. The variety of viewpoints and perspectives enriches the process, but may also delay completion and load the result with excess ideas and words.

◊ *A more complex decision process.* The varied information and perspectives available to the group are inputs to the group's decisions and must be understood and evaluated by group members. Personal values and other factors tend to make consensus difficult. Group member roles and their relative status make simple decision strategies such as majority voting problematic. Much more time and effort may be required for a group to reach a decision because of these factors.

Information Technology Functions Supporting Collaborative Work

◆ ◆

Information technology provides functions to support collaborative knowledge work. Examples are functions for communications, scheduling and coordination, shared data access, concurrent work, project or topic collaboration, collaborative authoring, and meetings.

Communications

Collaborative work relies upon communications. Although the traditional voice telephone network provides for synchronous, two-party communications, a much greater degree of flexibility and functionality through asynchronous and multi-party communication is provided by digital data networks. If workgroup participants are in close proximity (same building or campus of buildings) local area network (LAN) interconnection is effective and efficient. If participants are in different cities or different countries, a wide area network (WAN) is necessary. The communications that can be supported by these networks include:

◊ Voice communication (including multi-party voice conferencing and asynchronous messaging via voice mail)

◊ Facsimile communications of text and graphics

◊ Asynchronous electronic messaging (e-mail)

◊ Asynchronous imaging (documents, sound, or video) via e-mail or file transfer

◊ Asynchronous meetings (requiring stored results from prior meetings held at different times and saving results for future meetings at different times).

◊ Synchronous electronic meetings (video conferencing with imaging and voice). Specialized software provides functions frequently required for collaborative work.

◊ Voice communications group support. Software can facilitate creation and maintenance of group member directories, automatic or abbreviated group dialing, message forwarding, voice messages addressing for multiple recipients, and automatic voice message storage and retrieval.

◊ Facsimile communications group support. Software can support transmission of documents directly from a word processor, spreadsheet, or other software; creation and maintenance of group directories; automatic sending of faxes at optimal time; and even integration of received facsimile data and images into application packages.

◊ E-mail group support. Software can support group directories and addressing, automatic classification of both incoming and outgoing messages, storage structures for organizing and storing messages, acknowledgments and priority messages, and access to mailing lists and bulletin boards.

◊ Imaging group support. Software allows an online session to include images of documents to be displayed to two or more participants or may display full or partial-motion images of one or more participants. The part of the computer screen used for the documents or other images is often referred to as a white board because changes can be made and immediately displayed, as if the participants shared a white board.

◊ Video conferencing and electronic meeting group communication support. Software manages two-way video and audio so that participants can see and hear each other during an electronic meeting.

Scheduling and Coordination

One of the most time-consuming aspects of cooperative work is arranging the necessary synchronous interactions of workgroup members. In addition to the time lost finding mutually acceptable meeting alternatives, time is often lost because a work product may be stalled by the unavailability of a team member. Functions in scheduling and coordination software can simplify the process and greatly increase scheduling and coordination efficiency.

◊ Group scheduling software can search through each proposed participant's schedule, identifying mutual availabilities, and reserving time intervals.

◊ Scheduling software can include resources (such as meeting rooms and equipment) and coordinate their use with participants' schedules.

◊ Scheduling software can integrate with e-mail facilities to communicate tentative schedules, confirm reservations, and distribute documentation such as agendas, minutes and summaries, and other workgroup products.

◊ Scheduling and coordination software can assist in rescheduling when conditions change, such as key participant availability.

Shared Data Access

A workgroup will generate and access data in the form of spreadsheets, word processing documents, graphics, and databases. If such data and work products are stored on a central computer or departmental server, they may easily be made available to any member of the group. If they are stored on one or more individual computers, software for shared access must be used. Functions in **shared-access software** can provide several levels of support, from simple file sharing to simultaneous file updating.

◊ Peer-to-peer local area networks allow workgroup members access to data stored on each other's computers. No central control or coordination is needed to manage this form of shared access.

◊ Workgroups can be assigned common group facilities on a network with ability to access and share data. The network can span the organization or be limited to a department.

◊ Bulletin board and discussion group software allows workgroup members to conduct asynchronous discussions following topical "threads" even when separated by long distance.

◊ Document database software allows workgroups to maintain and organize relevant document and multimedia data to share across time and space. One current technology providing such facilities is illustrated by Lotus Notes™. A second technology consists of Web pages for the work of a group, maintained on an internal network (intranet).

◊ Remote document access software stores messages and documents on a workstation connected to a LAN. Remote users may perform searches, receive copies of documents, add new documents, and forward documents to other users.

Concurrent Work

Two or more members of a workgroup may need to work on the same data, document, or spreadsheet at the same time. If workers are face-to-face in the same location, data sharing is simple. When team members are separated in space, functions in **concurrent work** software can support their needs either by allowing them to view team actions in real time or by managing the effects of changes:

◊ **Version control software** may be used to keep track of the elements of a joint work product such as chapters of a report. Elements are checked out and checked in, and the progression of changes to each element are tracked.

◇ **Simultaneous access software** can operate over networks. Both the work product and each person's actions are displayed. Team members can view each member's actions and react in real time.

◇ Concurrent work technology can support multi-party views of work-in-process together with audio and video. Such concurrent work support technology is particularly effective when participants are separated by long distances.

Example

Collaboration with video conferencing and white boards: Two knowledge workers working jointly hold a video conference. Each faces a video camera mounted on top of his or her computer, and has a telephone headset to speak and listen (see Figure 4-3). As they speak, each person's picture is digitized, compressed, transmitted, and displayed on the other's computer, along with pertinent documents, graphs, or other data. The communication of voice, video, and documents simultaneously may employ an ISDN (Integrated Services Digital Network) line that transfers digital data at high speed. The workers discuss the document on the white board (the part of the screen

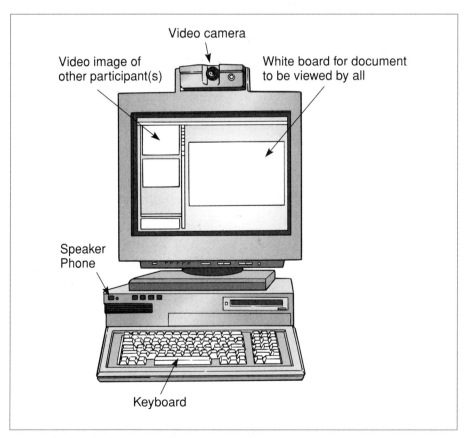

FIGURE 4-3 *Desktop for video conferencing*

used for this purpose). Changes on the white board made by one are displayed immediately on both screens. As they exchange views on the voice connection, their faces provide visual clues to each other about their reactions. Video conferencing methods work best when the participants know each other and, therefore, know how to get information from visual and verbal clues. The scenario can be extended to more than two participants. ◆

Other examples also illustrate the technology:

Examples

A lawyer working closely with a client who also has video conferencing facilities can discuss legal documents and make changes during the exchange. ◆

Two accountants with complementary expertise can discuss the form and content of a financial statement being prepared for release. ◆

A professor can grade a paper by talking with the student about the content while pointing to the specific text. ◆

In each case, the exchange eliminates the need to be in the same place, but provides an essential combination of voice, video for visual clues, and document.

Project or Topic Collaboration

A workgroup is not a permanent organization. This means that workgroups are constantly being formed for projects or assignments, workgroup membership is frequently changed as people join and leave projects, and projects are eventually completed and workgroups dispersed. Extensive communication among workgroup members must be supported throughout a project. Members need access to archives of past discussions and documents. Archives must include a variety of retrieval methods, and must be managed to support access without excessive duplication. In addition to work-in-process and project archives, there is increasing recognition of the need to support managed access to external information. Problem or topic-based data that may be relevant to a project is not constrained by organizational boundaries. Software that supports collaboration may need to maintain external data or at least organize and support external data references. Examples of requirements that can be met by collaborative support software include:

◊   Establishing forums on topics that have interest and value among members of the workgroup. Those who are members of a project or who have interest in a topic may access and add to its contents. Information may be added from any source including company files, news-wires, and e-mail. Documents may include spreadsheets, images, graphics, and sound and video clips. Examples of uses for topics or forums are project notes, reports plus comments and other feedback, and contact lists.

◊ Compiling collections of completed projects and other exemplary work products to support new projects. "Best practices" and other contents may be available to support new projects.

◊ Enabling workgroup members to view, access, and contribute to a discussion or forum from any location at any time.

◊ Using software mechanisms to simplify reading and make sense of project or topic files. Examples are:

  ♦ message threading that shows the relationship and sequencing of messages

  ♦ text searching and retrieval tools

  ♦ searching across multiple topics or forums.

To examine the use of project or topic collaboration software by a project group, assume a group of knowledge workers are assigned to a software design project.

Example

Each person is assigned a part of the project, but part or all of the group needs to communicate about factors such as requirements, alternative solutions, enhancements, and user interfaces. The group members have several meetings, but employ conferencing software for most communication. A moderator is appointed to create the main topics and control access to the messages. The software organizes the messages from each participant by topic. Comments are indented and attached to topics. A discussion will have a "thread" that progresses from start to finish. Each participant can choose what to view. Options include messages for a topic from selected days, from selected members, or associated with keywords. Design information, comments, and ideas are communicated rapidly and are available for easy retrieval. ♦

There are software products that provide facilities for users to create, access, and share information in a discussion forum. They include a mail agent to enable users from other locations to participate in the forums and software to replicate forums in remote offices and between companies.

Examples

Lotus Notes™ is a widely-used example of current collaboration support technology. It is designed especially for sharing unstructured information. Notes supports e-mail, conferencing (such as sharing notes, asking questions, and offering opinions), routing documents, accessing document databases, sharing files within a workgroup, tracking status of work-in-process, and repository management. An individual Notes user creates, maintains, and shares information collections (called databases in Notes terminology). Workgroups have the same database creation and maintenance capabilities. Access and delivery—especially over local and wide-area networks—is a major facility of Notes. Notes is also a platform for building and delivering applications, although such development usually requires professional developers.

The Notes system takes care of managing the databases. It has interactive two-way replication, which means that when something is updated on one server, it is replicated on other servers in the network. The software expands workgroup communication because it allows topics to be created and made available whenever a need arises. It can even affect the structure of an organization because information flows more freely and without regard to organizational boundaries.

For instance, using Notes, an insurance broker tracks "critical brokerage information, such as insurance company profiles, marketing information, live news, technical expertise, and profiles of more than 100,000 companies." This information is provided to 1,700 users. The Notes application provides customized, filtered, and categorized information based on workgroup and individual user requirements.   ◆

An intranet applies the technology of Web pages that began in the Internet for internal communications. In a simple application, reference data can be maintained on Web pages. This can include plans, assignments, schedules, and standards. An intranet application can be expanded to include work documents such as project notes, report drafts, and memoranda.   ◆

Collaborative Authoring

In collaborative authoring, group members work together to write reports, programs, analyses, or other outputs, often from distant locations. More than one person may write and edit the same section, often working concurrently. Software can support collaborative authoring in two ways: by controlling access to versions of components being written and by aiding simultaneous work from different locations.

Access or version control to prevent work on outdated versions is provided by a checkout system. An individual working on a product makes that product unavailable to others (except perhaps in read-only mode) until it is checked back in. Some version control systems permit simultaneous checkout of a component and facilitate conflict resolution when the different versions are checked back in. More elaborate systems can reconstruct the history of each change to every component, complete with date and time stamps, author identification, and "notes in the margin."

Users of a version control system must partition their work product into manageable components and adhere to the check-out/check-in requirements of the software. Version control systems are common especially in software development, where most products are the result of collaboration and time pressure is usually severe.

If more than one person must work on a work product at the same time, software support must operate in real time as well. **Simultaneous authoring tools** can display a baseline document on more than one system. Typically, changes are displayed in different colors to reflect their author's identity. In addition to simultaneous viewing of the work-in-process, simultaneous authoring usually requires audio and even video communications among the authors. A record of changes must be supported by this software to enable backtracking.

Another form of collaborative authoring involves simultaneous reviewing. In many cases, multiple reviewers add comments and suggest changes and improvement, which are then assimilated and used or discarded by the original author. In this example, reviewers do not need to see each others' efforts, but the person making the revisions would like to see all comments and suggestions at the same time, in context. Software that supports simultaneous reviewing may present the document to reviewers in finished form and accept suggestions in the form of posted notes or links that appear in place.

Meetings

Electronic meeting systems support a variety of different purposes from idea generation through assessment and decision making. They may be used to support either small or large groups and may support work separated in space and/or time. A major category of electronic meeting systems is called group systems or **Group Decision Support Systems (GDSS)**.

Most electronic meeting systems tend to focus on same time, same place work. Special purpose electronic meeting rooms commonly include a workstation for each participant, a shared display, a facilitator, and software to capture the work product and provide aids for various meeting activities (see Figure 4-4). Extensive research has evaluated the process gains and losses when electronic meeting systems are used.

The benefits from electronic meeting systems are:

◊ Simultaneous participation. Each participant has a terminal and can make suggestions or comment on other participants' ideas.

◊ Equal opportunity for participation. In many meetings, a few individuals dominate the discussion. With electronic meeting systems, all participants have equal opportunity. The system discourages domination by one person or a small group.

◊ Enhanced idea generation. More ideas are generated in idea sessions than with manual alternatives.

◊ Facilitates use of a variety of software-supported techniques and methods. For example, ideas and suggestions can be evaluated through voting, rating, and ranking with instant results.

◊ Captures the ideas expressed in the meeting (provides an organizational memory for the meeting).

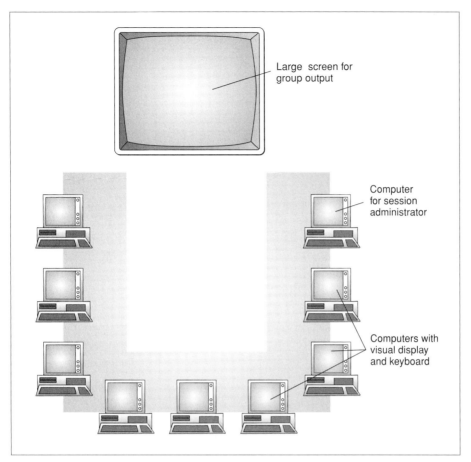

FIGURE 4-4   *Electronic meeting room for small group planning and decision support*

◊   Allows more people to participate in a meeting without increasing meeting length. Coordination and communication requirements for meetings increase exponentially with group size. Meeting length, therefore, increases with meeting size. Because electronic meeting software allows parallel processing of comments, it reduces the time for everyone to participate.

In an electronic meeting system or GDSS, a typical process for decision making consists of four steps:

1. *Idea generation.* Each person makes suggestions about an issue. This is equivalent to electronic brainstorming. Suggestions are saved and displayed

on the shared screen. Each person can comment on ideas made by others, expanding the list of ideas and suggestions.

2. *Idea organization.* Ideas and comments stored in the computer are organized into a list of key suggestions and issues.

3. *Prioritization.* Key suggestions and issues are prioritized by using the ranking facilities of the meeting system software. The results are available immediately.

4. *Follow-up.* Suggestions are captured by the meeting system software for accomplishing the top ideas that have emerged.

Process losses often observed in group meetings are reduced with such tools. For example, domination, pressure to conform, and incomplete task analysis are reduced. The system does not eliminate all group meeting process losses, however. For instance, it does not prevent participants from failing to be active. Some information is lost since participants do not talk aloud and provide verbal and body language information to the meeting. On balance, however, an electronic meeting system can be very effective at eliciting ideas and suggestions. It assists in ranking ideas and bringing the meeting to a conclusion, and it provides a record of the meeting for subsequent use.

Analyzing Collaborative Work Support Requirements

◆ ◆

An explicit analysis of support requirements for collaborative work will help individuals (and groups) use existing software functions more effectively and acquire and implement additional software. The analysis is also an input to infrastructure design (Chapter 15). The analysis worksheet (see Figure 4-5) records cooperative work requirements for each task. The requirements are specified in terms of extent of need for seven different functions, as explained in the previous section and summarized in Table 4-1.

The worksheet provides a view of requirements by task. Each column has a set of evaluations relative to the need for support for each cooperative work function. If, for example, one or more tasks had a high need for cooperative authoring, investment in cooperative authoring support may be justified. If no tasks require it, that support need not be implemented. Between these two extremes of high need and no need are mixtures of low or medium use. The decisions in these cases reflect individual judgments.

Name _____   Date _____

Task	Importance of Software to Support Functions in Collaborative Work (Indicate None, Low, Medium or High)						
	Communi-cations	Scheduling & Coordination	Shared Data Access	Concurrent Work	Project or Topic Collaboration	Collaborative Authoring	Meeting Support

FIGURE 4-5 *Worksheet for analyzing collaborative work requirements*

Table 4-1 Summary of Collaborative Work Functions	
Collaborative Work Function	*Explanation*
Communications	Electronic communication with others
Scheduling and coordination	Coordinate work schedule with others
Shared data access	Share access to data and work products
Concurrent work	Communicate while two or more are working on the same or related product
Project or topic collaboration	Communicate ideas and progress on project or topic
Collaborative authoring	Work concurrently on same document
Meetings	Electronic support for meetings

Factors Underlying Requirements for Knowledge Work Management

◆ ◆

As explained in Chapter 2, significant improvements in knowledge work productivity can be achieved by managing such factors as work environment, task structure, and scheduling. Knowledge work management is, therefore, a key part of a strategy for improved productivity by individuals and groups. An underlying assumption is that human time and cognitive resources are scarce. The limits on time and cognitive resources are not absolute. They are affected by motivation. Knowledge workers who are highly motivated may both increase the time allocated to important activities and also increase the cognitive resources applied to them. Given limits to time and cognitive resources, high productivity is achieved by methods and technology that increase motivation to sustain effort and minimize unproductive use of resources. The objectives of the work management methods and technology are to increase motivation to sustain work, schedule and switch among tasks in a way that minimizes productivity loss, and minimize the costs of establishing and maintaining readiness to work.

Limits on Time and Cognitive Resources

As described in Chapter 2, conserving individual cognitive resources is vital, since humans have limited capacity to concentrate on a task. A key factor in resource conservation is making activities as automatic as possible. Other factors include increasing availability by motivation and reducing losses by scheduling.

When humans perform an activity, they perform (at the extreme) with either full attention or automatically (no attention). Human attention consumes time and energy; therefore, attention is a scarce cognitive resource. The opposite of attention is automatic processing. Activities become automatic when they have been learned well enough so that they can be performed without continuous attention. Automatic processing of an activity may require attentional resources only to initiate or to deal with problems that may occur; otherwise, it has low cost relative to attention.

Conservation of attentional resources is achieved (and productivity improved) in knowledge work by establishing work routines that can be learned and repeated automatically. Many supplementary activities can be automatic. Typing is largely automatic after "touch typing" is learned. Some types of analysis are largely automatic once a problem has been formulated (although problem formulation always requires high attention). For example, scanning a body of literature for specific indicators may become a nearly automatic activity.

Motivation to Sustain Productive Work

A person who is motivated is able to apply more physical and mental energy to knowledge work. There are a number of environmental and work conditions affecting motivation. This section focuses on conditions affected by knowledge work scheduling, namely, the effect of frequent completions that produce completion motivation, effect of deadlines, and effect of individual cycles of performance.

Completing a necessary activity, no matter how small, is motivating. Deadlines are a variation on this theme. A deadline forces completion, and there is motivation in the completion. From a motivational standpoint, the ideal knowledge work consists only of short jobs with well-defined deliverables or outcomes. The effect of short jobs on motivation is illustrated by research on the work of high level managers. These managers tend to have an activity mix consisting largely of short jobs (a few minutes each) such as reading and commenting on memoranda, interviews, discussions, and responses to questions. They tend to be very motivated and are able to sustain a high level of attention.

Since short jobs provide more motivation, long jobs can be divided into smaller intermediate jobs with deliverables. A programmer assigned to develop a large program requiring six months to complete can achieve improved completion motivation by creating short jobs based on deliverables such as design documents and tested modules. Based on experience with programmers, subdivisions into one-week deliverables produces better results than longer jobs. Even short clerical activities completed by knowledge workers produce completion motivation.

In addition to short jobs versus long jobs for motivation, people have both daily and weekly cycles of performance. While all people have performance cycles, cycle timing is an individual phenomenon. Scheduling can take advantage of these cycles to schedule difficult, high attention work when attentional resources and motivation are at their peak. For example, a person may have a daily cycle that has high performance potential in the morning until lunch, with a lower potential immediately after lunch, and a high potential again in the late afternoon. This concept suggests that short jobs with immediate completion gratification should be scheduled during times when energy levels and motivation are low. More difficult work requiring sustained attention should be scheduled for peak times.

Random and Scheduled Interruptions

Interruptions are a part of the work environment for most knowledge workers. A single task may be scheduled, but random interruptions may break into the task activities and introduce some new, unscheduled task. Although a single task was scheduled, more than one task is active because of the random interruptions. In other cases, the knowledge worker explicitly schedules concurrent work on more than one task. Managers often expect to have more than one task active and switch among them.

Interruptions can be scheduled or unscheduled. Scheduled interruptions in the form of breaks or rest periods are important to sustained productivity. The effects of random or non-rest interruptions depend on the activity being performed. Interruptions have very little effect on productivity with some activities; for others, interruptions break concentration or otherwise interfere with performance. An example of an activity with little adverse effect from interruption is a supplemental clerical activity such as typing or filing. Key entry can usually be resumed with little productivity effect after an interruption. An example of an activity that is adversely affected by an interruption is a *persuade* activity. Since persuasion usually obtains results through a sequence of arguments and evidence, a break in the presentation may cause listeners or even the persuader to lose the thread of the argument sequence.

Since interruptions will certainly occur, the issue is how to reduce the productivity loss that occurs because of a break in the continuity of attention. Each time there is a switch among tasks, there is a switching loss. The switching loss for intentional switching among active tasks may be reduced by methods for managing the form of the interruption. The switching loss for random interruptions may be reduced by methods for recovering to the level of attention existing prior to the interruption.

There are individual differences in ability to switch from one task to another. Some knowledge workers seem to be able to handle short interruptions without significant loss of task continuity; others switch slowly and recover slowly. Different methods, including the use of information technology, can reduce the rate of interruptions and the severity of loss of task continuity.

Switching Among Tasks

Humans cannot *simultaneously* perform more than one activity, but they can perform more than one activity *concurrently*. The difference is in doing two things at the same time versus appearing to do them at the same time. It may appear two activities are being performed simultaneously, when in fact they are being done concurrently. Humans achieve this concurrency by switching back and forth between activities. The switching can be done based on an interrupt condition or rotation:

◆ *Switching based on an event or condition interrupt.* This is the most common. When more than one task is being performed concurrently, only one is using the worker's attention. If a second task is being performed automatically and needs attention, there is an event or condition that interrupts the first task, puts it on "hold," and focuses attention on the second. For example, a person may be authoring at the same time a print job is being run. When the print job is done, the worker hears in the background the completion of the printing and interrupts the attentional work to unload the printer. A person at a meeting in which a relatively unimportant discussion is taking place may put the meeting on automatic (or with low attention monitoring) and devote attentional resources to thinking about some other problem. Full attention is returned to the meeting when some event or condition, such as a switch in topic or a vote, signals the need.

◊ *Switching based on rotation.* This is essentially a timed or scheduled interrupt. When two or more jobs are being done concurrently, the attentional requirements of the jobs may allow the worker to switch between the jobs, rotating attention among them. For example, a person may rotate between watching a news program and scanning the newspaper based on timing of commercials. A person may schedule a time for returning phone calls, switching to and from this activity based on the time period.

Research suggests that performing two high-attentional activities concurrently results in an overall performance reduction because **task switching** must be frequent. Significant additional mental attention is required to recover an attentional task that has been put on hold and begin again at the point of last switching. When switching involves an automatic task, however, relatively little attention is required to recover the automatic task. Because of this difference, concurrently performing one high-attention and one or more low-attention (automatic) activities can be especially productive.

The implications of attentional processing, automatic processing, and switching based on interrupts or rotation are that task mix, work procedures, and the information system can be designed to support improved productivity. Such a design will facilitate a combination of activities with only one high-attention activity at a time. Where switching among attentional activities is required, the information system may facilitate switching and recovery.

Establishing and Maintaining Readiness to Work

A number of actions performed frequently maintain a readiness to work. These are maintaining availability of resources within a physical workspace or an information technology workspace. For example, reference materials and reports must be placed where they can be retrieved. Address books, contact lists, and calendars must be updated. Computer software must be loaded or the latest updates obtained and added. Files must be safeguarded by backup procedures.

Many startup actions take very little time, but are done so often that small improvements in time to perform yield significant benefits over time. For example, the procedures to start the computer, load software from a network server, and sign on to the mail take little time, but they can be automated to reduce time and errors. The savings may be only a minute a day, but 240 work days yields 240 minutes or four hours of savings a year. The same principles apply to accessing commonly used functions in software packages. If the common method is to find the function on the third level of a menu, an alternative such as a keystroke, icon, or high level menu item can reduce access time by a small amount each time. If access is frequent, these savings can be significant over time.

Methods and Software for Knowledge Work Management

◆ ◆

Knowledge work management can make use of a number of methods; it can also benefit from the use of software. There is a body of literature on time management based primarily on a discipline of establishing priorities and scheduling use of time to meet them. An important, useful assumption of time management is that explicit setting of priorities and schedules improves performance over performing tasks scheduled intuitively and implicitly. This section focuses on **work management software** support as it relates to establishing scheduling methods; automating simple, repetitive work management actions; and establishing and maintaining readiness to work.

Methods and Software for Maintaining Work Motivation

Since completion motivation is important, scheduling methods may be used to develop and track short, frequent activity completions. **Scheduling software** may also be used to protect high productivity times of the day for concentrated, high-attention work.

Deadlines create motivation and are developed by scheduling methods. Along with the scheduling methods must be reporting mechanisms that report actual progress and compare it to planned progress.

Motivation methods are needed to overcome natural tendencies to avoid hard mental work. Since attentional resources are limited, and performing work with attentional resources is tiring and perhaps difficult, there is a natural tendency to avoid high-attention work. There is also a tendency to not sustain high-attention work. It has been demonstrated, however, that those who are able to sustain motivation to do high-attention work achieve higher productivity. For example, authors with high productivity have reported use of mechanisms such as scheduled times with a single focus and without interruptions. This dedicated time with a single task motivates sustained high-attention writing activity day after day.

Methods and Software for Setting Priorities and Scheduling

Knowledge workers employ a variety of mechanisms for scheduling such as calendars and "to do" lists. Calendars and "to do" lists can be supported by computer software. In addition, scheduling systems can be used to record estimated and actual task durations and completion dates, record progress, and identify schedule completion problems.

Software can be used to set priorities. However, simple lists and ranking may suffice for most knowledge workers. **Personal Information Management (PIM) software** packages contain facilities for maintaining a calendar and developing and maintaining lists of priorities. If future activities and events signaling completion are complex, it may be appropriate to employ software with more complex scheduling methods.

The requirements for progress tracking and reporting can be met with a broad range of techniques and tools. When activities are completed in sequence and very few tasks are concurrent, a simple report or graphic approach such as Gantt charts may suffice. A Gantt chart can easily be created with a spreadsheet package. (A Gantt chart is a bar chart with time—days, weeks, or months—in the horizontal axis and a bar for each activity showing time to start and time to finish.)

If activities take place in parallel and there is a more complex network of activities, special purpose project planning and tracking tools may be more productive. These packages use a PERT/CPM network method and require significantly more effort to input data for planning and tracking tasks and activities. PERT/CPM charts show how the starting of an activity is dependent in completion of prior activities. The dependencies allow analysis of the activities in a critical path.

Methods and Software for Switching Tasks

A requirement for having more than one application available at the same time can be supported by an operating system that allows more than one application to be active at the same time and, therefore, reduces the time to deal with an interrupt, switch among applications, and return to a previous application. The concurrent applications can be different packages (such as electronic mail active along with word processing) or concurrent activities within the same software package, such as more than one spreadsheet active at the same time or more than one document active in a word processor.

Interruption can be handled in a variety of ways. To avoid random interruptions, stored message technology can be applied. A system might support this with voice mail, electronic mail, and other ways for people to leave messages without interrupting work. For example, the combination of voice mail and a phone bell that can be switched off may be all that is needed to prevent interruptions of critical tasks or activities. Technology for cooperative work (such as calendaring application) can support methods that enable co-workers to identify when others are available for meetings and schedule times during their interruptible periods.

In analyzing activities that must be performed concurrently with others or that must be interrupted, the criteria or triggers for switching among them should be considered. There is a significant cost in interrupting an activity that requires high attention. Remembering the problem state and returning to a mental representation of that state after dealing with an interruption may take significant time and attention. There is some risk of not being able to reconstruct the problem state and, therefore, losing potentially valuable knowledge work products. Whenever possible, it is probably more productive to schedule low-attentional activities for concurrent work and reserve uninterruptible blocks for high-attention work. For example, many knowledge workers schedule time outside of the regular work day "to get some real work done."

Many activities involve obtaining work from others and passing results on to others. Other activities involve concurrent, collaborative work with sharing of data and concurrent work on analyses or reports. The infrastructures can be designed to support collaborative work (discussed earlier in chapter). This may include cooperation via networking so that one person can access and work on the same data, analysis, or report on which another is working.

Methods and Software for Establishing and Maintaining Readiness to Work

Maintaining readiness to work may involve use of software features to automate sequences of operations; provide an easily available notepad, card file, calendar, reminder, and clock; and specialized icons, bars, and menus to reduce search and access time for commonly used programs. It may also include software to maintain backup protection.

Operating systems and many software packages have functions to automate sequences of operations and make them available in macro commands, menus, buttons, or keystrokes. Some automated system management procedures may be selected when software is installed or selected by an option selection procedure. Other automated procedures must be developed by methods such as macro or script recording (described in Chapter 9). Procedures such as sign on, sign off, backup, and error recovery are candidates for automation.

In the course of a day, a knowledge worker may have frequent need for personal information management (PIM) functions. These functions include a notepad that is easily accessed for keeping notes, a card file, a calendar, a reminder list, a clock (including, perhaps, a world clock that shows the time at remote locations, such as a plant in Singapore). The card file may be used for items such as topics and contacts (a function also termed a "contact manager"). The card file may be connected to a phone dialer to automate calls when a contact number is accessed. The calendar may be part of a group calendaring system that allows members of a group to request times to be scheduled on the individual calendars. These calendars may be printed for convenience and ease of access. A reminder list (including a "to do" list) assists in setting priorities. The system can display reminders of meetings and "to do" items when they are due.

Backup can be specified within some packages. However, more comprehensive backup to removable media requires special methods and software. (This will be described further in Chapter 6.)

Since each user has a specific set of software, the time to find and retrieve frequently accessed packages can be reduced with the help of features such as specialized icons, task bars, and menus available at the operating system level. These features can also be used within a software package to reduce the time required to access commonly used features. (This is explained further in Chapter 9.)

Analyzing Support Requirements for Knowledge Work Management

◆ ◆ ◆ ◆ ◆ ◆ ◆ ◆ ◆ ◆ ◆ ◆ ◆ ◆ ◆ ◆ ◆ ◆ ◆ ◆

Based on the concepts and methods related to knowledge work management, users can analyze their tasks to identify requirements for scheduling, switching, and readiness to work by using a worksheet (see Figure 4-6). The person filling out the worksheet is asked to identify the need for the most common software support for task management. The worksheet focuses on support for scheduling and tracking progress, concurrent access to software and files, time and priority management support, contact management support, automating of system management, and automating of backup and recovery.

When the worksheet is completed, the requirements can be analyzed to evaluate how they can be met by procedures and software functions. High-value, important requirements may justify custom software if the requirement cannot be met with packaged software. Low-need requirements may be met at low cost with features of existing software, since these requirements

Name _____ Date _____

Task Management Requirements

Software functions in support of task management	Importance to Task Management for Knowledge Worker			
	Low Importance	Medium Importance	High Importance	Notes on Need
Scheduling, tracking, and reporting: Simple sequences (Gantt) Complex networks (Pert)				
More than one software package/file active at same time				
Time management support (calender, "to do," priority setting, reminder)				
Notepad, card file, address list, contact management, automatic dialer, and similar record keeping				
Automated procedure support and icons, task bars, keystrokes and menus to reduce access time				
Special backup and recovery software				

FIGURE 4-6 *Worksheet for analyzing the importance of knowledge work management software*

probably do not justify an investment in finding and learning specialized software. Requirements of medium importance can probably justify only modest search and learning investment in specialized software.

ummary

◆ ◆ ◆ ◆ ◆ ◆ ◆ ◆ ◆ ◆ ◆ ◆ ◆ ◆ ◆ ◆ ◆ ◆ ◆

◆ The chapter surveys concepts, methods, and software related to collaborative work and knowledge work management. It defines information system requirements that depend on these activities.

�◊ Collaborative work is very common in organizations. Since many tasks are too large for a single individual who may not have the required expertise, organizations establish teams, committees, and workgroups to accomplish the tasks. There are benefits from collaborative work, but there are also added costs of communication and coordination. Information technology can be used to reduce these costs and increase the effectiveness of collaborative work.

◊ Knowledge work activities identified for a project may be divided among members of a workgroup, but this may alter some of the activities. The process also introduces new activities required to coordinate and schedule the work, share information, and review and integrate work-in-process. Collaborative work may be synchronous (at the same time) or asynchronous (separated in time). Collaboration may take place in one location or separated in space. Collaborative work increases interdependencies in the work, increases the need for coordination due to division of work, increases the number of inputs to consider in achieving the final work product, and complicates the process of decision making.

◊ Important workgroup technologies are communications networks and software, scheduling and coordination software, shared access software, concurrent work software, and group meeting software. The full range of technologies may be employed, including voice mail, conferencing, facsimile, e-mail, imaging, and electronic meetings. Information technology support for collaborative work provides a wide range of media choices for communication.

◊ The systems supporting collaborative work provide for project or topic collaboration, collaborative authoring, shared access to files and databases, and electronic meeting systems. These systems support increased productivity and reduced collaborative work losses using software that manages the storage, access, and interactive exchanges for collaborative work. Project and topic collaboration systems maintain project and topic files and provide methods to organize data for meaningful retrieval and use. Collaborative authoring systems support concurrent work on documents by maintaining records of changes and by showing concurrent work. Shared access to files and databases allows team members to maintain files on individual computers and make them available to members of the group. Electronic meeting systems support group meetings for decision-making processes with software that allows parallel processing of group member inputs, parallel processing of comments, and voting.

◊ The productive management of a knowledge work environment and knowledge work tasks is supported by time management principles and methods. They explain motivation to sustain productive work, handle interruptions, switch among tasks, and establish and maintain readiness to work.

◊ Motivation can change the physical and mental energy applied to knowledge work. Although there are numerous motivational conditions, the primary conditions focus on factors such as completion, deadlines, and cycles of performance capability. These are affected by scheduling, an activity supported by software.

◊ Interruptions are a part of the knowledge work environment. However, interruptions can reduce productivity. The effect of scheduled and random interruptions differ. Both are affected by work design and use of software to schedule uninterrupted times and software that allows fast switching back to an interrupted activity. Simple scheduling can use calendar software, but more complete scheduling can use scheduling software to produce Gantt charts or network charts.

◊ Switching is required because humans cannot perform two tasks simultaneously, although they can work on more than one task concurrently by switching. Switching is normally due to an interrupt, but some switching is based on rotation among tasks. Operating systems and applications that allow more than one application or file to be active reduce switching times.

◊ Readiness to work requires activities to establish and maintain a work environment. This consists of a physical space environment and an information technology environment. Activities include loading software, startup and shutdown, and backup and recovery. Methods are applied to automate sequences of operations and reduce access time by the use of specialized icons, task bars, menus and keystrokes. Personal information management (PIM) software facilities are useful in improving productivity. These facilities include notepads, card files, calendars, reminders, and clocks. Specialized software is also available to increase productivity in backup operations.

EXERCISES

1. Prepare an analysis of a task you performed that involved significant collaboration. Prepare an analysis by activity of the costs of collaboration and the benefits. Identify how information technology was used. Explain whether more information technology would have been valuable.

2. Prepare a collaborative work requirements worksheet. Analyze the results and identify the software functions that are important for supporting your collaborative work.

3. For a period of time (such as an hour or a half day), identify times when two or more tasks are active at the same time. Identify the activities that are mainly automatic. Identify activities that can be automatic if they are repeated.

4. Use a software package for collaborative writing of a short paper. Evaluate the benefits and problems with its use. Explain how your writing methods might need to change in order to achieve higher productivity in cooperative writing with the software.

5. Investigate the network software management policies where you work and evaluate their effect on workgroup productivity.

6. Investigate the benefits of using calendaring software within your workgroup. If it has been rejected or tried and dropped, evaluate the reasons for the rejection or failure.

7. There are companies (such as Kinko's) that offer video conferencing facilities. They are less expensive on weekends. Assemble a group to participate in a video conference. Caution: There is an extra cost.

8. Prepare a knowledge work task management requirements worksheet. Prioritize the software support. Write a short paragraph defending the priorities.

9. Write a short evaluation of the value to you of each of the following personal information management (PIM) functions: calendar, clock, world time clock, "to do" list, reminders, note cards, contact/address list, and dialer.

10. Identify the capabilities of a personal computer operating system for having more than one software package loaded and available for use. Specify how a user switches among them. Also identify the capabilities of your word processor to have more than one document loaded and available.

11. *External Data Exercise:* Do Exercise 4 in Chapter 8. (Chapter 8 focuses on accessing external data on the Internet. The External Data Exercises included in Chapters 1-7 are designed to prepare you for the more difficult exercises presented in Chapter 8.)

Data and Software Management for Knowledge Work Productivity

◇　◇　◇　◇　◇　◇　◇　◇　◇　◇　◇　◇

Data access is at the heart of knowledge work. Without data, a great proportion of knowledge work tasks cannot be performed. Efficient and effective processes for analyzing data requirements, organizing and managing individual data, and accessing organizational and external data are fundamental to knowledge work productivity. Related to management of data is the management of software resources. These resources may be on an individual system or accessible to it. Since accessing data and providing results of analysis frequently depend on communications capabilities, these requirements are closely associated with data access and use.

Part 2 covers four key topics on data and software management and explains how to manage and access data in organizational databases and external sources. How to build and manage individual databases using database software will be covered in Chapter 12.

Chapter 5, Analyzing Data and Communications Requirements This chapter analyzes data and communications requirements. It explains how individuals and small groups can analyze data and communications requirements associated with knowledge work tasks. The chapter presents concepts related to these requirements and provides a technique for eliciting requirements that is robust enough to yield a correct and complete set of data and communications requirements, but also simple enough to be repeated whenever tasks or conditions change.

Chapter 6, Organizing and Managing Software and Data This chapter focuses on organizing and managing software and data. It illustrates how the quantity of software and data on both individual and remote systems will naturally grow at a significant rate. Without proper management of these resources, access time and errors in access will increase, reducing productivity. The chapter also presents concepts and methods for

managing software and data. These include organizing directories and files, establishing naming conventions to aid organization and retrieval, and maintaining accessibility. One of the problems of data management is the use of the same data in different applications. The chapter describes methods for sharing data across applications in a way that increases productivity and reduces errors.

Chapter 7, Accessing Organizational Data This chapter focuses on methods used by an organization to maintain databases containing a wide range of data about the organization and its transactions. It emphasizes that knowledge workers have frequent need to access databases structured and maintained by the organization and to retrieve various types of data. Individual access may be to operational databases or to extracts of operational databases, termed a data warehouse. The chapter explains the concepts related to organizational data and databases and describes procedures for accessing data.

Chapter 8, Accessing External Data This chapter explains that much of the data for environmental scanning, problem formulation, and analysis comes from external sources. Examples of these sources are Internet Web pages, newsgroups, and external databases. The external databases are maintained by government agencies or private organizations. Since much of the data is in text form, the chapter emphasizes text searching concepts and methods.

The management of data and software topics in Part 2 provides information supporting the topics in the next part of the text. Part 3 describes concepts and methods for designing and implementing productivity enhancements with information technology and emphasizes using software and building solutions.

CHAPTER 5

Analyzing Data and Communications Requirements

◇   ◇   ◇   ◇   ◇   ◇   ◇   ◇   ◇

CHAPTER OUTLINE

OBJECTIVES

After completing this chapter, you should be able to:

◆ Explain requirements for collections of data and sources of data.

◆ Describe need for communications.

◆ Describe two simple, systematic methods for identifying and documenting individual data and communications requirements.

◆ Explain how to extend the methods to collaborative work data requirements.

◆ Explain how to create a data and communications worksheet.

KEY TERMS AND CONCEPTS

This chapter introduces the following key terms and concepts, listed in the order in which they appear:

real-time data	transaction/event data	database
stored data	relationship data	databank
existence	database dictionary	synchronous communication
business event	meta data	asynchronous communication
accessibility	file	critical success factors
overload	physical file	Data and Communications
filtering	logical file	Requirements Worksheet

Having analyzed knowledge work tasks and activities by means of a Task/Activity worksheet (Chapter 3) and analyzed collaboration and work management requirements (Chapter 4), the next step is to analyze data and communications requirements.

A critical need in knowledge work is access to data. Data may be available locally or may be accessible only by electronic communications. Note the importance of data and communication in the definition of knowledge work:

> Knowledge work is human information processing in which the dominant activities are expected to generate useful information, *depend on knowledge accessible by the individuals performing the work,* employ a mental model of process and output, and require significant concentration and attention.

Knowledge workers increase the value of their work by the way they perform processes and procedures and by knowing how to obtain and use relevant data. Much of the data that a knowledge worker uses is not stored electronically. Paper files and books are important. Finding data in books and paper files is a vital part of knowledge work. Using library and non-electronic documents may be as important and critical as electronic information retrieval. This chapter focuses on data processed and stored by computers.

Data may be generated or received during an activity, or it may be retrieved from storage. Retrieval and use of stored data is limited not only by its existence and accessibility, but also by limits on human attention to the data obtained. Individual knowledge is vital in determining the availability of data, selecting data for retrieval, and limiting the amount of data presented for human attention.

The need to have and maintain collections of data leads to files and databases. These collections exist on both organizational and individual systems. Sources of data for use by knowledge workers include creation during processing, re-entry of data, and retrieval from internal and external databases. Data communication resources allow an individual to be part of a number of networks and engage in collaboration with remote colleagues. Data communication resources are used not only in communicating among individuals and groups, but also in obtaining data and storing and distributing results.

An analysis of data and communications requirements is preceded by a process to identify and document the requirements. Two approaches may be used. The first is simply to document current use. The second is a discovery process to systematically consider the reasons for data and communications and derive a statement of requirements. This chapter explains both methods.

The process of preparing a data and communications requirements worksheet begins with the tasks and task activities documented in Chapter 3. The sources for computer-based data requirements are identified. Communications requirements include communication to obtain data and distribute outputs. The worksheets documenting data and communications requirements will be useful in organizing local data (Chapter 6) and specifying an information infrastructure (Chapter 15).

Stored Data

◆ ◆ ◆ ◆ ◆ ◆ ◆ ◆ ◆ ◆ ◆ ◆ ◆ ◆ ◆ ◆ ◆ ◆ ◆ ◆

Stored data is significant in knowledge work. Not all data comes immediately from the situation or event; much data must be retrieved from storage. However, there are limits to the scope and amount of stored data. There are different categories of stored data which guide collection, storage, and retrieval.

Immediate Data versus Stored Data

Immediate or contemporary data is captured or arrives at the beginning of or during a task activity. Immediate data may be captured or obtained either in real time or in the period close to the activity. The term "real time" is applied to data capture, use, and processing operations that take place during an activity and are able to change its performance. Consequently, **real-time data** is processed as it is entered into the computer system, rather than stored for execution at a later time. For example, in customer order entry, data is real time if it is provided fast enough so that the dialog between the customer and company representative is supported and order/commitment decisions are influenced. Some activities rely entirely on real-time data. For example, a police officer directing traffic will employ only real-time observed traffic data (and personal expertise). Immediate data collected during an activity does not have to be used in real-time responses. It may be captured or obtained in real time but may not be used at that time. It may be stored for later use. For example, a customer inquiry may be made in the morning, but may be temporarily stored and not processed until the afternoon.

Stored data is data that has been accumulated prior to the task that employs it. Data may have been collected and stored specifically for use in the task. For example, financial transactions affecting taxes are collected for that purpose throughout a reporting period. Data is also collected and stored for other uses or potential uses. Transaction data items, for example, are stored as records of routine business events. Transaction data is often the basis for analysis tasks and is used to make non-routine decisions.

In knowledge work, immediate data inputs from activities are generally not sufficient for tasks. Stored data must be accessed and incorporated in task activities. Immediate observations frequently cannot be evaluated or processed without stored data. For example, a bond trader cannot make high-quality decisions based on only buy and sell orders observed in real time. The trader needs historical data on the bonds being traded, their quality, the inventory of bonds available, trends in the market for bonds, trends in interest rates, and analysis of call dates.

The bond trader example emphasizes a very short task processing/decision time for each trade. However, many knowledge work activities require a fairly long time period over which inputs are processed and outputs developed. For example, an analyst may be given ten days to perform a complex analysis. The ten days becomes the immediate time for the task. During the period of analysis, new data may be obtained through observation and interviews, but much of the data needed will come from stored data.

Limits to Retrieving Stored Data

Three characteristics limit or constrain the retrieval of stored data: existence, accessibility, and overload.

Existence refers to data that has been captured and stored. The primary source for internal organizational data is recording of business events or transactions.

A **business event** is typically rich in content and has a large number of attributes. Some are easily measured, such as time of day, products ordered, and prices agreed on. Others are not easily measured, even though they clearly are important. Examples are personal attitudes of the parties to the transaction, extent of personal confidence displayed, negotiation behavior prior to transaction closure, satisfaction of various parties, and personal assurances given. In recording a business transaction or event, only certain attributes are captured. The basic set of attributes recorded are those required by subsequent events, such as delivering products ordered and billing the customer. These vital attributes are specified by the chart of accounts for an organization which specifies the mandatory attributes to be recorded for each transaction. Transactions are usually limited to those that affect the financial records, either by specifying subsequent events that have a financial impact or by specifying a direct financial effect.

Examples

A salesperson loses some sales and closes others. If no sale is made, there will be no event recording, even though the reasons for the lost sale may be meaningful for analysis. If the sale is made, the quantitative details of the sale will be recorded; the attitude of the customer, the questions raised during the negotiation, the level of customer confidence in the supplier and its products, and similar important information will not be part of the transaction record. ◆

A customer who had purchased a car from an automobile dealership noted for its customer service orientation had a problem. The temperature gauge showed the cooling fluid was too hot. The problem might be a faulty gauge or a worn thermostat that was not opening properly. The service representative indicated the dealership was fully booked with advance service appointments for two weeks and made no attempt to deal with the emergency situation of an overheated engine that could result in serious damage. The transaction was not recorded, yet the event reflected badly on customer service response and the way the dealership was organized to deal with emergencies. ◆

A sales representative is given data that should influence billing procedures. Since the information does not fit within the selling procedures, the sales representative does not record them. ◆

Some data may be captured and used during transaction processing, but discarded after the event. A person taking telephone orders may listen to customer complaints and respond with assurances and apologies, but the complaints may not be recorded and stored for analysis. ◆

Not everything about business events can be recorded. There are too many rich details. There must be some selection of the important attributes to record and store. For example, the color of the suit worn by a customer is probably not important. The decisions about which attributes to record limit the existence of data.

Accessibility refers to the availability of data to a user. Data may have been stored, but still not be accessible. A user may not be aware of the data. If the user is aware of the data, it may not be accessible if it is in a form that makes it impossible to find, given reasonable time and cost. For example, an analyst may be asked to evaluate the sales performance of males versus females for certain types of products over the past year. Sales are not on commission, so salesperson identification is not part of the recorded transaction. The original paper sales tickets contain the salesperson's identification, but not gender. Data collection for this analysis might be too costly and time consuming (although alternatives such as statistical sampling might still be used in a cost effective way).

Overload refers to an excess of data. Retrieval can access more data than can be processed by the knowledge worker. (The limits to human attention were discussed in Chapter 1.) Limits must be set. **Filtering** can be used to reduce the amount of data requiring attention. A filter is a device or program that separates data, signals, or material in accordance with specified criteria. Overload occurs in many tasks. It easily happens when computer-based search procedures provide low-cost retrieval. Data stored as a part of business or other activity may be difficult to access with sufficient selectivity. Too much data can make a knowledge work task just as difficult to complete as the opposite condition of insufficient or nonexistent data.

These three concepts—existence, accessibility, and overload—constrain retrieval processes and procedures. This means that knowledge workers must understand what data exists, how to access it, and how to select only the desired data to avoid data overload.

Classifying Stored Data

Stored data is fundamental to knowledge work. Stored data items allow the past to influence the present. This influence is specific, based on its use. This contrasts with the use of knowledge and expertise codified as more general principles and procedures. Knowledge and expertise are important in identifying and selecting relevant stored data for use. Important categories of stored data are transaction/event data, relationship data, summarized data, reports and analyses, and meta data.

1. *Transaction/event data.* This represents "raw data" from business activity. Transaction data has usually been validated and may have been preprocessed to classify the type of transactions or events. **Transaction/event data** can be re-processed to suit the needs of the knowledge worker. Its limitations are in what is recorded about each transaction or event and the purpose and quality of recording, processing, classifying, and storage.

2. *Relationship data.* Organizations collect, store and maintain data about entities such as customers, suppliers, employees, and products or materials.

Transactions and events pertain to **relationship data** and are often applied to change its values. For example, a credit sale will increase the "balance due" in stored relationship data for that customer. Only predefined attributes of relationships are stored.

3. *Summarized data*. Transaction and event data items and relationship data are often categorized and summarized. The user makes inferences from the summaries about the business activities and relationships. Summaries may be simple tallies and totals. Descriptive statistics may also summarize underlying transactions, events, or relationships.

4. *Reports and analyses*. Rather than retrieving and using raw data or summarized data, a user may rely on reports and analyses that interpret the underlying data. This requires reliance on the expertise of those designing or creating the reports and analyses.

5. *Meta data*. Data about data includes location, method of storage and retrieval, and expectations of quality and timeliness. A **database dictionary** is a form of **meta data** that describes the contents of a database. Meta data may be broader and more extensive. For example, meta data may indicate that corporate sales are retrievable from the corporate database, whereas comparable competitors' sales are only retrievable from an external financial database. Meta data describes how to understand or interpret the data. For example, SIC (standard industry classification) codes are used to classify business activity. A description of the coding scheme is important to any analysis that employs SIC coding. Data requirements for a knowledge worker include such meta data related to current and potential tasks.

This classification of stored data highlights the fact that different types are significant. Transaction data, relationship data, summarized data, and reports and analyses are commonly found as stored data. The need for meta data beyond that ordinarily contained in database dictionaries is sometimes overlooked. The result of poor meta data is that sources of data are unknown to many potential users and, if known, the data might be used inappropriately because of lack of understanding about the data and its quality.

Requirements for Collections of Data

◆ ◆

In information processing, such terms as file and database are in common use. There are other technical terms to describe data more precisely, but this chapter will use the commonly accepted terms for collections of data.

Collections of Data as Files or Databases

A **file** is a collection of data with some common characteristics that are meaningful for the user. In other words, a user defines a collection of data as a file because the data belongs together for user purposes. A file is usually given a name that describes the basis for the collection. Examples of files are data about clients, customers, purchases, receivables, payments, projects, products, books, and policies. The term "files" is also used to designate word processing documents, spreadsheets, and multi-media presentations that are named and stored separately. (See Figure 5-1.)

Some computer software packages apply the analogy of folders to refer to collections of data. The terminology comes from the way knowledge workers

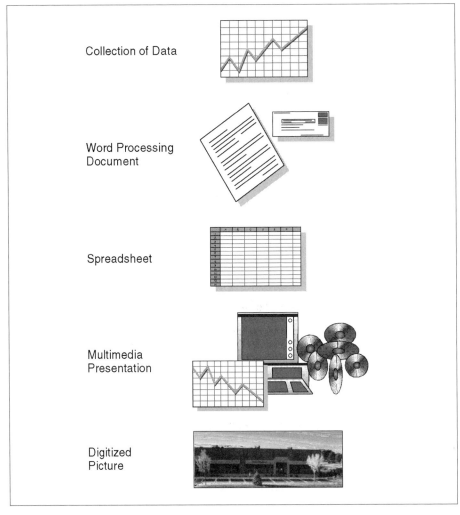

Collection of Data

Word Processing
Document

Spreadsheet

Multimedia
Presentation

Digitized
Picture

FIGURE 5-1 *The term "file" refers to many different collections of data*

deal with noncomputer data. In working with physical documents defined as belonging together, it is common to place them in a folder and to refer to that collection as a file. Other software uses the term "folder" to mean a container for related documents or spreadsheets that are individual files. Whatever the terminology, the concept of file is a collection of data treated as a unit.

Files may be physical or logical. **Physical files** can be observed in physical space. Examples are a file drawer containing folders, a collection of documents in a tray or pile, or a collection of books on a topic in the same section of a bookshelf. Files are organized in some way to support access. Usually file organization follows the primary interest of its maintainers and users. A major difficulty with physical files is that access is limited to one topic or criterion. A physical file of customer records cannot simultaneously be accessed as if it were a file of products sold.

The concept of **logical file** arises because of the flexibility of computer storage of data. If data records are organized properly, the same set of data can be accessed using more than one topic or criterion. It appears to the user as if there are different physical files. While there may be only one physical representation in computer storage, the user can work with the data as if there were more than one file. The concept of logical file will be important in data organization (to be discussed in Chapter 7).

The term **database** is sometimes equated to a file, but should usually be thought of as a broader term that refers to a collection of data about more than one thing. A large, extensive database is usually organized around some major theme or objective such as an organizational unit or organizational function. Examples include the personnel database or the customer database. A database may be stored as one or more physical files. It can represent many logical files. The term "database" is used especially in cases in which data records are stored, managed, and retrieved using packaged database management software.

The term **databank** is sometimes used to refer to a repository of text or non-record oriented data about a major topic of interest. For example, there may be a databank of government documents. There is no clear difference between a databank and a database, so the term "databank" is used less often.

Need for Individual System Data Storage

Much of the organization's data is captured, processed, stored, and made available to individual users by the formal, organizational information system. There are a number of reasons for allocating additional data storage on a knowledge worker's personal computer system or personal storage area on a departmental computer:

◇ *To provide data not stored by the organization, but needed for additional processing and analysis or for inquiries.* Past records may be needed for current activities and potentially for future use, and questions may arise about past analyses, actions, or status of events. Data to respond to such inquiries may come from records of past actions including source data, analysis methods, immediate results, drafts, and final reports.

◇ *To accumulate data for periodic processing.* Data needed in business processes may be accumulated in a batch until the work is performed. For example, employee suggestions requiring evaluation may be stored until a session is held to select the best of a batch.

◇ *To hold processing results as intermediate output to await future events and decisions.* For example, a file of unpaid invoices is stored until payments are received. Documents redesigning a process are stored until decisions are made to adopt, reject, or modify the proposed redesign.

◇ *To store data to reduce access delays or difficulties.* Even though data may be available elsewhere in the organization or from external sources, local storage may be used in order to have the data available locally and to avoid communication and access delays. For example, a portfolio manager might retain daily performance data in a series of spreadsheets simply because local availability makes analysis quicker and easier.

◇ *To retain data that is potentially useful.* For example, a manager may retain departmental performance reports indefinitely because an analysis of growth, expense, or other performance trends may be requested in the future.

◇ *To store data temporarily until a task is completed.* There are many tasks in which it is good practice to preserve all initial and intermediate data until the job is completed. For example, the drafts of a report may be saved until the final report is prepared. The final report may be saved for permanent reference; the drafts are either discarded or archived.

Need for Stored Data for Collaborative Work

Collaborative work adds new stored data requirements. As explained in Chapter 4, the needs center on data related to projects for collaborative assignments. Some of the most significant reasons to store data for collaborative work are:

◇ *To store data related to the work and work product of the project.* This includes project specifications, progress reports, notes, memoranda, and analyses.

◇ *To store data related to project scheduling, coordination, and management.* This includes project schedule and availability of staff members.

◇ *To store reports and other products being worked on.* This enables group members to work on the latest version without transfer delays, or to work on products concurrently.

◇   *To store reasoning and results from collaborative planning and decision-making meetings.* This provides a record of decisions made and allows group members to proceed with work rather than wasting time re-evaluating prior decisions.

Sources of Data for Individual or Collaborative Information Processing

◆ ◆ ◆ ◆ ◆ ◆ ◆ ◆ ◆ ◆ ◆ ◆ ◆ ◆ ◆ ◆ ◆ ◆ ◆ ◆

An important step in analyzing data requirements is to identify the sources of data used in information processing. Data sources can be classified at a high level as internal or external (see Figure 5-2). Data from internal sources may have been created during processing, re-entered from reports and other documents, or may be retrieved from internal files or databases. External data are files or databases from external sources that have been copied onto user systems, external databases accessed directly using electronic communication, and data accessed on networks such as the Internet.

Data Created During Personal Processing

Documents and records may be created by original data entry or by data processing. Such data is a product or byproduct of other tasks and activities. Examples include reports, spreadsheets, and presentations that have been created by the individual.

Re-entered Data

Data from internal or external reports and analyses may be available in a stored file, but often such data items are re-entered. Why would anyone enter

Internal	External
• Created by personal processing • Re-entered from reports and documents • Internal files — individual files — department files — organization files	• From business partners (customers or suppliers) • External databases — installed on individual system — accessed by communication • Networks such as Internet

FIGURE 5-2   *Sources of stored data for individual information processing*

data that was already stored in a computer system? It is frequently done for either of two reasons: (1) the cost of re-entry is lower than the cost of obtaining it from storage, or (2) it may not be technically feasible to obtain a machine-readable copy. Re-entry may be preferable when the data source is external to the organization and there are no provisions for doing a computer extraction of the required data.

Data Retrieved from Internal Files and Databases

An organization maintains much of its data in separate information systems: user files, workgroup or departmental files, and corporate files. These are often three different sets of technology:

1. *User files.* As part of an individual information processing infrastructure, an individual will maintain many files.

2. *Work group or departmental files.* If a department or workgroup has its own network or system, individuals in that department or workgroup will probably share data, perhaps via client/server technology. Departmental data is often quite accessible, although it is subject to more constraints on modification and retention than individual data.

3. *Corporate or organization data on corporate files.* Usually, access is restricted to those with demonstrated need for access and controlled by password privileges. Subsets of organizational data are often made available for analysis in separate files or databases known as data warehouses.

External Files and Databases

Files and databases are available from a variety of external sources. These include companies with which the organization interacts, governmental and commercial databases, and electronic network sources.

Files belonging to business partners, including vendors, customers, and financial institutions. Access privileges are restricted to specified data. Most access is read-only, although there are some cases in which outsiders are allowed to enter orders and make similar changes. For example, a vendor may allow a customer read-only access to a file showing the status of that customer's orders. Banks may allow read-only access to a customer's file of deposits made and checks cleared.

Public and private databases on user systems. Databases built and maintained by external sources are available for local use on an individual user system. Such databases may be provided on media such as magnetic tape or CD-ROM (Compact Disk-Read Only Memory). They can provide an individual with local access to reference files, public and private statistical and informational databases, and library resources. Many organizational and departmental systems also provide access via a local area network to such sources.

Public and private databases accessible by communications.   Many public agencies have files that can be accessed directly via network or dial-up communication. For example, files of laws, agency regulations, status of rulings, and statistics are provided by many governmental units. Private companies maintain and market databases of statistics, corporate and government data, and financial statistics. Private vendors also provide online access to library resources, such as journals, books, reports, and dissertations. These databases are usually directly accessible via electronic communications.

Electronic networks.   Electronic network services can be provided by the organizational system or by an external vendor of such services. Commercial vendors provide access to their own systems and to large networks such as the Internet. The information available on the networks is very extensive. There are files and databases on specific topics, records of discussion groups, reports, and commentaries. (These will be described more fully in Chapter 8.)

An example of the use of external data sources is an accountant responsible for financial reports to shareholders and regulatory authorities. The job makes frequent use of information about how other companies deal with complex issues in their financial reports. The accountant can use reference books, but a more efficient approach may be to access such information from computer files. Access to reference data on computer files may be achieved in several ways. For example, the analyst may access the financial reporting files electronically through computer-to-computer communications with a commercial service that provides reference data for online search. Another possibility is to purchase a copy of the financial reporting references on CD-ROM. Once file access is achieved, the analyst must still be able to search using terms that identify the issue being investigated.

Computer Communications

◆ ◆ ◆ ◆ ◆ ◆ ◆ ◆ ◆ ◆ ◆ ◆ ◆ ◆ ◆ ◆ ◆ ◆ ◆

A computer system has facilities for input, processing, storage, and output. Outputs may take a printed or "hardcopy" form or may be transferred for use in electronic form. Electronic communication extends the capabilities of a single computer by enabling input from remote sources, remote storage, remote data access, and output to remote receivers. The remote sources and receivers are not just computers; a wide range of devices may be used. Through communications, the individual computer becomes part of a network of information sources and destinations. This section provides background information on two issues related to requirements for data communications in knowledge work tasks: how communications are used and how the volume of data to be communicated can be determined.

How Communications Are Used in Knowledge Work Tasks

Communication technologies are used in knowledge work for obtaining and transmitting a broad range of data: text, pictures, graphics, sound, and video in addition to voice communication. Data communication allows data to be obtained from or sent to other computers. The connections can be direct from user to source or via a shared private or public network.

Computer communications between individuals can be interactive, meaning that both the sender and receiver are available simultaneously. Consequently, the receiver of a message can respond immediately to the sender. The result is a synchronous session, since both parties must be available simultaneously. A telephone conversation is an example of **synchronous communication** which features interaction that often clarifies the meaning of the conversation.

An alternative to synchronous communication is **asynchronous communication**. Messages (such as e-mail or voice messages) are received and stored by the communications system until the recipient elects to read them. Data asynchronously retrieved in response to a request is stored pending use. There is always a delay in reading and responding to stored voice and e-mail messages. A delay in retrieving data requested for a task means the process requiring the data will be delayed. Processing delays are not inherently undesirable. They allow work to be scheduled and processes to be performed without interruptions. A person who always answers the telephone when it rings is frequently interrupted. If that person's activity involves mental concentration, it might be better to respond to stored voice mail messages during a rest period.

Examples

Electronic messaging has numerous advantages and disadvantages compared to the telephone. It is asynchronous rather than synchronous; therefore, it is not necessary to interrupt the recipient or synchronize schedules. A second advantage is the documentation of messages that is available with e-mail. A disadvantage is the loss of that portion of meaning that is conveyed by elements such as tone of voice and inflection in a conversation. A second disadvantage is the loss of interaction and clarification that may be achieved through synchronous communication. ◆

Although both are asynchronous, electronic mail is much faster than regular mail. E-mail tends to be less formal than other forms of written communication. The greater informality of e-mail increases the rapidity of communications, but can also result in less precision in conveying meaning. ◆

To determine communications requirements, examine each task and the requirements for accessing or transmitting data directly with other computers or through networks. Determine the need for synchronous human communication to obtain inputs such as data and instructions and to deliver outputs such as reports and decisions. Will synchronous communications improve the efficiency and effectiveness of work? Might asynchronous communications be more suitable?

In addition to the question of synchronous versus asynchronous communication, it is useful to define the purpose of communications. Examples are to access data, inform or collaborate with others, and to distribute task results.

Electronic Communication Volume

The requirement for data communications is rising rapidly and technology changes are providing dramatic improvements. (The technology is discussed in more detail in Chapter 14.)

Communication volume must be considered in relation to the capacities of the available technology. A simple distinction between low and high volume is useful in understanding requirements.

◊ *Low volume.* A single textual report, a few spreadsheets, or some simple graphics can be transmitted electronically with little problem or delay. Low-volume data is often included as an e-mail attachment.

◊ *High volume.* As the data to be communicated grows to hundreds of text pages, or thousands of records, special provisions may need to be made for its communication. Inclusion of graphics and other images, sound, or video also tends to require high-capacity communications. High-volume data may be more easily or economically transferred physically (express mail) than via electronic means.

Two Methods for Determining Data and Communications Requirements

The objective of determining data and communications requirements is to document the data and communication needed for efficient, effective, and timely knowledge work. The processes described are also applicable to information processing applications involving more than one individual, but this chapter emphasizes the documentation needs of an individual knowledge worker.

There are essentially two methods for defining data and communications requirements:

1. *Document data currently used and communications currently employed.* The logic is that the data currently used has evolved through experience and, therefore, the current collections of data represent a complete set of requirements. The same logic may be applied to current use of data communications. The method is simple and direct.

2. *Employ a discovery method to elicit a correct and complete set of data and communications requirements.* The logic is that current data and communications use may reflect reasoning that is no longer applicable and may not be taking advantage of current data and communications opportunities. Creative uses of data and communications may emerge if requirements are not limited to what has been done in the past. The discovery process provides the rationale for each requirement.

Both methods may be used in a complementary fashion. All data and communications currently used may be documented. A discovery method may then be applied to identify data and communications needs for tasks and activities without regard to current practice. The two results are compared. Current use that did not emerge in the discovery process may have been overlooked or may not be necessary. New requirements from the discovery process should be evaluated for feasibility and cost. Those that are feasible and within cost limits may be implemented.

◢◆ Discovery Method for Data and Communications Requirements

♦ ♦ ♦ ♦ ♦ ♦ ♦ ♦ ♦ ♦ ♦ ♦ ♦ ♦ ♦ ♦ ♦ ♦ ♦ ♦

Arriving at correct and complete requirements can be difficult and time consuming. The method described in this section is simple and can be repeated when re-analysis of requirements is indicated. The method employs overlapping questions, so there is a high probability of arriving at complete requirements. The method can be easily tailored for an individual. Questions or sets of questions that are not applicable may be omitted. The method can be applied to requirements determination for larger systems, so the experience gained in evaluating requirements for an individual system or project may also be applied to these systems.

Using Questions to Elicit Requirements

This method is based on systematic inquiry using a set of questions based on the tasks performed. Each question elicits data and communications requirements. For each requirement, questions are asked about its relative importance and whether it is already available. After all task information requirements have been elicited, the sources are organized into groups corresponding with noncomputer data sources, organizational or subunit computer databases or files, personal system databases and files, and external data sources.

Why use predefined sets of questions? Why not just list all data and communications needs? The reason is that most knowledge workers rarely think directly about data communications needs; they think about how they use information and information technology. Therefore, the questions used to elicit requirements should ask questions related to needs.

When a question is asked, it may not evoke a complete response. The person or group may need a different question to trigger the mental processes that elicit the rest of the requirements. The questions can be designed to be overlapping in their effect. If one question does not elicit recall of a requirement, another may do so.

Three Characteristics of Tasks as Sources of Requirements

A knowledge worker needs data and communications to accomplish tasks. Characterizing tasks assists in eliciting requirements. Three characteristics of tasks are associated with management processes, organizational processes, and products and services provided by the organization. For some tasks, more than one characteristic may apply, so the questions for more than one characteristic may be used in analyzing requirements (see Figure 5-3).

1. *Tasks as part of organizational management processes.* Examples of knowledge work activities that support management processes are analysis, evaluation, planning, scheduling, control, and decision making. Tasks that are dominated by these activities usually involve access to data and extensive use of information processing functions to analyze data and prepare various types of reports and memoranda.

2. *Tasks as part of organizational processes.* Organizational processes (often called business processes) perform organizational tasks. These tasks frequently involve more than one person and often cross business functions. The processes involve accessing documents, files, and other information, and exchanging data with others. Examples include making a purchase, processing an order, hiring an employee, or preparing a proposal. Improving these processes typically involves reducing cycle time by combining steps,

eliminating process delays, and providing information to empower employees to perform a more complete set of activities and thereby streamline the process.

3. *Tasks associated with products and services provided by the organization.* Goods and services may include information to help customers select features or configurations before a sale and respond to customer questions and problems after the sale. Specialized information may be included with the product or service. An example is information provided by a pharmacist about the effects of a prescription drug and information on interaction effects with other prescriptions being taken. Providing these services requires access to data.

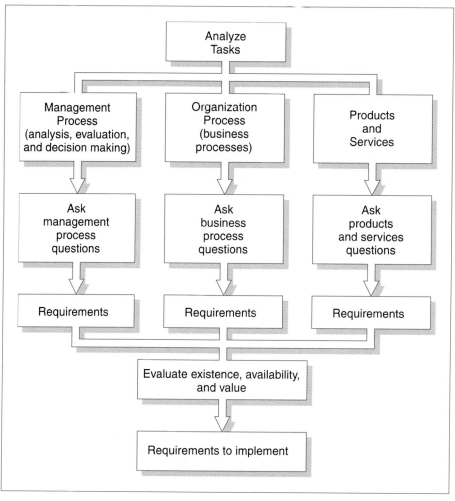

FIGURE 5-3 *Discovery approach to requirements*

Steps in Data and Communications Requirements Determination

The following method has demonstrated good results in identifying correct and complete requirements. There is a set of questions for each of the sources of requirements to help an individual think about data that can profitably be used and whether it is available. Not all three sources of requirements will apply to every knowledge worker.

1. *Analyze each of your tasks in terms of the three task characteristics.*
   a. Is the task associated with support of management processes?
   b. Is the task part of a business process?
   c. Does the task involve goods or services?
   A task may involve more than one of these sources; if so, use all of the task questions that apply.

2. *Relate questions to each applicable source of requirements for each of your knowledge work tasks.* The questions do not ask for requirements directly. They focus attention on the reasons data and communications facilities are needed. These needs allow data needs to be specified. The data needed can be described in very specific terms (customer name and address) or in general terms (data about customer past purchases). Need for communications facilities can be noted. For each item or class of data, record also responses to the following:
   a. How important is the data? A simple classification into *critical, generally useful,* and *somewhat useful* will be sufficient. If the data items are not useful, remove them from further consideration.
   b. Are these data items available now? If "yes," describe the source.

3. *Identify new data items for support of work.* Identify the sources.

4. *Analyze requirements not met with current or planned data or communication.* For future action, analyze requirements not expected to be met with current or planned resources. Record reasons for not meeting such as constraints of cost, difficulty, or uncertainty as to value.

5. *Record data or communication currently available or planned for implementation on a data and communications requirements worksheet.*

Requirements Associated with Management Processes

The following five sets of questions overlap in their coverage of data requirements for management and those who assist management with analytical, evaluation, and decision support. The questions also elicit data requirements for monitoring or evaluating management processes.

1. What problems do you deal with? What information do you need to solve each problem you identify?

2. What decisions do you make? What information do you need to make each decision?

3. What are your **critical success factors** (five to seven things that are most important in evaluating you as being successful)? What information do you need to monitor your critical success factors?

4. What are the "ends" for your processes and activities (what are the outputs—tangible or intangible results of your efforts that establish whether or not you are effective)? What information do you need to measure and monitor your "ends" or effectiveness?

5. What resources (such as time and monetary expenditures) do you employ in your processes and activities (efficiency in your use of resources to produce outputs)? What information do you need to measure your efficiency in use of resources?

Requirements Associated with Organizational (Business) Processes

The following sets of questions refer to business processes in which you participate either by performing work or supplying information to others who are performing the work. Identify those processes and then ask the questions about each:

1. What data do you receive from others? How could it be supplied with less delay? What data could you store on your system in order to reduce information delays?

2. What problems do you have in information processing for the process? What data and communications facilities would assist you?

3. What parts of the process could be performed in parallel (in order to reduce cycle time)? What data and communications would you need in order to do your work in parallel with others?

4. What errors occur frequently in the input or process? What improvements in data or communications would reduce errors?

5. What parts of the process could be combined for greater efficiency and reduction in cycle time? What communications and information would you need in order to do a larger part of the process?

Requirements Associated with Products and Services

Identify the products or services you provide or consider your interaction with customers or suppliers before or after a sale or service. Customers or clients can be external to the organization or within the organization. Products or services can be physical products, information products such as reports, or advisory or analytical services. Ask the following questions for each product or service:

1. What information is associated with or contained within the product or service? What additional information would be valuable to customers or suppliers?

2. What are the most common questions or inquiries from customers or clients? How could this information be provided more easily?

3. What uncertainties are faced by clients or customers relative to the selection, purchase, or use of the product or service? What information could you provide that would reduce their uncertainties?

4. What information would allow you to improve the product or service you provide?

Extending the Discovery Method to Collaborative Work Data Requirements

The discovery method using questions about the reasons for data can be applied to collaborative work involving project teams, collaborative assignments, etc. The analysis is simple enough that it can be repeated for each new project or other collaboration. The objectives of the collaborative effort are defined. The project or team objectives are analyzed in terms of relevance to management processes, business processes, or products and services. The appropriate set of questions can then be asked. The context of the questions is the project and its objectives.

After discovery of requirements, they can be analyzed in terms of importance and current availability. Items not currently available can be evaluated relative to cost and feasibility of obtaining them. The final step in analysis is to decide on methods for providing the data to the workgroup and managing the requirements within the time and cost constraints of the group tasks.

Creating a Data and Communications Requirements Worksheet

◆ ◆

The requirements process for data and communications needs can be summarized on a **Data and Communications Requirements Worksheet**. This worksheet provides a description of data needed for each task and documents the tasks needing communications support. A few facts about each of the data and communications requirements are recorded. The worksheet is organized around the tasks to be performed (as was done on the task/activity analysis of Chapter 3). An example of the layout of a data and communications requirements worksheet is shown in Figure 5-4.

Items on the Data and Communications Requirements Worksheet

Following are descriptions of the columns listed on the Requirements Worksheet and some notes about filling in the data for your requirements.

1. *Task.* Enter a task from the Task/Activity Analysis (Chapter 3). List each task in the left-hand column (but insert just one at a time because several rows may be needed for each task). The list of tasks may be expanded to include some that were not included in the task/activity analysis (because it included only the most important).

2. *Task type.* Indicate whether the task is primarily associated with management processes (M), organizational (business) processes (O), or products and services (P). If more than one, list them all.

Task	Task Type	Data Needed	Identification for Source of File/Database	Location of File/Database	Use of Communication Network in Task	Communication Volume (low or high)

FIGURE 5-4 *Knowledge worker data and communications requirements worksheet*

3. *Data needed.* Specify the data items by name or descriptive term for a group of items.

4. *Identification for source of file/database.* Name the files/databases accessed for data input. Also list any non-computer data sources such as books, reference manuals, etc. The identification should be a name that is descriptive of the contents, such as invoices, clients, address book, etc. Be complete but reasonable in amount of detail. Access to general purpose files or other material need not be defined. For example, reference to a dictionary or thesaurus would not normally be included on the worksheet. Access to a dictionary of medical terminology would be listed unless that was part of normal knowledge work environment.

5. *Location of file/database.* Where are source databases or files located? Identify external database vendor as part of location. If there are any access restrictions or limitations, note them.

6. *Use of communications network for task.* Indicate whether communication is synchronous or asynchronous. Note primary and important uses of communications in the task. Examples are data access, communicating or collaborating with others, or distributing task results.

7. *Communication volume.* Distinguish between low and high volume.

Note that size of files is not specified. In most cases, this will not be critical because storage is relatively inexpensive. However, if storage requirements are very large, they should be noted. Storage requirements may be significant for graphics, pictures, voice, and video.

Summary of Data Sources

The data sources required to document knowledge work tasks are summarized in Figure 5-5.

1. *Noncomputer sources of data.* Documents such as books, papers, reports, checks, and business transactions. In some cases, a data source may be a specific individual.

2. *Organizational databases and files.* These sources will be accessible online or subsets may be extracted for use on an individual system.

3. *Department or workgroup databases and files.* These sources may be accessible on a departmental or workgroup computer system.

4. *External databases.* These can be commercial databases, governmental databases available to outside organizations, and customer/vendor databases which allow access.

5. *Your own databases and files.*

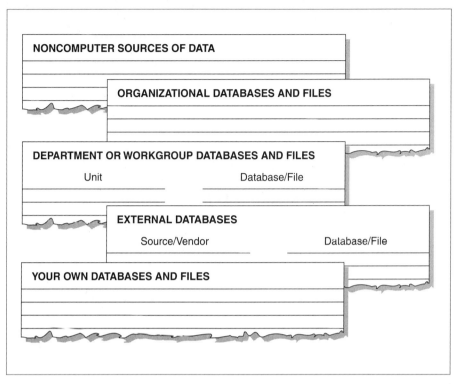

FIGURE 5-5 *Summary of data sources*

Data and Communications Requirements for a Director of Software Sales

◆ ◆

Figure 5-6 describes the requirements for data and communications for a director of sales for a software company. The organization currently uses a central database, Lotus Notes™, with broad organizational input. The Notes package stores comments and documents. It also stores discussion notes in a form that makes it possible to follow a discussion on a given topic.

In interpreting the results, the director indicates an extensive use of asynchronous communication. While efficient, he is concerned that this reliance keeps him from various face-to-face management processes. He also commented on the importance of informal information sources and meetings with information content, but no formal data sources.

Task	Task Type	Data Needed	Identification for Source of File/Database	Location of the File/Database	Use of Communication Network in Task	Communication Volume (low or high)
JOB SPECIFIC						
Develop and sell resellers on our software	P	Contact database	Resellers database	Mac Server	Asynchronous	Low volume-2 meg file
Maintain accurate database of reseller contacts	O	Contact database	Resellers database	Mac Server	Asynchronous	Low volume-2 meg file
Communicate with management regarding customer feedback and recommend modifications to software	M,O	Lotus Notes database: Customer and development database	Customer issue database; development database	Lotus Notes server	Synchronous	Low volume-documents in Notes database
Generate new leads	P	New reseller listings	Trade mags, 3rd party lists, Internet, customers	Internal and external sources, Marketplace CD ROM, List services	Asynchronous	High volume-hundreds of thousands of contacts and related info
KNOWLEDGE BUILDING & MAINTAINING						
Continue education on Internet, firewalls, TCP/IP, Lotus Notes, etc.	P	New articles found by me and by others	Notes technology database, ComputerWorld, Wired, PC World	Notes server, Computer Source (3rd Party periodical CD), periodicals	Asynchronous	High volume, lots of articles and pictures
Analyze competition	P	Press releases and product info	Notes competition database, Selling Magazine	Notes server, Computer Source (3rd Party periodical CD), periodicals	Asynchronous	Low volume, minimal competition
Maintain knowledge of our products and competitive sales management systems	O	Press releases and reviews	Notes SFA database, Selling Magazine, other PC magazines	Notes server, Computer Source (3rd Party periodical CD), periodicals	Asynchronous	Low volume, only a few possibilities
Keep current on reseller industry	P	Lots of articles from all sources	Notes technology database, VAR Business, Computer Reseller News, Internet	Notes server, Computer Source (3rd Party periodical CD), periodicals	Asynchronous	High volume, tremendous amount of info on industry; changing rapidly
KNOWLEDGE WORK MANAGEMENT						
Maintain computer manuals, etc.	O	WIN 95 reference manual	Help files on computer, Internet resources	CD ROM, internet, magazines	Asynchronous	Low volume; only a couple of manuals
Manage time and schedule	O	Day Timer & software; Company schedule (Now up to date)	My time schedule file; Company schedule	On my PC and on company network	Synchronous	Low volume

FIGURE 5-6 *Knowledge worker data and communications requirements worksheet for a director of sales for a software company (M = management processes, O = organizational (business) processes, P = products and services)*

Summary

◆ ◆ ◆ ◆ ◆ ◆ ◆ ◆ ◆ ◆ ◆ ◆ ◆ ◆ ◆ ◆ ◆ ◆ ◆ ◆

◊ The information recorded on the Data and Communications Requirements Worksheet is useful in evaluating requirements and generating input for the design of an information management infrastructure.

◊ Concepts of data distinguish between immediate data and stored data. Both are typically needed. Retrieval of stored data reflects existence, accessibility, and overload considerations.

◊ A file is a collection of data with some common characteristics meaningful to the user. The term "folder" is sometimes used to refer to a file or collection of files. Computer technology allows physical files to be accessed in a variety of ways, so that it appears to the user as if there were many files. A database is a collection of data organized around a theme or objective.

◊ Individuals need stored data for future processing, to hold data for periodic processing, to hold data for future events, to keep data otherwise difficult to access, and to store data until a task is completed.

◊ Project groups and teams employ stored data facilities to retain data about the project, store project management data, store reports and other products being worked on, and store results of collaboration meetings.

◊ The sources of data may be internal or external. Internal sources are created during processing, re-entered from prior processing, or files obtained or accessed from users, workgroups, or organizational systems. External sources include business partners, public or private databases either installed on user systems or available by direct electronic communication or network services such as the Internet.

◊ Computer communications can support both synchronous and asynchronous human communication, remote input or output, and file transfers. Communication speeds required for an individual system will depend on the type and volume of communications needed.

◊ There are two methods for determining requirements: documenting existing data and using the discovery method. Both methods may be used in a complementary approach.

◊ A Data and Communications Requirements Worksheet is employed to record data about requirements. The format is simple and focuses on recording requirements and sources, locating data files and databases, and recording use of communication networks.

EXERCISES

1. Identify your data and communications requirements *as a student.* Use a copy of the Data and Requirements Communications Worksheet plus an additional sheet for notes that add documentation and explanation to the worksheet. Use the tasks you defined in Exercise 1 of Chapter 3. Write two or three paragraphs interpreting the results.

2. Identify your data and communications requirements *in your current position or in the position you expect to hold when you graduate.* Use the worksheet plus a notes sheet to add documentation and explanation to the worksheet. Use the tasks you defined in Exercise 2 of Chapter 3. Write two or three paragraphs interpreting the results.

3. Analyze the effect of asking several indirect questions rather than a single direct question about requirements. For the three types of requirements, analyze how many of the same requirements were elicited by different questions, and how many were unique to a question.

4. Use the discovery approach to analyze data and communications requirements for a project involving collaboration.

5. *External Data Exercise:* Do Exercise 5 in Chapter 8. (Chapter 8 focuses on accessing external data on the Internet. The External Data Exercises included in Chapters 1–7 are designed to prepare you for the more difficult exercises presented in Chapter 8.)

Organizing and Managing Software and Data

◇　◇　◇　◇　◇　◇　◇　◇

CHAPTER OUTLINE

OBJECTIVES

After completing this chapter, you should be able to:

◆ Describe the hierarchical approach to creating and naming directories and subdirectories.

◆ Describe issues and methods in managing and controlling packaged software.

◆ Describe methods for locating files.

◆ Explain the differences between the various types of backup procedures (full, selective, differential, and incremental).

◆ Explain the reasons for file archiving.

◆ Describe the basic methods for protecting individual systems from unauthorized access and computer viruses.

◆ Describe the following processes: file appending, file importing, cutting and pasting, embedding, and linking.

KEY TERMS AND CONCEPTS

This chapter introduces the following key terms and concepts, listed in the order in which they appear:

directory
subdirectory
folder
peer experts
backward compatibility
directory structure
hierarchical search process
user-defined keywords
full backup

selective backup
differential backup
incremental backup
archiving
encryption
viruses
file appending
file importing

ASCII (American Standard Code for Information Interchange)
Rich Text Format (RTF)
embedding
Object Linking and Embedding (OLE)
linking

Continuous increases in computer capability, performance, and storage capacity permit and encourage continuous expansion of individual programs and data. An increasing collection of programs and data can reduce efficiency in computer use and lower productivity. Software program files and data files must be organized for effective use and efficient access. The difficulties from poor management of software and data increase over time as the amount of software and data increases. There is an increase in the number of software packages that are useful to an individual. The trend is for each new version of an existing software package to increase in size, capability, and complexity. Data files grow over time in size, variety, and scope. Careful planning and ongoing attention to software and data storage reduces frequency of access problems such as inability to locate data, access errors, and excessive access time.

Managing data and programs maintained at the departmental or corporate level is outside the scope of individual responsibility because these resources are organized and maintained by information systems specialists serving a variety of users. Although the information system function may manage some software and data on individual systems, this chapter assumes that individual knowledge workers are expected to take primary responsibility for individual data access and storage and for programs stored on their systems. Organizing and managing individual programs and data can be more simple than organizing and managing programs at the organizational level because these programs are smaller and require inputs from only one individual (or a small workgroup). The individual generally defines or controls system installation. The individual also decides what data to collect, what to save, how to organize data for access, and how to determine the data to be archived or discarded.

The explanations in this chapter use the term "file" in the generic sense to refer to any collection of data treated as a unit of storage by the computer operating system. The terms **directory**, **subdirectory**, and **folder** are essentially synonyms and refer to a collection of files that are or appear to be stored together. The files in a directory or folder belong together because of some common characteristic.

The chapter contains concepts, principles, and practical suggestions for five topics related to the management of individual software and data:

1. *Managing software package versions and upgrades.* Software packages undergo frequent upgrades and revisions. These changes require installation and training time for users, who must become acquainted with the new features. To minimize this time, individuals should have a decision strategy for installing new versions.

2. *Organizing directories for software and data.* Storage of both programs and data should be designed to support the process of subsequent access, which involves remembering, finding, and retrieving activities. These mental and physical activities are supported by directory structure and file naming. The directory structure should be simple to implement and maintain, and the directory names should reflect the way people remember names.

3. *Finding directories and files.* Programs or data files are not useful if they cannot be found quickly. Excessive search time reduces productivity. If search time is too long, the program or data files are less useful and may not even be used. The methods should be simple in both concept and operation.

Example

A complex letter must be written to a customer who made a complaint. A similar letter was written a few months earlier to another customer with the same complaint.

If the previous letter can be found quickly, it will reduce the time to formulate a response. ◆

4. *Ensuring data availability.* The number of stored files increases over time and is limited by the individual system data storage. The individual needs an approach to deciding what data to keep current, what to discard, and what to archive. Discarded data items can never be recovered; archived data items are expected to have infrequent use. Ensuring availability of data retained in an individual system requires regular backup, since equipment failure can result in loss of stored data.

5. *Moving data between files and applications.* Data should not be re-entered for a new file or application if it can be moved from an existing source. Data from one application may need to be used by another application. In some cases, the user wants updating of results in one file to result in automatic updating in other files. Moving data and automatic updating can improve productivity and, if used properly, can reduce errors.

This chapter emphasizes basic concepts, but will often illustrate the concepts with features found in personal computer software. Some new versions of operating systems reduce or eliminate many of the limitations of widely used systems. The principles explained in this chapter apply in the context of both limited and newer operating systems.

Managing and Controlling Packaged Software

◆ ◆ ◆ ◆ ◆ ◆ ◆ ◆ ◆ ◆ ◆ ◆ ◆ ◆ ◆ ◆ ◆ ◆ ◆ ◆

There are three important management issues concerning personal computer software packages: (1) the locus of control of packaged software, (2) what to do with old versions when new ones are installed, and (3) how to decide when to install a new version.

The Locus of Control over Software Packages

Individuals in organizations do not usually have complete control of personal computers. The costs of package acquisition and installation, training costs, and issues of data sharing are too significant to permit each knowledge worker, manager, or support person to choose his or her own software tools. In many organizations, the software decision is departmental rather than corporate.

Individuals may still have choices, but they are typically constrained to an approved subset of software.

When software is acquired in volume, the distribution channel frequently delivers something other than the "shrink-wrapped" product purchased at retail. Consequently, the installation and administration processes differ. Volume software is typically sold as a license for a particular number of users, e.g., a "10-pack." Often what is delivered is one copy of software and one copy of documentation. Additional documentation may be available at additional cost.

In some organizations, individual users may still be responsible for the installation and organization of the software. Because of the relationships between software and data, and because of the persistence of software, the individual user should carefully integrate new software with existing packages, directory structures, and naming conventions.

An individual may prefer custom installation focusing on individual preferences, but this may involve significant organizational costs. Tools are available that support central installation, setup, and control of packaged software. This suggests that for major software packages used by many individuals and groups, individual users may have little or no control over the type and version of software used, nor where and how it is installed.

Version Control of Software Packages

When a new version of a software package is installed, it will frequently replace an existing version. This usually is satisfactory. In some cases, however, new versions will need to coexist with previous versions of the same package. Why would a user want to retain a prior version? One reason is to protect against new versions that do not work the same as older ones, either in their processing of older input data or in certain features. For example, macro programs written for use with a prior version may not work with a new one. A second reason is that the new version may have changed so much that training is required. In such cases, an older version may be retained for those not yet trained. If prior versions of a package must be retained, two possibilities exist:

1. Reinstall the previous version when it is needed.
2. Install the new version in a directory with a different name from the previous version, or move the old version to a directory with a name indicating its old status. Because of the complexity of many applications, it may not be possible to operate two versions of some packages on one computer.

Old versions should only be kept when required, since they take storage space and may be mistakenly used.

Decision Processes for New Versions and Upgrades

One approach to new versions or upgrades of software is to upgrade whenever a new release is available. The opposite extreme is to not upgrade until problems with the existing version force a change. Of course, corrections to software, in the form of "bug fixes" should usually be installed immediately. Upgrades to new "improved" or "enhanced" software versions are more problematic. Many users reason it does not make sense to work with old versions when new ones are on the market. The upgrade package cost is usually modest at the individual level. Vendors offer upgrades at reduced rates for existing users of their software or their competitors. Occasionally, upgrade discounts are limited to a short time period in an attempt to encourage rapid upgrades.

The problem with new versions of software is that the full, actual cost is much more than just the software and installation costs (see Figure 6-1). Upgraded versions usually provide new capabilities and features, but these require learning or training. Keep in mind that full productivity is usually associated with sufficient training and experience so that the use of the software (at least the most frequently used features) is largely automatic, allowing

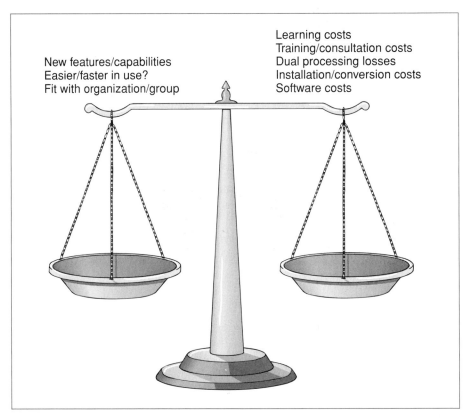

FIGURE 6-1 *Trade-offs in decision to install new version of software package*

the user to focus attention on the task rather than the software. When a new version introduces new features and operations, the user is temporarily faced with "dual processing loss" which causes reduced productivity. (As previously described, "dual processing loss" occurs when two high-attentional tasks must be done at the same time: the task of the problem being worked on and the task of learning the changes in the software.)

The way that upgrades and new versions have been managed on large mainframe systems provides insight for an individual system. Well-run installations typically schedule upgrades to new versions ("bug fixes" may be installed immediately). The schedule of changes is managed to reflect the tradeoff between the cost of the change and the benefits. Research has shown that frequent software upgrades, even to fix problems, can introduce new problems and difficulties for software users. Six- to twelve-month intervals between upgrades are common with large systems.

Organizational Considerations in Package Selection and Upgrades

For an individual, the tradeoff decision is also affected by organizational policies and procedures. If the organization makes a change in software versions or is planning to do so, the importance of consistency suggests that an individual make the change at the same time. The value of the consistency is based on two value/cost considerations: training and cooperative work.

1. *Training.* Organizational training in new versions or new software packages is often most effective with groups rather than individuals. Also, much of the training for software use is by **peer experts** (individuals within a department or group who have superior expertise and/or experience). The usual tendency in a group is to ask a peer expert before seeking help from the formal information systems support function. The advantage of the peer expert is knowledge of the general domain (such as accounting) and knowledge of the problems being worked on. Since the peer expert can often give advice in minutes, there is no need to wait for a remote expert to respond. The peer expert approach is less effective if members of the group do not use the same software package and the same version.

┣•xample

An organization selected a new spreadsheet processor as the standard for its knowledge workers. Training was provided. However, there was no strong organizational pressure on individuals to adopt the new standard. The result was a mixed situation in which many individuals used an old package that was no longer supported by the organization. The value of peer expertise was reduced because the peer experts moved to the new package, and there is an ongoing loss of productivity because of the mixed use of old and new packages. ◆

2. *Cooperative work.* There are many situations in which the work of one individual is transferred to another in the form of worksheets or files. If the cooperating individuals are using different software, there is a loss of productivity because results between packages must be converted. In addition, there are potential problems because of miscommunication resulting from the lack of a common understanding of how the results were obtained.

Example

A worksheet developed on one major spreadsheet processor can be transferred to another individual using a competing spreadsheet processor. However, the translation process takes time and may introduce problems because not all features can be translated directly. Modifications to the converted spreadsheet may result in incomplete and inaccurate computations. ◆

Most software packages include **backward compatibility** so that data can be exchanged between versions of the package. Many packages even provide two-way data compatibility with competitive packages. In some cases, however, version compatibility is one-way (data accessible under the older version is converted for the upgrade and can no longer be accessed by the prior version). This complicates the upgrade decisions.

Example

A faculty member upgraded her personal copy of a database package. Subsequently, she found that students in the school's computer lab were not able to complete assignments, since the data she prepared in the new package could not be accessed by the older version. ◆

Approach to Individual Analysis of Replacement Packages and Upgrades

When organizational considerations do not dictate the software package or version, the individual must analyze the tradeoffs in adopting new packages or versions. A conceptual approach to the analysis is to consider a replacement package or upgrade as the contender, and the existing package as the defender. This approach essentially says that the contender must demonstrate sufficient advantage compared to the defender to justify the time and full cost of the change. In other words, a replacement package is not evaluated on the features common to both packages, but only on the incremental benefit of new and improved features. The costs of lost productivity due to the learning effort required and the cost of any training needed must also be considered.

The upgrade or replacement package cannot be evaluated entirely at a single point in time. Most categories of software are still evolving rapidly. The implication is that nearly every package will have to be upgraded eventually. Vendors eventually stop supporting older versions. Even though the individual may not need a new version, others in the workgroup may need it. Given these considerations, an individual should consider immediate replacement, delayed replacement, or skipping a version.

There is no exact formula for costs and benefits, but the considerations listed below may be useful. The list is support for explicit analysis, even when the costs and benefits are imprecise. The explicit consideration of soft data helps overcome the natural human tendency in intuitive analysis to underestimate the *costs* of change and overestimate the *value* of change.

Costs

◊ Training costs of formal courses including costs of trainers, training materials, and time costs of participants

◊ Installation costs including conversion of files, if required

◊ On-the-job training costs by users as they develop skills to the same level of automatic processing as with the defender package

◊ Time cost of peer expert consultation as less proficient users are brought up to the same level of proficiency as with the defender package

◊ Costs of correcting errors caused by improper use of new software features

Benefits

◊ Estimated value of new features in reducing time, effort, and errors

◊ Estimated value of new features in providing capabilities not found in defender package

◊ Estimated reduction in cost of transferring data and results between packages if features of contender package meet this need

◊ Estimated reduction in peer expert consultation and central user support in aiding users with problems, if features of contender software are a better match with user visualization of problems and solution procedures

◊ Estimated value of more responsive vendor support (through help line, manuals, and online help screens)

◊ Estimated value of improved reliability of contender software (if relevant)

◊ Estimated value of compatibility of contender software with related software relative to user interfaces (if this is a benefit of the contender)

Organizing Directories

◆ ◆ ◆ ◆ ◆ ◆ ◆ ◆ ◆ ◆ ◆ ◆ ◆ ◆ ◆ ◆ ◆ ◆ ◆ ◆

A fundamental requirement for finding data is some method for naming and organizing data files. A directory or folder is the basic container for a collection of files. It is a list of files stored under an identifying name. The directory concept works best if the things in the directory belong together. The collection of data units organized under a directory name include files of records, program files, spreadsheet files, documents, and graphic images. Directories can be more than simple sequential lists. Computer operating systems use a hierarchical directory structure with directories containing subdirectories.

A **directory structure** should be organized to support an individual's work (including the way the individual thinks about the work). The objective of supporting the way a person works is generally the overriding one for directory organization. A secondary consideration is interaction with other personal systems in a network or with the organizational system. Because of illness or other emergencies, it may be necessary for someone besides the owner to find files stored on an individual system. Consequently, the directory structure and file naming conventions should also facilitate meeting these secondary needs for others to be able to locate data on systems not their own.

Conceptual Basis for Directory Structure

The conceptual basis for the organization of directories is the principle of simplifying complex systems by hierarchies. There are other ways to organize data, but hierarchies are very effective (see Figure 6-2). When a person is looking for specific data, a **hierarchical search process** is often the most natural. In a hierarchy, the top level is the most general and consists of broad categories. At the second level, each broad category is subdivided into a number of more specific subcategories. The process continues until further subdivision is not profitable.

Directories or folders in computers provide a hierarchical storage structure consistent with theories of human organization of information. They provide a hierarchical structure through multiple levels of subdirectories, or folders within folders. The use of subdirectories can usually extend down an indefinite number of layers. (In most operating systems, there is no limit to the number of levels of directories, but there may be a limit to the *overall length of the name of a file,* including the directory path. This constraint limits the length of file names and often presents subtle problems in PC-DOS.) The hierarchy can be visualized as an inverted "tree" with a single root, large

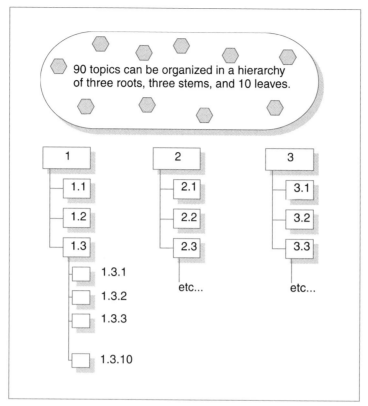

FIGURE 6-2   *The power of a hierarchy in reducing complexity*

branches dividing into smaller branches, and leaves at the end points. The branches, smaller branches, and leaves are often terminal nodes.

Example
A professor keeps a directory of course lectures. The number of files can become quite large and search can be difficult. An alternative is to have a directory/folder for course lectures and a subdirectory or subfolder for each course. The directory structure would consist of two levels:

Level 1:   Directory for course lectures
    Level 2:   Subdirectory for lectures in Course 1
          Subdirectory for lectures in Course 2
          etc.   ◆

Consider, however, a professor who teaches a number of different courses and stores lots of data about the lectures, students in the course, and overhead slides. A different directory structure with three levels might be used:

Example

Level 1: Directory for courses
    Level 2: Subdirectory for Course 1
        Level 3: Subdirectory for lectures in Course 1
                Subdirectory for students in Course 1
                Subdirectory for overhead slides in Course 1
    Level 2: Subdirectory for Course 2
        Level 3: Subdirectory for lectures in Course 2
            etc. ◆

Since directory structures are hierarchies, some general principles of organization or classification for design apply to them:

◊ Levels in the hierarchy should proceed from general to specific.

◊ Each node in the hierarchy that is not a leaf node (the lowest level) should have a limited number of nodes in a sub-tree under it. The number should fit within the guidelines of what a human can easily distinguish. This suggests an upper limit of fewer than the maximum that can be displayed on a directory list at one time.

◊ Files are stored under leaf nodes using descriptive names. Intermediate nodes in the hierarchy are used to simplify the directory structure and often do not contain files.

A Task-oriented Directory Structure

The directory structure should reflect how an individual works and conceptualizes work. Since knowledge work is based on tasks performed, a logical basis for a directory structure is task structure. Data and programs should be stored so that they can be easily located when a task is begun (Figure 6-3).

A recommended approach to directory structure is a hierarchy with the root directory at the top of the hierarchy followed by separate subdirectories for the operating system, software packages, and user data. The software package's subdirectory has subdirectories under it for each software package. The user data subdirectory has subdirectories under it for each major task. Task subdirectories may be subdivided further, depending upon the size and duration of tasks and the amount and diversity of task data.

Example

Level 0: Root directory
    Level 1: Operating system directory
    Level 1: Directory for user software
        Level 2: Subdirectory for each software package
    Level 1: Directory for user data
        Level 2: Subdirectories for each major task
            Level 3: Subdirectories under task subdirectories ◆

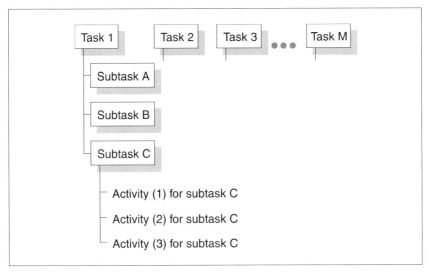

FIGURE 6-3   *Directory structure with tasks at top and activities at leaves*

The recommended directory structure separates the software to perform activities (the software packages) from the tasks that store the task results.

Directory Structures and Software Packages

Personal computer software vendors make certain assumptions about the way their products are used. One assumption often made is that each software package works in isolation or as the only function of the computer. This assumption, if implemented, may have negative consequences for a personal storage structure. The negative effects come from the installation programs for the software packages.

PC software package installation programs typically create a directory for the software under the root directory. The installation default method is to specify storage of outputs from package use in the package directory or in a subdirectory under the software package directory. For example, the software package installation program for a spreadsheet package installs default options to store spreadsheets in the same directory as the spreadsheet package or in a subdirectory under the spreadsheet software directory. The default action can lead to two potential problems: (1) the root directory may become cluttered with many different package subdirectories, and (2) both programs and data files are stored in the same directory structure. This is equivalent to making the directory structure the reverse of knowledge work task structure. It is essentially task within activity:

Example

Level 1:   Package (activity) directories
    Level 2:   Tasks (files associated with tasks)   ◆

This approach is not consistent with the concepts of knowledge work. This file organization means that data files are related to the software used to create them, but they are *not* easily related to the task or project to which they belong. Data files for tasks may be scattered throughout the directory structure. This is especially the case when, for example, database files are used to create a spreadsheet which might, in turn, be the basis for tables and graphs in documents. The data files would be stored in one directory hierarchy, the spreadsheet files in another, and the documents in yet another.

This problem in personal computers can be contrasted with older, more established large computer operating systems. Mainframe and minicomputer systems were developed with multiple users in mind. Mainframe directory structures are organized for software sharing and individual privacy. One result is that mainframe software is stored separately from data. Another is that mainframe users have their own directory hierarchy for data. In this type of large computer directory structure, users tend to naturally order their directory structures by task rather than by type of software.

The general solution to the personal computer software practice of associating data files with software package structures is to store each software package in its own subdirectory and have a separate task-oriented directory structure for data files. This usually means overriding default directory options in software packages and specifying (with the software option menu) where the data files for the software results are to be stored.

Example

A tax preparation package automatically creates a directory for the files produced by the software. If these are the only files associated with the task of income tax preparation, the directory structure may be satisfactory. However, if the tax preparation involves spreadsheets and other documents, it would be more consistent with the task nature of knowledge work to have the following directory structure:

Level 1: User data
   Level 2: Tax preparation (a task)
       Level 3: Tax preparation software (software here because it is task specific)
       Level 3: Tax preparation data files

   If the software is being used over a number of years, an alternative might be:

Level 1: User data
   Level 2: Tax preparation (a task)
       Level 3: Tax preparation for year 19xx
           Level 4: Tax preparation package for year 19xx
           Level 4: Tax preparation data files for year 19xx
       Level 3: Tax preparation for year 19xx+1   ◆

This directory structure based on tasks assumes that the user has tasks with a variety of different files produced by different programs, such as a word processor or spreadsheet processor. This is the case for most knowledge workers. In isolated cases, however, the software package default may be acceptable because most or all work is produced with a single package.

Individual versus Workgroup and Organizational Directories

The preceding discussion assumes that the directory structure is entirely up to an individual and, therefore, can reflect the way that individual conceives of and manages work. There may be other considerations that affect the directory structure. These include workgroup interactions, data sharing, and providing access to others. Software is often installed only on a network server, so that all users share a single copy of program files. In many organizations, software resides on the hard drives of personal workstations, but is centrally administered.

A workgroup (or an entire organization) may need to share data files. One method that supports sharing is to store data that must be shared by the workgroup on a central network server in a directory structure that supports access by multiple users. Often private user data subdirectories as well as separate workgroup subdirectories are assigned to support sharing.

Another alternative to support workgroup computing is to provide operating or network services that allow shared access to files wherever they are located. Such services are common in various "peer-to-peer" network operating systems. With such systems, the "owner" of a file or subdirectory declares its availability to specified individuals or groups. A problem with such systems is that access depends on availability of the system on which a particular file resides. In a large workgroup, not all computers may be available at all times.

In organizations where software is centrally stored or administered, individual users may have little or no choice about the way in which programs are accessed. However, the organization of data storage directories is still an important infrastructure task for every individual knowledge worker and for every workgroup.

Finding Directories and Files

◆ ◆ ◆ ◆ ◆ ◆ ◆ ◆ ◆ ◆ ◆ ◆ ◆ ◆ ◆ ◆ ◆ ◆ ◆ ◆

A task-oriented organization of directories and files establishes an appropriate framework. Over time, however, the number of directories, subdirectories, and files may grow beyond the ability of humans to easily access their contents when needed. It may be difficult to locate a file or a collection of files concerning a particular task or topic. A directory hierarchy and file names are the first approach to locating a desired file. The hierarchy works by localizing the search to a small part of the directory structure. If this approach fails, it may be necessary to employ search software.

The set of possible names for directories and files is virtually limitless. These names can be thought of as entries in a code book for naming and retrieving files. The larger the number of terms in the code book, the harder it is to select the set of words that will locate a file. In order to constrain the set of file and directory names and increase the likelihood of retrieval, an individual should establish naming conventions.

Naming Conventions

The operating system limits file and directory names. The widely used Microsoft DOS operating system has directory naming limits of eight characters and file naming limits of eight characters, plus an extension (suffix) of up to three characters. The filename extension is ordinarily used to indicate the type of file based on the software package that created it. For example, an extension of XLS indicates a Microsoft Excel spreadsheet file.

Because of the limits imposed by the short DOS file name, many users have devised their own private naming schemes. They often use the file name extension as part of the identification. This practice of using the extension does not cause problems when a majority of files are created and maintained with one software package. A common example is word processing software, where most of an individual's files have the same type because they have all been created by the same package.

Most other operating systems support file and directory names with more than eight characters. Various "add-on" software packages for use with DOS allow longer and more meaningful names associated with each file and directory. Although the primary approach to searching for files relies on file names, many operating systems and software packages provide additional methods for locating a file. One method employs **user-defined keywords** that describe the contents of a file. A second method is a search of the contents of files to locate words or phrases known to be found in the file to be located.

A keyword method for search information consists of a set of keywords defined by the user when a file is created. The software stores the keywords in a special search directory along with the name of the file to which they apply. This method allows the user to search for a file based on keywords rather than the name of the file.

As another alternative to finding a file by its name, the contents of files can be searched to find one or more that have selected words or phrases in them. Since such a search can be time consuming, some directory management software packages create indexes of words in documents filed in a system. These reduce the time to search for a file based on its contents.

A well-structured hierarchy of directories helps users locate data even though file names are short. The directory hierarchy establishes the general content of the files within it. For example, a directory named TAX already establishes the fact that the files in this directory and subdirectories relate to taxes. The individual file names do not need to repeat this general information. Thus, even within the DOS limitations of 8-character names, it is possible to establish a naming convention that will be useful in managing individual data. Following are some principles that apply to both long and short file names:

◇ *Names should result in a grouping and ordering that will be useful for an individual.* For example, to group files together, the names should begin with the same character, since operating systems usually present them in sequence by name.

◇ *Names should be meaningful in identifying the contents.* The directory and subdirectory hierarchy establishes the general content group. The file name should allow a user to locate a file within the content group of the directory.

◇ *Names should be designed to facilitate file retrieval rather than reflect file creation.* Some suggestions reflect this concept:

◆ *Use first characters to sequence the file in natural retrieval order.* For example, if major sections of a report are numbered, the numbers should appear in sequence as the first one or two characters in the file name. (See Figure 6-4.) If year is the differentiating characteristic, the first two characters should indicate the year. For example, tax notes for Schedule C for 1993 would be **93SCEDLC**. The same type of notes for 1994 would be **94SCHDLC**. If the program supports larger file names, the files could be saved as **93SCHEDULEC** and **94SCHEDULEC**.

◆ *Compose descriptors of contents rather than generic names (such as section, chapter, document, or report).* For example, a report on pollution would be better named **POLLUTE** than **PREPORT**. If the report is divided into multiple sections, use one or two characters as numbers for sequencing. Make the name meaningful for retrieval. Rather than **TRIPRPT** for reports on various trips, use **FRANCE** and **NEWYORK**, or **FRANCTRP** and **NEWYKTRP**.

◆ *Consider including the version number as part of the name.* In much knowledge work, preserving prior versions is important. For example, each succeeding draft of the report on pollution could include a number to indicate version, such as **POLLUTE1** and **POLLUTE2**.

◆ *If the operating system allows only short names, use phonetic naming to make short names represent longer terms.* For example, the name for the pollution report might be **POLUTION** (using only one L keeps

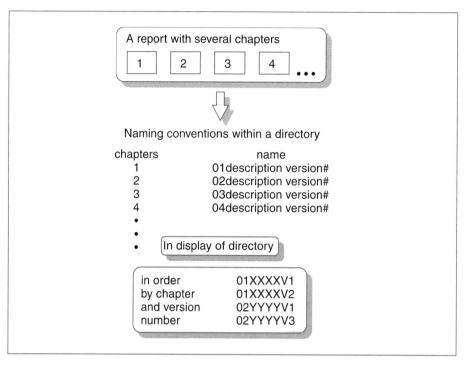

FIGURE 6-4 *Examples of using naming conventions to support file retrieval*

a meaningful name), **POLLUTN** (using N for ION retains a meaningful name), or **PLTN** (eliminating vowels often retains a phonetic equivalent). Using the phonetic option, chapter 4, version 2 of the pollution report could have the meaningful name **PLTN0402**.

Retrieval Methods

If a user employs a hierarchy of directories to group files, retrieval space (at least initially) can be limited to the directory in which the file is expected to be found. Using consistently appropriate naming conventions, the file can often be directly accessed. If the name does not allow the file to be located, the search within the directory may be extended by using one of the following methods:

◊ *Sorting and displaying directories by the date the files were last written.* In the case of documents, persons often remember the approximate date. Therefore, presenting a list of documents in date order assists retrieval.

◊ *Sorting on file attributes other than name and date.* The directory list can also be sorted and displayed by file extension (the suffix) or by size (in bytes).

◊   *"Viewing a file" without opening it.* In the "View" mode, a small section of the file can be viewed to check its contents without incurring the delay of loading the software package.

If these search methods fail, file names or contents may be searched for key words or strings of characters. A search key can be a few characters or a word. The search may be within a single directory, within a hierarchy, or within an entire hard disk.

In formulating words or character strings to locate a file, the search key conventions of the search software must be followed carefully. Following are some conventions governing search keys:

◊   *Upper and lowercase.*   Search software may allow a user to search with case specified, or it may rely on different conventions in searching. For example, a convention might be "case sensitive" to uppercase letters in the search key but match lowercase to both upper and lowercase contents. If this convention applies, the search term "Software" would retrieve a file named "Software" but not one named "software." A search term "software" would find "Software," "SOFTWARE," and "software."

◊   *Wildcard for one character.*   A question mark (?) is a character in a search string that represents one unknown character. For example, to search for the word "organization" or "organisation" (British spelling), the string could be "organi?ation."

◊   *Wildcard for one or more characters.*   An asterisk (*) is a character in a search string that represents one or more unknown characters. For example, the search string "comp*" will retrieve all files that begin with the characters "comp," such as computer, computing, computation, and computerization.

◊   *Phrases.*   One convention is to enclose any search term containing a space in quotation marks. For example, searching for "Integrity of Data" may require the quote marks.

Maintaining Integrity of Data and Software

◊ ◊ ◊ ◊ ◊ ◊ ◊ ◊ ◊ ◊ ◊ ◊ ◊ ◊ ◊ ◊ ◊ ◊ ◊

Procedures to deal with software packages and directory and file management are critical to maintaining personal work space. Data and software integrity issues include error recovery, recovery from data loss, archiving, restoration of data and software, protection from attack, and security. These issues are reflected in questions such as the following:

◊ How can data destroyed by a **Delete** command be restored (undeleted)?

◊ If files are destroyed by user accident, sabotage, or equipment malfunction, can they be restored?

◊ Can old data and software no longer in active use be retrieved, if necessary?

◊ Can confidential user data be protected?

◊ Can users protect data and programs from destructive software viruses?

This section reviews the value of software facilities and user procedures for dealing with these issues. It emphasizes the importance of these procedures in managing individual information systems and illustrates the value of automatic processing for frequent, simple activities such as backup.

Undoing or Undeleting Mistakes

It is easy to make a mistake and delete important work (see Figure 6-5). The most commonly used software packages now provide commands that enable users to undo work or recover (undelete) material deleted erroneously. Some packages allow undoing of only the most recent command or perhaps the two most recent, but others allow undoing of an unlimited sequence of most recent commands. Many operating systems provide for temporary storage of deleted files via a feature such as a "wastebasket" or "recycle bin." This provides an option in case a file was deleted in error. Files are kept in this temporary storage until they are explicitly discarded. Low-priced software, shareware, or even freeware may be available to provide this function for older operating systems.

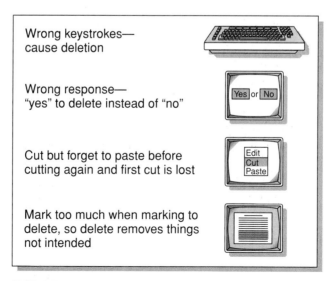

FIGURE 6-5 *Oops—and wrong things are deleted*

These **Undo** and **Undelete** commands and wastebasket/recycle bin features are important for reducing the cost of mistakes. When new software is installed, the undo and undelete commands should be part of initial training in order to avoid loss of work during early use.

Backup and Recovery of Data

Personal computers are increasingly reliable, but accidents do happen. Users make mistakes, there are power interruptions, and technology failures destroy data and programs. Managing individual information resources should include technology and procedures for protecting data and software from the consequences of human errors, adverse environmental effects, and equipment failures. This section focuses on two critical areas: data backup and recovery.

The concept of backup and recovery is simple: data is saved (i.e., a copy is made) at a designated point in time, or after a certain amount of work has been completed. The saved copy allows recovery of the data starting from that backup point. Assuming there were a simple tradeoff between cost of backup and cost of recovery, the frequency of backup would be set so that the cost of backup over a period of time equaled the expected cost of recovery. However, while the cost of backup can be easily calculated, the cost and frequency of failures requiring recovery from backup storage is difficult to compute. Backup can be made relatively routine and automatic, but failure and recovery usually seem to occur at inconvenient times, interfere with other important activities, and impose significant stress.

Managing knowledge work includes scheduling work. "Paying" for insurance against unscheduled, stressful backup with small, regular backup activities may be considered a good knowledge work management bargain. Therefore, backup should be done at least as often as the frequency that is calculated from an analysis of backup versus recovery costs.

Example

A knowledge worker who takes three minutes to back up data each day may consider it good insurance against a failure event that may require five hours (300 minutes) for recovery without backup, even though the expected failure rate of once in 250 days (.4 percent) suggests that spending more than the break-even point at 1.2 minutes of backup time per day is not economical. The backup computation is similar to fire insurance. Fire insurance costs are almost double the expected loss over all insured (because of administrative costs). However, the disastrous effects of having an uninsured fire makes insurance attractive. ◆

Data backup can be implemented during data entry or processing, at the end of an entry or processing session, or periodically based on a time interval. Managing data resources includes providing procedures for all three cases. In each case, software functions and tools are available to facilitate backup.

As illustrated in Figure 6-6 and described in the following paragraphs, managing data resources includes applying "save" and "backup" functions for each case (see Figure 6-6).

1. *Save while working.* This backup saves the work, but does not create a backup file on a separate medium, such as a diskette or tape. In some software, work may be saved automatically via timed backup functions. It may also be saved manually at frequent intervals. Saving work manually can be based on time intervals (such as every 30 minutes). An alternative method is to build a habit of saving work whenever certain events occur, such as interruptions, breaks in the work, or changes in the nature of the activity. Backup generally requires only a few seconds after the use of the backup function has become automatic.

Examples

A widely-used financial management package records each transaction when it is entered. If there is a failure, every transaction has been saved in the file. ◆

A timed backup for a word processing work package saves work based on a parameter set by the user. A 10-minute backup specification means that no more than 10 minutes of word processing will be lost if there is a failure. ◆

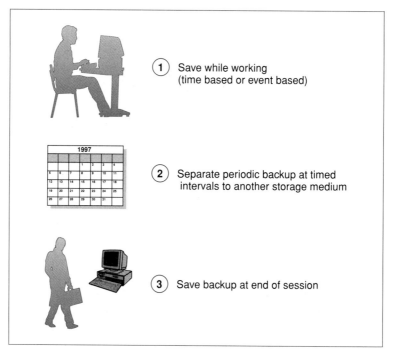

FIGURE 6-6 *Three cases for save and backup functions*

A widely-used tax package saves the work to a file only if the user specifies it, but a message prompts saving before a session is ended. ◆

2. *Separate periodic backup at timed intervals to another medium.* The most complete protection is provided by periodic backup to another medium such as tape, diskettes, or another computer.

3. *Save backup at end of session.* Most software packages for knowledge work expect the work to be saved and request the user to verify if it is *not* saved. Saving preserves the work of the session, but it does not provide a backup copy on a separate medium. Therefore, if the work and the backup are both saved on the computer hard disk and there is a failure with the disk, the file may be lost. A separate medium requires an explicit backup procedure. Some packages prompt frequent session backups to a diskette or tape. For example, the Quicken™ financial management package prompts users to backup to diskettes. Taxcut™, a tax preparation program, includes a "backup to diskette" option. Session backup is most important if the results have a high cost of recovery.

Backup to diskettes can be accomplished without special software by periodically copying all the files in active directories. Specialized backup software reduces the time and cost of periodic backup. The software can be instructed to copy only the changes since the last backup, and data compression methods may be applied to reduce the number of diskettes required for backup storage. The main disadvantage of backup to diskettes is the time required.

Since much data may be created or modified in a short time, diskette backup may be too time consuming to be practical. Low-cost backup tape drives may be impractical for the same reason. An emerging option is recordable CDs (compact disks), a high-capacity removable storage medium.

Example

One of the authors has an old, small hard drive left over from a system upgrade. The extra drive is used for backup. A schedule process built into the operating system finds and copies all data files that have been changed on the main hard drive to the backup hard drive. This process runs every day at 5:00 A.M. ◆

Periodic backup to another networked computer is another desirable alternative. When a computer is connected to a network, the network file server often provides backup at low time cost because it can be done at high speed. Network software may be employed to automatically read and backup data files in computers on the network to the file server computer.

Example

A university provides a network backup service for $10.00 per month. The service guarantees restoration of the contents of a hard drive within four hours of a restore request. To use the service, the computer must be left on at night for backup processes from the network. ◆

There are several types of backup. These include *full, selective, differential,* and *incremental.*

◆ A **full backup** is the most complete and includes backing up data files, software files, and operating system files. A full backup can be used to completely replace a failed drive.

◆ A **selective backup** usually bypasses software and operating system files, but includes user data and (in most cases) software settings files. The volume is usually only a fraction of that of a full backup. To restore files, the operating system and software must be reinstalled and reinitialized.

◆ A **differential backup** copies all files that have changed since the last full (or selective) backup. A differential backup usually replaces the contents of the previous differential backup. A complete restore operation requires the last full backup plus the differential backup to completely recreate the contents. The combination of a periodic (weekly, monthly, or quarterly) full backup, plus an automatic differential backup, can be very efficient.

◆ An **incremental backup** resembles a differential backup, except that it copies only files that have changed since the last backup of any kind. An incremental backup results in a new incremental backup file each time it runs. A restore operation requires the previous full backup and the entire sequence of incremental backup files.

As these examples illustrate, backup costs can be reduced significantly if the backup procedure can use software features and the procedures are used frequently enough to be automatic. Recovery procedures are implemented infrequently, so they are unlikely to become automatic. However, since recovery procedures may need to be implemented under stressful conditions, it is worthwhile to try out these procedures to gain some experience in using them before they are required (much like having a fire drill to simulate the real situation). This is the same concept as the organizational practice of having simulated computer disasters that require employees to follow disaster recovery procedures.

Archiving and Retention

Archiving is based on an explicit decision to remove unused data and software from active storage (on the hard disk), but to retain it in case there is a subsequent need. (Data and software not expected to have any further use is discarded rather than archived.) Every computer user should define a retention policy and then follow it. Files that are not needed should be discarded.

Retaining unneeded files "just in case" is costly not only in terms of hardware cost, but also in terms of extra time required to locate and distinguish current from out-of-date data.

Examples

In working on a task, one of the authors always creates a new copy of a file when its contents are changed. Usually, when a task is completed, he deletes all but the current, most up-to-date version which can then be archived. However, when he forgets to do this at the completion of the task, the obsolete versions are hard to find and delete. ◆

A colleague's policy is to never save an extra, old copy of any file. So far (about 15 years), she has not lost any functionality as a result of this policy. ◆

These two examples illustrate two different retention policies. Probably an intermediate policy between these extremes would be most prudent and efficient. However, every knowledge worker should consider the risks and create a suitable policy.

An archive consists of inactive data and little-used software. The decision to archive should reflect both the expected benefits and the costs of effort to decide on items to archive, copying to the archive, and marking and storing data for retrieval.

Why archive anything? The cost of storage is so low that data with very low expectation of future use can be stored very economically, considering the cost of archiving. Users who neither discard nor archive data will find that storing and retrieving data becomes increasingly time consuming. If a hundred memoranda are stored, they are simple to manage and search for retrieval. If the number rises to one thousand, the difficulties are not too significant, but may sometimes be troublesome. But if the file of memoranda rises to ten thousand, there is an increase in both management and retrieval costs. One way to reduce complexity is to transfer some of the data to an archive. For example, if memoranda more than two years old are worth keeping but are not likely to be accessed, they can safely be archived.

If archiving requires the user to examine each file, the archiving effort may be too high. With some preplanning of directories, all files in some directories may be organized for archiving or discarding.

Example

An individual works on several projects. Each project results in a directory of files. The user creates a permanent project master directory with a short file name describing each project and containing vital historical data. All other directories and files for each completed project are archived (or discarded) after a defined period (such as one, two, or three years). ◆

Various media may be used for archiving. These include diskettes and magnetic tapes. High capacity (20MB (megabyte), 100MB, or more) removable media are also available and effective for archiving, and recordable CD technology is another option. Diskettes are inexpensive and have reasonable capacity for data files when using compression software. Since the cost is low, separate diskettes may be used, and only partially filled, in order to simplify retrieval from the archive. Magnetic tape is not an ideal archiving medium because it can deteriorate in just a few years.

If a good file management approach has been followed, files that belong together are in the same directory. Archiving of files can be based on several criteria:

◆ Archiving all files for a completed project

◆ Archiving all files within a directory older than a certain date

◆ Archiving all files that document the progress of a project

If the archive is small, carefully labeling the diskettes may be sufficient; if the archive starts to grow, it may be useful to maintain a small directory to the archive.

Archiving software is usually fairly simple. When software is loaded, the diskettes or CD-ROM containing the software can be stored as the archived copy in case the software must be reloaded. Removing software may involve not only removing the software from the directories, but also removing all the links to it in the program management software. This is most easily done with specialized removal software (uninstallers) or removal facilities included with most newer program management packages. When software has been significantly customized, it may be possible to copy settings files so they can be restored if the software is reinstalled.

Individual Data Security

One design objective for structuring and naming directories and files (or folders) is reducing the time required to locate stored work. This process should support access by a co-worker, if necessary. However, there may be data files that should not be accessible except by designated individuals.

Security for personal information systems can be at the physical access, system access, application access, or file access levels. Physical access means restriction by physical barriers such as locks, keys, or access cards. The other access protection methods typically employ user names and passwords.

There is a basic tradeoff with passwords between ease of recall and effectiveness. A password that is easy to memorize and recall is either short or has personal meaning (such as mother's name or telephone number). A password that is most secure is generally long, completely random, frequently changed, and contains no personal information. For transaction systems involving high risk, organizations employ frequently changed, randomly generated passwords. To maintain security, organizational policy may require a user to memorize the password rather than write it down on a note placed on the computer or in a desk drawer.

For an individual system without physical security, the use of passwords should reflect the risk to the individual and the organization. For example, an individual with only a few files that require protection might use one or more of the following methods to maintain security:

◊   A simple, easily-remembered password to allow access to the system. This password would be available to other authorized supervisors or co-workers.

◊   Hidden directories and files for moderately sensitive data.

◊   A moderately difficult, random password, plus encryption for highly sensitive files. **Encryption** recodes the data, so it is meaningless without the key to restore it. The password and encryption key would be provided only to persons authorized to see the files.

Protection from Viruses

Viruses are destructive (or bothersome) programs that enter an individual system from any external source, most often from diskettes. They may be relatively benign or cause complete destruction of system data and programs. There are two ways to protect a system from the effects of virus programs: avoidance and detection. *Avoidance* means never copying or executing programs from an untrusted source. This includes diskettes as well as networks. Since viruses are programs, data files may be copied without risk. However, it is not always easy to distinguish between data and programs. The "Microsoft Word Virus" of 1995 is a data document containing a macro program that executes when the document is loaded. Destructive forms of this data-propagated virus have recently been found.

The second method of protection is to use virus protection software. This may be included in the operating system or installed as a software package. Virus protection software can be run periodically or can be set to check every diskette when mounted. Virus protection software can also be set to scan any program file accessed via a network.

New viruses or variations of old viruses appear at a rate of more than one per day. Therefore, virus protection software should be upgraded at least once per year. When there is a high level of data or program exchange, virus protection software should be updated more frequently.

Sharing Data Among Applications

◆ ◆

A common issue in knowledge work is reuse of data. Data in one file may be needed in another. Several files may use the same data and updating one file requires updating all. The question is how to share data at the lowest cost with the fewest errors. The least productive method is to re-enter the data in each new application. This is not usually desirable except for the most simple cases. However, in order to achieve productivity in sharing data between applications, a knowledge worker must invest time in learning to use tools that support the transfers. This section describes four generic approaches to data sharing: (1) file appending/file importing, (2) cutting and pasting, (3) embedding, and (4) linking. These approaches are supported by the features of all major software packages. There are both industry open standards and proprietary standards to support data movement and linking among applications.

An example of a common task that requires data movement is a word processing document that incorporates part or all of a spreadsheet. This example, illustrated in Figure 6-7, will be used to explain the various considerations guiding the approach to be employed. These include the following:

1. *Is part or all of the data being copied?* Copying the entire file and moving it to another essentially creates a new merged file. For example, copying

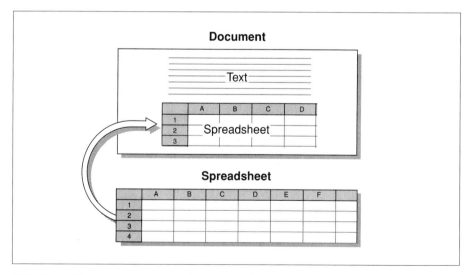

FIGURE 6-7 *The common requirement to move data between a spreadsheet and a document*

an entire document into another document essentially creates a merged document; copying a spreadsheet into another creates a merged spreadsheet. Copying part of a file involves cutting and making a partial transfer.

2. *Are the two sets of data of the same type (such as text, worksheet, chart, picture, or bit map)?* If they are not the same type, the data being transferred may need to be converted in order to be placed in the application receiving it.

3. *How will the copied data be changed in the file receiving it?* A problem arises if the files are not of the same type. If the data being copied into a new file will be altered, there are two general approaches: (1) convert the data into a form that can be manipulated by the software for the receiving (containing) file, or (2) embed the copied file in the receiving file, but maintain a connection to the software that created it. For example, in the conversion approach, a spreadsheet is copied into a document and edited using the table tools of the word processor. In the embedding approach, the spreadsheet is placed in the document, but is edited and changed by using the spreadsheet processor software.

4. *Is the data being copied at a point in time (a "snapshot"), or should subsequent changes in the data being copied also be made in the application receiving the copy?* A single, static snapshot can employ a different approach than a dynamic copy. The linking of applications so that changes in one application can be automatically made in any other application with links to it is a powerful method for dynamic placement of data. It can reduce errors because updating may be forgotten, but it can also introduce errors when changes are propagated automatically. For example, a document that incorporates analysis from a spreadsheet can be static and not reflect subsequent spreadsheet changes, or it can be dynamic and reflect changes.

File Appending and Importing

File appending results in merging two existing files. This works easily if the files are of the same data type (both word processing documents, both spreadsheets, or both pictures). The instructions for moving the data from one file into another may be termed "copying" or "retrieving and appending." The file being moved can be inserted at any place in the receiving file. The file being appended is copied. After the file is appended, the data exists in its original file and as part of the new file.

If the storage formats of the files are not the same, data can still be transferred by using the conversion or **file importing** facilities of the receiving application or a standard format. In the conversion approach, the receiving application is instructed about the format of the data being copied, and the conversion is made by the application package. For example, spreadsheet processors use different storage formats, but all of them will convert and copy other formats. The same applies to word processing and database packages. As another example, package importing facilities can be used to copy a part of a spreadsheet into a document. Once the spreadsheet has been imported, it can be altered or edited using the word processing commands (Figure 6-8).

In the standard format approach, the data to be moved into another application is converted to a standard such as **ASCII (American Standard Code for Information Interchange)** or coding based on extensions of the ASCII code. Virtually all application software can append such coded data to an existing file. The problem with this data transfer is that much of the formatting in the data being copied is lost. For example, converting a spreadsheet to ASCII will result in copying the data, but not the formulas or the formatting into rows and columns. Some software packages have facilities to assist reformatting of imported data. For example, a list of customer names that are to be used as row labels in a spreadsheet can be imported into the rows of a spreadsheet. If the imported data contains both names for labels and data, there may be commands to divide the imported data and place it in appropriate cells in a spreadsheet (often called "parsing"). As an example, a financial report prepared using a word processor may be moved into a spreadsheet using the **Import** and **Parsing** commands.

Pasting

Pasting is a very simple approach to taking selected data from a source (either **Cut** or **Copy**) and placing it in another document or spreadsheet. It is similar

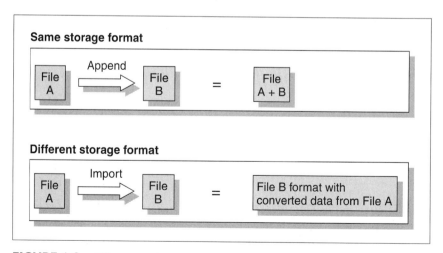

FIGURE 6-8 *File appending versus importing with conversion*

in concept to file appending by copying or importing. The usual procedure is as follows: (a) Mark the data to be cut or copied. (b) Do a **Cut** or **Copy** command. (c) Transfer the data to the receiving file. (d) Move the cursor to the location where the cut or copy is to be placed. (e) Select the **Paste** command.

The difference between cut and copy is that **Cut** removes the data from the source document (after the cutting, the data is not found in the source) while **Copy** leaves the source document intact.

Example

Copying a document or report and pasting it into a spreadsheet will, in many applications, place the report columns in spreadsheet columns. In the Quicken™ financial management package, a report may be copied and posted to a spreadsheet processor. The columns in the Quicken report become columns in the spreadsheet.   ◆

The usual approach to cutting/copying and pasting is for the software to hold the cut or copied segment in temporary system storage (a "clip board") until a **Paste** command is given. This allows a segment to be cut or copied and for other work to be done until the user is ready to paste. Since the **Paste** command does not erase the stored **Cut/Copy**, it can be pasted as many times as desired. A new **Cut/Copy** command will replace the existing **Cut/Copy** (Figure 6-9).

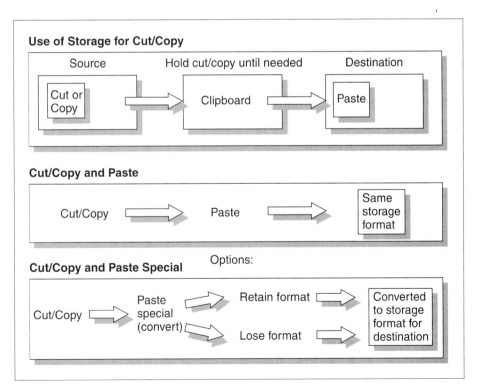

FIGURE 6-9 *Paste and paste special*

If the data types of both files are the same, pasting is very simple. If they are different, then the insert must be converted to fit the containing file. For example, a spreadsheet segment can be pasted into a text document as formatted or unformatted. If unformatted, the data items are pasted, but not in a row/column format. If formatted, the rows and columns are preserved and the table can be manipulated as a word processing table. If a picture is pasted, it is converted to the word processor format, enabling the user to access the word processor graphic tools. Although terminology may differ somewhat, most **Paste** options include those described in Table 6-1.

Embedding

Importing data normally results in the data being converted to the format of the destination file. For example, a spreadsheet or spreadsheet segment that is imported or pasted into a word processing file can no longer be manipulated as a spreadsheet. In some cases, this is not desirable. One approach to subsequent changes is to make the changes on the spreadsheet with the spreadsheet software and then re-paste the revised version into the document. This is cumbersome and relies on human memory about changes to be made and requires manual intervention. A more productive alternative is to embed the spreadsheet into the document rather than importing or pasting it.

Table 6-1 Paste Options Provided in Generalized Software Packages	
Option	*Explanation*
Rich Text Format (RTF)	Transfers and preserves format. In the case of transfer from spreadsheet to word processor, the table format is preserved and the table handling facilities of the word processor can be applied. This may be a default option for *paste*.
Unformatted	Transfers data without preserving the format. A spreadsheet table transferred to a document will lose column formatting.
Embedded object	Transfers an object from the source file to the destination file. (This is explained in the next section on embedding.) The object retains all or most of the characteristics it had in the source.
Paste link	Creates a link for automatic updating of pasted data. (This is explained in the section on linking.)
Picture or bitmap	Stores different graphic representations (such as pictures).

The concept of **embedding** is simple. The data moved into the containing destination is not converted; instead, it is placed in the file as a separate object that can only be manipulated by the software that created it. In other words, embedding is useful when the destination file and the file or segment being placed in it use different software. For example, a spreadsheet that is embedded is manipulated and changed through the use of the spreadsheet software. The action of embedding establishes the connection to the spreadsheet software. Subsequent changes do not require going to the spreadsheet package, making changes, and re-embedding them. Instead of going to the software, the software is brought into use by the embedded data or "object."

An embedded object, when copied, does not depend on the source file. If the source file changes, the object does not change. This means that embedding should only be used when the data or graphics are fairly stable, or when the source file may not be available for changes. Since all data is copied to the receiving file where it is embedded, the destination file size increases by the size of the copied data (see Figure 6-10).

The most widely used current approach to embedding is Microsoft **OLE** (pronounced Oh-lay). The term stands for **Object Linking and Embedding**. The OLE standard is a *de facto* standard based on Microsoft™ specifications. An alternative standard developed by IBM, Novell, and Apple is termed *Open Doc*.

Linking

In **linking**, the data to be used in the receiving file is not copied; instead, a link is established to the source. A representation of the current data is displayed when the receiving file is opened and used (see Figure 6-11). Linking (or dynamic data exchange) is a way of automatically updating data being

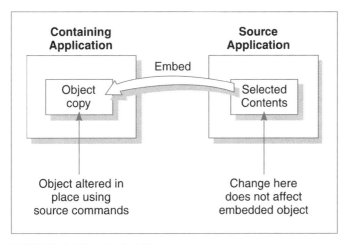

FIGURE 6-10   *Embedding*

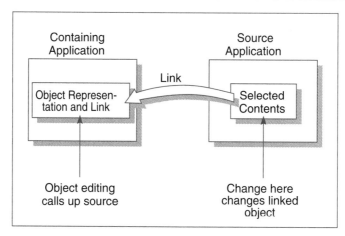

FIGURE 6-11 *Linking*

used in a containing file when the source is altered. Changes are made only in the source, but the dynamic link means the latest version is always used by the destination application.

Linking is desirable when the latest version of source data should always be used.

Examples

A spreadsheet budget is incorporated in a management report prepared with a word processor. If the budget is changed in the spreadsheet, the linked data items in the management report are changed when the management report file is opened. ◆

A report is created using data extracted from a database system. If the extracted data items are linked, any changes in the database data will be made in the document containing the linkage to the database extracts. ◆

The use of linking can reduce the size of a file. For example, pasting or embedding a video clip or sound clip may take significantly more storage because a complete copy of the insert is added. With linking, the application using the clip contains only the linkage.

Automatic propagation of changes can reduce effort and eliminate the problem of making changes in all of the places data has been used. However, it should be limited only to uses that benefit from dynamic updates. Most documents with copied data reflect the data at a point in time and, therefore, should not be changed unless there was an error in the original. The facilities for dynamic linking usually provide a list of links. These can be displayed for a file.

Automatic linking is useful but error prone. It can easily result in unintended changes. To reduce the possibility of errors, the software can be set to display a message before opening a document with automatic links (to verify that linking should take place). There are commands to change from automatic updating to manual updating in which updating must be explicitly specified.

Summary

◊ ◊

- ◊ The basis for managing data and software is a hierarchy of directories/ folders. This reduces the complexity of both storage and retrieval. The logic of organizing and managing data and software supports a hierarchy based on tasks at the top of the hierarchy and activities at the leaves.

- ◊ The management of software reflects tradeoffs between the costs of implementing a new version and the benefits from the new software features. The costs of implementing a new version are primarily in costs not explicit in the records of the organization, such as productivity loss from training and dual processing and extra advisory services.

- ◊ A directory/folder structure provides the containers for data. Naming conventions support retrieval by creating names that help users recall content and by organizing the display of files in a meaningful way. In addition to directory structures and naming conventions, there are software functions that allow users to search file names, key words, or the full content.

- ◊ A major objective of data management is maintaining the integrity of data by protecting against loss during processing or after a processing session is completed. The basic methods are archiving and backup. Other accessibility concerns relate to security and viruses. These methods and meeting these concerns involves both software and manual procedures. In order to reduce the complexity and size of stored data, it is often desirable to remove data and software, but maintain accessibility in an archive on tapes or diskettes.

- ◊ Productivity is improved if data in one application can be placed in another application without re-entering it. Four methods are employed to achieve this objective: (1) file appending/importing, which is essentially merges files with the same storage formats or imports them when the storage formats are not the same; (2) cutting and pasting, which achieves the same objective, but with selected parts of a file (Data being moved can be pasted in a way that retains the format of the original data or in unformatted form.); (3) embedding, which enables the data pasted (an object) to remain connected to the software that produced it (An embedded object is changed by causing the object to call the source software application.); and (4) linking, which does not move the data to the destination file; instead, it provides linkage so that any changes in the source application data are made in the destination application file (automatically or when manually approved by the destination application).

EXERCISES

1. Define a directory/folder structure for your personal information system.

2. Compare your existing access and directory structure to the structure defined to meet your needs. Define a strategy for migration to this ideal structure.

3. Create a half-page document and a small spreadsheet of about 4 rows and 3 columns. (The word processor and spreadsheet processor can be from the same or different vendors.) Include all information for turning in the assignment as part of the document. Do the following to demonstrate your understanding of transferring data among applications: (Print out the results of each step in the exercise. You will need to read the appropriate paste, paste formatted, paste unformatted, embed, and link instructions in the software you are using.)

   a. Paste the spreadsheet into the document using
      (1) The formatted RTF spreadsheet conversion
      (2) The unformatted spreadsheet conversion
   b. Embed the spreadsheet into the document. Make a change in the spreadsheet without going back to the spreadsheet processor.
   c. Link the spreadsheet to the document. Make a change in the spreadsheet and then reopen the document. The change should appear there if you have linked correctly.

4. Create a small spreadsheet (approximately 5 × 7 cells). Copy and paste it into a document. The default option is probably RTF. If so, use your word processor table facilities to alter the table layout. Print the spreadsheet and the table before and after alteration.

5. Copy a small spreadsheet segment in unformatted format to a document. Use your word processor to format the data in the document. Show the data after the unformatted transfer and after formatting.

6. Embed a small spreadsheet segment in a document. Click on the embedded object and make a change. Describe the effect.

7. Embed and link a spreadsheet. Observe and explain the effects of the following:

    a. Making a change in the source spreadsheet

    b. Making a change in the embedded object spreadsheet

    c. Removing the link and repeating (a) and (b)

8. Perform the transfers in Exercise 3 using package software from different vendors. Comment on differences.

9. Export a report from a financial management package (such as Quicken™) into a spreadsheet.

10. Create a short document. Copy the document and paste it with links to a second document.

    a. Make and store changes in the original document and note the changes that occur automatically in the second document.

    b. Look up links in the second document (probably under the **Edit** menu). Break a link and make a change to verify it has happened.

11. *External Data Exercise:* Do Exercise 6 in Chapter 8. (Chapter 8 focuses on accessing external data on the Internet. The External Data Exercises included in Chapters 1–7 are designed to prepare you for the more difficult exercises presented in Chapter 8.)

Accessing Organizational Data

◇   ◇   ◇   ◇   ◇   ◇   ◇   ◇   ◇

OBJECTIVES

After completing this chapter, you should be able to:

◆ Explain some of the methods used to organize and search databases.

◆ Describe the differences between various types of databases.

◆ Describe data entities, attributes, and relationships.

◆ Describe online analytical processing (OLAP).

◆ Describe data structures in terms of records and files.

◆ Explain the need for constraints on accessing organizational databases.

KEY TERMS AND CONCEPTS

This chapter introduces the following key terms and concepts, listed in the order in which they appear:

Structured Query Language (SQL)
Query By Example (QBE)
database administrator
database management system (DBMS)
data manipulation language (DML)
database query language
data definition language (DDL)

enterprise database
client/server database
data warehouse
relational database
entity
entity instance
attribute
identifier
key
relationship

field
data type
data structure
record
data structure diagram (DSD)
collating sequence
sorting
online analytical processing (OLAP)
pivot table

A knowledge worker uses data from multiple sources: personal, organizational, and external. It is not sufficient for knowledge workers to rely solely on data obtained by individual activities; they must also access and use data stored by the organization and retrieved from external sources. This chapter explores issues in accessing data maintained by the organization. The next chapter will describe access to external data sources.

Data to be accessed may be *structured* (such as data files, database records, or database tables) or *unstructured* (such as document or text files). Although both kinds of data may be found in organizations and in external sources, organizational data tends to be structured and external data tends to be unstructured. Therefore, access mechanisms for structured data will be explained in this chapter on organizational data. Access considerations for unstructured data will be described in the next chapter.

Organizational data may be stored in enterprise-wide databases or in local databases. Subsets of organizational databases are often made available specifically for access and retrieval by knowledge workers in a process called "data warehousing." Organizational databases are also made available to individuals through client/server technology.

This chapter explains how organizational databases are structured and how a knowledge worker can access organizational data. In order to provide a background for understanding structure and access, some organizational data issues are also explored. The chapter explains the terminology typically employed to describe and define organizational data and surveys some of the processes employed in building organizational databases and providing for retrieval by individual users.

Individuals who access organizational databases work with data that has already been processed and structured. The principal problems are how to conceptualize retrieval (given the existing structures) and how to formulate retrieval instructions. Organizations generally establish relational databases so that data can be made available to knowledge workers. The retrieval tools available to individuals are generally based on the standard database language **SQL** (**Structured Query Language**, pronounced "sequel"). Therefore, this chapter explains some of the characteristics of the SQL language and how it is applied to access structured organizational data. Retrieval tools generally conceal some of the complexities of SQL through user interfaces such as **QBE** (**Query By Example**). The chapter also introduces the general category of user data retrieval and reporting tools and explains controls and restrictions organizations may impose on individual access.

Managing Organizational Data

◆ ◆ ◆ ◆ ◆ ◆ ◆ ◆ ◆ ◆ ◆ ◆ ◆ ◆ ◆ ◆ ◆ ◆ ◆

Organizational data is based on the functions of the organization. Transaction systems maintain records of the entities involved in organizational functions, such as customers, employees, materials, products, and suppliers. Records of events (the transactions resulting from the organization's operations) are also gathered, processed, and maintained. Transaction data is analyzed and summarized to support management. Some of the results of this data aggregation are also maintained in the organizational databases.

Data from transactions in early business data processing applications were organized in separate files. Each file contained the set of records associated with the purpose and "ownership" of the file. The concept of a file as a set of related records tended to result in physically separate files with "owners" for each file. For example, the personnel department was responsible for person-nel records, and the payroll department was responsible for payroll files.

Since separate files may contain overlapping information, this system had diffi-culties. For example, a personnel file includes employee name, address, and date of employment, and a payroll file also includes employee name and address. Because different processes are used to collect and maintain these two files, there are always differences or inconsistencies between them (see Figure 7-1).

Problems with Separate Files and File Ownership

File ownership and responsibility can be a useful organizational control on the quality and use of data. However, it tends to restrict data access and results in duplication and incompatibility. When records of identical entities or events are maintained in separate files, they are updated at different intervals from different sources by different processes with different quality control proce-dures. The result is that data item values for identical entities will frequently disagree.

A major problem with separate files is the difficulty of correlating the same data maintained in several separate files. Data that references the same busi-ness entity or event may not agree across two or more files. The difficulty of

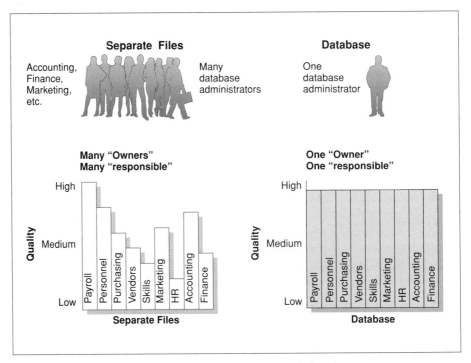

FIGURE 7-1 *Differences between separate files and databases*

reconciling such differences may make retrieval difficult or retrieval results unusable. There are many other difficulties in working with separate files. Different data definitions and different processing may make files incompatible. The benefit of separate file ownership, therefore, is usually more than offset by the problem of differences in business facts presented by separate files.

The Database Solution

The solution to the retrieval problem when separate applications maintain their own files is a database that includes all related data. A high, uniform level of quality can be obtained through data quality assurance procedures applied consistently and by coordinated updating. In this way, all applications access the same data and all users receive the same information with the same quality and recency.

A database requires an organizational authority to control it and software to manage it. The **database administrator** is the person who has authority over definition and use of the database. A **database management system (DBMS)** is a software system that manages the creation and use of databases. Stored data must be accessed through the database management software. Access facilities are provided: one for applications and for programmers doing application development, and one for data users.

Application programmers doing development write instructions using a programming language containing a **data manipulation language (DML)**. The DML instructions define the application interface to the database management system. The DBMS in turn translates data manipulation commands into database instructions that insert, modify, retrieve, or delete stored data. All data is processed through the DBMS to assure consistency.

A user wishing to access the database for a query or special report uses a **database query language**. The query language has facilities to formulate the query and format the output. Thus, the database management system should be viewed as the only "door" to the physical storage of data in the database, as depicted in Figure 7-2.

Another important component of a database management system is a **data definition language (DDL)**. The DDL is used to define the structure or schema of the database. It has facilities for coding the names, descriptions, and structures of the data in the database. The language commands are used to define relationships, integrity rules, and data processing procedures associated with units of data.

Reporting and application development facilities are often bundled with DBMS software. One example of a development facility is a report generator that helps users extract information from a database, sort it, and format reports. Another example is an application program generator designed to operate with the DBMS. It may include development software to design user

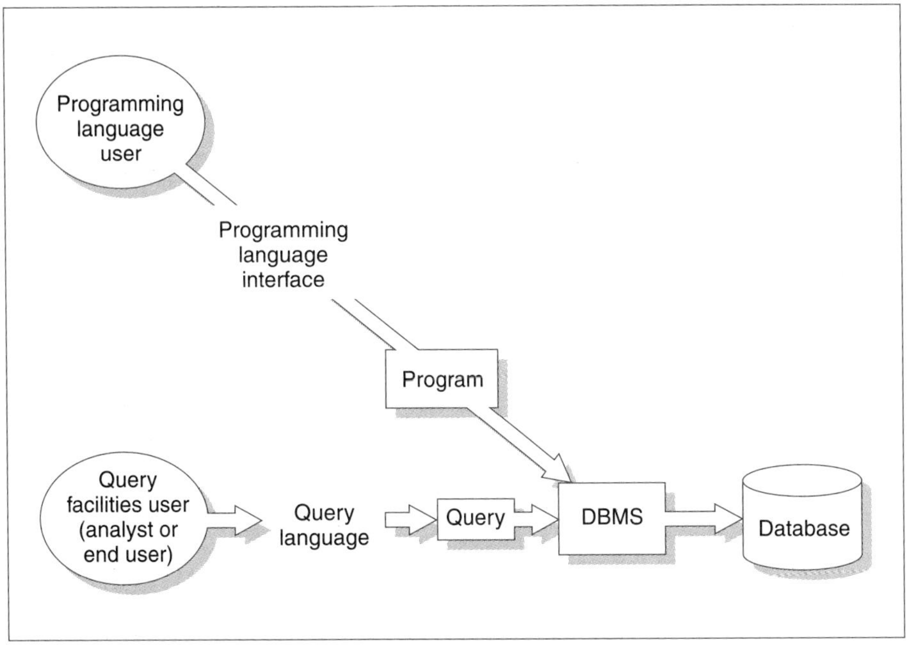

FIGURE 7-2 *DBMS as the way to access data*

screens, generate data retrieval commands, and handle logic associated with the application. The DBMS software is, therefore, one approach to developing information processing applications.

Enterprise Databases

The concept of an enterprise-wide database is a logical extension of the benefits of an application or departmental database: eliminate data redundancies and inconsistencies across the entire enterprise. A powerful argument in favor of **enterprise database** planning is that the objects of interest for an organization (and, therefore, the reasons for database systems) are not easily partitioned into departments or functions; they are much more likely to be needed across departments and functions. By defining a single enterprise-wide database with its models, structures, and rules, the problems of duplication, inconsistency, and unavailability can (in theory) be eliminated.

Enterprise databases have intuitive conceptual appeal, but are usually not fully implementable. A central database planning group cannot cope with the complexities of modeling data for an entire organization. In the time it takes to collect all the information for a data model and coordinate it, the organization and its environment are likely to change.

A centralized enterprise database raises several issues. When databases are associated with a coherent group of primary users, these users tend to take responsibility for its completeness and accuracy. When there is only one organizational database, who is responsible? A central data administration group can take some responsibility, but user perceptions of responsibility for completeness and accuracy tend to be diminished. A large central database reduces problems of coordination in updating and correcting the database, but the risks from failure or security violation may be increased by centralization.

An alternative to the centrally planned enterprise database is to create separate data models and design databases around organizational units, geographic locations, or business functions. For example, the vendor database primarily used by purchasing may be designed, operated, and maintained as a separate database that is the responsibility of the purchasing department. Plants at two different locations may have their own local databases covering their operations. It may still be necessary to communicate between the separate databases to maintain consistency and control redundancy, but with careful planning the proportion of data that must be transferred or copied may be relatively small. Having multiple databases introduces issues of coordination because the databases will have some common information that must be maintained at multiple locations.

Client/Server Databases

The enterprise database has tended to be more of a conceptual ideal than a complete implementation objective. The availability of computing power at the desktop, plus the networking of the organization's computer systems has led to an alternate database model termed the client/server model.

The **client/server database** model allocates data to a database server and assigns local responsibility for its maintenance and integrity. Input and data processing, and querying, retrieval, and reporting are allocated to local networked computers. This change by itself does not add new capabilities, but it may improve performance by replacing a centralized bottleneck. The use of networked computers on the desktop allows more computing power to be applied to user interfaces. Knowledge workers are able to access client/server data just as though it were stored on their personal computers.

An added benefit of the client/server model is the ability to cope with the demand for portions of databases at different geographic locations. Client/server database systems are able to maintain consistency among partially or completely replicated databases. This capability means that data can be physically maintained at locations near its use, even though it may be used at more than one location. The effect of client/server database software is that the database can appear to be local to the user who needs to review data.

Data Warehousing

The organization's databases are essential to operational and management functions. Business functions are dependent on computer applications that in turn depend on timely access to the appropriate databases (or data files). Operations and transaction processing have priority if there is insufficient computing power to meet all user and processing demands at all times. It is often necessary to restrict *ad hoc* query and retrieval during peak activity hours to avoid interference with those business processes. In order to provide support for knowledge work, many organizations have created an alternative source for those desiring access for analytical purposes. The alternative data source is termed a **data warehouse**. It is a database created specifically for retrieval by knowledge workers. The emphasis of the data warehouse is on making selected data available for query, retrieval, and analysis whenever needed without interfering with normal database processing activities. Figure 7-3 depicts the data warehouse concept, which rests on two key premises:

1. Data needed for knowledge work is based on transaction data.
2. Data needed for knowledge work does not have to be based on the most current transaction data.

Requirements for analytical use define the contents and organization of databases to be used for retrieval. The databases are usually organized as relational databases to facilitate rapid access and retrieval. Data warehouse mapping programs are created that periodically extract data from production databases and files, and create or update the data warehouse. For example, student registration data at a university might be copied into the data warehouse only once per semester if the uses are largely statistical. On the other hand, transaction summary data from stores of a chain of electronics retailers might be extracted every night for analysis the following morning.

The data warehouse approach is often combined with the client/server approach. This means access to the data warehouse is effectively the same as access to a database on the desktop computer.

Review of Data Concepts

◆ ◆

Data for organizational use may be structured in various ways. Some methods are especially suited to transaction processing; others are applicable to data access and retrieval. The most common organization of databases for access and retrieval by knowledge workers is the **relational database**. This section

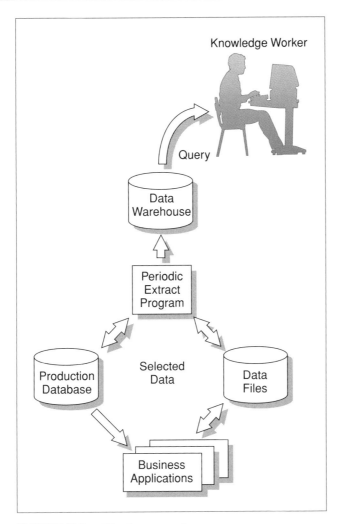

FIGURE 7-3   *The data warehouse concept*

focuses on data concepts and terminology associated with the relational model of a database. The relational model will be applied in both this chapter and a later chapter (Chapter 12) to build a solution using a database management system. This chapter will provide sufficient background of terminology, principles, and operations for individual access to organizational data already organized and stored. The emphasis will be on retrieval and report generation. Chapter 12 will extend the discussion to the process of building an individual relational database. In other words, this chapter will focus on obtaining data and building simple reports using relational databases provided by the organization. Chapter 12 will explain how to build a relational database and how to apply database software tools to the development of an individual application.

Information systems (IS) professionals have a precise technical language to describe data, the fundamental commodity of information systems. This chapter presents a few of the data concepts and terms employed by the custodians of organizational data such as entities, attributes, and relationships; data items, records, and files (terminology used in Chapter 3); ordering or sequencing of data; and traditional types of files. Familiarity with these terms and concepts will help knowledge workers communicate with computer professionals. It will also help them understand instructions related to the use of relational database management software.

Entities, attributes, and relationships are more abstract terms than the common business terminology of records and files. These abstract terms are very useful because they provide a way to think about critical issues of organizational data management. This section defines these terms, relates them to common, traditional terms, and explains the links between the two.

Entities, Attributes, and Relationships

Organizations cannot collect and store data about everything. Consequently, they identify objects of interest (or entities) and collect data about them. The objects of interest are those things and events that the organization must deal with in some way, such as in buying, selling, and producing, or hiring and firing. As illustrated in Figure 7-4, entities are the subjects of transaction processing, reports, analyses, and decisions.

An **entity** or entity class is any type or category of objects about which data is collected. An entity may be a thing, person, abstract concept, or event. It can also identify the role of objects such as customer, employee, or component part. An entity is a category; an individual instance within the category (about which data is collected and stored) is an **entity instance**. Examples of things about which to collect data are products, orders, and customers. Examples of persons are employees or applicants. Examples of abstract concepts are ideas for textbooks. An example of an event is the sale of an item.

If an organization finds it useful to keep files about something such as products, parts, or employees, a file is built for each entity (**PRODUCTS, PARTS,** or **EMPLOYEES**). The individual records in each file are entity instances. For each entity, there are characteristics that uniquely identify each entity instance. A part is distinguished by its part number, description, and cost; an employee is characterized by employee number, name, social security number, and date hired. There are many characteristics of parts and employees that are not of interest to an organization. In fact, different organizations may decide on different sets of characteristics in which they have an interest. Characteristics of interest are termed attributes.

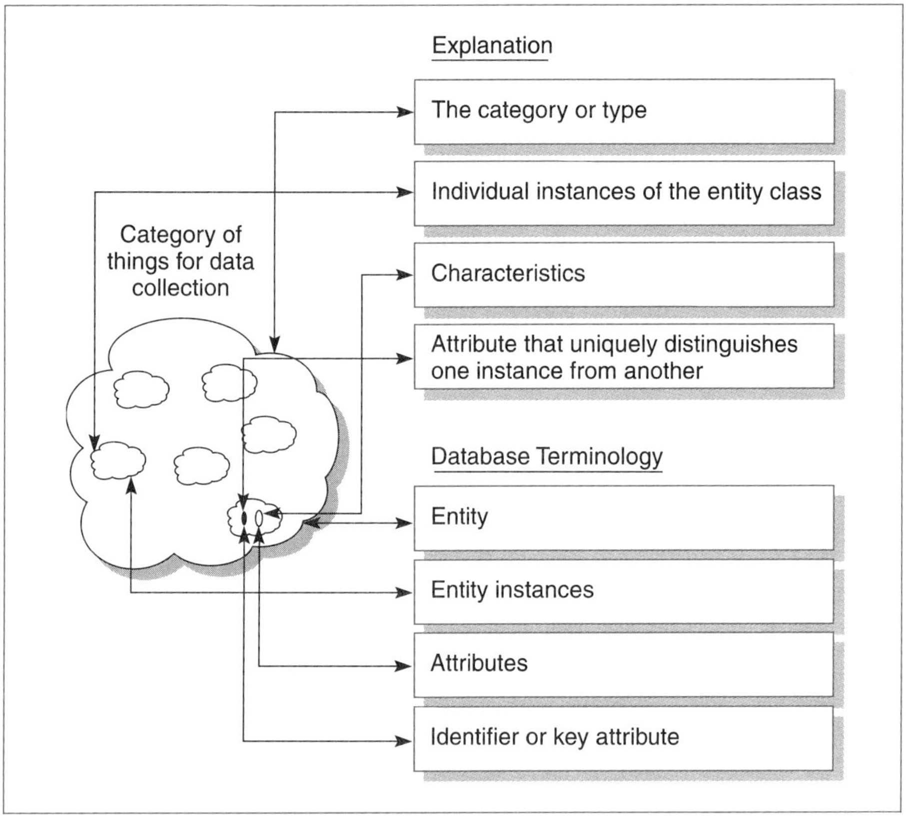

FIGURE 7-4   *Database terminology*

An **attribute** is a characteristic of interest about an entity; the set of attributes describe a particular entity. An instance of the entity is represented by a set of specific values for each of its attributes.

The list of attributes for an entity should include all that are of interest to different parts of the organization. For example, in addition to part number, description, and cost, the production scheduler may be interested in attributes of replenishment order policy, lead time, and planning responsibility.

Each entity must have at least one identifier, an attribute or set of attributes whose value uniquely differentiates each instance of the entity. In other words, the attribute that distinguishes one employee from another is the **identifier** or **key** for the entity EMPLOYEE. An identifier may be a natural attribute, such as a person's name, but is usually an artificial attribute such as an employee number that is created for just that purpose. Most data items cannot be record identifiers because they do not have unique values. Customer name may be unique for a business customer, but not for individuals because more than one person may have the same first, middle, and last names. An identifier may be composed of multiple attributes. For example, a sale may be uniquely identified by the composite of date, shop number, time, and sales register number.

Examples

A name is not usually a good identifier because it is not unique. However, it is very convenient. If used, it must often be supplemented by other attributes. A video rental store maintains a database of approved customers. The customers are issued a number contained on a customer card. However, many customers do not carry the card. Customer rental records can also be accessed by name, but since names are not unique (there are two persons with the name Gordon B. Davis in their file), the address or phone number is used as an additional attribute to locate the right record. ◆

A mail order company has a customer identification number, but most customers do not remember it. The phone order personnel ask for the mail code (zip code) and last name. If only one match on these attributes is found, the customer record match is verified over the phone. If more than one person meets these two attributes, customer address is used to decide among the possibilities appearing on the order screen. Once a match has been verified, the order process proceeds with the correct customer record. ◆

Entities do not stand alone. There are associations or relationships among them. An entity may have relationships with one or more than one other entity or among its own instances.

A **relationship** is a correspondence or association between entities. When two entities are related, there are really two relationships because of the different directions for the relations. For example, a customer *places* orders and orders are *placed by* a customer. The two relationships are *places* and *placed by*. The *degree* of a relationship is characterized by the largest number of instances on each end of a relationship. The degree of a relationship may be one-to-one (1:1), one-to-many (1:M), or many-to-many (M:M).

Example

The degree of the relationship between *customer* and *customer order* is 0:M (a customer may have placed zero, one, or more orders) (see Figure 7-5). The relationship between *customer order* and *ordered product* is one-to-many (1:M) because an order may be for more than one product: it contains multiple "order detail" lines. The relationship between *product* and *ordered product* is also one-to-many, since a given product may be specified on an order detail line on more than one order, while an order detail line always specifies just one product. ◆

This definition of relationship is also a way of encoding business rules. A business with only one product per order might have a very different data model. Its business rules could result in a data model that relates a customer order directly to a product and might not use the entity class *ordered product*.

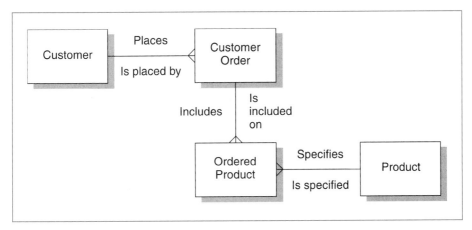

FIGURE 7-5 *An entity-relationship diagram depicts the four entities involved in a typical customer order and the relationship between entities.*

The concepts of entity, attribute, and relationship provide a powerful way to describe the objects of interest about which data should be collected and stored. The entities describe what things are of interest. Attributes describe the characteristics of the entities; their values must, therefore, be stored with each instance of each entity. Relationships define the ways in which entities are likely to be interconnected for business rules and for reports and analyses. The entity-attribute-relationship model of data provides the concepts and terminology necessary to describe and discuss data without regard to the way in which it is stored, processed, or otherwise physically manipulated.

Relating Entity Terminology to Files, Records, and Data Items

The terminology of entity, attribute, and relationship may not be used in ordinary organizational conversation. It is more likely that people will refer to data using the terms file, record, and data item or data element. Individuals in the organization refer to the sales file (the records of sales events), the employee file (about people in the role of employee), the customer file (about people or companies in the role of customer), or the product file (about things produced or sold). In other words, the term *file* usually corresponds to the more abstract concept of an entity.

The term "record" may be used in ordinary conversation to refer to entity instances. Each record in a file describes one instance or occurrence of the object of interest. There is a record for each sale, employee, customer, or product. Records are usually thought of as structured. Each record has within it a number of data items or data elements. These data items are implementations of the concept of attributes. One (or more) of the attributes is the record key;

this is equivalent to the term entity identifier. The data items **employee name**, **employee number**, and **department assigned to**, are attributes of the entity employee. The data item **employee number** is the unique identifier or record key in this example.

The terms "data item" and "data element" have some physical storage connotations. A data item or element is sometimes referred to as a **field**, but the latter term is used more precisely to refer to the set of storage locations assigned to a data item (or the spaces on an input or output medium to be occupied by the data item values).

Data Names

An attribute (or data item) is assigned a name in order to refer to it in storage, retrieval, and processing operations. Two or more data items may be assigned a single name for data processing purposes if they are sometimes referenced as a unit. This depends on how the user views the data. For example, there may be two elementary data items for **FIRSTNAME** and **LASTNAME**, but the data name **FULLNAME** may be assigned to the pair of elementary items **first and last names**. In a search or retrieval operation, **FIRSTNAME** will try to match only the first name; **FULLNAME** addresses the combination of first and last names.

Associated with each data item is a set of possible values (domain of values). The set of possible values is defined in a general way by the type of the data, but the domain of values may be restricted to a small subset of listed values, limited values within a specified range, values computed by some algorithm, or specified values or value ranges with exceptions (such as zero).

Example

If gender is coded as M for male and F for female, any other code is invalid. The two codes represent the domain of values. In a date code, no day of month may be greater than 31 or less than 1; month codes must be between 1 and 12. These rules define the domain of values for dates. ◆

Data Types

Every item or element of data consists of a particular data type such as **integer**, **real**, or **date**. Aggregations of data items are also of a particular type. The concept of data type is routinely and intuitively used in everyday arithmetic. For example, numbers of data type integer are used for counting, but numbers of data type currency are employed for accounting. In computing, data type is an explicit notion and must be specified in some way for every elementary item and every aggregation of data items.

Data type is a definition of the storage structure and the operations that can be performed on data. All data has the type property. Programming languages also include built-in types for common operations. Most modern computer languages also provide support for user-defined data types that specify the characteristics of unique data items.

Data type differentiates important characteristics of data relative to representation in storage, appearance, and operations permitted. The concept of data type is important for users and programmers mainly because of the operations permitted and appearance. For example, it makes sense to perform arithmetic using numeric data types, but not with items of text data type.

Example

A data item declared as type Currency has a fixed decimal point. A data item declared as type Integer can represent only whole numbers. The output appearance of an item of type currency will include "cents" while an item of type Integer will be displayed with no fractional part.   ◆

Data Structure

The term **data structure** is used to describe combinations or aggregations of elementary data items. A knowledge worker accessing organizational data may need to interpret data structure documentation. Therefore, two notations will be described and related to a business document.

The **record** is the most common example of a data structure. A record data structure is an aggregation of data elements (or other structures) that may themselves be of differing types. This definition of a record as a data structure is consistent with the earlier definition of a record as the collection of attributes pertaining to an entity instance. The record data structure allows users to name, refer to, and operate on a meaningful aggregation as a unit. An example of use is in a program that reads, creates, or saves a record in a file or database.

Data structures exist outside of data stored by the computer. One of the applications of data structures is describing or defining business documents. Figure 7-6 shows a typical transaction document which represents data that pertains to several entities and contains many of their attributes as data items. The entity relationship diagram presented earlier (Figure 7-5) is an abstract model of the entities and relationships incorporated in this document. For many purposes, a less abstract model of the data structures of this document will be useful or necessary. Two such models or notations for describing data structures are the "algebraic data description language" and the "graphical data structures diagram."

The algebraic notation is a way of describing data structures in text. Figure 7-7 is an example of this notation. The terms on the left of the equal sign are composed of the elementary structures to the right. The algebraic notation is useful and compact. However, it is difficult to use to visualize the relationships among the elements of a data structure. Figure 7-8 is an example

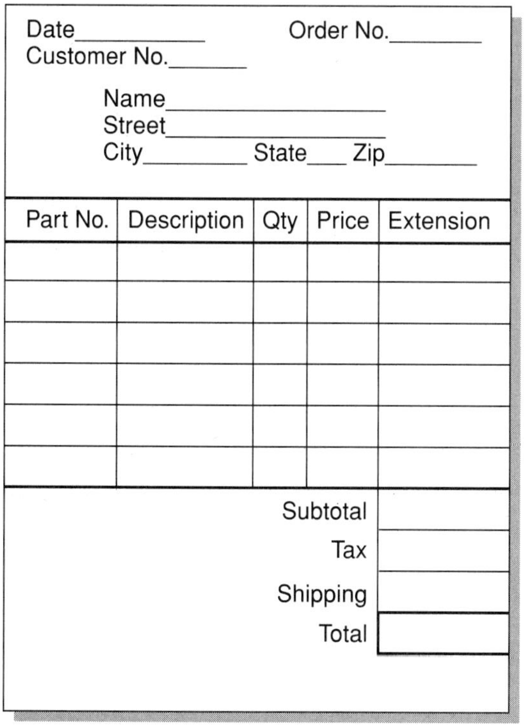

| Date_____ | | Order No._____ | | |
| Customer No._____ | | | | |

    Name_____
    Street_____
    City_____ State____ Zip_____

Part No.	Description	Qty	Price	Extension
		Subtotal		
		Tax		
		Shipping		
		Total		

FIGURE 7-6 *A customer order example*

of a graphical representation—a **data structure diagram (DSD)** of the data in Figure 7-6. A DSD shows the composition of a data structure as a hierarchy.

The algebraic notation and data structure diagrams illustrate two ways of describing and interpreting data structures. Most analysis and design support tools maintain data structure information using some variant of the algebraic data definition notations. A user will often need to make use of that type of documentation to understand data structures. When analyzing or designing data structures, the ability to visualize interrelationship graphically can be very useful. Even though DSDs may not be maintained in documentation, an analyst, designer, or programmer can readily translate from an algebraic notation to a DSD.

Data Order

The concept of data order or data sequence is very significant in data retrieval, storage, and maintenance. A report must present its contents in a specified order or sequence to convey the intended meaning. While order seems like a

```
order     = heading + body + totals

heading   = orderno + order date + customerno + name + street + city + state + zip

body      = {partno + description + quantity + price + extension}

totals    = subtotal + (tax) + (shipping) + total
```

- + is used to mean "and." C = A + B means data structure C consists of the sequence of data units A and B. Example: order = heading + body + total.

- [|] are used to show a choice of one of the bracketed elements separated by the vertical bar. C = [A | B] means C consists of either A or B.

- ( ) are used to show an optional item. A = B + (C) means A consists of B and sometimes C. Example: tax is not always required in totals.

- { } is used to show repetition. A = {B + C} means that A consists of an unspecified number of repetitions of the sequence consisting of B and C. Example: body.

FIGURE 7-7   *An algebraic data description of the customer order example in Figure 7-6 and an explanation of notation*

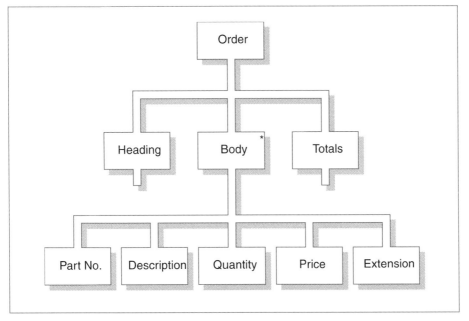

FIGURE 7-8   *A graphical data structure diagram (partial) of the customer order example in Figure 7-6*

simple and straightforward concept, there are many hidden complexities that can mislead the retriever of data. There are two concepts that are important to working with order: collating sequence and sorting.

A **collating sequence** is a definition of the precedence of one value of an atomic unit of data over another. In a character data type, the atomic units are single characters. Characters have a collating sequence that corresponds to the alphabet. However, computer collating sequences are not as simple as the alphabet. Should capital letters be ordered before all lowercase letters, or each before or after their lowercase equivalents? Should numeric characters be sequenced before or after alphabetic characters? What about special characters? Where should they appear in relation to digits and letters?

The most important standard for sort sequence is ASCII (American Standard Code for Information Interchange). ASCII has been extended from an original 128 to 256 characters. Part of the basic ASCII sequence is:

Space

Special characters ! " # $ % & ‘ ( ) * + ’ , - . /

Numerals 0 through 9

Special characters : ; < = > ? @

Upper case alphabetic characters

Special characters [\ ] ^ _ `

Lower case alphabetic characters

Special characters { | } ~

Note that spaces appear first in an ascending sequence followed by numbers. Another standard code, called EBCDIC (Extended Binary-Coded Decimal Interchange Code) is used on IBM mainframes.

Most software packages use some modification of the ASCII code. For most applications, the differences in sorting sequence are not visible or not important, but a user should be aware of the effects of sorting differences. These are illustrated in Table 7-1. Note, for example, that the default for the packages is lower case alphabetics before upper case. However, a sort feature may allow the user to change the order. The major differences in Table 7-1 are in the space character (space F) and special characters.

The process of placing data into a particular order or sequence is termed **sorting**, a significant activity in transaction data processing. To sort, one or more data items are designated as a sort key. There are a variety of useful sequences or orders for presenting data depending on the purpose of an output report. Such reporting sequences have no necessary relationship to the physical sequence in which the data records are stored.

Table 7-1 Collating Sequence from Ascending Sort Command in Four Packages			
Microsoft Word 7.0	*Microsoft Access 7.0*	*Microsoft Excel 7.0*	*WordPerfect 7.0*
*I	F	I	+I
\b	*I	123	*I
+I	+I	F	\b
123	\b	*I	123
a	123	\b	a
A	a	a	A
A_B	A	A	A_B
anderson	A_B	A_B	anderson
Anderson	anderson	anderson	Anderson
davis	Anderson	Anderson	davis
Davis	davis	davis	Davis
F	Davis	Davis	F

Example

Sales reports require many different sequences and subtotals to satisfy the requirements of sales analysts. Historical sales data may be ordered and subtotaled by product, product type, customer, customer type, location, or sales representative.   ♦

Sorting is an important decision in preparing retrieval and reporting requests. In addition to understanding collating sequence issues, the user should understand the effect of sort key specification. The primary sort key orders the data; within the primary sort, there may be many records with the same primary sort characteristics. These can be further sequenced based on a secondary sort key. The process may be continued with many keys. In retrieval software, the primary sort key is listed first, the secondary key is listed second, and so on.

Example

A state of Minnesota file sorted by last name will have many Andersons; a second sort key will put "Anderson, Anders" before "Anderson, Sven." A third sort on middle name or initial will place "Anderson, Anders A." in the list before "Anderson, Anders S."   ♦

Relational Databases Maintained by the Organization

◆ ◆

While there are other data models especially suited to high volume transaction systems, the relational model is preferred for databases that support user access to the data. The relational model has rules that must be applied when building tables in order to avoid errors. Since this chapter assumes the tables have already been designed and built, these rules are not considered here.

In retrieving data from an organizational database, a user may retrieve part or all of a single table, or part or all of several related tables.

◊ *Part or all of one table.* An entire table may be retrieved. The output will include all entity instances and all attributes for them. The size of many organizational databases prohibit retrieval of entire tables. The alternative is to retrieve only a subset of the records and only specified attributes for the selected records. The selection of part of a database table is based on record selection criteria. Selection criteria are often based on values of key attributes, although the values of one or more non-key attributes may also be used as selection criteria.

◊ *Part or all of several related tables.* Tables that have predefined relationships can be combined in a retrieval. Relationships are implemented by interconnecting tables using redundant identifiers. When a relationship between two tables is implemented, one end of the relationship is the key attribute for that table. A matching nonkey attribute must be included in the related table. This linking attribute is the foreign key. In Figure 7-9, each row of the orders table is linked to a particular customer because it includes the primary key (**Customer No.**) as a foreign key.

The process of finding and extracting data from organizational databases consists of five steps:

1. Identify the tables containing the data of interest.
2. Lay out the format of the output or report for the results.
3. Determine the criteria to use to select and order the desired table rows.
4. Form and execute a query in the database retrieval language provided.
5. Validate the query results.

Identifying the Tables of Interest

The first step is to select a table or related tables that contain the data of interest for a query or a report. A description of the contents of each table

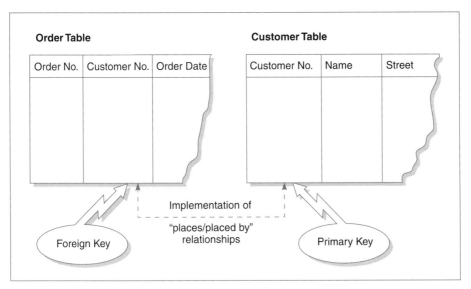

FIGURE 7-9 *Implementation of two tables and the two-way "PLACES" relationship*

should be acquired. This includes the names of attributes and information that explains the meaning of the attributes. Constraints on the data such as period of time represented and source of data may be valuable.

Where more than one related table will be "joined" in the query, the relationship should be clearly defined. The keys and foreign keys that join the tables should be identified. A simple diagram may be useful in this regard (see Figure 7-10).

Formatting the Output or Report

The format of the output depends on what is to be done with it. In general, there are three ways the data from an organizational database will be used by individual knowledge workers:

1. *Data for use in spreadsheet analysis.* Output is selected and moved directly into a spreadsheet file. This is a common output for business analysis.

2. *Data for use as part of a document.* The output may go to a file or directly into a word processing document where it can be manipulated as needed during document editing.

3. *Report output.* The output can be a table or a report in final print format. Either output can be used as is or be the basis for further manual report preparation. Reports can be designed for printing and distribution with headings, date of report, subtotals, and totals.

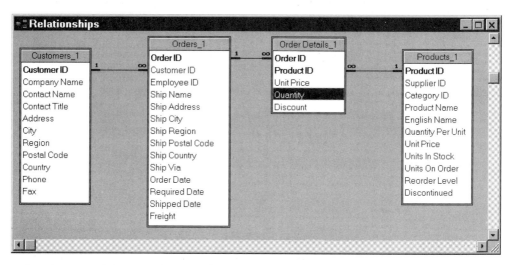

FIGURE 7-10 *Diagram showing the relations between tables*

When the data being retrieved is to be used in a spreadsheet, the layout of the output is a table. The table is exported to a spreadsheet. Once in the spreadsheet, the data can be processed in the same way as data entered directly. Since the transfer from the database query results to the spreadsheet file maintains the table format, it may require little or no formatting. In most cases the query can be used to select and order the data and reduce the need to manipulate it in the spreadsheet. For example, selecting only the records and attributes needed for the spreadsheet application will eliminate deletions after the transfer has been made. Ordering the table eliminates the need for sorting in the spreadsheet.

Data from a query can be used as part of a word processing document. There are several alternative approaches to consider. Selected data may be placed in the word processing document as a table in RTF (Rich Text Format) or as text. The table format makes use of the word processing table facilities. Data selected as a table by the query is inserted as a table in the word processor. Data may also be inserted into a document in text format where it can be processed the same as other text entered from the keyboard. In order to reduce editing in the word processing document, the appropriate alternative should be carefully selected.

Selected data can be output by a database query for direct use as a table or a report. A report format or a table can be presented directly as a business report. Database query report output is designed using the report generator facilities of the database package. Some reports are designed using templates provided by the DBMS; these are often useful without further processing. Others are designed by the user. The user design can be a modification of a report template provided by the system, or it can be created entirely by the user.

Report design includes decisions about report titles, ordering and grouping of data, headings for groups, subtotals, record counts, and header and footer text on each page.

Determining Selection and Ordering Criteria

Except in the unusual case of needing to output every row of a table, criteria are used to select only the desired rows. Selection criteria are based on the values of data attributes. A simple selection will specify a condition on a single attribute. For example, a user may need to select all orders dated "this month." Selection criteria may also be based on multiple attributes. A report may include only orders in the previous three months that have total amounts greater than $1,000.

Selections may also be based on the results of table attributes that do not directly enter the desired output or report. An example of this type of selection is to choose orders from customers with ZIP Codes greater than 80000. In this case the data to be selected is in the orders table, but the selection criteria is based on customer. In effect, a subset of customers is selected first and this subset is the basis for selection using additional criteria.

The order of outputs must be specified as well. Often the primary key of a table is appropriate for ordering. Most retrieval tools use the primary key as the default for sequencing outputs. Multiple ordering criteria may also be used. For example, order totals may need to be analyzed by customer. Output order would then be order number within customer number.

Related to ordering is grouping, often with subtotals. In the preceding example, orders might be grouped by customer with a heading line and total line for each customer.

Forming and Executing a Database Query

Relational database retrieval tools are based on the language SQL, a complete command language designed to manipulate relational tables. SQL is an international standard, although there are differences among vendor implementations. SQL tends to be used primarily by database professionals. Users generally use some form of "Query By Example," (QBE), a simpler query language, or a graphical query design procedure. Especially where graphical user interface tools are available, the knowledge worker is likely to be shielded from the intricacies of SQL. However, the capabilities of SQL underlie the retrieval language used in QBE and in graphical database retrieval software. The following paragraphs introduce a few of the features of SQL.

An SQL instruction enables users to select rows based on one or more conditions (such as equal to, greater than, or between). Columns are specified by data name in an SQL statement. The results of an SQL operation may be ordered according to specified column values. Built-in functions allow for various computations, such as counting rows, summing column values, or finding the maximum or minimum value in a column. Other SQL instructions can change a table or perform other manipulations.

Example

Create a spreadsheet section that contains a list of all customer names and the order numbers of every order greater than $1000 during the current month. ◆

SELECT CUSTOMER_NAME, ORDER_NO, AMOUNT
FROM ORDERS
ORDER BY AMOUNT **DESCENDING**
WHERE AMOUNT > 1000 **AND** MONTH = CURRENT_MONTH

The components of this SQL statement are first the keyword **SELECT**, followed by a list of the columns to be retrieved, and the name of the table from which to retrieve. The ordering clause specifies that the result is to be arranged from high to low by amount. The **WHERE** clause provides the selection criteria.

Example

Create a report that lists each product on order (from ORDERED_PRODUCT table). For each listed product, include the order number (ORDER_NO) and quantity ordered (QUANTITY), plus additional details about the product from the PRODUCTS table. ◆

SELECT ORDER_NO, ORDERED_PRODUCT.PRODUCT_NO,
ORDERED_PRODUCT.QUANTITY, DESCRIPTION, SUPPLIER
FROM PRODUCT, ORDERED_PRODUCT
ORDER BY ORDER_NO, PRODUCT_NO
WHERE ORDERED_PRODUCT.PRODUCT_NO = PRODUCT.PRODUCT_NO

This query is similar to the first, but it selects columns from two tables. (In relational terminology it "joins" the tables.) In the list of fields in the **SELECT** clause, the columns **PRODUCT_NO** and **QUANTITY** have been "qualified" with the table name (the part preceding the period). This must be done because the same names exist in both of the tables involved. The **FROM** clause then lists both of the tables involved. Finally the select clause specifies the matching pair of key and foreign key fields that implement the relationship.

It is useful to think of the result of this query as yet another table. The result of the join may be called a "view," or "user view." That is, the definition of the query is a definition of a table. When it is executed as part of a retrieval, the view is delivered. The view or result table does not have a separate existence in storage. It is a "virtual" table.

The SQL language has great power and precision, and can be used to define queries of significant complexity. It includes many additional features such as the ability to insert data items and rows, or to modify or delete them. It includes functions such as counts, totals, and averages that may be used as results or as intermediate products in queries. It can also produce errors, some obvious, but others very subtle. Direct use of SQL is generally left to database specialists and programmers.

This brief introduction to SQL provides some insight into the value of friendly user-oriented packages that formulate queries for users. The user can describe the query using graphical tables and simple specifications.

Validating Query Results

Query results are subject to several types of errors. These are based on either misunderstanding the composition of the tables or on incorrectly specifying the syntax of a query. Users must make a habit of evaluating the correctness and completeness of results. In the following list, the first five suggestions are generally advisable; the last three are useful in a period of learning or testing and when the results require extra validation.

1. *Estimate the number of records to be retrieved prior to the query operation.* Base the estimate on independent knowledge of the data, if possible.

2. *Inspect or print a sample from each of the tables being used in order to review your understanding of the tables and their values.* Apply database functions to inspect various attributes and get a count of the number of records having each valid code (or those that have a blank or miscoded attribute).

3. *Make rough estimates for any calculations such as totals that will result from your queries.*

4. *Compare your results with previous queries or with estimates by others in your workgroup.*

5. *Do a complex query by starting with the simplest part and adding query elements one by one.* Examine the results after each addition.

6. *Sort results so as to highlight possible errors or omissions.* For example, sort by a financial amount and inspect the high and low values. Sort by names to identify duplicate or misspelled identifiers.

7. *Perform a second query using independently formulated conditions to verify that the* **WHERE** *clause and other parts of the expression have been processed as expected.* Compare the results to see if they make sense.

8. *Consider a complementary selection (or at least a count).* For example, if the desired selection obtained 150 records from 2500, reformulate the query to count the number of records that do not meet the condition.

The sum of the two queries should yield the total number of entity instances in the table.

Online Analytical Processing (OLAP)

◆ ◆

Even though graphical user interfaces provide easy access to relational databases, some software vendors now provide a combination of analytical and retrieval software. In other words, rather than formulating a query, obtaining the data, and doing the analysis, the software formulates a data query based on an analytical question. The process is online without intermediate steps, so the type of software is termed **online analytical processing (OLAP)**.

The OLAP analysis is often termed multidimensional analysis using multidimensional databases. Data is represented as user-defined dimensions rather than tables. A sales analysis database might organize data by product, territory, customer, and other dimensions important to sales managers. A multidimensional database can have multiple hierarchies. Time is a common dimension in analytical applications, and multi-dimensional analysis can extract data for specified dimensions and time periods. Computations such as moving averages, growth rates, period comparisons, or cumulative statistics can easily be made. The most common applications are in marketing and financial analysis.

The advantages of OLAP lie in a simpler approach to analytical exploration of data. Results may be analyzed using a variety of techniques and a number of presentation methods, such as graphs, tables, and spreadsheets.

Constraints on Accessing Organizational Databases

◆ ◆

Unlike personal systems, the organizational system is available only to those in the organization who are authorized and have computer access. The organizational system and its database system maintain controls or authorization tables that specify who can access different parts of the organizational data. Access privileges may be for an entire database, selected tables, or specified attributes.

Privileges are established by the database administrator or equivalent. User passwords are the typical method for validating authority to access data. Some systems limit queries to certain time periods. The reason for such time limits, when these exist, may be to avoid degrading the performance of the online transaction system. Data warehousing is a way of bypassing this reason for limiting access to transaction data.

The databases and files maintained by the transaction systems reflect the most current state of the organization and its environment. Data in the data warehouse provides the most current data available for queries. Since these databases reflect an up-to-date, current, and official state-of-the-organization, they must be considered the primary information source for business decisions. In most cases, data should be retrieved directly from these databases.

Are there situations when an individual should copy selected data into a personal computer system? The answer is yes, under some circumstances. It may be necessary to do analysis over an extended time period. In that case, a static "snapshot" of the data is needed, rather than access to continually changing transaction data or a periodically updated data warehouse. It may be convenient to work with a snapshot when the use of the data does not require updating during the period of use. The tradeoff is between timeliness and the cost of executing a fresh query.

Example

An analyst is asked to do extensive analysis of the customer list at the end of the year. By selecting only those attributes of interest for the analysis, the analyst can download a copy of the file at the end of the year. The limited set of attributes makes the file easier to use. The downloaded copy can be used without taking the time and effort to make a separate query for each question. ◆

Knowledge Work Productivity in Accessing Organizational Data

◆ ◆

Concepts about organizational databases have been presented in the chapter. This section will explain issues of efficiency in using data access software and describe three common ways the data from organizational databases are employed in knowledge work tasks: direct use, spreadsheet analysis, and word processing document.

Efficient Use of Data Access Software

Data access efficiency is improved by using software that best matches the activities to be performed. There are software packages that offer database access as a part of the functionality of the package. In evaluating alternatives, user efficiency objectives include reducing effort required to obtain data, reducing errors in obtaining data, eliminating redundant operations such as re-entry of data, and eliminating redundant data storage.

Desirable features of software used for database access include easy-to-use graphical interfaces for formulating queries, ease of learning, and user help facilities. Graphical interfaces for queries and ease of learning are closely related. A graphical interface for query design reduces both initial learning time and relearning time if the task is performed infrequently.

User help in formulating a query or report (often termed a "wizard" or "assistant") is based on common operations and formats. For example, a report assistant may suggest common options based on the data, such as format or headings. The assistant improves productivity because the preselected choices reduce the report design effort.

The productivity from specific software used for database access may also depend on the way the data will be employed. Three common ways to use the data are direct use of the results without further processing, use of data in spreadsheet analysis, and use of the data in a document prepared with a word processor. In the latter cases, the data access features should support efficient data transfer to a spreadsheet or document.

Obtaining Data for Direct Use

The facilities of all database packages provide for retrieval and printout of a database table or query in table or report format for direct use. The report format reduces effort to prepare a report for use. Its features allow a user to specify headings and subheadings, sort data, calculate subtotals, page totals, and grand totals, insert page numbers, and perform other functions more easily than with other software. A graphical user interface for query and report formulation can reduce the time and mental effort to select data and define report characteristics. It can also reduce query formulation errors.

Example

A typical graphical user interface for formulating a query asks the user to specify the tables to be used. The user selects from a list of available tables (reducing errors in entering table names). The tables included in the query are shown graphically and the keys that allow tables to be joined are displayed graphically with connecting lines. This reduces errors in deciding which tables can be joined for a query. The user selects the data names of the attributes to be used in the query and specifies whether the attributes are to be included in the output. The use of the list reduces effort to locate attribute names and eliminates errors in writing the names for the attributes in the query. If an attribute is to be used in selection, the selection criteria is entered. For example, a query to select high-value orders may specify a criteria of greater than 1000. The notation employed for query criteria generally follows simple mathematical conventions, such as ORDER TOTAL > 1000. ◆

Obtaining Data for Spreadsheet Analysis

Spreadsheet software is frequently used to analyze data from a database. The database software provides the best capabilities for data management and the spreadsheet software provides the best data analysis facilities. Being able to transfer data from a database to a spreadsheet allows the best facilities of both packages to be employed. Productivity is enhanced by accessing an organizational database and transferring rather than re-entering data.

Transferring data from a database to a spreadsheet can involve transfer from a single database table or involve selecting data from one or more tables. The most common transfer is the data resulting from a query. The transfer (frequently termed "export" or "output to") converts the tabular data of the database tables, query tabular results, or query report into the cells of a spreadsheet. Table labels on attributes (column headings) are generally transferred to the spreadsheet along with the data values. The spreadsheet may be automatically assigned the name of the database table (or query table) or the user may be asked to assign a name. Once the transfer is made, there is no further connection between the database and the spreadsheet. If the database is updated, the spreadsheet is not changed. All of the data analysis features of the spreadsheet may be applied to the data. The records may be analyzed and summarized in a wide variety of ways and the data presented as graphs or charts.

After importing a data table to a spreadsheet, a user often needs to summarize data. A productive feature for this is a **pivot table**, which enables users to perform tasks such as the following:

◊   *Summarize data with subtotals and totals.* The analyst specifies the basis for summarization and rows meeting the criteria are grouped together with subtotals and totals.

◊   *Select rows and columns to be included in a summary table with subtotals and totals.*

◊   *Pivot the data so that rows become columns and columns become rows.* The pivot table can use selected rows and columns.

The pivot table allows an analyst to easily examine a number of different ways to organize, summarize, and present data.

Example

A table from a query retrieves records of sales. The records contain **salesperson**, **product sold**, **dollar value of sale**, and other data. When the table is exported to a spreadsheet, pivot table functions can be used to summarize the records, grouping all sales for each salesperson with subtotals by salesperson for each product. Using two salespersons, called A and B, and two products, called x and y, the function will summarize all records as follows if the analyst specifies sales dollars by product for salespersons.

Sum of Sales $		
Salesperson	Product	Total
A	x	12
	y	21
A Total		33
B	x	33
	y	20
B Total		53
Grand Total		86

By simple specification, the table can be pivoted to make **Salesperson** a column on the analysis. The data in this case is the same, but the presentation has changed.

Sum of Sales $	Salesperson		
Product	A	B	Grand Total
x	12	33	45
y	21	20	41
Grand Total	33	53	86

Obtaining Data for Word Processing Documents

Productivity is improved by accessing an organizational database and transferring data rather than re-entering it. Only the data needed for the document is transferred. A number of options are generally available when transferring a query result or a report result from database software to word processing. The data can be transferred as delimited data (data items separated by tab settings or characters such as commas), formatted data in tabular form, and rich text format (table format). The export format depends on how the data will be used in the report. If the table format is to be maintained in the report, the RTF option is useful. If the tabular format is to be maintained, but some word processing changes are to be made, a formatted data in tabular form may reduce effort. If the data is to be used in the document, but the tabular format of the query or report output is not to be maintained, then delimited data may provide maximum flexibility.

Summary

◊ ◊ ◊ ◊ ◊ ◊ ◊ ◊ ◊ ◊ ◊ ◊ ◊ ◊ ◊ ◊ ◊ ◊

◊ The organizational approach to databases is important since most knowledge workers will retrieve data from corporate databases and rely on it for many of their individual tasks.

◆ Rather than having separate files for the records of an organization, databases are used for related sets of data. A high uniform level of quality is obtained by quality assurance procedures applied consistently and by coordinated updating. All applications can access the data, and all database users receive the same information with the same quality and recency.

◆ The logical concept of a database requires a database management system and a database administrator.

◆ Current technology is migrating databases from central systems to more accessible client/server systems. Transaction-based data may be selected and copied from production databases into a data warehouse for retrieval by knowledge workers.

◆ Organizations capture and store data about entities of interest. These entities correspond roughly to objects for which organizations maintain files or database tables. Each entity instance (like a record) has attributes or characteristics that describe and differentiate it from other instances.

◆ The attributes (characteristics) of entity instances are assigned data names. Attributes belong to a data type that defines data operations. Data items are combined into data structures that may be described by algebraic data definitions or by graphical data structure diagrams. Data are ordered in a useful sequence, as needed.

◆ Organizations tend to provide data access to users based on the relational model. In the relational model, each entity is described as a table with columns for each attribute, rows for each entity instance, and a key attribute that uniquely identifies each row (entity instance).

◆ Database query languages are provided with each database system. The standard, underlying language for database queries is SQL (Structured Query Language). SQL is powerful and complex. Most query languages employed by users provide a simpler approach, including Query By Example in systems with graphical interfaces. To create a query, a user identifies the tables needed, determines selection and ordering criteria, creates and executes a query, and checks to be sure results are correct.

◆ Database software for access to organizational data can improve knowledge work productivity by reducing time and effort to obtain data, eliminating re-entry time and errors by use of transfer or export functions, and preformatting data for subsequent use. Query and report output is commonly used in the form provided by the database software, exported to a spreadsheet for further analysis and processing, or exported to a document.

EXERCISES

1. In accessing organizational data, an individual user does not need to worry about setting up the relational tables. The data exists as relational tables, so the user focuses on how to access and use the data effectively. The first exercise is a "learn-by-following" exercise.

   This exercise will refer to Microsoft Access™, Excel™, and Word™ to illustrate the principles of access, export to word processor or spreadsheet, and the underlying SQL code. However, the same learning exercise can be applied to other packages and sample databases. The packages (database, spreadsheet, and word processor) do not need to be from the same vendor. A different spreadsheet package and word processor may be employed with the sample database with the same results.

   The database for the exercises is the Northwind™ database provided with the Microsoft Access database package. It is found under subdirectory **Sampapps** under the Access directory. The database for use is called **nwind.mdb**. There are eight tables in the Northwind database. Select **nwind.mdb** to bring up the screen with the tables, then proceed as follows:

   a. *Open tables.* Open each of the eight tables to see what the table looks like. Use **Design** to examine the design view of the **Employees** table. The design view will be important for establishing your own database (as described in Chapter 12).

   b. *Open saved queries.* Click on **Query**. The list of queries represents "saved queries" that can be used again. **Open** will run a saved query. **Design View** shows the way the query selection was established. Clicking on the SQL icon (or selecting SQL under **View** on the menu bar) shows the SQL statements generated for that query. Examine both the Design View and SQL for the query "Category list."

   c. *Open saved reports.* Click on **Report**. The list of reports represents "saved reports" that can be used. A report uses the results of a query, so there is no report without a table from a query. Examine the report for **List of Products by Category.** Examine its design view, which shows the layout of the report. Note the use of elements such as report header, page header, category name, and detail line.

   d. *Move query results to a spreadsheet.* Do the report for **List of Products by Category.** Go to **FILE** on the menu bar and select **OUTPUT TO.** Select Microsoft Excel. Store it. Open Excel and then open the file you just stored. In other words, transfer data from the report output of Access to a spreadsheet in Excel.

   e. *Move query results to a document.* Repeat the report for **List of Products by Category** and **FILE** and **OUTPUT TO.** Select Rich Text Format (RTF).

Select a name and store as a Word word processing file. Open Word and examine. Note that the output is in a table format.

f. *Select some rows on a single table.* Select Query and do a "New" query on the **Employees** table. Add the **Employees** table to the query list and close. Select **Last Name** for the first field, sort in ascending order, and enter the following selection criteria:

> Last Name   Like "S*" or Like "B*"

This will select only the employees whose last name starts with S or B.

g. *Select a few rows of related tables.* Combine two tables, but select only a few fields. Combine Products and Suppliers tables, but select only **Product Name** and **Company Name** (of supplier). Print in **Product Name** ascending order.

h. *Examine SQL statements and modify them.* Repeat the query for (g). View the SQL statements. Delete the **ORDER BY** clause. Note the change in result. Print only the first page.

2. Tailor a report using database report facilities. The description is based on the Northwind database, but the exercise can be adapted to other database packages and sample databases.

a. Use the **Products** table for a query to produce a list of products starting with the letters A, B, or C. List the **Product Name** and **English Name**. Store the query.

b. Use the **Report** facilities. Do a New report. Use the query from (a). Use the Report Wizard™ first to produce a standard report in tabular form. Change the order of the fields in the report. Sort by **English Name**. Print the report.

c. For the same report as (b), go to **Design View**. Change the names for the two columns. Print the report.

3. Assume you have access to any data stored by your organization (or the university if you are a student). State two or three problems that can be addressed by data analysis. Describe the data to be retrieved, the analysis to be performed, and the format (including headings, sorting, subtotals, and totals) of the report.

4. Explore the report facilities of a personal computer database package. Formulate three queries. Use the query results to prepare reports. Do the reports in three formats:

a. List the query results as a table.

b. Create the report using Report Assistant™ or Report Wizard.

c. Create the report based on custom specification facilities provided by the package.

5. Obtain specifications for two or more OLAP products and compare them. Evaluate their usefulness in your organization (or by university administrators).

6. Using a database available to you, formulate an interesting analysis for the data. Extract data and export it to a spreadsheet. Analyze the data and prepare a graphic analysis. Write a short report defining the problem and the answers developed from the analysis. Illustrate the analysis with graphs where useful.

7. Compare the collating sequence used by your word processor and spreadsheet processor. Create a list of the following with one item per line in a document and one item per cell in a column in a spreadsheet: Alpha, alpha, gamma, Gamma, $, %, <, ?, /, +, =, and #. Hint: You can use what you learned in Chapter 6 about copying and pasting to enter the list of data only once (for example, in the word processor) and paste it to a spreadsheet column. Sort each list in ascending order. Compare the results. What are the implications for typical reports? What are the implications in sorting codes containing special characters?

8. Repeat Exercise 6, using the sample database provided with Microsoft Access. The database has eight tables for a hypothetical wholesale company, Northwinds Trading Company, that imports food and beverage products. Your task is to analyze a history of individual shipments of products to decide which products are most deserving of a limited promotion budget. There are a number of stored reports included with the Northwind sample database, but there are no reports to evaluate sales trends over time.

   The database is organized by individual shipment. To do an analysis, sales should be summarized by quarter. To reduce the scope of the exercise, consider two full years of data (eight quarters). Assume that the analysis is to decide on the promotion budget for only the beverages product line. Then proceed as follows:
   a. Identify the tables and attributes of records to be selected.
   b. Formulate a query to obtain the records that meet the selection criteria.
   c. Export the records to a spreadsheet.
   d. Manipulate the data to analyze quarterly sales for eight quarters. Consider using the data modeling or pivot table feature of the spreadsheet software. This allows you to summarize the data with little extra effort.
   e. Use graphs to present results. (Decide which results can be meaningfully presented on the same graph.)

9. *External Data Exercise:* Do Exercise 7 in Chapter 8. (Chapter 8 focuses on accessing external data on the Internet. The External Data Exercises included in Chapters 1-7 are designed to prepare you for the more difficult exercises presented in Chapter 8.)

Accessing External Data

◆   ◆   ◆   ◆   ◆   ◆   ◆   ◆

OBJECTIVES

After completing this chapter, you should be able to:

◆ Describe the various categories of external data used by knowledge workers.

◆ Explain the address structure for Internet addresses and World Wide Web URLs.

◆ Describe some of the resources available on the World Wide Web.

◆ Explain the role of bulletin boards and discussion groups in information sharing.

◆ Describe the role of Telnet, FTP, and Web browsers in accessing remote data.

◆ Explain the process of file searching via various search and navigation facilities.

KEY TERMS AND CONCEPTS

This chapter introduces the following key terms and concepts, listed in the order in which they appear:

ASCII (American Standard Code for Information Interchange)

MIME (Multipurpose Internet Mail Extension)

PDF (Portable Document Format)

HTML (Hypertext Markup Language)

URL (Uniform Resource Locator)

BBS (Bulletin Board System)

FAQs (Frequently Asked Questions)

firewall

Telnet

Web browser

FTP (File Transfer Protocol)

Internet

WWW (World Wide Web)

stopping rule

The data on a personal computer or in office files is a small part of the data needed for knowledge work. Data is also obtained from additional sources, such as:

◆ Organizational files and databases

◆ Noncomputer documents and reference materials (from a knowledge worker's professional library, company library, or public libraries)

◆ External computer files and databases

Chapter 7 described procedures for accessing organizational data. Although non-computer data sources are important, the emphasis of the text is on effective use of information technology. Therefore, this chapter focuses on external computer-accessible data.

External data access follows the general steps for locating and retrieving data. The difference between internal and external access is in the breadth of options. Following are the general steps for accessing data:

1. Recognize that data appropriate for the task does or might exist.

2. Locate the data source(s) by using general search strategies to define the domain of search.

3. Test processes to confirm the existence and location of the desired body of data.

4. Search to isolate the relevant data by formulating and applying effective search parameters.

5. Retrieve relevant data in a useful form for the task.

External data sources provide transient data, published literature, descriptive and reference data for individuals and organizations, government data, statistical data, and discussion data from bulletin boards and networks. Different search and retrieval strategies and techniques are needed depending upon the type of data and its source.

Knowledge-building and maintenance tasks include the process of building and continually upgrading awareness of external data. It is not a simple task. Partial automation may be used to assist. Software methods such as "intelligent agents," "lenses," or "search robots" assist knowledge workers in locating, screening, and acquiring relevant data.

So much data is "out there" that knowledge worker productivity in searching and acquiring data is a relevant concern. It is all too easy to get lost in the data search and retrieve too little or too much. When the needed data exists, being productive means acquiring the data relevant to the issue at hand as efficiently as possible. It requires understanding the data marketplace and being skilled in using information technology to locate and acquire the right data.

Data Presentation and Transfer Standards

When data is transferred to or from an external source over communications facilities, there must be protocols: coding conventions that are understood by both source and destination. In addition, files may need to be compressed to reduce transmission volume and speed data transfer, especially in the case of pictures, graphs, audio, and video. Since such files must be decompressed at the destination, compression standards are required. Standards, protocols, or agreements for data presentation are also important in reading and working with external data sources. Several important protocols or standards are ASCII, MIME, Postscript, PDF, and HTML. Only a brief introduction is provided here since the details of these protocols and standards are hidden in software.

ASCII (American Standard Code for Information Interchange) is a nearly universal standard seven-bit code. It encodes the characters on a typical keyboard (numbers, upper- and lower-case letters, punctuation marks, and special characters) plus a number of control characters. The limitations of the seven-bit ASCII code are lack of additional alphabetic characters found in some alphabets (such as á, â, ä, å, à). The International Standards Organization (ISO) adds a series of character sets that make up eight-bit code sets that extend the concept to languages with different character sets, such as Greek, Cyrillic, Arabic, Japanese, and Hebrew. There are also sets of codes for mathematics and graphics characters.

The advantage of the ASCII code is that it is widely used for text and, therefore, accepted by all word processing and communications software. Since it is limited to text and standard English characters, other conventions must be applied to documents with extended character sets, graphs, pictures, sound, and video.

An Internet standard called **MIME (Multipurpose Internet Mail Extension)** specifies additional character sets, plus encoding for other forms of data so that they can be transported as if they were text. Pictures, graphics, sounds, and video clips are MIME encoded before transfer and decoded before presentation. MIME encoding is built into many communications packages, so that various types of data appear to move easily between server (where the data is stored) and client (the system accessing the data). The MIME standard is linked within electronic mail systems and also World Wide Web browsers in such a way that the encoding process is usually hidden from the user.

An important requirement with some data is the ability to transfer the precise form of a document via e-mail or file transfer. Postscript™ is a language for coding documents as commands in plain ASCII text to retain the exact formatting of a transmitted document. Postscript is primarily used to transfer document formatting to a printer. Some documents available on the Internet are formatted in Postscript. Such documents may be transferred and printed exactly as the author intended. Packaged software is available for many systems to allow on-screen viewing of Postscript documents.

Another method for transferring documents is to encode them in a **Portable Document Format (PDF)**. The encoding is done with Adobe Acrobat™, a software package designed for this purpose. The file to be encoded may contain formatted text and multimedia content such as pictures, graphs, audio, and video. A person receiving a PDF file reads it with an Adobe Acrobat reader, a free software package. The file can be read, displayed, and printed exactly as originally written. PDF files cannot be altered. This fact, plus the free reader, has helped make many complex documents widely available.

HTML (Hypertext Markup Language) is the document encoding and presentation standard of the World Wide Web. Versions of HTML have been approved as International standards, but newer alternatives in widespread use have not yet been standardized. HTML coding describes some but by no means all format information. Web browsers have great flexibility in displaying contents, sometimes leading to unreadable displays. HTML pages are encoded in seven-bit ASCII and are quite compact. HTML's simplicity and compactness has been a major factor in the growth of the World Wide Web.

Interpreting Addresses for Accessing External Data

◆ ◆ ◆ ◆ ◆ ◆ ◆ ◆ ◆ ◆ ◆ ◆ ◆ ◆ ◆ ◆ ◆ ◆ ◆ ◆

This chapter points to many sources of external data. In many of the examples, specific addresses are included. Although it is not necessary to understand the structure of addresses in order to use them, it may helpful to better identify data resources. There are two common forms of addressing that it will be useful to understand: (1) Internet addresses and (2) World Wide Web addresses.

Each computer on the Internet has a globally unique numeric address called an IP address (IP stands for Internet Protocol). It is these 4-segment numbers that are used by underlying networking equipment to convey messages between computers. While computers use numeric addresses to address one another, humans prefer descriptive names. Thus addresses such as **csom.umn.edu** are used to refer to the Carlson School of Management at the University of Minnesota. These addresses are called *domain names.*

The domain names have a hierarchical structure. At the top of the hierarchy, on the right-most part of the domain name, there are site designations such as **.com** (commercial), **.gov** (government), and **.edu** (educational), and then country domains such as **.se**, **.au**, **.uk** (country specific domains are always two letters long). The United States does not use a country domain. Dots separate the segments of a domain name. Going down one level in the hierarchy (or left one dot), there are specific company or organization names, such as **ibm.com**, **umn.edu**, or **ieee.org**. Organizations outside the United States use three levels before an organizational name—for example, **essex.ac.uk**, or **qut.edu.au**. The hierarchical structure of domain names serves two purposes. First it gives humans a rough guide to the type, and maybe location, of the organization a name is associated with. Second it helps the Internet's domain name service relate IP addresses to domain names.

Examples of addresses illustrate the hierarchical structure:

ntu.edu.sg	identifies Nanyang Technological University, an educational institution in Singapore
csom.umn.edu	the Carlson School of Management at the University of Minnesota
qut.edu.au	the Queensland University of Technology, an educational institution in Australia
ibm.com	IBM, a commercial enterprise
ieee.org	The Institute of Electrical and Electronic Engineers, a nonprofit organization

World Wide Web addresses are the second form of addresses and embed Internet domain names. Addressing is one of the fundamental technologies in the Web. **URLs, or Uniform Resource Locators**, are the technology for addressing documents on the Web. A URL includes the type of resource being accessed (e.g., Web, gopher, WAIS), the address of the server, and the location of the file. The syntax is:

> type://host.domain/path/filename.extension

where type may be one of: file, ftp, http, gopher, mailto, and others. Type specifies the type of data transfer protocol to use. It is (almost) always separated from the second component by a colon and two forward slash characters.

The second part, host.domain, is one of the standard Internet domain names described above.

The third part is often omitted. It specifies the location of the document and its name as it is stored on the specified host computer. It is always offset with forward slashes, and includes a complete filename and extension. The filename extension is used to indicate the type of file, so the Web client program knows how to process it. When only parts one and two are specified, a "default" document is usually sent (instead of an error message).

Examples illustrate World Wide Web URLs (Pronounced "you-are-ells," not "Earls."):

http://www.ssa.gov/   The Web site for the Social Security Administration of the Government of the USA

http://www.ibm.com/   The top Web document of the IBM Corporation

http://www.ncsa.uiuc.edu/General/Internet/WWW/HTMLPrimer.html   The first page of the *NCSA Beginner's Guide to HTML* at the The National Center for Supercomputing Applications of the University of Illinois at Urbana-Champaign, an educational institution in the USA

http://www.windows95.com/apps/antivirus.html   URL of the virus software pages in the application pages of Microsoft's Windows95 support service

The World Wide Web allows access to information organized with hypertext links. A hypertext link is a word or set of words marked to show that it provides a link to a related idea, concept, file, or Web page. By placing the cursor on the marked word(s) and indicating a transfer by a keystroke or mouse click, the system will transfer from the marked text to the connecting data at the same site or at another site. The same concept applies to other media, such as graphs, pictures, and sound.

External Data Categories and Sources

◆ ◆

External data is defined from the viewpoint of an individual user. An organization's internal databases often include data obtained or derived externally. For example, the organization's strategic intelligence function may monitor clients and competitors, collect and disseminate relevant data, and maintain an internal strategic intelligence database. In some organizations, such databases are part of the formal information system. They are managed by the MIS department and routinely support specific decision-making functions. An example is a database of competitor products and prices to support a firm's product development and marketing functions.

External data used by individual knowledge workers can be loosely classified into six categories (see Figure 8-1). These are described briefly in the following paragraphs and explained in more detail in subsequent sections.

1. *Transient data.* Data such as market prices and closings, news stories, and weather often have high value for many tasks, but usually have very short useful lifetimes. Accounts of natural events such as weather or disasters may be critical to many business decisions in the short term. Access to transient data has several unique characteristics based on its short useful life and need for timeliness.

2. *Periodicals.* Published literature including magazines, books, trade and research journals, reports, and newsletters. The information explosion has resulted in a doubling of the volume of information in this category every few years. Alternative methods and services to access these resources have also been increasing at an accelerating pace.

3. *Reference works.* Organizational, association, and individual descriptive and reference data. The low cost and wide accessibility of World Wide

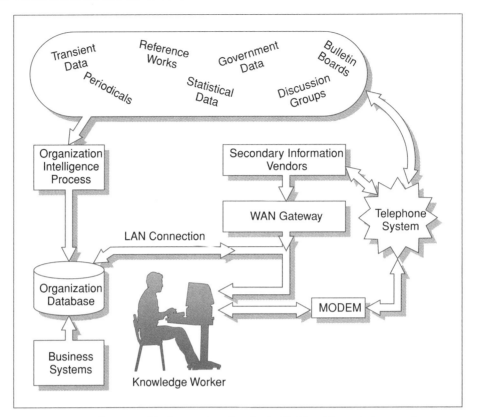

FIGURE 8-1 *Sources of information for the individual knowledge worker*

Web pages has prompted many organizations, associations, and individuals to place descriptive and reference data on Web pages.

4. *Government data.* Governments at all levels accumulate data that is often available free or at low cost. Government data of value to the knowledge worker may range from simple statistics such as the census to new, complex analytic models developed by agencies or subcontractors. Government data is also processed and made available by data resellers.

5. *Statistical data.* Includes both government and private data. Many knowledge work tasks benefit from statistics gathered and maintained by both government and private organizations and institutions.

6. *Bulletin boards and discussion groups.* These have a similar objective of sharing information and allowing comments and ideas to be made available to interested participants. They may be used for posting information such as announcements, alerts, and product releases plus posting comments from readers. They may also be used for discussion groups or forums around a topic or issue. They may be open, public groups or private, limited access groups.

Transient Data Including News and Markets

One of the important attributes of information is timeliness. Transient data has high value when it is current, but loses its value rapidly. Valuable transient data may include market data, general news data, and weather. An important class of transient data, at least with respect to computer access, is data released in both electronic and paper form. Examples are financial reports, earnings estimates, and product announcements. Very rapid electronic access to such data may add significant value for decision makers.

Electronic access to external transient data is usually accomplished through the services of a third party provider. Thus, an organization that needs access to financial market data may contract with each of the markets or with a service that is able to provide a single access point to multiple information sources. It has been common, especially in the financial services industry, for the information systems function to contract for, manage, and provide such support. The IS function is then responsible for internal distribution of such external data. The spread of network information service providers, however, has made access to many information sources available at the individual level.

Many network vendors provide access to market data. For example, the three largest online service providers—CompuServe, America Online, and Prodigy—provide stock market data on a fifteen-minute delay to all subscribers. They also carry many fee-based market information services. In general, fee-based access to network services is available via a local phone call. Since 1991, the Internet has rapidly added commercial services. Virtually any electronic news and information service available online is available on the Internet, including market data. Since the Internet is international, market and news data from all parts of the globe are available.

Example

ClariNet™ is one of the primary news services available on the Internet. ClariNet is a commercial venture begun in 1989 that acquires online news feeds from news services such as AP (Associated Press) and UPI (United Press International). ClariNet organizes the news into newsgroups and then sells subscriptions to all or selected segments. News in advance of TV broadcasts or newspapers is available by monitoring ClariNet. ◆

Two inhibitors limit access to external, transient data: (1) lack of knowledge of availability and (2) the difficulty of selecting only relevant data. Network providers and the Internet add new features almost every day. Locating a source of transient data requires reliance on online documentation, search engines, and published guides. The individual who has a potential need for this class of data must develop personal knowledge by scanning and experience. No single guide is likely to point to the specific information needed, based on available data. Rather, a guide can point to likely sources or perhaps the type of sources for the information sought. Likewise, no single search engine is likely to provide the coverage and selectivity needed, so users must understand the capabilities of several different search engines. In addition to specific, directed queries, a user may find relevant data by browsing, asking questions in newsgroups, and looking for references in other material.

Users can select relevant data from transient services manually by scanning titles (the equivalent of headlines) periodically. Whenever specific topics to be monitored can be defined (such as company names), a monitoring service (a program that processes the news feed against a table of keywords or search arguments) can be used to perform the scanning. When an item is selected, it can be e-mailed to the individual subscriber. An individual can, of course, install his or her own monitor program. Service providers provide such monitors for the Internet.

♦xamples

Reference COM **(http://www.reference.com/)** is a free filtering system that searches Internet newsgroups and electronic mailing lists. It is accessible by anyone on the Internet through e-mail or a World Wide Web interface form. The user provides query data (keyword, organization, author, or newsgroup) which is used to create a user interest profile. The filter then matches the profile against the daily newsgroup exchanges and e-mails the user a report of the matched messages, including the first twenty lines of each message. A user can request a full message, give the filter feedback, and give other filter management commands. ♦

PointCast™ is an innovative, free Internet application that can be tailored by the individual to select market, news, sports, and weather data of interest **(http://www.pointcast.com/)**. PointCast automatically updates data in each selected category hourly (or as tailored). The PointCast interface can be used as a "screen saver" that displays headlines, a stock and sports ticker, and advertising. Advertising supports the free distribution. ♦

Published Literature: Books, Magazines, Journals, and Reports

Journals, reports, and books are being published at an increasing rate. In addition to traditional library reference sources, there are two important electronic methods for accessing published data: online databases and CD-ROM reference publishing. Online databases are operated by many organizations, including governments, professional organizations, research institutions, private developers, and third-party providers. Online databases are sometimes available directly from the producing agency but more often from information distributors. Three commercial information providers (DIALOG, Ovid Technologies, and LEXIS-NEXIS) illustrate these services.

◊ The DIALOG Information Retrieval Service, a fee-based service from Knight-Ridder Information, Inc., has been available online since 1972. It includes access to over 450 databases from a broad range of disciplines. The databases reference millions of documents drawn from scientific and technical literature, full-text trade journals, newspapers, and news wires. Services are described on their Web pages (see Figure 8-2):
http://www.dialog.com/dialog/dialog1.html

◊ Ovid Technologies is a commercial provider of search services to over 80 databases. It includes databases for current contents, biomedical, sciences, engineering, arts and humanities, and social and behavioral sciences. Services are described in their Web pages:
http://www.ovid.com/

◊ LEXIS-NEXIS is a commercial provider of search services to external databases covering legal, business, and government information. The databases

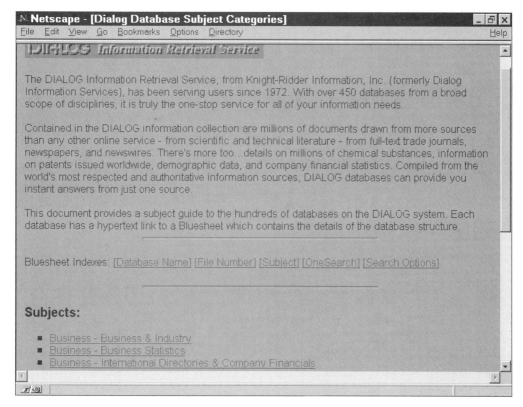

FIGURE 8-2 *Dialog Information Retrieval Service database subject guide on the World Wide Web*

are extensive and include full text of documents, articles, regulations, and reports. Services are described in their Web pages:
http://www.lexis-nexis.com/

The number and size of databases available have introduced an additional layer of information service: organizations that do searches of the databases and information provider offerings. Such search services include reference librarians, search firms, and search programs. They accept search criteria, select the most likely database sources, search, and often provide the selected original documents. Many search firms subscribe to multiple databases and other information sources. Their products include topical searches and periodic or special reports based on contracted search criteria and specified sources. Many organizations subscribe to one or more of these services. Such services are also available to individuals.

Example

A service named Current Contents distributes title pages and article abstracts on over 6,000 scientific journals each month. Content monitoring services can search Current Contents and forward selected information to subscribers. ◆

An alternative to online database and search services is the purchase of the databases for organizational, departmental, or individual system use. CD-ROM storage has made this alternative feasible. Purchasing a database offers two key advantages over many current online services: data can include more than simple ASCII text, and it can be reproduced at relatively low cost. CD-ROM disks can be used on individual workstations and on LANs to provide low-cost access to very large data files. The low cost of CD-ROM equipment means that LAN administrators are able to stack multiple CD-ROM drives on a LAN, making the contents of four, eight, or more CD-ROMs available online to all their network users.

Example

PC Magazine is one of the highest circulation specialty publications in the information technology field. In addition to the printed magazine, the publisher sells a quarterly CD-ROM containing all editorial content for the prior twelve months. Much of this content is available at the PC Magazine online World Wide Web site:
http://www.pcmag.com/ ◆

Organizational, Association, and Individual Descriptive and Reference Data

Creating and maintaining Web pages once a Web site has been made available is relatively inexpensive. Organizations, associations, and individuals have created information pages. A set of Web pages may be descriptive and/or contain information such as schedules and reference data. The quality of data in Web pages differs widely. Many Web pages are not up-to-date, and pages may be dropped or moved, "breaking" links. The Web provides a huge archive of external data. In early 1996, some analysts estimated there were 50 million pages accessible on the Web.

Example

A student interested in enrolling in almost any college or university can find current data on programs, faculty, course schedules, syllabi and assignments, campus maps, and placement office statistics by accessing the Web. ◆

The variety of information on the Web can be overwhelming. Therefore, it may be useful to classify Web resources as directories, reference data, individual pages, descriptions and activities, and association calendars. The following examples with their URLs (Uniform Resource Locators) illustrate this concept:

◊ *Directory and reference data.* An example is the MISRC/McGraw-Hill Directory of MIS Faculty. It is available for search on a Web site (and also as a printed directory):
  http://webfoot.csom.umn.edu/isworld/facdir/home.htm

◊ *Individual pages.* Faculty members and students can place personal descriptions, pictures, and resumes on Web pages.

◊ *Descriptions and activities.* Companies, educational institutions, organizations, and societies have Web pages to describe their activities and calendars of events. An example is the Management Information Systems Research Center at the University of Minnesota:
  http://www.misq.org/misrc/misrc.htm

◊ *Association calendar information.* An example is the description and calendar information for the Association for Computing Machinery (ACM):
  http://info.acm.org/

Government Data

National, state, and local governments are large information collectors and producers. Many agencies make information publicly available via document libraries, online information providers, and transportable media (such as magnetic tape and CD-ROM). Many agencies, legislatures, and executive offices make their data available via Internet access tools.

Example

One of the main reasons the United States Securities and Exchange Commission (SEC) was created was to act as a library for corporate information and make this information available to investors. The SEC uses the Internet to make available its public database of corporate information within 24 hours of filing. According to SEC

Chairman Arthur Levitt, in a speech on August 27, 1995, "Technology is so advanced that the cost to the Commission is quite modest. With a personal computer and a modem, you'll be able to have the entire SEC Public Reference Room in your own living room. You'll be able to research information and download documents. Nothing could be better for investors—and nothing could be better for the market, which thrives on accurate information."
http://www.sec.gov/ ◆

Because governments collect and generate so much information, many commercial organizations obtain information from government units and organize, classify, and disseminate it. In some cases, government agencies sell data directly to recover some of the costs of producing and processing it.

Examples

High-resolution photographs of the earth's surface by the Geosat satellite, sold by mail for many years, are now available via the Internet:
http://edcwww.cr.usgs.gov/ ◆

The Telecommunications Act of 1996 is the first major revision of telecommunications law in almost 62 years. The Telecommunications Act of 1996 has the potential to change the way we work, live, and learn. The FCC maintains a WordPerfect Version (335 pages) of the completely updated Communications Act of 1934, as amended by the Telecommunications Act of 1996:
http://www.fcc.gov/ ◆

Statistical Data

Statistical data such as the United States census has been available in electronic form for a number of years. Recent technology including online access and CD-ROM have improved accessibility. Like other reference material, statistical data is available directly from its developers and from numerous third-party information vendors.

Example

The U.S. Census Bureau maintains social, demographic, and economic information for the United States. For information about the statistics and access:
http://www.census.gov/ ◆

In some cases, data is being made available in spreadsheet form for further analysis and modeling. For example, using the Internet, agricultural economic statistics are available from a university library in the form of Lotus 1-2-3™ compatible ".WKS" format spreadsheets. Researchers can copy the spreadsheet and load and analyze it on their personal computers:
gopher://mann77.mannlib.cornell.edu:70/11/data-sets

Large statistical data sets are available on other media including magnetic tape and CD-ROM. When comprehensive datasets such as market statistics are needed online, access must currently be provided within the organization, but accessibility is changing rapidly as mechanisms for charging for data access evolve on the Internet.

Bulletin Boards and Discussion Groups

Three different types of information sharing groups have evolved: (1) bulletin board systems, (2) commercial discussion groups, and (3) personal discussion groups.

1. *Bulletin board systems.* **Bulletin board systems (BBS)** are independent systems created and operated by entrepreneurs or organizations. There are thousands of private and quasi-public bulletin board systems. Many BBSs are fee-based, and many specialize in providing just a few types of information, for example, IBM-PC shareware. Most BBSs are loosely interconnected. They are also increasingly connected to the Internet.

2. *Commercial discussion groups.* These include information services and the major commercial online vendors such as CompuServe, America Online, and Prodigy. Their services are marketed to individuals for a relatively low monthly fee and hourly charge. CompuServe is one of the primary sources for technical information provided by information industry vendors. Vendors assign staff to follow Compuserve bulletin boards specific to their products, post replies, announce problem solutions, and post upgrades. The first source of technical information for many network administrators is CompuServe's discussion groups. Many vendors are moving to Web pages.

Example
The primary source of information about the many software products of Microsoft are the Microsoft forums or discussion groups. Anyone whose job involves supporting these software products can find answers and post questions to the appropriate forum. Microsoft employees monitor the forums to gain feedback and provide support. ◆

3. *Personal discussion groups.* The primary example of personal discussion groups is Usenet News. Usenet News is a collection of thousands of discussion groups made available through BBS systems, commercial online services, and the Internet. Some Usenet discussion groups lack coherence and discipline in the types of comments made and adherence to the topic of the discussion. Other groups are followed by a relatively small number

of users. It is often possible to obtain a prompt answer to an obscure technical question from someone on the other side of the world.

Search tools are available for discussion groups and bulletin boards. Many Usenet news group discussions are archived, that is, contents are permanently retained. One such archive supports full-text searching of past discussions at http://www.dejanews.com/. A user looking for information that might have been discussed in a particular news group can search its archive and retrieve relevant comments. In some newsgroups, volunteers accumulate important information and periodically post it as **FAQs (Frequently Asked Questions)**.

Bulletin boards are commonly supported within organizations. Most electronic mail systems support bulletin boards. These may be used to access and disseminate useful information within the organization.

Accessing External Data Sources

To access external data sources, users must first be connected to a data provider. Connectivity is available in many different ways including direct connections, third party access providers, and internal, organizational networks. If users are connected via the Internet, one network connection can provide them with access to a broad range of services. While most data sources and services are connected via the Internet, direct and third-party connections are alternatives.

External Connections

An information source can provide two types of connections: a direct connection or a connection via the Internet. A direct connection requires a dial-up modem call. In some cases, a long distance or "800" call is necessary, but the vendor will usually arrange a local "Point-of-Presence" (PoP). Many database vendors and the commercial online service vendors use or operate a "Value Added Network" (VAN) to provide local dial-up modem access. This form of connectivity allows the user to connect via a local number, even though the information provider's database may be distant. Most dial-up connections support high-speed modem access. In addition to dial-up connection from an individual's personal computer, an organization may provide individuals with modem-based access via a modem pool attached to a LAN, mainframe, or the internal telephone system.

Connectivity via the Internet means that the user obtains Internet access and then connects to the information source through the Internet facilities.

The rapid growth in the Internet has been accelerated in part because it has become a single point of connection to many different sources of information. Users can connect to the Internet through an individual modem or a local area network connection.

Internet Service Providers (ISP) provide a local dial-in point-of-presence. An individual may obtain modem access to all Internet services economically via an ISP. Organizations can also connect to the Internet via dial-up modems to ISPs, but often arrange for higher capacity direct (non-modem) connections to meet usage requirements. Individuals within the organization may then be authorized to use Internet services, subject to internal policies. Organizations may arrange direct connections to external information services in the same way: a connection of specified capacity direct to the service provider.

The organizational connection to the Internet or other external data source is usually distributed to departments and individuals via internal networks including LANs. An issue in connecting internal networks to the Internet is security. Organizations have concerns about allowing the Internet community access to internal computing, data, and network resources. (They also have concerns about making the Internet available to individuals.) Technologies such as Internet "firewalls" and "proxy servers" are available to reduce connectivity risk. A proxy server is an application gateway that mediates traffic between a protected, internal network and the Internet. A **firewall** is a network program that monitors all incoming and outgoing Internet connections. Only authorized connections are allowed to proceed; others are blocked. Thus, a network administrator can use the security software to allow selected users to access only specified information sources and bar all other Internet traffic.

Data Access Interfaces

The three most common methods for accessing data stored on a remote computer are Telnet, Web browsers, and FTP (File Transfer Protocol).

Telnet is a remote access program that emulates a "dumb terminal." It allows remote login to a host computer and supports character-based interaction. The user enters command words or characters to instruct the remote computer. Since Telnet software is widely available, it has been the standard for remote access for many years.

Web browers are programs that allow access to data on remote computers permitting such access. Web browsers are superior to Telnet because they have graphical interfaces and hyperlink capabilities. Data on web pages at a remote computer can be copied and files can be transferred using a file transfer protocol. Additional functions of Web browsers are explained in the next section.

FTP (File Transfer Protocol) is a widely used, simple, and reliable method for obtaining files from a remote computer. It will be explained in more detail later in the chapter.

Methods for Accessing External Information

◆ ◆

There are several methods that can be used to access data. Computers are critical to these methods. Transferring data between computers over a connecting network requires a computer to send the file, a computer to receive the file, and a communications network to perform the transmission. To make such a system work requires rules, procedures, conventions, and standards that allow users to employ the same approach with different data sources.

A communications protocol defines standards for transmitting data. These include the formatting or framing of data; error control; sequence control for the parts of a message; utilization of network resources; initiation, connection, and termination; and recovery from losses, errors, and abnormal conditions. A significant difference between protocols commonly used in communication is the technique for defining a unit of transmission (also termed "framing").

A number of standard methods for storing data and enabling external access are available, as well as proprietary methods established by some vendors. These include access protocols and methods for providing remote access through a local computer, file transfer, and combined file search and transfer. Information locations, forms, and search and access tools are evolving rapidly. This chapter provides an overview of these concepts. It includes illustrations and examples of current technology but does not describe all available methods.

Internet and World Wide Web

The **Internet** was developed as part of a United States government project by the Advanced Research Projects Agency (ARPA) to develop a network to share research results. The Internet protocol breaks each transmission into numbered packets that can be sent by different communication paths. The packets are reassembled at the receiving site. The protocol is robust in the event of failure of one or more communication paths because the missing packets can be identified and resent. The addressing structure for Internet sites was described earlier.

The **World Wide Web (WWW)** was developed to use the Internet to allow sites to provide access to multimedia data organized as pages with links to allow easy movement from a reference or term in one page to related material in other pages. A protocol was developed for transferring pages with hypertext links and multimedia. A World Wide Web address is termed a URL or Uniform Resource Locator. The URL specifications that indicate the hypertext transfer protocol and world wide web access were described earlier.

The number of Web sites and proliferation of information has resulted in a need for user-oriented tools to search Web sites and keep a directory of useful sites. These tools are termed Web browsers. Examples are Netscape and Microsoft Internet Explorer.

Web browsers link to search software. A large number of search packages (also termed search engines) are available. Although each search engine may find the same result for a user, each has characteristics that make it more appropriate in terms of finding the most relevant information. A few examples of search software available with Web browsers are Yahoo, Lycos, Magellen, Infoseek, Excite, Alta-Vista, and WebCrawler. Internet users should explore the features of the different search engines and employ the ones that provide the best results for the searches being conducted. A search service that lists a large number of search engines and index services is BRS Search available at: http://www.escape.com/~brs/search.htm

Remote Access Through a Local Computer

With a modem, a user can dial in to a computer from almost any location. Sometimes access to the desired computer requires access through another computer. This access method may be used to avoid long-distance charges, or it may be the method provided from a LAN. The long-distance situation applies when a user is distant from the remote computer and telephone charges are high or modem speed is slow. A local computer to which the user has or can get access privileges may be used to access the remote computer. Once connected to the local computer, the user works on the remote computer just as if it were accessed directly.

File Transfer

An information provider may make data available in the form of a file to be copied by anyone who has access privileges and access software. Copying a file from a remote computer often involves significant data transfer. Therefore, the transfer must be efficient.

The most common copying method is the File Transfer Protocol (FTP). FTP is built into many communication software tools and is available as a separate software package. (See Figure 8-3.)

FTP is employed to transfer data files, program files, software corrections, manuals, and a variety of other data. The transfer can be in either direction. For example, many software providers establish files that users can download with FTP in order to get software modifications. The software modifications obtained in this way are used in the same way as modifications on diskettes. In general, a user must know whether the data in the files is text data or binary coded, as this affects the options for file transfer.

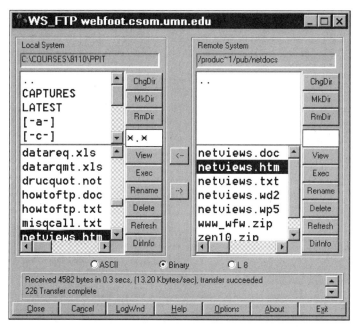

FIGURE 8-3 *Anonymous FTP supports file transfer between a local computer and a remote computer*

The most frequent use of FTP for information retrieval is known as anonymous FTP. In this convention, the operator of the FTP server (information source) establishes an account named "anonymous." Users (clients) connect to the account using "anonymous" as a user name. For security reasons, most anonymous FTP servers only permit file reading and copying. Many current versions of FTP client software and Web browsers hide technical and procedural details from their users and make anonymous FTP connections automatically. The user may use a graphical interface to specify transfer to or from a remote computer directory and a user directory.

File Search and Transfer

There are a number of methods to search for and selectively transfer data from remote files. A commonly used method that illustrates the functionality needed by users is Gopher, developed in the early 1990s at the University of Minnesota. Gopher is a client-server protocol and software for both servers and clients (World Wide Web clients can also access information on Gopher servers). With Gopher, documents and other files reside on servers on the Internet. Gopher client software presents users with a hierarchy of items and directories that appear much like a file system. The Gopher interface was designed to resemble a file system since a file system was considered to be a good model for organizing documents and services. The Gopher client differentiates directories or folders from documents. Users employ the Gopher protocol to access files stored on other computers and make selective transfer of data that can include electronic files, documents, pictures, sounds, and video clips.

Locating Data Sources

◆ ◆ ◆ ◆ ◆ ◆ ◆ ◆ ◆ ◆ ◆ ◆ ◆ ◆ ◆ ◆ ◆ ◆ ◆ ◆

The knowledge worker locating information online to some extent assumes the functions of a reference librarian. Searching productivity requires efficient use of online indexes, indexing services, and search agents. Two such sources are interactive versions of paper indexes and search tools and agents.

Online Versions of Database Indexes

Most database services provide information about their contents in an easily accessible form on the World Wide Web. In addition to accessibility, the information may be much more current in its online form than in paper indexes. An individual may use the Internet indexes to decide on the database service to access.

Examples

The DIALOG Information Retrieval Service provides descriptions of each of its databases on "Bluesheets," a loose-leaf documentation series. The Bluesheets are now available on the Web (with a blue background!) at:
http://www.dialog.com/dialog/databases/netscape1.1/bls.html ◆

Information Handling Services (IHS) specializes in providing its customers with on-site and online access to detailed technical information from government and industry, including vendor catalogs, electronic components data, and U.S. military specifications and standards. IHS has a system of collecting, cataloging, collating, indexing, and cross-referencing documents into their information retrieval system. Information about these services is available at:
http://www.ihs.com/ ◆

Search Tools and Search Agents

Indexing and search tools and agents form a category of database locating tools. This class of tools generally has two components: (1) a search and index method that compiles indexes of directories, folders, and documents based on titles, comments, and perhaps even on contents, and (2) a search tool that responds to a query with a list of descriptors. These search tools usually do not differentiate between databases and database contents, leaving it to the user to select sources from query results.

Examples

Wide Area Information Servers (WAIS) was developed as a project of Thinking Machines, Apple Computer, Dow Jones, and KPMG Peat Marwick. Client applications request information using keywords. Servers search a full text index of databases, returning the identifiers of the most likely databases to contain the requested information. The user may then search those databases for the desired information. WAIS will return a list of documents (ordered by relevance) that match the search arguments. The client may then request the server to send a copy of any of the documents found. The WAIS system was designed to support infrequent users, such as executives relatively untrained in search techniques. WAIS uses English language queries augmented with relevance feedback. Versions of WAIS software are available free and may be used in private databases as well as public systems.
(http://www.wais.com/) ♦

"Veronica" is the name of a resource-discovery system providing access to information resources held on most of the world's Gopher servers. In addition to native Gopher data, Veronica includes references to many resources provided by other types of information servers, such as WWW servers, Usenet archives, and Telnet-accessible information services. Veronica queries are keyword-in-title searches. ♦

Archie is a system or tool for gathering, indexing and serving program file information on the Internet. The current version provides a collection of filenames found at anonymous FTP sites, as well as a smaller collection of text descriptions for software, data and other information found at anonymous FTP archives. Users run a client program to connect to an Archie server and issue search commands to find information in an Archie database. In the case of a file, this information can then be used to retrieve the file directly from the archive site using the "FTP" command. Archie is most useful for locating sources of software and other files where the file name is known or can be partly guessed. ♦

Yahoo! is an Internet search service that collects and indexes World Wide Web information. Yahoo!'s search engine enables users to find information about topics of interest through simple keyword queries. Searches can be restricted to titles, Uniform Resource Locator (URL) addresses, or comments. Search results are returned along with their locations within Yahoo!'s hierarchical index.
(http://www.yahoo.com/) ♦

Searching Databases

Several approaches are used to locate specific items within databases. One of the most common approaches uses tagged fields with Boolean search expressions.

Another common approach uses Boolean search expressions, but does not require or allow the user to identify specific fields. An even simpler approach does not require a Boolean logic expression, but instead applies default assumptions about the structure of a query. A more technical approach using complex patterns called "regular expressions" is available in some cases. Many database search engines use some form of "proximity searching," wherein "hits" are weighted according to the patterns of occurrence of search terms in the target database. In some engines, proximity searching and Boolean logic expressions can be combined, allowing very precise expressions.

Perhaps the simplest form of database searching uses some form of word matching in tagged or specified fields. Many library and other reference systems provide a searching mechanism that works in this way. To search, the user must identify a data field and a word, partial word, or words to find required data. For example, the NOTIS system in use by many research libraries allows searches of the form

author=davis, g*

which means, "search for references authored by G Davis" (the asterisk prompts the system to search for any word beginning with the letter "g"). While simple and easy to learn, such searches may produce a high proportion of irrelevant data. In the example, a searcher who did not know Davis's full first name might need to be more selective. To do so, the researcher could create a more refined second query after examining the results of the first:

author=davis, gordon

Boolean logic is added to most search languages. It allows search terms to be combined to select more precisely using "and" or "or." For example, under the NOTIS system, one might search for

author=davis, g **and** subject=productivity

to look for just that work of g. davis classified under the subject of "productivity." Boolean expressions of arbitrary complexity can be built from strings of terms; parentheses are used to prevent ambiguities of interpretation. In addition to Boolean logic, some systems have extended the search argument to include the concept of proximity. Proximity, or nearness, is especially important in searching abstracts or full text. The search syntax allows the user to specify that two search terms must occur in the same sentence or paragraph. For example:

keyword=productivity **near** technology

Such systems often add a special character to help match alternative forms of a word, so that the previous example might become:

keyword=productiv? **near** techno?

Since the contents of each database interact with each search expression, the search process usually requires both trial and error and familiarity with the contents of each database. A search expression that finds far too many references in one database may find far too few in another.

◆xamples

The Wide Area Information Service described previously illustrates a relevance approach to searching. Instead of requiring a complex search expression, WAIS accepts keywords and returns the references it has found sorted by a "relevance score." WAIS presents its list of "hits" and allows the user to select any one for further inspection. It also allows a user to identify and return a subset of items found as feedback to a repeated search process. ◆

Infoseek Search is a widely used World Wide Web tool that appears on the Netscape search page. It has its own unique search syntax, with rules such as those illustrated in Figure 8-4. ◆

As indicated in Figure 8-4, there are many search tools available with new search services being introduced continuously. Before using these tools, users should ask themselves two key questions: (1) what content do they cover? (or what do they index) and (2) what search syntax do they use? For example, one search engine may index HTML titles and URLs, while another may index partial or even full contents. Most casual users of these powerful tools use only the default search criteria. When a list of search terms is provided by a user, search engines tend to treat each word as a separate term and assume an implicit "and" between each.

◆cquiring Data

◆ ◆ ◆ ◆ ◆ ◆ ◆ ◆ ◆ ◆ ◆ ◆ ◆ ◆ ◆ ◆ ◆ ◆ ◆ ◆

A number of different forms of delivery are available for external information. Files may be downloaded via FTP. In some cases, a search will identify items that may already be available locally. Many libraries, database vendors, and other services provide delivery of full-text or photocopy documents. Often documents may be ordered online for delivery by an express mail service.

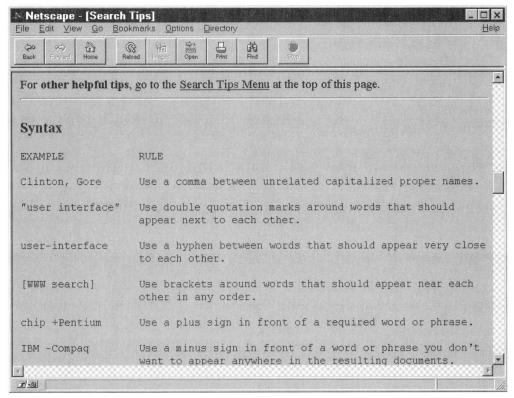

FIGURE 8-4   *Search syntax example from Infoseek*

Example

One of the authors subscribes to far more journals than he has time to read. Sometimes they pile up in a backlog and there is never enough time to catch up. A search service, Current Contents, provides the title pages of selected journals via e-mail. It is much more efficient to scan just the title pages in this consistent, electronic format than it is to leaf through the physical journals. Therefore, the backlog of journals is simply filed and accessed only when the Current Contents title and abstract suggest an article will be worthwhile.   ◆

Planning and Stopping Rules in External Access

◆ ◆ ◆ ◆ ◆ ◆ ◆ ◆ ◆ ◆ ◆ ◆ ◆ ◆ ◆ ◆ ◆ ◆ ◆

Knowledge work productivity principles apply in processes for finding and retrieving external data. The rich potential of external data mean that a knowledge worker can increase search time almost without limit. High productivity is achieved if search time is matched with requirements for completeness and cost of added search does not exceed the marginal improvement.

The nature of the problem is indicated by the fact that a short search period may find half of all useful data. To achieve 80 percent of useful data may require double the time required for 50 percent. To reach 90 percent may mean an additional doubling. Doubling again may achieve only 95 percent. In other words, using one search unit as the base measure (for example, 30 minutes), 80 percent will require 60 minutes, 90 percent will require 120 minutes, and 95 percent will require 240 minutes. The point is not the accuracy of these estimators, but the principle that each added increment of completeness costs more than the previous. The question is when to stop. The **stopping rule** (which defines the extent of search) should be planned based on requirements. The rules can be based on limits to search time, number of sources, number of references or data sets, or useful data increments achieved with each added source that is searched. The requirements should be decided on before search processes are begun (or after an initial limited, exploratory search).

Planning has been described as a knowledge work bargain. Time spent in planning is repaid by reduced task time and improved effectiveness. Planning has a high payoff in external search. The planning process clarifies requirements, and defines the extent of search and the search strategy. The search strategy defines the most likely sources and the order of search. The search strategy may be modified during the search as sources are found and examined, but the initial planning establishes an efficient and effective process.

Summary

◊ ◊ ◊ ◊ ◊ ◊ ◊ ◊ ◊ ◊ ◊ ◊ ◊ ◊ ◊ ◊ ◊ ◊ ◊

◊ External data is that which is not delivered or provided by the organization, but must be located and accessed by the individual knowledge worker. There are six categories of external data: transient data, published literature, organizational and individual data, government data, statistical data, and discussion groups and bulletin boards. The individual may need to access data from one or more of these categories to complete a job-specific task or to build knowledge.

◊ External data access requires connectivity. The individual may be connected to a data source directly or via a third party provider using a dial-up modem. The individual may also be connected via some form of gateway from the organization or department LAN. External data sources are often directly accessible via the Internet.

◊ One of the most difficult aspects of external data access is knowing where to locate sources of data. A number of search tools are available, both directly or through commercial service vendors and via the Internet. Many agents, robots, or "Web crawlers" are in operation on the Internet, compiling indexes accessible to Web browser or other client tools.

◊ The search model of indexes, guides, and search tools is an extension of the reference library approach. Database searching can be more specific after users locate appropriate databases. There are a number of different approaches to locating specific items. In addition to Boolean logic search arguments, some tools feature proximity searches, relevance rankings, or other schemes. Data may be acquired in a number of different ways, including electronic delivery of printed output from a vendor.

◊ A search for external data is knowledge work that benefits from planning and stopping rules. Planning clarifies requirements, develops an initial search strategy, and defines stopping rules. Stopping rules explicitly describe the extent of the search.

EXERCISES

1. Look at a few examples of Web pages. Print out a page and explain the contents of the pages.
   a. Louvre museum: http://www.louvre.fr/. Access this site to find out about the Louvre, its hours, and admission cost.
   b. Social Security Administration: http://www.ssa.gov/
   c. Edgar database. Look up most recent 10Q (quarterly report) for 3M: http://www.sec.gov/
   d. Internal Revenue Service (Note: forms may be downloaded using Acrobat):
      http://www.irs.ustreas.gov/prod/
   e. Access archives of CNN's daily news almanac for an item that is of interest to you:
      http://www.cnn.com/almanac/daily/index.html

2. Explore the following Web pages. Turn in one example of data you found interesting. Be sure the source is identified.
   a. Search Usenet News using Reference.com at http://www.reference.com/
   b. Explore facilities offered by DIALOG:
      http://www.dialog.com/dialog/dialog1.html
   c. Explore availability of photos of the earth's surface:
      http://edcwww.cr.usgs.gov/eros-home.html

d. Explore economic census data:
http://www.census.gov/ftp/pub/epcd/www/busstat.html

e. Explore capabilities of Yahoo: http://www.yahoo.com/

f. Explore WAIS: http://www.wais.com/

3. Choose a narrow topic of interest to use in this exercise, then formulate queries.

a. Use a WWW search engine—print a few examples of results.

b. Use the search facility to locate information on a technology of interest to you. Use the IBM home page: http://www.ibm.com/. Look at the information on the IBM search methodology.

c. Use a Gopher search mechanism. Print a few examples of results.

d. Use an electronic search of books and articles. Print a few examples of results.

4. You are asked to explore tour ideas for a tour to be used as a reward for salespersons and their spouses. Make the assignment more specific as to type of trip and location and then define a search strategy. You are asked to give some ideas and then explain how you will proceed (with the Web) when the management selects one idea. You may want to explore a few travel sites before defining your strategy. A few examples to start the search are:

a. http://www.travelocity.com

b. http://www.fodors.com

c. http://www.royalcaribbean.com

d. http://www.cntraveler.com

5. Your company authorizes you to purchase a laptop computer (and be reimbursed). They expect you to do some comparison shopping. Develop specifications for memory, modem, speed, and hard drive. You should use the Web browser search tools. Look at sites for vendors, such as IBM, Toshiba, and Dell, and shopping sites such as
http://www.NotebookMall.com/ and http://www.notebook-inc.com/

6. Web browsers enable users to create a file of frequently used web site addresses (URLs). These files are referred to as "bookmarks." However, users who continually add new addresses to their **Bookmarks** file may create a file so large that it becomes difficult to search. If an individual is a frequent user of the Internet, the URLs should be organized as a hierarchy of files or folders in order to reduce search time. Create a folder structure for the bookmarks with your web browser. Store two or more bookmarks in each folder. Print out the list of folders and bookmarks. Explain why the file structure you selected fits your use of the Internet.

7. The Internet can be used to transfer data internally and also to share data with selected external parties. For example, a person whose responsibilities

include visits to many of the offices and plants of a company might create a web page to display an itinerary and an explanation of the objectives of the visit. The web pages might also include a photo and vita. Creating web pages has been simplified by packages that convert a word processing document to HTML format. Create a short web page for such a visit using the Internet publishing features of your word processor. (Optional: Add a photo and short resume.) Place documents in files to be downloaded and printed at remote locations.

8. Explore some Internet features discussed in the chapter.
   a. Access a bulletin board and analyze the last 50 messages.
   b. Get information and look at photos of the authors of the text. Access http://www.csom.umn.edu/ and select faculty. Then select Information and Decision Sciences. Select Davis or Naumann in the faculty list. What are the current interests of these faculty members?
   c. Join a forum about a topic of interest to you. Report on the messages exchanged by forum members during a one week period.

9. Explore the home shopping features of the web. Use the search facilities of the browser to find several shopping sites. Select three sites and compare their features.

10. Find people you know who have moved. Use the search facilities of the browser to find web sites for the search. Two starting possibilities are

    http://www.yahoo.com/search/people/
    http://www.switchboard.com/

11. Find sources of current news. Compare three sources for coverage and ease of access. Also explore the availability of comic strips in http://www.unitedmedia.com/comics/ Print a favorite strip from those available.

12. If you have had experience with the Web, think of the task of training a new person to do the kind of Web searches you do and to do them efficiently (in terms of time) and effectively (in terms of relevant data). The report from this assignment should be in good form to share with others.
    a. Provide a short description of the search task you perform.
    b. Define search strategies with tips, guidelines, and stopping rules.
    c. Give a specific example with desired results, sites, reasons for selection, and stopping rules.

13. Create a competition among small groups of three or four people. Have each group list four topics on which another group is to find information from the Web. Exchange the lists. Score each group on the number of relevant items of information they found, with extra points for interesting sites.

Designing and Implementing Productivity Enhancements

◆ ◆ ◆ ◆ ◆ ◆ ◆ ◆ ◆ ◆ ◆ ◆ ◆

Part 3 (Chapters 9 through 13) focuses on achieving individual productivity with application software, i.e., individual and group software supporting tasks and activities. The material in these chapters is based on the following propositions:

1. Software packages (generalized and specialized) are the most cost effective method of obtaining software functionality to support individual tasks and activities. They include many valuable productivity enhancements that have not been realized because the features are not understood or their productivity implications are not recognized.

2. Software packages feature many options that allow them to be customized to fit the preferences and work habits of individuals and groups of users to make package use more productive.

3. Software packages can be supplemented by procedures (macros) that extend package functionality and enhance productivity.

4. Custom programs can provide unique functionality for more productive knowledge work. Custom programs can be written as macros within a software package or developed as free-standing applications.

5. Complete systems or applications are usually implemented with database functionality at their core. Understanding database software helps make more effective use of systems and applications. Complete custom applications may be implemented around database software packages.

6. There are trade-offs involving cost, time, and risk in selecting options, developing macros to automate sets of operations, and developing custom programs and applications. A significant personal investment is needed to achieve the knowledge necessary to obtain these productivity benefits.

Given the availability of software packages for knowledge worker use and the possibility of custom development, personal and group productivity with software applications requires knowledge and elementary expertise in five areas:

1. *Using productivity features generally found in both generalized and specialized packages.* Examples include common

menu items and overall menu organizations; search and edit tools; cut, copy, and paste tools; and application linking and embedding features. Part 3 introduces many of these features, but to obtain the full benefit, individuals must explore and experiment with package features.

2. *Customizing options to make software package use more productive.* The text explains the logic and purpose of options and suggests many that may be useful. Full benefit for productivity comes from additional exploration and experimentation.

3. *Extending the functionality of software packages by using macros that automate simple sequences of actions and macros that provide full program logic.* The text explains how to record macros and how to add control logic. A strategy for personal productivity will include development of skills at both macro recording and macro editing.

4. *Using database software packages for record-keeping.* Database software packages include many systems-building features that can automate tedious and

error-prone activities. Managing individual data requires an understanding of the relational database model and of the facilities and features provided with these packages.

5. *Customizing programs developed in a programming environment.* Part 3 emphasizes the role of graphical user interfaces (GUIs) and implementing applications that build on its features. Some of the important features of GUIs can be implemented in user-written macros. For most users, custom programming will be limited to simple programs, GUIs, and macros with simple control structures. Part 3 introduces custom programming and graphical user interfaces although it does not provide in-depth instruction in custom application development.

The objectives of the five chapters in Part 3 are as follows:

Chapter 9, Selecting an Approach to Computer Solutions This chapter surveys the alternative approaches and methods to achieve productivity with software. It describes two methods in detail: selecting package options and recording macros.

Option facilities allow users to select productivity enhancements provided by the package and to fit the package to a specific work environment. Recording macros is essentially "programming by doing" and is, therefore, valuable in automating sequences of actions.

Chapter 10, Developing a Simple Program
This chapter introduces programming concepts and program control structures. The emphasis is on essential program structure. The chapter explains how programming principles can be used to develop and refine macro programs with decision logic and repetition capabilities. It focuses on modular design and implementation in macros and programming and introduces the concepts of event-driven and object-oriented application development.

Chapter 11, Designing and Implementing a User Interface
This chapter focuses on a programming environment for user-developed programs. It covers the design and construction of user interfaces for event-driven applications and explains how user interface functions can be developed in macros as well as in free-standing programs. It also describes the use of interface objects and their properties and interactions, and explains how these concepts are applicable to many different software packages used on personal computers.

Chapter 12, Developing Solutions Using Database Software
This chapter focuses on database software package capabilities and features and describes these packages in the context of record-keeping applications. It covers the use and customizing of standard package features, as well as techniques for database application design and implementation.

Chapter 13, Evaluating, Refining, and Integrating Applications
This chapter presents ways to refine applications to make them more complete and robust. It also describes ways to enhance and interconnect applications. It explains that as applications grow to become part of the work environment, they must evolve toward increasing reliability and flexibility. It also illustrates how these concepts and techniques begin to bridge the differences between personal applications and more broadly used departmental and organizational systems.

The productivity enhancement approaches presented in Part 3 increase in complexity (with increasing cost, time, and risk) by moving from simple option selection and macro recording to programming and using a programming environment for graphical user interfaces. The database software chapter extends the concepts of accessing structured corporate data presented in Chapter 7 to use of a database management package to develop and manage individual or small group databases. Part 3 ends with a discussion of methods that can be used to incorporate more robust and error-free features into software programs and to extend applications with more advanced features.

In each chapter, the materials presented provide a conceptual framework for productive use of packages and programming environments. The emphasis is on developing a long-term understanding of how productivity enhancements are designed and implemented. The exercises provide practical learning by applying the concepts within packages and environments that are currently available. The solutions provided are all within the context of personal computers and interactive operations.

Selecting an Approach to Computer Solutions

OBJECTIVES

After completing this chapter, you should be able to:

◆ Explain the range of alternatives for implementing useful, productive computer solutions for knowledge workers.

◆ Describe factors to be considered in choosing an alternative.

◆ Survey the process of custom application development.

◆ Explain customizing via package options and preference settings.

◆ Describe customizing via macro recording and how this option can be used to automate user procedures and achieve improved productivity.

◆ Explain the use of Help facilities.

KEY TERMS AND CONCEPTS

This chapter introduces the following key terms and concepts, listed in the order in which they appear:

custom application
  development
macro facilities
macro recording
systems development life
  cycle (SDLC)
stakeholder

prototype
requirements analysis
options and preferences
menu
tool bar
icon

button
keystroke
macro
macro editing
hypertext links
"just-in-time" learning

The most fundamental decision in obtaining a computer solution to support knowledge work activities is whether to "make" or "buy" application software. The "make" decision for application software is to do custom development of an application; the "buy" decision is to purchase an application software package. Custom development involves defining requirements and developing the application to meet user requirements. Using an application package involves some compromises relative to user requirements, since the package is designed to fit many different users and may not be an exact fit for any one user. However, software packages typically provide users with options that can be tailored and customized to meet individual requirements and preferences. These options include functions that influence individual productivity.

This chapter surveys three alternative approaches to productive computer solutions when requirements suggest a computer application (see Figure 9-1): (1) custom development of software applications, (2) customizing by selecting package options, and (3) customizing with macros. The choice among the alternatives should reflect functionality, productivity gain, implementation cost, and risk factors.

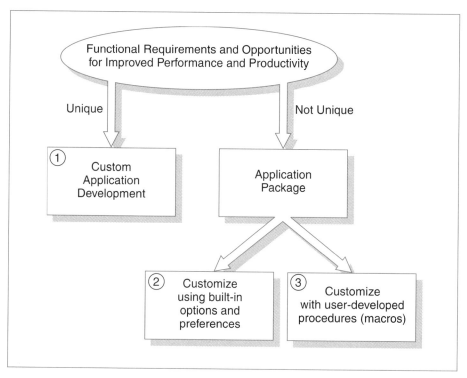

FIGURE 9-1 *Three alternative approaches to productive computer solutions*

◆lternative Approaches to Software Solutions for Knowledge Work

◆ ◆

Software applications can help knowledge workers improve productivity and enhance the scope, quality, and timeliness of their work. The selection of software is, therefore, an important individual and organizational decision. Assuming that a software solution is appropriate, there are three major alternative approaches to productive software solutions for knowledge work: (1) custom application development, (2) package software customized with built-in options and preferences, and (3) package software customized by user-written procedures.

Custom Application Development

A cost/effective software solution for individual users will generally be a software package rather than custom development. However, in some situations, requirements may be so unique that no software package can adequately meet user needs. **Custom application development** involves defining requirements, developing and testing programs, developing user procedures, and implementing the application. Custom applications require on-going effort (maintenance) in order to correct errors and add enhancements.

Custom development is more costly and more time consuming than acquisition of software packages, but unique requirements can be met. Although custom application development is generally not justified for a single individual, it may be worthwhile when a number of knowledge workers in an organization have the same unique requirements.

Customizing Packages Using Options

Both generalized and specialized software packages usually include a wide range of built-in options that allow users to customize the packages to reflect their tasks and activities, working environment, or other preferences.

Vendors of generalized software packages attempt to meet the needs of the broadest possible range of users. Therefore, they select default settings of options that meet most common basic needs. Since these settings are necessarily a compromise, they are not likely to provide the most effective setup for individual knowledge workers. Consequently, customizing options should be considered as possible productivity enhancements each time a new package is installed or when a package is used for a new purpose.

In many organizations, sets of options have been specified for organizational purposes. For example, a subset of available fonts may have been specified for a spreadsheet processor, or automatic backup may have been specified for a word processor. Since there is a trend toward central control of some software package options, individual users may be denied access to some options in the interests of organizational standards. In general, such constraints are appropriate to maintain organizational standards and to promote communication among individuals.

Customizing options are normally found under "preferences," "options," or "setup." Even though only a few options may be used, users should be aware of the features available to customize a software package to improve productivity. Figure 9-2 illustrates a screen for selecting some options with a word processing package. The types of options are explained later in this chapter.

Customizing Packages Using Macro Facilities

Additional customization may involve automating activities and adding functions. This level of customization employs macro programming facilities provided by the software package. **Macro facilities** help users develop routines or programs to automate sequences of activities and to add functions (sequences

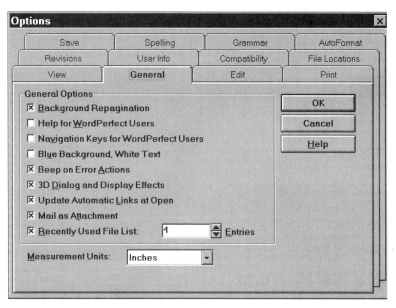

FIGURE 9-2   *A set of pages, each with many choices, for user-selectable options (Microsoft Word 6.1)*

of activities controlled by programmed logic). By supporting the use and development of these routines, macro facilities add programming capabilities to the standard package capabilities.

Two approaches can be used to develop a macro: macro recording and macro programming (see Figure 9-3). This chapter emphasizes automating routine, repetitive tasks with macro recording. More complex macros requiring programming logic will be covered in Chapter 10.

Macro recording is a method of programming by doing: the user performs the sequence of activities to be automated, and the macro facilities record the steps as the instructions of a program. For example, a user may perform a set of spreadsheet operations to create a heading, set fonts, define borders, and establish row and column headings. If these same operations are to be repeated frequently, they may be automated using a recording macro. The user defines a name for the macro, turns on the macro recorder, performs the activities to be automated, and turns off the recorder, which prompts the system to ask where to store the macro. Subsequently, when the recorded macro is "replayed," the activities are performed in exactly the same way. The advantage of macro recording is that the user need not understand the macro programming language since programming consists of performing the activities. The main disadvantage of macro recording is that only a sequence of actions may be programmed; no program logic to select from alternatives can be recorded. Because it is a fairly easy approach to automating a sequence of

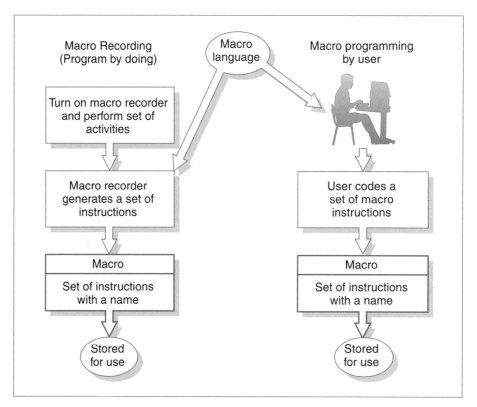

FIGURE 9-3 *Two approaches to macro programming*

actions, macro recording is an important capability for improving productivity in using computer software. (Macro recording procedures are explained in more detail later in this chapter.)

The second approach to macro development is writing macro program instructions. Macro instruction languages resemble conventional procedural programming languages designed to write the procedures the computer is to execute and the decision logic that governs the execution of the computer actions. A generalized software package may have a macro language that is unique to it, or it may employ a macro language used across a suite of generalized packages. (Writing macros with decision logic is explained in Chapter 10.)

A macro is stored as part of the software package used to create it. When users work with the package, they can specify the use of a macro by entering its name and selecting "Run" from the list of options. The macro is retrieved by the package and run. Running (often termed "playing") consists of executing the set of instructions stored in the macro (see Figure 9-4).

Macros are computer programs; however, they tend to be short and limited in scope. Since macros are developed and executed within a software package, they will not work without the package. Although most macros tend to be

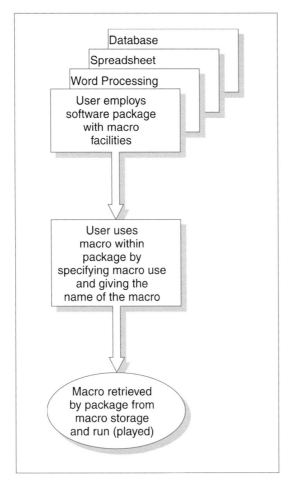

FIGURE 9-4 *Running a macro*

short, many large, complex applications have been developed using a macro language. Spreadsheet macros have been used for complex applications based on spreadsheet processes. In the case of database packages, the macro language is designed as a language for application development that uses the facilities of the database package for data storage and retrieval.

Many software packages include a set of prewritten macros for common functions. For instance, a word processing package may include a macro that displays a common memo format or performs operations such as printing envelopes.

Example

A widely used word processing package has a macro to print an envelope. It consists of several hundred statements organized into a number of separate subprograms. It allows users to select among numerous options for fonts, return addresses, and postal bar codes. ◆

In searching for productivity enhancements, users should examine the pre-written macros available with the software package. Table 9-1 lists some examples of macros available in WordPerfect 6.1 and 7.0.

Prewritten macros are not limited to those included with the packages. Independent software vendors often offer macros for widely used packages. User groups share macros, and magazines for users of specific packages include additional macros. For example, an issue of a magazine for a popular word processing package included macros to create an organization chart, change underlined text to italic, and copy text from an address database to envelopes.

Selecting Among Productivity Alternatives

◆ ◆

The previous section presented three alternatives for obtaining customized software: custom application development, customizing with options, and customizing with macros. Selecting among these alternatives involves four concepts related to the cost and value of software: (1) functionality improvement, (2) productivity gain, (3) implementation cost, and (4) implementation risk (see Figure 9-5). These concepts (introduced in Chapter 2) are applied in this section to selecting among productivity alternatives.

Table 9-1 Examples of Macros Available in WordPerfect 6.1 and 7.0	
ABBREV	Allows users to create and expand abbreviations
ENDFOOT	Converts endnotes to footnotes
EXPNDALL	Expands all abbreviations
FILESTMP	Places file name (including directory path) as part of a header or footer
FOOTEND	Converts footnotes to endnotes
READFILE	Reads a text file with voice output (requires voice output hardware)
REVERSE	Creates white text on black background or other colors
WATERMRK	Helps users create a watermark

Analysis factor \ Alternatives	Custom application	Application package with options	Application package customized with macros
Functionality	Can be best	Good	Better
Productivity effect	Can be best	Good	Better
Implementation cost	Highest	Lowest	Low
Implementation risk	Highest	Lowest	Low

FIGURE 9-5 *Summary of analysis factors for three custom options*

Functionality Improvement

One fundamental objective of applying information technology to knowledge work is to increase work effectiveness. The scope, quality, and timeliness of work can be improved by new functions or by extending the capabilities of existing functions. Information technology provides functionality to achieve task results that are infeasible or impossible without it. The potential to include additional information, to analyze it more thoroughly, to present it more clearly, and to include more current information are important to both organizations and individuals.

A characteristic of information technology is that improvements or additions to functionality are frequently obtained in generalized software packages with very little added cost. For example, when data items have already been imported, validated, and stored in a spreadsheet, performing more computations for analysis may return great value for low cost. Functionality of "what-if" modeling and presentation graphics may be included in a spreadsheet analysis with relatively little cost.

Some added functionality can be obtained through package options, but these are often focused on ease of use and appearance of results. Macro programming is effective in extending the functionality of a package. Well-designed macros may be reused to increase productivity in multiple applications. For example, a spreadsheet macro may be reused to provide additional functionality for all spreadsheets. However, if there are many unique requirements, a custom program may achieve greater functionality than a macro because it is not constrained by package context (the limitations of a containing package).

Productivity Gain

Another basic premise of individual computer use is that information technology can be used to improve human productivity by improving work efficiency. Two productivity features of software solutions for knowledge work are providing structure for work and automating activities.

Since structuring activities for knowledge work tasks and designing appropriate output formats requires significant human effort, software solutions that provide task structure can reduce human effort and allow attentional resources to be focused on analysis, decision making, and content. Structuring is evidenced in such forms as layouts, input specifications, input validation procedures, templates for performing activities, menus for selecting options, and output formatting.

◖Example

A tax program has alternative input procedures: one allows direct entry onto facsimiles of the tax forms, and the other uses a structured "assistant" to ask a sequence of questions. The tax assistant feature provides structure by the form, sequence, and content of the questions asked. This structuring feature allows the tax preparer to efficiently gather only the relevant information. ◆

Most knowledge work tasks involve numerous repeated activities. Many of these are clerical support activities that are necessary, but have low added value in terms of applying expertise to the task. Many of these activities can be automated by simple alternatives such as programmed procedures, data retrieval (instead of data entry), and anticipating inputs.

◖Example

A spreadsheet developed to analyze product defect trends requires entry of several data items. A macro automates the classification of defects during data entry via a set of questions used to arrive at the classification. The macro eliminates the need to look up the criteria for classifying each data item before adding it to the spreadsheet. This speeds the task and reduces the likelihood of data input errors. ◆

Achieving the goals of functionality and productivity from software requires a division of labor between humans and computer support. The computer should be used, insofar as possible, to reduce or eliminate activities that are routine, boring, error prone, or redundant. Human attention should be used for activities involving judgment, learning, creativity, pattern recognition, and logic. Productivity gains from choosing the best alternative reduce operating time and improve individual work style.

Implementation Cost

Software implementation costs include acquisition, customizing, and learning costs. The acquisition cost of custom software is the cost of development. A custom solution requires a thorough understanding of capabilities, recognition of needs or opportunities, and an implementation cycle. Developing custom software always takes longer and costs more than adopting a generalized software package.

The acquisition cost of a generalized software package is insignificant compared to the training cost involved in learning to apply it effectively. Training costs can be managed by careful planning and staging, but the time required to learn the new software must be considered in relation to the expected value from increased functionality. False economies are often applied to learning. A package may be selected for its advanced capabilities, but training is often terminated after only the basics have been introduced. Consequently, the added values are never obtained because the advanced capabilities are not applied.

The primary cost of customizing is time. In order to customize a package, the user requires time to be trained and to explore the package to learn what options are available. Additional time may be necessary to investigate these alternatives. Once the training and learning hurdle for a package has been passed, advanced capabilities (such as macro recording) make it possible to add significant functionality with relatively low effort. Direct programming of macros adds to the time and, therefore, the cost of customization.

Risk Factors

Customizing by selecting options is low risk. It takes time, but the alternatives are well specified, and errors in specification are quickly detected. Extending the functionality of packaged software by creating macros is more risky because of the possibility of incorporating errors that may not be easily detected. Since macro languages are programming languages, a broader range of errors is possible. A macro may contain errors of syntax, data, and programming logic. As macros increase in size and complexity, the effects of some of these types of errors may be subtle and difficult to detect.

Because macro languages allow solutions of high complexity, there is also some risk of attempting to solve a problem that, in the end, proves to be too difficult, resulting in lost time and effort. However, macro programming carries much lower risk than custom programming because the structure and basic functionality is already in place.

The risks associated with custom programming in terms of non-completion or excessive cost are much greater than with customizing packages or developing macros. There is also a greater risk that the solution will not be what was wanted or expected. This risk is compounded when multiple individuals are involved because of the likelihood of conflicting expectations and communication failures.

Custom Application Development

◆ ◆

This section surveys issues in developing custom applications and describes the development cycle employed in system development by information system professionals. It also describes the processes for identifying and documenting application requirements and contrasts large system requirements methods with methods appropriate to user-developed, individual systems.

Having identified application requirements, a user should not proceed to custom development until existing software packages and customizing of packages has proven unsatisfactory. (Subsequent chapters explain the processes for implementing custom solutions.)

System Development Life Cycle (SDLC)

The **systems development life cycle (SDLC)**—a logical sequence of processes for system development—begins with eliciting requirements based on a perceived need, problem, or opportunity. Requirements are documented and analyzed using representations (such as diagrams, charts, tables, lists, mockups of forms and reports, and narratives) that capture essential information. These representations are used to communicate among the various stakeholders for the application and to obtain feedback to refine the requirements and check them for completeness, consistency, and correctness. **Stakeholders** are those who have an interest in the application as users, users of outputs, providers of inputs, or providers of development funds.

Once requirements have been defined, the design process generates alternative designs. A tentative design is selected and documented using a representation that describes the system. The selected design is evaluated against requirements and checked for omissions, inconsistencies, and contradictions. Variations of the preferred alternative are also investigated to assure that the selected alternative best meets the requirements.

When a design has been selected, the implementation process begins. Implementation involves producing the desired system and developing documentation and training materials. It involves tests to assure that requirements have been met. The resulting operational system is installed. During the operational lifetime of an application system, system maintenance procedures are required to provide modifications and enhancements.

Figure 9-6 illustrates an idealized version of systems development life cycle phases (from feasibility assessment to operation and maintenance) via a high-level outline. In reality, these phases overlap and are incomplete. For instance, missing requirements may not be noticed until late in the implementation or

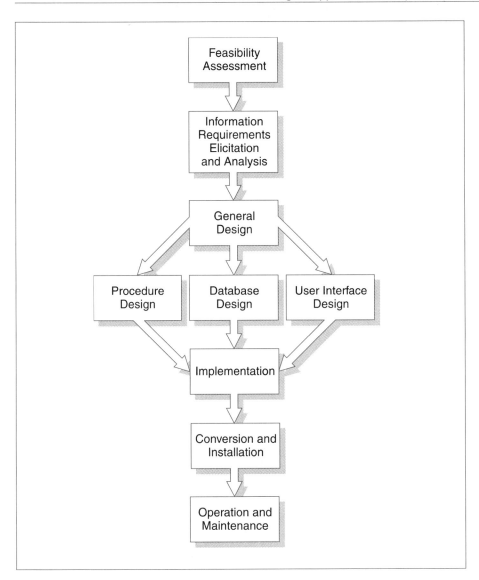

FIGURE 9-6   *The Systems Devlopment Life Cycle (SDLC)*

testing phase. Application prototypes may be developed to help elicit requirements. Often, existing application packages are the basis for requirements determination. In such cases, the requirements questions focus on needs or wants not covered in the package. Applications may at first meet only part of the total requirements, and several versions may be required to produce the desired results.

The sequential approach from requirements analysis and design installation works well if the stakeholders know their requirements and can describe them adequately. However, it is often not possible to define requirements correctly and completely in advance, since full understanding of the way tasks and activities interact with the system comes through use of the application. During this process, new requirements emerge and initial requirements evolve and change. Therefore, many systems development approaches incorporate various methods to improve the user's ability to formulate correct and complete requirements during the early phases of requirements elicitation and analysis. One important method is to provide for several iterations of the required steps. Another method involves the use of **prototypes** which enable users to visualize the actual systems before they are complete.

A prototype is a partially completed system that contains the essential elements from the user's perspective. Users can operate the prototype to see if the inputs and outputs are clear, complete, and meet requirements. Prototypes are incomplete by definition and usually must be replaced in the final system.

Application Requirements

Chapter 5 provided a series of questions designed to draw out an individual's information requirements. These requirements were broad and covered the entire scope of individual tasks. This section focuses on the specific, detailed requirements for individual applications. Asking an individual to specify requirements for a new application is likely to result in a combination of narratives, lists, sketches, and simple drawings. These provide a starting point, but in most cases they are incomplete and include parts that are incorrect and inconsistent.

A requirements analysis process organizes the requirements and represents them in a way that helps identify omissions, inconsistencies, and errors. The representation also aids design work. A formal, professional **requirements analysis** usually employs one or more formal methods and tools to represent and model three types of requirements:

1. *Process flow requirements* describe the flow of data and activities from input through processing and output.
2. *Data requirements* define and model the data used in inputs, files, and outputs.
3. *System behavior requirements* define performance, resource, control, and timing specifications.

Formal methods for representation are very useful in large, complex systems or in systems involving many stakeholders. The three types of requirements also exist in individual systems, but they may be represented in a much less formal manner.

Following is a simple approach for analyzing individual system application requirements, as illustrated in Figure 9-7:

1. *Describe processes with sentences.* Write (and rewrite) statements that describe the processes the application system is to perform. Use words that identify inputs, processes, and outputs. Where needed, amplify process descriptions for clarification.

2. *Mark sentences to identify processes and data.* Identify the processes (usually verbs) and data (usually nouns). Use some notation (such as underlining or highlighting text with colored pens). Create a list of processes with inputs and outputs for each. Identify data and data structures (organized sets of data).

3. *Sketch layouts of screens and documents.* Sketch the documents or screens to be employed for both input and output.

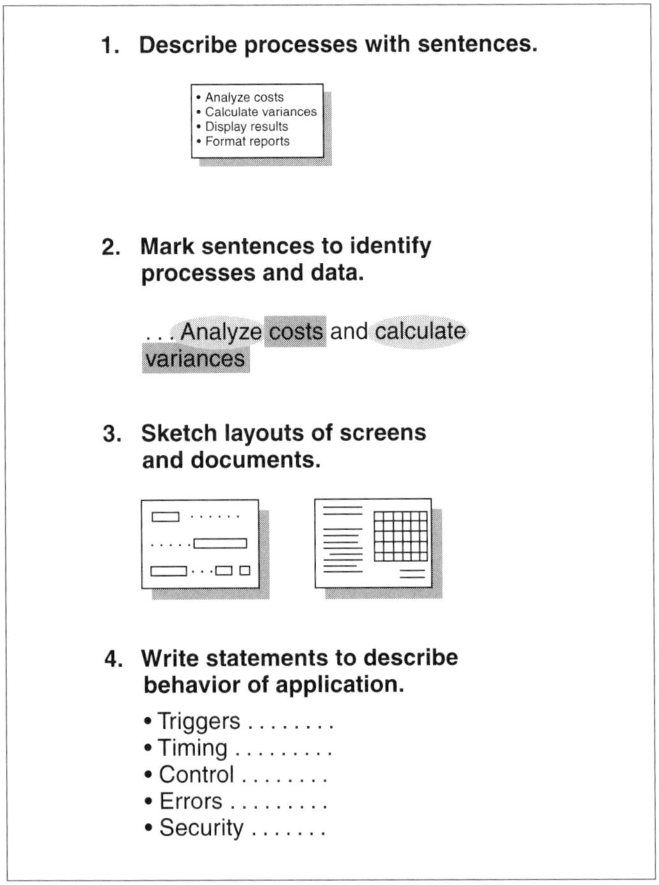

FIGURE 9-7   *A simple approach for analyzing individual system application requirements*

4. *Write statements to describe behavior of application.* The behavior statements should explain the events that trigger processing, the timing requirements, and the basis for controlling the operation of the application. Also describe errors that may occur and how they can be detected and resolved, and note any security considerations.

Visualize the process of using the completed system. Mentally "walk through" the tasks that will be accomplished with the system to check for completeness in the lists of processes and data, screens and input/output documents, and the behavior of the application with respect to control and timing. If possible, walk through the process of use with a colleague. Then revise and redefine the requirements until they fit the expected uses.

This requirements description is an initial basis for selecting an existing package, customizing an existing application package, or developing a custom program. The next two sections of this chapter explain the use of customizing options and the use of macro recording to automate sequences of keystrokes or mouse actions. Subsequent chapters describe more complex methods to customize packages and build custom applications.

Customizing by Selecting Package Options

Operating systems and software packages, both generalized and specialized, typically provide users with numerous **options and preferences** for customizing the package. Examples include options for the display, work environment, files, toolbar, status bar, menu bar, and keyboard. These options and preferences can be classified according to productivity effects or by the type of option (where they occur in the system).

Options and Their Productivity Effects

Some options and preferences (such as screen color selection) have little or no productivity effects. However, many options have potential productivity effects. As illustrated in Figure 9-8, there are five types of options relative to productivity:

1. *Options that match the computer to the environment.* These options eliminate special operations.

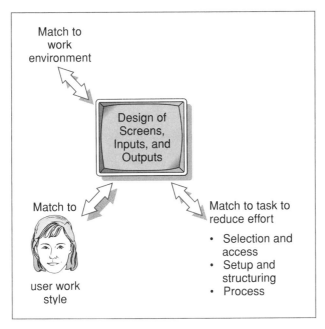

FIGURE 9-8 *Options for productivity*

Examples

If a user must produce most outputs in the international A4 paper size (slightly different than the common 8½ x 11 size used in the U.S.A.), the paper size can be set as the default option for printing. Otherwise, it must be specified for each output. ◆

An organization may opt to use the international format as its standard for writing dates (day-month-year). The date function will normally have an option for that format. ◆

Users may want to add specialized terms of a task environment to their spell check program. Frequently occurring terms or sets of words may be associated with an abbreviation. Entering the abbreviation will obtain the full term or expression. ◆

2. *Options that match personal work style.* These options reduce effort and errors.

Examples

A company with plants in Mexico, France, and Denmark creates correspondence in English, but uses special characters associated with the different languages for names. The special characters can be looked up in a table of characters when needed. Alternatively, users can configure a keyboard with the special characters assigned to key combinations. ◆

The keyboard can be tailored to fit a user's preferences. A user who enters text in Swedish may wish to have the keyboard configured to "Swedish" so that the three extra Swedish symbols (Å, Ä, and Ö) are associated with the same keys as on the Swedish keyboard. ◆

The outlining feature within a word processor may be set to fit the preferences of the user. Setting the outlining style to fit user preferences reduces effort and errors. ◆

Setting options for "beep when error" may reduce the possibility of overlooking error conditions. ◆

Setting default spreadsheet options to two decimal places for users who work with financial data eliminates a format specification step in every new spreadsheet. ◆

3. *Options that reduce selection and access effort.* These options are primarily special items on menus, icons, tool and button bars, and keystrokes.

Examples

The operating system can be tailored to automatically load commonly used software packages when the computer is turned on. ◆

A user can tailor the system interface with icons to speed access to software packages. ◆

A spreadsheet can be tailored to move the cursor to the next cell down for next entry (or right, left, or up) after entering data. ◆

An option may allow a user to create a custom keyboard. Keystrokes may be assigned to keys selected by the user. Both package and user-written macros may be assigned to user keyboard strokes. For instance, individuals who edit documents for publication often need to ensure that subtitles begin with a capital letter. A macro can be designed to perform this function and assigned to a special keystroke. Pressing the assigned key (such as Control + M) activates the macro. ◆

4. *Options that reduce setup effort.* The most common option in this category is reuse of templates. Documents and spreadsheets frequently employ a standard format that includes elements such as headings, date, and author. For spreadsheets, this may also include fixed data, as well as formatting and formulas for variable data. Establishing a template can automate activities that would otherwise need to be repeated manually.

Example

A template is established for an expense analysis. Fixed information, row and column headings, and formulas for summing columns and rows are incorporated. ◆

5. *Options that reduce process work effort.* The most common approach is reuse of procedures. Macros and scripts are two method. A script defines a

set of operations that must be performed in order to accomplish a designated task, such as accessing data. From a practical standpoint, a script is a type of macro. Some macros may be available as options, or they may be written separately. (These are explained in the section on recording and writing macros.)

Options and preferences that have a productivity effect tend to yield very small savings each time the feature is employed in information processing. The examples of configuring the keyboard to meet special needs, establishing a keystroke for a macro, or making the date appear in standard format save a few seconds with each use (compared to performing the operations without the option in force). However, the cumulative savings can be substantial if the operations are repeated often. Options should always be considered before any custom programming is performed. Frequently, an option can provide most of the benefits of a user-written macro or customized solution.

Example

An option that saves only 15 seconds per day yields a total savings of one hour per year.   ◆

Options for Hardware and Software Features

Another way to think about options (sometimes referred to as "properties" or "preferences") is in terms of the way the hardware and software can be customized for data entry, storage, and output. Following are examples of options available with generalized hardware and software:

Screen interface options. These allow the user to customize the appearance of the application to reflect work habits or to highlight the importance of specific features. For example, background and foreground colors may be changed to suit the user, and character size and style may be adjusted to fit the user's visual capabilities.

Keyboard options. As explained earlier, the user may select keyboard settings to reflect language use and to associate certain keystrokes with specific functions. The response characteristics of the keyboard (such as repeating key speed) can also be altered.

Menus, icons, tool and button bars, and special keystrokes. These may be customized to emphasize functions important to the user and to reflect personal preferences. Icons are employed to reduce access time; therefore, icons not used can be removed and new icons added as required. (Adding macros to menus, icons, or keystrokes will be explained later in this chapter.)

Storage options. The user may specify where data, backup, reference, and other files are to be stored. Default file names or naming patterns may also be specified. Work in process may be automatically backed up at specified intervals, and backup prompts may be specified.

Output options. The printer, printer fonts, color, style, alignment, and many other formatting options may be specified. Output options may also be set for e-mail, fax, or file storage.

Process options. There may be a selection among alternative approaches to solution processes and procedures. For example, incoming e-mail may be automatically directed to topic folders based on contents, or sequenced by arrival time to assist users in scanning and selecting data.

Handling of data and exception conditions. An example is displaying a 0 (zero) value when a cell has a zero value.

Some options are selected in connection with the operating system and are, therefore, applied to all applications that use the operating system's file and printer input and output management. Other options are associated with each generalized software package. Specialized application packages usually have fewer options.

Access Options

A user may tailor the user interfaces for accessing software to change the selection methods. There are essentially three methods for accessing software: menus, tool bars, and keystrokes.

1. *Menus.* A **menu** (or list of options) is usually organized as a hierarchy. Access to a high-level menu discloses a submenu; access to a submenu item may reveal a third level, and so forth. Menus provide an excellent means of helping users identify and select options. The disadvantage is the number of selection steps required.

2. *Tool bars.* A **tool bar** consists of a horizontal or vertical bar containing small graphical objects called **icons** (also termed **buttons**). An icon can be used to select software or functions within a software package. An icon can be set to perform an action with one mouse click that otherwise might require going through a set of menus.

3. *Keystrokes.* A **keystroke** (or combination of keystrokes, such as CTRL + a letter key) may also be used to access software. This option requires memorizing the keystrokes, but it can be very efficient since it can be done from the keyboard without the extra motion needed with a pointing device like a mouse.

Customizing Procedures Using Macro Recording

◆ ◆ ◆ ◆ ◆ ◆ ◆ ◆ ◆ ◆ ◆ ◆ ◆ ◆ ◆ ◆ ◆ ◆ ◆

A **macro** can be a simple sequence of operations, or it can be a complex program with selection logic and repetition structures. This chapter describes a simple method for automating a sequence of operations. Chapter 10 explains the process of developing a macro program with dialog, logic and repetition. As previously defined, macro recording is "programming by doing," since the user performs the actions that are to be programmed. Using the analogy of an audio tape recorder or VCR, the actions a user performs are *recorded* to create a macro; the macro is then *played* to perform the actions that were recorded. Macros are most often recorded and used within an application package.

Macro Recording Within a Package

There are numerous situations in which a sequence of steps must be repeated in exactly the same way. Macro recording software essentially builds a computer program by capturing the sequence of steps as they are performed and storing them for playback when needed. Recorded macros can be used to repeat the operations of a single job, or they may be saved and reused for other activities.

Building a program by executing a set of instructions employs the powerful concept of programming by doing. Since the sequence is executed during the building of the macro, any errors in the sequence of steps will be discovered immediately. Macro recording also has some of the positive aspects of prototyping, since a sequence of instructions is built and immediately tested. If it is not correct, the sequence may be repeated or the recorded macro may be edited and replayed. A significant advantage of this procedure is that a correct, well-formed sequence of instructions can be recorded by an individual who does not know the underlying macro programming language.

There are two fundamental reasons for automating a sequence of steps (such as keystrokes and mouse movements): (1) to achieve productivity by reducing the time required to repeat the sequence, and (2) to reduce errors by using a stored, validated sequence of instructions. Converting a sequence of steps into a macro adds functionality, since the software package now includes the recorded macro as an executable function. The cost in terms of development time is small and can often be offset fairly quickly by productivity gains. This discussion assumes that a recorded macro is produced by the knowledge worker who will use it. If a macro has been or must be developed by a third party, the development costs are higher because of the need to make the macro more general and more completely documented.

The macro recording process can be so easy to use that one-job macros are often feasible and cost effective. For example, an individual may need to make many repetitive changes to a document, but the changes may be complex or time consuming, using ordinary search and replace operations. To improve productivity, a macro recording may be made and replayed until each of the changes have been made, after which it can be discarded.

Example

Figure 9-9 shows a simple macro that locates the next WordPerfect text marked for the table of contents and makes it both bold and large. If this were something that had to be done many times in a document, recording the macro and playing it might save time and effort. ◆

Macros are usually created, used, and saved for repetitive use. In saving a macro, users have several options: (1) macros may be associated with only the specific data file, spreadsheet, database, or document in which they were created; (2) macros can be made available whenever the package is used; or (3) macros may be associated with a specific class of data.

Following is a general procedure for writing a program sequence by recording a macro:

1. Position the cursor at the point where the contemplated sequence of instructions applies.

2. Select the "Record Macro" function.

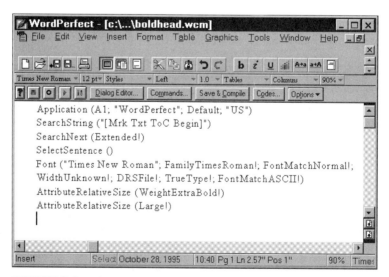

FIGURE 9-9 *A recorded macro to search for words marked for the table of contents and make them large font and bold (WordPerfect)*

3. Name the macro (a description of the macro can be saved with the name).

4. Start the macro recorder.

5. Execute the sequence of steps.

6. Stop the recorder.

7. Save the recorded macro.

Figure 9-10 illustrates the steps defined by a specific software package. The macro name is used to call the macro and execute the sequence of instructions. As explained later in this chapter, many generalized packages include several other options, enabling users to assign a macro to a menu, tool bar, or special key combination.

If a recorded macro needs minor changes, it may either be re-recorded or edited. When the sequence of steps of a macro to be recorded is greater than the limits of human short-term memory (about 5–7 steps), additional effort is usually required since human errors are frequent. Macro recorders generally have no way of undoing or reversing a step during recording. In most cases, users must terminate the recording process, delete the erroneous partial result, and restart the recording process. For any complicated sequence, a

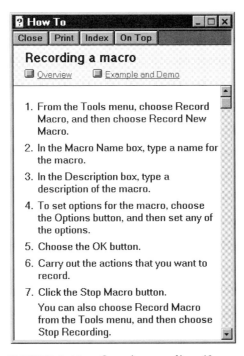

FIGURE 9-10   *Steps in recording (from Microsoft Excel Help)*

possible solution is to plan out the sequence of steps of a macro in advance and write them down. For macros of moderate size (10–15 steps) this may be feasible.

Software packages that support macro recording also support macro editing. Macro editing allows common recording mistakes to be corrected without a repeat of the recording. It may also permit more complex macros to be recorded in separate parts that are then combined using an editor. (Editing will be explained later in this section.) Some packages also allow users to record a series of small macros and then write another small macro that executes each macro in the series in turn. However, recording such multi-level macros requires additional planning.

Macro recording facilities are found in many generalized application packages such as word processors, spreadsheet processors, and database packages. The following examples illustrate the power and productivity effects of this customizing method:

◆ *Spreadsheet.* A recorded macro may be used to set up a spreadsheet so that specific elements are specified (such as titles, column size, data formats, formulas, and page and print setup commands). (See Figure 9-11.)

FIGURE 9-11 *A simple macro that turns off spreadsheet grid lines and formats a column heading (Microsoft Excel 5.0)*

◊   *Word processing.* A recorded macro may be used to convert a document's format (such as marking text for indexes or tables of contents, or changing the appearance of lists or paragraphs).

◊   *Database packages.* A recorded macro may be used to automate repetitious steps, such as applying calculated changes to each row of a selection.

Relationship of Templates and Macros

Templates were explained in Chapter 2. They enable reuse of forms, document formats, and spreadsheet formats (including formulas if these are part of the spreadsheet form or report). Templates like those explained in Chapter 2 can be produced by macro recording, but there are conceptual and practical differences in doing so.

A template is produced by preparing a spreadsheet document, or database form and saving it as a reusable template. When a user desires to employ a template, it is retrieved using a template access instruction. The template is copied, so the result is stored as a new document, spreadsheet, or database; the original template is not changed.

A recorded macro is developed by starting the macro recorder and performing a sequence of actions. The macro is saved using a user-defined macro name. A user employs the macro by playing the set of stored instructions. The execution of the instructions produces the result within a current document or spreadsheet.

Templates are more restricted in purpose and scope than recorded macros. However, saving a form as a template and saving a macro that creates such a form provide the same result for a user. The difference is that a template is saved as a form and a macro is saved as instructions to develop the form. For those situations in which either method is feasible, the template is easier to employ because the process of development allows the user to make changes until the form or layout is exactly as intended. Making such changes with macro recording is difficult or impossible.

Macro recording can be used for more purposes than templates can because a full range of instructions can be executed. Recorded macros can also be edited to add decision logic (to be explained in Chapter 10).

Editing a Recorded Macro

A recorded macro consists of a set of computer instructions in a programming language. The language may be used by several packages in a package suite or may be specific to a single software package. Macro recording generates well-formed statements that conform to the syntax of the language. Even information systems professionals find this capability to be very useful because it reduces the need to learn the details of programming language syntax. As illustrated in Figure 9-11, the statements of even a simple recorded macro can appear to be quite technical. Without the recording capability, writing even a simple macro is too difficult for a nonspecialist.

There are varying degrees of **macro editing** support. In some packages, editing is limited to cutting and pasting existing statements. Even this limited capability can be useful because a statement recorded in error can often be repeated correctly during the same recording. The erroneous statement can then be deleted without re-recording the entire sequence. More complete macro facilities include debugging help to identify and correct errors.

The most complete macro recording and editing facilities produce macro recordings in the form of statements in a general purpose programming language. Such facilities permit macro recording to be a regular part of extending the capabilities of a software package and building custom applications. They make it feasible for a knowledge worker to create a relatively complex program without becoming either an expert programmer or an expert in the specific macro language.

Macro editing is specific to the syntax of the macro language of the package. Following are some general guidelines for macro editing:

◊ *Be familiar with the editing capabilities and limitations of the package before recording a macro.*

◊ *Ignore or reverse errors made while recording a macro* (whenever doing so does not make repeating an operation impossible); plan to remove them in an editing step.

◊ *Record macros that operate on specific data or on a set of organized data;* make the procedures more general during editing.

◊ *When a macro must include decisions or other control logic, use macro recording to create each sequence of steps and add the control logic with the editor.* (This step is the subject of the next chapter.)

Reducing Access Time for Frequently-used Macros and Templates

Macros are written for use within a package such as a spreadsheet processor, word processor, or database package. They are usually stored in a file accessible from within the package. To run or play a macro, a user accesses it by a series of menu selections. For example, the user may select Tools from a top-level menu, select Macro from the drop-down menu, select Play or Run from the next menu, and then select the macro by name from a list of stored macros. If the list of macros is long, users may have to scroll through it to locate the desired macro. This four-step selection process via menus is efficient for seldom-used macros, but the access time and mouse motion may be reduced for frequently used macros. As illustrated in Figure 9-12, there are three major alternatives to multistep menu selection for reducing the time to access and run a macro:

1. Placing the macro on a high-level menu
2. Assigning the macro to an icon on a toolbar
3. Assigning keystrokes to run the macro

Each of these options is described in the following paragraphs. Since the concept is similar for templates, the explanation for macros can also apply to

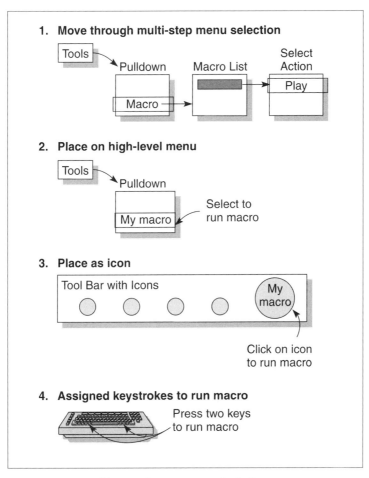

FIGURE 9-12 *Alternative access methods for macros*

templates. Implementation details will depend on the facilities of a specific application package. For example, to implement one of these approaches within a spreadsheet package, the user employs the specific procedures of the macro access facilities of the spreadsheet package.

Placing the Macro on a High-level Menu

Rather than placing a macro at the end of an access path with four levels of menus, a user may customize a high-level application package menu with the macro name. For example, a top-level menu bar selection of the Tools menu pulls down a second-level menu, enabling the user to place a macro name on the second-level list. A mouse click on this macro menu item will run the macro. This reduces access time significantly. Since menu space is limited, only frequently used macros should use it.

It is possible to create cascading menus of macros to allow access to more macros within an application package than can be placed on the **Tools** menu. In other words, the **Tools** menu would include a menu item to bring up a third-level menu with a list of commonly used macros. This is still a reduction in time if regular access requires scrolling to find the desired macro, since the menu approach contains only a few frequently accessed macros.

Assigning the Macro to an Icon

A macro can be assigned to an icon at two levels:

1. *On a high-level application package icon bar for common functions.* This is similar to the menu approach, but the icon is at the highest level on the application package screen. By clicking on the icon, users can run the macro written for a spreadsheet processor with any spreadsheet, run a macro written for a word processor with any document, and so on.

2. *On a spreadsheet, document, or query report.* In concept, a macro access mechanism may be placed directly on a spreadsheet, document, or query report. In practice, the most common use is on a spreadsheet. A user may place an icon on a frequently used spreadsheet to execute a sequence of operations. For example, a spreadsheet produced by an accountant may involve a two-step process of preparing the spreadsheet and selecting part of the spreadsheet for printing (including several print option selections). An icon may be placed on the spreadsheet. To print the spreadsheet, the user clicks on the icon. This prompts the system to perform a sequence of steps that include selecting the spreadsheet, selecting the **print** option, and printing the spreadsheet.

There is a key difference between a graphical object on a menu toolbar and on a spreadsheet: A graphical object on a menu toolbar is available whenever the toolbar is displayed; therefore, it can be applied to any spreadsheet. A graphical object on a spreadsheet is available only for the spreadsheet on which it appears, and only when that spreadsheet has been opened.

The procedure for creating menu icons, or icons on a toolbar depends on the application package. However, the general procedure for assigning a macro to a toolbar icon is to create the macro, name it, store it, and use a toolbar editing facility to select an icon, place it on the toolbar, and associate it with the macro. Menu placement follows a similar procedure.

Assigning Keystrokes to Run the Macro

Both the menu and icon approaches require one or more mouse actions. If the user is performing keystrokes, the mouse action interrupts the work flow at the keyboard. For macros to be accessed frequently during keyboard operations, the most efficient approach is to assign the macro execution to keystrokes.

The single keys on a keyboard are assigned to letters, numbers, and special characters. Macros are typically assigned to **ALT** plus a keystroke or **CTRL** plus a keystroke. (The two keys are pressed simultaneously.) Three keystrokes may be assigned, but this is more difficult to use. Keystroke execution of macros is especially useful in word processing because this method fits the keyboard nature of the task. Users can assign macros to keystrokes and apply the macro to various documents. A keystroke access can also be applied to a macro when many repetitive actions must be taken.

Example

A document is prepared on diskette for entry into a processing program. In the document, many terms must be marked with <XR> before the term and <XRE> after the term with no intervening spaces. Some terms will be marked during the initial draft, but many more terms must be marked during editing. A macro is recorded to place the <XR> at the beginning and assigned to ALT+s; a second macro is recorded to place <XRE> at the end of the term and assigned to ALT+e. When typing or editing a term, the user merely presses ALT plus s to place the code at the beginning of the term, or ALT plus e to place the code at the end. The macros eliminate errors (in entering an unusual code) and reduce keystrokes.   ◆

The general approach to assigning keystrokes is to prepare a macro and use the macro facilities to define a keystroke combination to assign to it. Since many keystrokes using **CTRL** and **ALT** are already assigned for the standard keyboard or by the package, these must be avoided. The package being used for the macro keystrokes will identify preassigned keystrokes. Some operating systems and packages such as word processors allow users to define one or more special keyboard definitions with unique keystroke assignments. These keyboard definitions are given names and can be selected when needed. This allows more complex sets of macros to be assigned. If there are different applications using sets of macros, this approach can create a set of macros tailored to the specific application. The keyboard definition can include both macro access and special character assignments.

Using Help Facilities

◆ ◆ ◆ ◆ ◆ ◆ ◆ ◆ ◆ ◆ ◆ ◆ ◆ ◆ ◆ ◆ ◆ ◆ ◆ ◆

The **Help** facilities of major application packages provide for both exploration of features and "just-in-time" learning. The **Help** contents are, in many cases, a substitute for a manual; in other cases, the manual is a supplement to the **Help** contents. The **Help** facilities also include assistance in developing applications within a package. These are represented by terms such as "Coaches," "Wizards," and "Experts." Unlike help topics that explain a single concept or term, the assistance facilities guide or coach a user in performing a complex function or building an application with the tools provided by the package.

Using Help to Learn Package Features

A manual may be read more quickly than a screen because of the necessity of manipulating a screen. However, a **Help** facility has two major advantages: (1) it can have **hypertext links** to immediately transfer to the explanation of a related idea or explanation, and (2) it provides search capabilities that are more efficient than an index. By using a combination of hypertext links and search terms, users can read a topic and related topics. The hypertext links are highlighted terms that transfer the user to further explanation by a mouse click on the linked term. The list of search terms for major packages can be very extensive and may include several hundred terms—or even full-text searches of **Help** contents.

The exploration feature of **Help** facilities helps users get started and get acquainted with software features. The feature usually includes an overall tutorial for the package, step-by-step instructions for common tasks, and "show me" examples. Many examples of programming functions display sample uses of the instructions. In the case of macros, the examples display the instructions included in the macro program. This allows users to copy the example code and make changes. The "copy plus change" approach can be very effective in improving productivity.

Many features can be learned on an "as needed" basis. **Help** facilities support this approach, generally referred to as **"just-in-time" learning.** For example, a user may not be ready to assign a macro to keystrokes. When a macro has been proven useful, the user can access the **Help** instructions to learn how to do it.

Given the existence of extensive **Help** facilities, a useful strategy for individual productivity is to make use of the high-level tutorial in the **Help** facilities to become familiar with major package features. Examples should be examined, and the search procedure learned and tested on some examples. With this framework, the **Help** facilities will support "just-in-time" learning. Figures 9-13 and 9-14 present examples of the contents page of **Help** facilities for a word processing package and a spreadsheet package.

Using Coaches, Wizards, and Experts

As part of **Help** facilities, software packages provide directed assistance for some activities. These facilities are often referred to as "Coaches," "Wizards," or "Experts."

♦xamples

The Excel 5.0™ spreadsheet processor has a Wizard to assist spreadsheet users in building a graph from spreadsheet data.   ♦

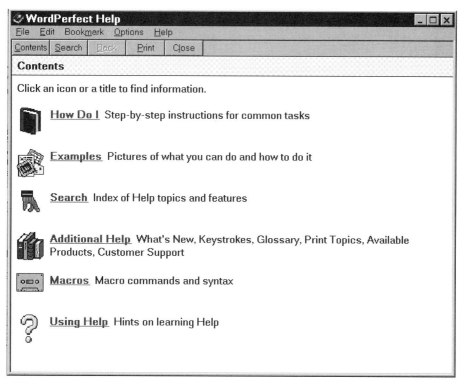

FIGURE 9-13   *Contents of Help facilities with WordPerfect 6.1*

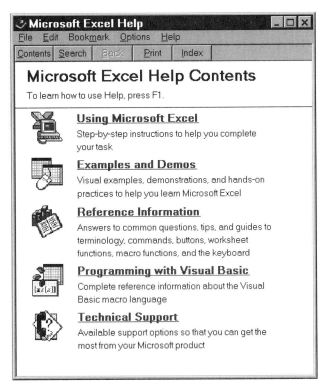

FIGURE 9-14 *Contents page of Help facilities with Microsoft Excel 5.0*

WordPerfect 6.1 has Coaches for a number of activities such as building templates, creating style sheets for documents, merging data to create letters, and inserting graphics. In WordPerfect 7.0, assistance is provided by a "Perfect Expert."

Summary

◆ ◆ ◆ ◆ ◆ ◆ ◆ ◆ ◆ ◆ ◆ ◆ ◆ ◆ ◆ ◆ ◆ ◆ ◆ ◆

◆ There are three alternative approaches to productive computer solutions when requirements suggest a customized computer application: (1) custom development of applications, (2) customizing by selecting package options, and (3) customizing by using macros. The choice among the alternatives should reflect functionality, productivity gain, implementation cost, and risk factors. In general, it is more cost-effective to use packages than to build custom programs.

◆ For custom development of applications, information systems professionals follow a general process called a system development life cycle or SDLC. The SDLC for large application systems is designed to ensure complete and correct requirements and tested software of high quality.

◆ Custom applications can meet the exact requirements of users, but the process of creating these applications is costly and has a fairly high risk of failure. Therefore, custom development is normally appropriate only when there are unique needs or many users to share the cost of development.

◆ Although software packages are generalized to fit a wide range of users, most packages include options and choices for users to match the packages more closely to the individual tasks and activities and to match individual preferences. Many of the options can have significant individual productivity effects when the software is applied in a specific setting. Customizing a package by selecting appropriate options and preferences is, therefore, an important element in achieving productivity benefits in package use.

◆ Macros at the elementary level are used to automate routine, repetitive tasks; more complex macros include control structures with logic and repetition. The chapter explains the use of macro recording and editing of recorded macros for automating routine, repetitive tasks. Templates (explained in Chapter 2) are similar to recorded macros, but more restricted. They enable users to save fixed parts of a spreadsheet or document for reuse.

◆ Access to macro programs or templates can be accomplished through the regular macro access facilities of a package. This typically involves several levels of menus. If macros are used frequently, other more efficient access methods may be employed: the macro may be placed on a high-level menu to reduce the search space or it may be placed on a tool bar as an icon so that a mouse action on the icon runs the macro. Icons may also be used to place macro access controls on a single spreadsheet or database report. However, their scope is limited to the spreadsheet or report on which they are placed.

◆ A macro may be assigned to keystrokes. This method is especially useful when the user is involved in entering data via the keyboard and a mouse action interrupts keyboard action. A specialized keyboard can be defined with assignment of keystrokes to invoke macros.

◆ Help facilities assist users in learning how to use a package effectively. They can also aid in "just-in-time" learning in which detailed learning is delayed until a need for a feature has emerged. Assistance in the form of Coaches, Wizards, and Experts provides "walk-through" help for selected activities. A productivity strategy will include exploration and effective use of Help facilities.

EXERCISES

1. Examine the properties a user can assign to the operating system environment. For example, for Windows 95™, examine preferences for each item in the control panel. List and explain preferences that may have a productivity effect.

2. Examine the options (preferences) available with your word processing package. Make two lists. In the first, note five options or preferences that fit personal preferences, but have minimal productivity effects. In the second list, identify five options that can have a productivity effect. Explain how the productivity might be achieved with each of the latter.

3. Examine the tailoring options for your spreadsheet processor. The options will be found on one of the drop-down menus. For example, Microsoft Excel™ has **Options** under **Tools**. The **Options** menu has 10 parts. What types of options are available to you? Look for options that perform the following: custom list, move selection after **Enter** key, fixed decimal, and zero values display. Try them, and explain how they might have a productivity effect.

4. Examine the applications you use with reasonable frequency. Identify at least five opportunities for automating sequences of operations. List the opportunities and explain why automation would improve functionality or productivity.

5. Select one of the opportunities in Exercise 4 (with only a sequence of operations). Use recording to develop a macro to simplify the execution of a specified sequence of actions. Use macro editing to remove errors. Print the macro. Explain the effect of each instruction (in general, since it executes the action you performed).

6. Examine the macros provided with your word processor. Select two and explain what they do and how they could be useful to you. Demonstrate their use.

7. Record a macro in a spreadsheet to perform the following functions:
   a. Place titles over five columns.
   b. Set their fonts to large and bold.
   c. Adjust the size of the columns to fit.
   d. Add a line (border) beneath the titles of all five columns.

   Use your own titles of varying lengths. Print out the macro program code that was generated. Mark the statements that perform each of the four separate actions above.

8. A small business that prints about 20 checks per week uses a spreadsheet instead of an adding machine tape to create a list of the checks for the

bank deposit. The list is printed in two copies. One copy is retained with the record of receipts. The other is attached to the deposit slip for the bank (after cutting it to size).

The list has a heading on it to identify the depositor, bank, and deposit date. (The deposit date may be different than the date of preparation.) The format of the heading and slip is as follows:

Small Business Firm
FOR DEPOSIT ONLY
First Snoose Bank
Minneapolis, MN
Acct 1 123 456 7899

(deposit date)

999.99
etc.

a. Record a macro to create the heading (not including the date). The macro should format the spreadsheet with columns 12 spaces wide. Make the cells of type **NUMBER** with two decimal places and a comma for thousands. Move the cursor to the **date** field and make it data type **DATE**. End the macro by positioning the cursor to enter the date of the deposit.
b. Run the macro and print the result
c. Print the macro
d. Edit the macro by adding a statement to turn off the gridlines before printing. Also add some comment lines in the macro with your name. (Comment lines usually start with an apostrophe, but check the package being used.)
e. Run the revised macro and print the result.
f. Print the revised macro.

(Hint: Two ways to find out how to write the line to turn off gridlines are to record a macro to do it and find the action line, or locate an example in the **Help** facilities.)

9. Make the recorded macro from Exercise 8 more easily available:
   a. Place the macro on the menu. Run the macro from the menu bar.
   b. Alter the macro to specify keystrokes to run the macro (such as **CTRL+d** or **ALT+D**). Run the macro using the keystrokes.
   c. Add the macro as an icon on a tool bar. Run the macro using the icon.

10. Do the deposit form from Exercise 9 as a template. Explain the relative advantages of macro or template for this simple form.

11. Many word processors have features such as Auto Correct that replace abbreviations with a longer term or phrase, but these can also be done

with recorded macros. Check the facilities of Auto Correct. For the following, create your macro, bring it up in Macro editing mode, and print the recorded macro. Make the macro run with a keystroke to do the following. Then include a screen capture of the window under Tools, Customize, Keyboard showing that your macro has been assigned to your chosen keystroke.

   a. Insert the Swedish name using Swedish characters for a subsidiary called Två Användare Aktiebolag when a keystroke is used.

   b. Insert the company product name that is trademarked along with a ™ symbol from the typographical symbol table. Use a product name of YUCK™.

12. Create a one-page spreadsheet macro for an expense report. Use it to set format, labels, page layout, and formulas. Prepare an example using the macro.

13. Use the assistance facilities (Coach or Wizard) available with a spreadsheet processor to create a bar chart and a pie chart. For example, using "expenses per day," create a bar chart showing components of total. Use a pie chart to show parts of "total for week."

14. Do the following and print the macros to demonstrate your work (not the output of the macro, but the macro itself):

   a. For a word processing application, assume you receive and capture data as unformatted text. Mark the data, use a recorded macro to implement the table function of the word processor, change the font to bold, and outline the table.

   b. For a spreadsheet application one column of a table is calculated as a percentage, but not using the percentage format. Select the column to be formatted, record a macro to change the format to percentage with two decimals, bold the result, and place a dark border around the column. *Hint:* Since you do not want to restrict these changes to a specific area on the spreadsheet, record using the **Relative Address** and do not include any "selection" activities while recording the macro.

Developing a Simple Program

OBJECTIVES

After completing this chapter, you should be able to:

◊ Describe the three major levels of program design (architecture, organization into modules, and internal design of modules).

◊ Describe the three approaches to program architecture (structured design, event-driven design, and object-oriented design).

◊ Explain the conventions used for coding operations, naming variables, and coding simple input.

◊ Explain program control structures.

◊ Add control structures and input dialog to recorded macros.

◊ Describe how to achieve modularity with macros.

KEY TERMS AND CONCEPTS

This chapter introduces the following key terms and concepts, listed in the order in which they appear:

program architecture	implementation level	method
hierarchical procedure design	event	sequence control structure
event-driven design	encapsulation	alternation structure
object-oriented design	inheritance	repetition structure
module	global data structures	infinite loop
decision logic	order of execution	indexed repetition
control structure	concatenation	recursion
program design architecture	Boolean operations	nested control structure
structured approach	object	parameters
pseudocode	property	

Individual information technology users may be able to achieve all important productivity objectives with packages, package options, and macro recordings. However, there may be opportunities for productivity enhancements that involve some knowledge of programming. This knowledge may be applied in the development of macros that have more functionality than can be achieved with recording. It may also allow users to write simple application programs. This chapter presents fundamental program design concepts, applies them to building more functionality into recorded macros, and describes the process involved in building a program using a program development system.

Program design occurs at three different levels: (1) program architecture, (2) organization of a program into modules, and (3) internal design of modules. This chapter surveys each of these design levels, explains program control structures for internal design of modules, and illustrates how these control structures may be added to recorded macros to create a program with alternation and repetition logic.

The top level of program design is **program architecture**. There are three different architectural design approaches for software: (1) **hierarchical procedure design** (often called structured design or traditional design), (2) **event-driven design**, and (3) **object-oriented design**. These three approaches are not independent. The structured design approach contains fundamental ideas that are incorporated in the other two. However, the event-oriented and object-oriented design approaches introduce new concepts that affect program architecture. Understanding the concepts in the three architectural approaches is important background for designing and structuring a program.

The next level of design is the organization of a program into program design units called **modules**. Much of the activity at this second level of program design is concerned with determining what functions should be defined as modules. A program will be simpler to construct, test, and maintain if program modules are well organized and interrelated. Although the different program architecture approaches may result in different module designs, the concepts underlying well-formed modules are universal.

The lowest level of design is the internal structure of the module design units. The module consists of program statements that define sequences of actions plus statements that specify decision or control logic. **Decision logic** allows conditional choices to be specified and actions to be repeated. **Control structures** are ways to write program statements, so that the logic is simple and unambiguous. Following rules of good programming practice in writing control structures reduces errors, aids program debugging, and assists in subsequent changes and enhancements.

Building macros that contain decision or control logic is the simplest and probably the most cost effective approach to programming by individual users (or small groups). One reason is that the macro is contained within the operations of a package, so many application functions are provided by the package. Therefore, the macro can be constrained in scope. A second reason is that macros with significant functionality can be constructed by starting with macro recording and adding decision and control logic. Extending the basic sequence of macros is simple enough to be applied by individuals who are not experts in programming, and powerful enough so that expert programmers can use it to improve their productivity in responding to simple program requests.

Programming Knowledge for Users

◆ ◆

A user can achieve productivity with information technology without being able to write a program. Learning to use the productivity features of packages, making use of package options and preferences, templates, and automating sequences of operations with macro recordings can be accomplished without a knowledge of programming. However, a knowledge of programming may be useful to an individual who is not a programmer for three reasons:

1. *As a useful background for understanding information technology.* A modest amount of understanding about programming may add significant understanding to individual computer use. Some productivity enhancements are easily implemented if the user has a modest knowledge of programming.

2. *For writing programs, either by programming a macro within a software package or for programming a separate application.*

3. *As a background in working with information systems specialists.* This interaction may be as a user on an applications development project. Another interaction may be as a specifier of requirements or as an evaluator of information systems functions.

Programming knowledge for an individual user may be divided into two areas:

1. *Writing program statements.* This chapter explains the process involved in writing program structures and statements.

2. *Creating user interfaces.* The user interfaces most important for individual users with personal computers are graphical user interfaces (GUIs). They consist of objects on the computer display screen. The design of screen objects and graphical user interfaces is simplified by software for GUI development. (The concepts of user interfaces and the use of user interface development software are presented in Chapter 11.) The principles and methods of user interface design are also important in connection with user-written macros and some features of software packages.

To an individual user, there may appear to be a proliferation of programming languages and user interface development systems. A person who is not a programming specialist cannot be expected to learn any of the many different languages and interface design procedures. As a practical matter, it is possible to learn the basics of a language and then use **Help** facilities for "just-in-time" learning of additional features. This enables users to write macros, user interfaces, and simple programs within a reasonably short time. This involvement is possible for several reasons:

◊ Although there are many programming languages, the basic instructions for common operations and control structures are very similar. There may be differences in conventions for naming variables and different object, property, and method names, but the arithmetic commands and control structure commands have similar patterns.

◊ An individual does not need to learn an entire programming language to write simple programs; a subset of the language may be sufficient.

◊ There are program development tools that automate parts of the program development process. For example, as described in Chapter 11, the program commands for graphical user interfaces are produced by an interface development tool, enabling the user-programmer to use simple commands to effectively operate the development tool.

◊ It is possible to learn how to write instructions by examining existing program statements (program code). The use of recorded macros as building blocks for a macro program allows a user to examine the program statements generated by the macro recorder as part of a learning process.

A strategy for individual development of elementary programming knowledge starts with an appreciation of the principles of programming, approaches to program architectures, and principles of program modules (see Figure 10-1). The next step is to learn conventions for program objects and variables and the form of common procedural statements for the programming language in use. (The statements generated by a macro recording can be used in this learning exercise.) The third step is to learn the basic control structures and use the manual or **Help** facilities of the language to code the control structures in that language. The programming skills developed in the first three steps can be applied to writing a macro with decision and control logic. Other skills such as modular design, testing, and documentation may be learned through building macros. (This strategy does not include user interface design and development. This topic will be explained in the next chapter.)

The **Help** facilities for the software package being used can assist users in learning to program. The trend is to place the manual for the package in the **Help** facilities. One advantage of an online manual is computer aided search to locate the description of a feature. A second advantage with many online manuals is a text with hypertext links. While reading a description, related programming topics marked with hypertext links may be accessed directly (see Figure 10-2). Examples are useful as templates for user-developed programs.

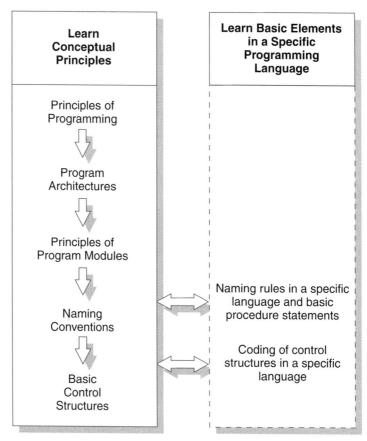

FIGURE 10-1 *A strategy for developing elementary programming knowledge*

Program Architectures

◆ ◆

Principles of programming are directed at producing correct or "well-formed" programs. A well-formed program is one that meets the following criteria:

◆ It has a clear and understandable structure.

◆ It performs its intended tasks with no unanticipated side effects.

◆ It does not contain errors.

◆ It can be modified when task needs change.

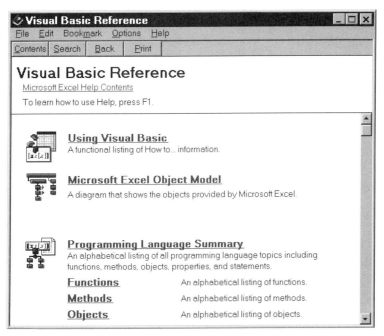

FIGURE 10-2   *Reference screen for a programming language*
(Visual Basic in Microsoft Excel 5.0)

Principles of programming to achieve these objectives are reflected in the design of modern programming languages and in the procedures and practices prescribed by development methodologies. In addition, there is a body of knowledge about good programming that is expressed in terms of guidelines for good practices or preferred style.

A concept underlying principles of programming is that programs should be designed and written so as to be understandable to humans. It is not sufficient that a program is correct in terms of steps to be performed; it must be understood by a human reader because programs will need to be changed, either to enhance their function or to fix errors. The computer can correctly interpret a program that has poor structure, uses meaningless names for data and procedures, or uses cryptic abbreviations. However, these defects make it difficult for humans, including the original author, to locate errors or modify the program. Future modifications to such a program are likely to introduce many new defects.

Making a program understandable to human readers requires the application of principles of clear communication. The principles that apply to writing, literature, and speech are also relevant to programming, since all deal with the processes and methods of crafting understandable communications. Therefore, a useful program design principle is to apply what a person knows about writing clear papers, reports, and speeches to writing effective programs.

This chapter presents three main approaches to program architecture, presented in the sequence in which they have been introduced. Structured design was adopted as the **program design architecture** of the 1970s, event-driven design reflected changes required by new technology introduced in the 1980s, and object-oriented design is coming into use in the 1990s. Although such terms often have marketing use, they also reflect real changes. As illustrated in Figure 10-3, the earlier approaches have contributed to the later ones.

Structured Design

As a program increases in size, it becomes much more complex. The basic approach for dealing with complexity is to create a hierarchy. Hierarchies can be observed in the natural world as well as in artificial systems created by humans. An example of a hierarchical structure in nature is a tree with its trunk, branches, twigs, and leaves. Another example is the human body with its major systems and subsystems.

A program of even moderate complexity should be structured into a hierarchy of procedures in order to deal with its complexity. There are several methods of organizing the program hierarchy. All of the hierarchical design approaches are called structured, even though they differ in appearance, design rules, and results. As illustrated in Figure 10-4, the result of any structured architecture is a hierarchy of modules that resembles an organization chart.

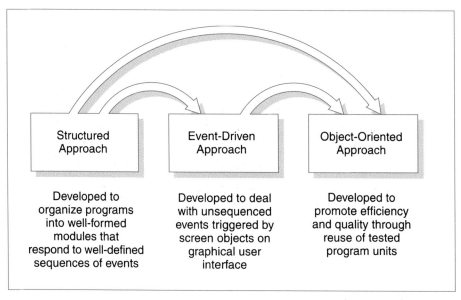

FIGURE 10-3 *Relationship of three approaches to program architecture*

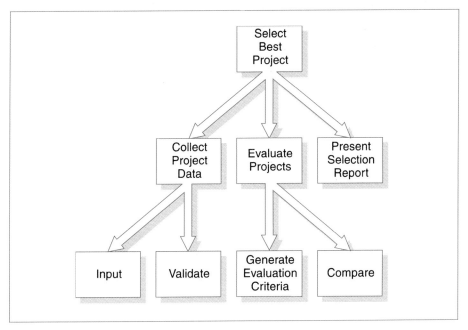

FIGURE 10-4   *Example of a program structure chart with hierarchy of modules*

The organization chart analogy is used throughout structured design. Upper-level modules make decisions and control the flow of processing, while lower-level modules perform detailed actions on specific units of data. Communication among modules is minimized and usually follows the hierarchy or chain-of-command. Each module is specialized to carry out its assigned function only. Organizational concepts such as limited span of control and depth of organization can be used to evaluate structured designs.

The structured design approach can be characterized by the systems development life cycle process it uses and by the various tools used in each major life cycle stage.

◊   In requirements determination, the structured approach tends to use diagraming methods for data models and data flow diagrams. Data models define data and data relationships; data flow diagrams describe process flows. There are many variants of each diagraming method. These diagrams are supplemented by form and report layouts, data dictionaries, and other documentation.

◊   Program architecture design or general design is accomplished by transforming the processes described in data flow diagrams into a program organization. The results are structure charts that define program modules and their relationships with each other.

◊ Detailed design in the **structured approach** expands the general module structure into detailed program structure. It tends to use some form of pseudocode or action diagram to specify the procedures within each module. A **pseudocode** description defines the flow of procedures and program logic. It employs a general notation that is not tied to a specific program language, but is a guide to writing program statements. In Figure 10-5, for example, the pseudocode defines a module to evaluate projects. It operates on data about projects in a table of projects and produces a table of criteria for evaluating the projects. It repeats computations on each project until all projects have been evaluated (or rejected because data items are incomplete).

◊ At the **implementation level**, the modules of the design specified using pseudocode are translated into programs and subprograms. The languages for coding are usually high-level procedural languages.

The emphasis of structured design is on producing understandable and maintainable modules that are clearly organized to provide the desired functionality. The principles of structure are incorporated in event-oriented and object-oriented approaches.

Event-driven Design

The structured design approach was developed in an environment in which programs responded to well-defined sequences of events. The event-driven design approach assumes that a program acts primarily in response to external stimuli that can occur in unpredictable order. With current technology, events are usually generated by a graphical user interface, although other resources such as timers, clocks, or networked computers may also trigger events. With graphical user interfaces, there are frequent interactions between the user and

```
module GenerateEvaluationCriteria (NofProjects, ProjectCriteria
        Table: ProjectCriteriaTable)
    while more projects are left
        if ProjectCriteriaTable(i) values are incomplete
            Insert FailureMessage in ProjectCriteriaTable(i)
        endif
        compute Payback and NetPresentValue of
            ProjectCriteria Table(i)
        insert reults in ProjectCriteriaTable(i)
        next i
    endwhile
endmodule GenerateEvaluationCriteria
```

FIGURE 10-5 *Example of pseudocode to define procedures within a module*

the program. At any point in time, the user may select among many alternative actions. Each such action is an event. An **event** can be movement or clicking with a mouse or other pointing device. It can also be keystrokes used to enter data or select a menu item. Other events may occur as the result of system timers, database or file conditions, or errors and exceptions. The key characteristic of an event-driven design is that its architecture is dictated by the need to have a response for every possible event that can happen regardless of the previous event, i.e., every possible event in random order.

Programs developed in this architecture are quite different from those developed by hierarchical structuring. The most important difference is that the focus in event-driven design is on the user interface. In fact, event-driven design applies primarily to the user interface. At the level of system architecture, event-driven interfaces may include other elements such as access to a database. Even though the controlling mechanisms are very different from those used in the structured approach, the individual modules can exhibit clear structures.

The approach to event-oriented development differs from the structured design approach in that the emphasis is on the events and the procedures invoked by each event. This emphasis influences the requirements process, the design process, and implementation.

◆ The requirements determination process focuses on events associated with user tasks and activities. Event requirements are defined by eliciting and modeling the tasks and activities of the user. These have events associated with them. Many event-driven applications involve selection and retrieval of data from databases. Describing and modeling user tasks, activities, and database access are important to the event-driven approach.

◆ Design uses a prototyping approach. The design is developed rapidly and modified through cycles of user interaction, feedback, and revision. The components of event-driven design are screen objects of various types (see Figure 10-6). Each type of screen object has a particular function. An example is an input box on a screen that can accept a single input value. Associated with each screen object are object properties that determine appearance and many aspects of object behavior. Each object may respond to a set of events. Some event responses are built in and others require user-developed procedures. These procedures are generally written as modules that perform the action triggered by the event. When complex procedures are needed in response to an event, their design follows the structured design approach. The result is one or more hierarchies of modules that work together to complete an action triggered by an event.

◆ For implementation, object properties are specified and modules are coded in the implementation language. The process of prototyping often results in complete coding at the end of the design process. Languages designed

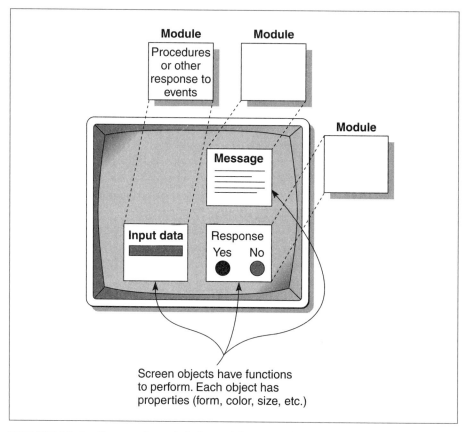

FIGURE 10-6 *Event-oriented design with screen objects and modules associated with screen object events*

to support event-driven programs often support incremental testing and integration. With this kind of language and development environment, partial programs and even partial modules are executed and modified as they are being implemented.

Object-oriented Design

The object-oriented approach extends many principles of program design and incorporates features of both structured and event-driven design. Each element of an object-oriented program is an object. Each object consists of data structures plus the operations, called methods, that can be performed on its data. Objects are activated by messages from other objects or are triggered by external events. Objects interact only by exchanging messages (that can include data). Containing both data and methods within an object is called **encapsulation**, one of the main principles of the object-oriented approach.

The effect of encapsulation is that data can only be affected through the methods of the object containing it.

Another important characteristic of objects is **inheritance**. Once an object has been defined, a descendant object may be created that automatically inherits the data structures and methods of the original object. Much of the power and potential of the object-oriented approach comes from inheritance. New types of objects are created by making specialized versions of existing, tested objects. Development productivity improvements of more than 10 to 1 have been claimed for object-oriented design and implementation with heavy reuse of objects.

The object-oriented design approach influences the requirements determination process, the design of applications, and the implementation process.

◊ Object-oriented requirements determination resembles data modeling. The analyst begins by identifying the real world entities that the system must represent, together with their properties. Object-oriented analysis extends the data modeling notion with the concept of methods. In addition to entities and properties, the behaviors or operations associated with each object are defined as its methods.

◊ The design phase of the object-oriented approach focuses on using existing stored object definitions. This implies that only those objects, data structures, and methods that are new and unique must be created. To the extent possible, an application consists of previously defined objects whose characteristics (data structures, properties, and behaviors) are inherited. Detailed design of individual modules follows the structured design approach. Methods may consist of assemblies of objects, but they may also be designed as hierarchies of modules following the principles of structured design.

◊ In implementation, object-oriented methods must be coded in languages that support the object-oriented approach. The two most widely used object-oriented languages are Smalltalk and C++. Each of these language systems provides complete development environments tailored to the needs of object-oriented implementation. Testing and integration in the object-oriented approach may be quite different from either structured design or event-driven design. The differences are based on the integration of objects into an existing, well-tested object hierarchy during design. This means that much of every new program has already been tested.

Figure 10-7 compares several characteristics of the three program architectures. The preceding discussion and the figure emphasize differences among the three design approaches. They can also be understood in terms of evolution in response to the changing dynamics of computer use. The change emphasizes efficiency and quality through reuse of tested software modules.

Design Approach — Characteristic	Structured	Event-Driven	Object-Oriented
Dominant view of the problem	Sequence of transactions	Random stimuli	Independent responses to messages
Organizing structure	Hierarchical processes and data in the background	Interface objects	All communicating objects
System components	Procedures and data	Interface objects and database	Objects containing data and methods
Design principle	Decomposition	Prototype	Inheritance and specialization
Design process	System development life cycle	Database design and user prototype	Object design and incremental build

FIGURE 10-7 *A comparison of three program architectures*

Program Modules

◆ ◆

To the computer, a program being executed is a sequence of machine language instructions. But from the standpoint of a designer or programmer, a program consists of a program architecture in which program statements, modules, objects, and other abstractions are organized. Intermediate level constructs such as modules, functions, subprograms, objects, and methods are needed to deal with program complexity.

A program that does useful work is not just a simple sequence of instructions to be followed from start to finish. There are always numerous choices that must be made during program execution, such as decisions based on the data being used, the previous actions taken, and various error conditions encountered. Even a fairly simple program must do a variety of things and will have a variety of execution paths. In terms of possible instruction execution sequences, program complexity is combinatorial. For example, a program that contains twenty instructions making either/or choices has over a million (2^{20}) theoretical paths through the program. While many of the theoretically possible paths are not feasible, the number of combinations is still very large.

There is no natural, sequential order in which to present or read an entire program. On the other hand, programs must be understandable to the human programmers and those who maintain existing programs. This points out some of the difficulties of understanding even relatively small programs by reading program statements.

Human understanding of a large complete program in terms of its instructions without any intermediate structure to aid comprehension is not feasible. Only when instructions are combined and organized into units, each of which carries out some program function, can program units be meaningful for humans. Therefore, an important objective for designers is to formulate program units or modules that are meaningful to humans.

Modules may be organized into a hierarchy that forms an organization chart for the program. To the extent possible, each module should have a single, well-defined and easily understandable function. It is not always possible to achieve this ideal, and there are situations where the concept of single purpose is sacrificed in favor of other structural considerations. However, in general, every module shares a set of common characteristics:

◊ *It involves a single function.* This means that it is possible to name a module with a simple, clear, and unambiguous declarative sentence that describes its purpose (an action verb plus an object).

◊ *It is appropriately sized.* A module is not too large to understand, nor so small as to be trivial. One rule of thumb is a size that will fit within one page or screen of program statements.

◊ *It requires single entry/single exit.* This implies that there is an integrity to each module. It can be used only as a whole module and never as a collection of parts.

◊ *It contains its own data definitions.* This supports the concept of encapsulation. If a module needs an element of data or a data structure internally or to exchange with its subordinate modules, the data should be defined locally within that module.

◊ *It communicates by passing parameters.* Sharing of structural information about data among modules is limited to specific exchanges needed to carry out the functions of the modules.

A compromise in the functional ideal for modules in which each module contains its own data is the limited use of **global data structures**. Global data structures are independent of single modules. Future changes can sometimes be made easier by defining some data and data structures so that they are visible to and shared by all modules. This is most often done with constants and variables that can be modified or revised at a single point, but are referenced and used by many modules.

Program Operations and Variables

When writing program statements, a programmer must know the syntax for the programming language being used. The syntax specifies how the words and symbols are placed together to form a program statement. For example, the general syntax for a statement to add the values associated with two variables and store the result under the name of another variable is the result variable name followed by an equal sign, the variable name for one operand, a plus sign, and the variable name for the other operand. The statement reads as follows (if the result variable name is Alpha and the two operand variable names are Beta and Gamma): Alpha = Beta + Gamma.

In computer programming, the equal sign (=) is used in ways that do not mean "equals" in the mathematical sense. The equal sign in a statement means to assign the result of the operations to the variable to the left of the equal sign. In the preceding statement, Alpha = Beta + Gamma may be interpreted as "sum the values associated with the variable names Beta and Gamma and assign or associate the sum with the variable name Alpha."

Arithmetic, Comparison, and String Operations

Most programming languages employ the following standard symbols for operations such as arithmetic:

+	Addition
−	Subtraction
*	Multiplication
/	Division
^	Exponentiation

In some cases, either a symbol or a word may be used to specify the operation. For example, in one programming language, either a plus sign (+) or the word ADD may be used.

Order of execution is implied by an order rule: exponentiation is performed first, addition and subtraction are performed next (from left to right), and multiplication and division are performed last. Rather than relying upon this implied order of operation rule, parentheses are used to make order of execution explicit. The operations in the innermost parentheses are performed first followed by the next set of parentheses, and so forth.

Comparison operators (symbols and sometimes letters) are used to define a comparison operation between variables:

Symbol	Comparison	Letters
>	Greater than	GT
<	Less than	LT
>=	Greater than or equal	GE
<=	Less than or equal	LE
<>	Not equal	NE
=	Equal	EQ

Additional programming symbols define operations on strings of characters, such as names and text.

    &   **Concatenation** (linking two strings together). For example, concatenating a first name and a last name will give a full name.

    Len ( )   Function that gives the number of characters in a string.

Logic or Boolean Operations

Boolean operators are often used in search and selection statements as explained in Chapter 8. They are also used in programming Boolean expressions in a computer program. A Boolean expression (a variable or an expression with variables separated by operators) is either TRUE or FALSE. The three basic **Boolean operations** (sometimes referred to as logic operations) are defined by the following terms:

AND   The result of a statement is true if both variables connected by AND meet the criteria.

OR   The result of a statement is true if either of the variables connected by OR meets the criteria.

NOT   Reverses the truth or falsity of a variable or operation if placed in front of it.

Variable Types

In programming, a variable refers to a storage location that can contain data. The contents of the variable storage location can be modified during program execution. Specifying the type of variables is important because type defines the operations allowed for the variable. For example, an integer variable can only represent an integer result (no fractional results); a real or floating point type variable can represent both integer and fractional results; and a string or character variable can only represent character strings. Many languages autoatically define a general default variable type to cover both numeric and character data. A user may explicitly define data types in order to define the operations allowed.

For example, in Microsoft Visual Basic™, there are seven fundamental data types:

1. *Integer*
2. *Long* Integer
3. *Single* precision floating point
4. *Double* precision floating point
5. *Currency*
6. *String*
7. *Variant* (default general type that can store other types). It can have subtypes such as Date.

In addition, a user can create a user-defined data type.

Constants can be defined in a program by writing them in a statement. Arithmetic constants are written as numbers; string constants are commonly enclosed in quotation marks.

Variable Names

Since data or results of operations are referenced in a computer program by variable names, the names of different variables must be unique. Variable names generally follow some naming conventions and have some restrictions. In older programming languages, the number of characters in a variable name was limited to a few characters. More recent programming languages allow much longer names. Variable names may be established by just using the names in a program, or by specifically declaring them at the start of a program. The advantage of declaring the variable names is that only those names may be used in the program. If a variable name is misspelled, the error can be detected; if variables are not declared, the program will assign the misspelling as a new variable. If a declared variable of a certain type is used as though it were another type, this error will be detected.

Variable names can refer to arrays of variables. For example, a list of sales might be called **SALES**. To identify the different sales variables, each cell in the list is identified with an index. **SALES(1)** references the data in the first location of the list; **SALES(2)** references the second location, and so forth. If the array has two dimensions, there are two indexes. The first refers to the row and the second the column. If **SALES** referenced a two-dimensional matrix, **SALES(3,4)** would reference the variable location in the third row and fourth column. A variable is identified as an array by a declaration. For example, in one language, the statement to define **DELTA** as a two-dimensional array with 5 rows and 4 columns is: **DIM DELTA(5,4)**.

Example

In Microsoft Visual Basic™, a variable name is limited to 255 characters, must start with an alphabetic character, and may not have periods embedded in the name. Upper and lowercase may be used to make names easier to read. To illustrate:

FirstName = "Gordon"   Defines a string and assigns it to the variable **FirstName**.

SalaryLimit = 450.00   Assigns a real value to variable **SalaryLimit**.   ◆

The name assigned to a variable or object may not only describe the kind of variable or object, but may also be used in statements that set or retrieve properties associated with the variable or object. Names are then combined so that the property name follows the variable or object name as a suffix, separated by a character such as a period. Two examples illustrate the variable/object name plus property:

txtDisplay.FontBold   name for a variable or object named **txtDisplay** that has a property of **FontBold** (a bold font)

Text5.BackColor   refers to a variable or object named **Text5** that can have different background colors

Procedure Names

Units of execution or modules are also named and their names must follow the syntax of the programming language. Names that clearly describe the function of the program should be used, as for example, **DisplayPicture**. In an event-driven program, procedures (subprograms) are written for each event that can occur. The name of the procedure is the name assigned by the programmer, plus a suffix that applies a predefined event name. For example, a procedure to define the logic when a change occurs in a scrollbar will have the event suffix **_Change**, and a procedure to respond to a keystroke will have the name suffix **_KeyPress**. If the scrollbar object is **InterestRate**, the procedure to define logic for a change in the scrollbar is named **InterestRate_Change**.

Object, Property, and Method Names

The event-driven and object-oriented approaches do not necessarily follow a hierarchical program structure. One of the implications of their different program structure is that units of data and units of execution must be distinguishable from all other units. In both approaches, three units that are associated together in naming are objects, properties, and methods. (Names are assigned to each of these.)

1. *Objects.* Object names for screen **objects** (such as forms, check boxes, and text boxes) are often assigned by the programming environment. For example, in Visual Basic™, a form object is named **Form**, a check box

control object is named **CheckBox**, a scroll bar is identified by **HscrollBar**, and a text box object by **TextBox**.

2. *Properties.* Properties of objects also have assigned names. **Properties** are the attributes of the objects, such as size, color, screen location, and visibility. Examples of property names are **Value** for the value property of an object, **Text** for a text string property, and **Visible** for a property of being visible on the screen.

3. *Methods.* A **method** (procedure that acts on an object) also has a name. For example, **Print** is a method to print text of an object and **FindFirst** is a method to find the first record that matches specified criteria.

The object, property, and method names are combined in a hierarchical "dot" notation. This notation is used in event-driven and object-oriented languages to assure that the correct objects, properties, and methods are referenced. For example, the following names refer to objects on the user screen and properties or methods of the object:

SampleInputBox.Label	Refers to the property "label" of the object "SampleInputBox."
PictureViewer.Display (filename)	Refers to the method "Display" of the object "PictureViewer."
lblMyBox.Font Size	Defines a label object on the screen and its font size property.
imgFrown.Visible	Defines a graphic object called imgFrown that has the property of being visible on the screen.

The names in the last two examples illustrate a useful but not required naming convention. Since there are different types of objects, it is useful to use the name to show this. In the two examples, the first three characters of the name identify the type of object (a label object or an image object on the screen).

Dialog and Data Input for a Macro Program

◆ ◆ ◆ ◆ ◆ ◆ ◆ ◆ ◆ ◆ ◆ ◆ ◆ ◆ ◆ ◆ ◆ ◆ ◆ ◆

In even simple macros, the user may need to enter data as part of the program. The data may be input for processing or data used to control program execution. Since user programs operate with graphical user interfaces, data entry is in response to a request or other event. The entry of the requested data also constitutes an event.

As an introduction to data entry for an event-driven program, this section explains a simple mechanism for data entry. An object in the user display screen requests an input by displaying a message to the user and accepting the user's input via the keyboard or mouse. The input instruction in the program must include the message to be displayed to the user. The message should indicate the data to be entered and any conditions that will help the user make a correct entry. For example, the following are user input messages that are explicit, clear, and concise:

Key in order date (MM/DD/YY format) and press **ENTER** key

Key in employee identification number and press **ENTER** key

Key in amount of order and press **ENTER** key. After last order, key in END and press **ENTER** key

Example

A simple approach to data entry in Microsoft Visual Basic™ is the InputBox function. The InputBox prompts a user for input by displaying a box with a message. The user inputs the data in a predefined location in the box. The following example illustrates the function in its simplest form:

Variable where result is to be stored = InputBox (message to user)

For example:

EmployeeIdentification = ("Key in employee identification number and press **ENTER** key")

The input box presented to the user by execution of this statement is shown in Figure 10-8. ◆

Program Control Structures

◆ ◆ ◆ ◆ ◆ ◆ ◆ ◆ ◆ ◆ ◆ ◆ ◆ ◆ ◆ ◆ ◆ ◆ ◆

A control structure is a pattern for organizing a set of program instructions to control execution within a module. Three control structures are sufficient to code any program module: sequence, alternation, and repetition (see Figure 10-9). The sequence control structure is the same as the result of macro recording: the statements are coded as actions to be completed one after the other. Both alternation and repetition are decision structures. The computer evaluates a conditional expression to be either true or false. Program execution follows one path or the other, depending upon the result of that evaluation.

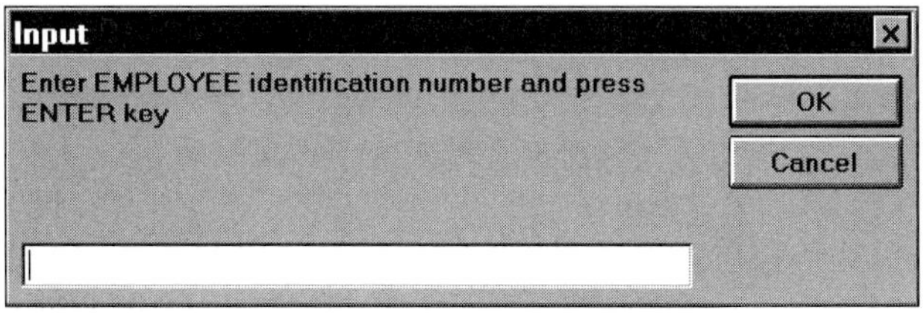

FIGURE 10-8 *Input box in Visual Basic. Message to user prompts input.*

The detailed design of a program and its control structures is developed in pseudocode, which has a format similar to simplified high-level computer instructions. Therefore, it is rather straightforward to transform pseudocode into the instructions of a specific high-level language. High-level programming languages have syntax elements (ways to code instructions) that are equivalent to the control structures used in a pseudocode. With pseudocode the program designer can focus on the program design rather than the syntactic details of a particular programming language. After learning the general form of each control structure, a programmer learns the way the control structure is implemented in the language being used.

In using pseudocode and also in writing computer instructions, it is good practice to use indentation to reveal the program structure. The control structure keyword is aligned at the left margin or left indentation if one control structure is nested within another. The statements on lines contained within the control structure, following the structure keyword, are indented. This visually shows the range of statements within the control structure, as illustrated in Figure 10-10. The structural elements of control structures are keywords, such as **if**, **endif**, and **while**. In pseudocode, a typographical convention such as boldface is usually used to make keywords stand out.

Sequence Control Structure

The **sequence control structure** is one instruction after the other, executed from beginning to end with no possibility of change. The instructions in a sequence are processing instructions such as arithmetic, operations on strings of characters, retrieval of data, or display of outputs.

Alternation Control Structure

The **alternation structure** is the way choices are controlled. The basic implementation of alternation is **if-then-else-end if**. There are a number of additional implementations of alternation. The additions are conveniences and each can

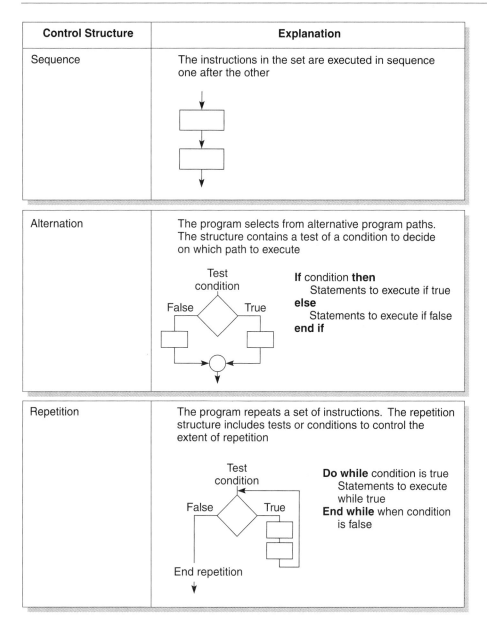

Control Structure	Explanation
Sequence	The instructions in the set are executed in sequence one after the other

Alternation	The program selects from alternative program paths. The structure contains a test of a condition to decide on which path to execute
	
	Test condition False True
	
	If condition **then**
	    Statements to execute if true
	else
	    Statements to execute if false
	end if

Repetition	The program repeats a set of instructions. The repetition structure includes tests or conditions to control the extent of repetition
	
	Test condition False True End repetition
	
	Do while condition is true
	    Statements to execute
	    while true
	End while when condition
	    is false

FIGURE 10-9   *Three control structures are sufficient to code any decision control logic.*

be translated to the basic **if-then-else-end if** control structure. Following is an example of the basic alternation structure. An example in the Visual Basic™ language is shown in Figure 10-11.

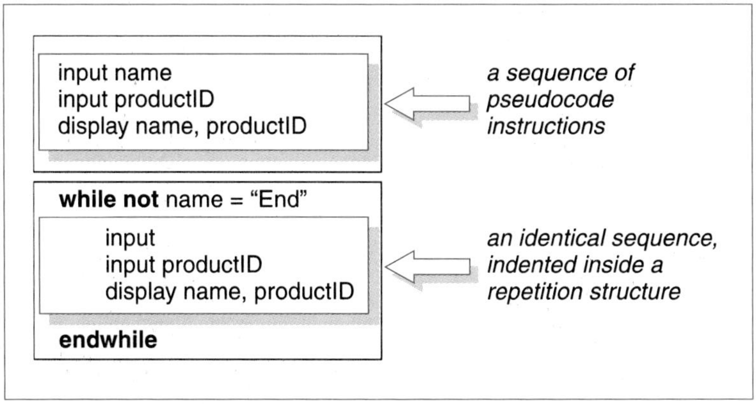

FIGURE 10-10 *Example of indentation in pseudocode*

```
if conditional expression then
    Sequence of statements if condition is true
else
    Sequence of statements if condition is false
end if
```

There is a frequently occurring special case in the alternation control structure where no action is to be taken when the condition is evaluated to false. In other words, perform actions if condition is true, but do nothing if it is false. In this special case no **else** statements are specified.

```
if conditional expression then
    Sequence of statements if condition is true
end if
```

Case is an extension of alternation that may be used to select among more than two possible actions. One and only one action is selected based on the value of a condition. A case statement has the following structure:

```
If salary < 1000 Then
        RetirementContribution = .03*Salary
Else
        RetirementContribution = .05*Salary
End If
```

FIGURE 10-11 *Alternation control structure in Visual Basic language. If the value of Salary is less than 1000, the retirement contribution is 3 percent; otherwise it is 5 percent.*

select case conditional expression
   case value-1
      Sequence of statements to be executed if the expression evaluates to
      case value-1
   case value-2
      Sequence of statements to be executed if the expression evaluates to
      case value-2
   ...
   case value-n
      Sequence of statements to be executed if the expression evaluates to
      case value-n
   case else
      Sequence of statements to be executed if none of the above apply
end select

Repetition Control Structure

The **repetition structure**, often termed a loop, is a way of conditionally repeating a sequence of instructions. The repetition structure evaluates a conditional expression with every iteration of its loop. Thus the statements within the loop effectively control the number of repetitions, since they alter the values being tested by the conditional expression.

The following example illustrates a basic repetition structure:

do while conditional expression is true
   Sequence of statements to be executed
end while

In the **do-while** control structure, the value of the conditional expression is evaluated before any action is taken. If it initially evaluates to false, the entire control structure is bypassed. If it is true, the sequence of statements is executed and control returns to the beginning, where the conditional expression is evaluated again. If a conditional expression is initially evaluated as true and the condition is never changed, the result is an **infinite loop**, a common type of programming error.

There are several useful variants of the basic repetition structure. One of the most common is the **repeat-until**. The following example illustrates the *repeat-until* structure:

repeat
   Sequence of statements to be executed
until conditional expression is true

The **repeat-until** variant is the same as **do-while** except that the sequence of statements is always executed once because the statements are executed before the conditional expression is evaluated.

An example of the *repeat-until* structure in the Visual Basic language is shown in Figure 10-12. In the example, the **repeat-until** structure is coded using the words **Do-Loop Until**. Each programming language may use slightly different words, but the structures are equivalent.

A third repetition variant is used when a sequence of statements is to be executed a predetermined number of times. The following pseudocode illustrates the **for** loop structure:

```
for index initial value to index ending value
    Sequence of statements to be executed
end for
```

The for loop is often called **indexed repetition** because repetition is controlled by a variable (called an index) that is incremented at each execution.

An important control structure related to repetition is **recursion** in which modules in effect repeat themselves. Since recursion structures are implemented differently, they are not used in the type of programming described in this text.

Nesting of Control Structures

Control structures may be "nested." A **nested control structure** is a control structure that is wholly contained within another. Overlap of control structures

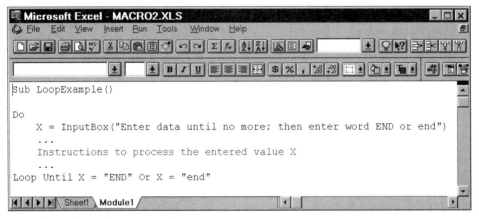

FIGURE 10-12 *Repeat-until control structure in Visual Basic language. Program segment requests input from user until the user enters the word "END" or "end."*

is never permitted. Control structure keywords mark the beginning and end of a control structure. Indentation is employed to further define nesting of control structures. Figure 10-13 presents two examples of nested control structures. One is a simple repetition within a repetition; the other is an alternation within a repetition. These examples reflect the structure of low complexity modules.

Other Control Statements

Two other control statements are often used. One transfers control from within a module to a subordinate module. Another permits immediate exit from a repetition structure.

◊ **Call** transfers control to a subordinate module. The **call** statement also specifies parameters. **Parameters** are the data to be transferred to and returned from the subordinate module.

◊ **Exit** statement to exit directly from within repetition and module structures. For example, a condition may occur within a repetition structure that means the repetition should cease prior to the condition established by the repetition structure. The exit statement is used for that purpose. The exit statement is most useful in dealing with exceptions.

```
           Repetition Nested within Repetition

do while input is not 'END'
      Input name, product number, and number of items
      Display input
      for INDEX = 1 TO number of items
            Input data for each  item into a matrix
      end for
end while


           Alternation Nested within Repetition

do while employee records
      Input employee name, status, dependents
      if status = retired then
            Compute health benefit cost for retired
      else
            Compute health benefit cost for not retired
      end if
      Display employee name, status, dependents, health benefit
end while
```

FIGURE 10-13 *Nested control structures*

Adding Control Structures and Dialog to Recorded Macros

◆ ◆ ◆ ◆ ◆ ◆ ◆ ◆ ◆ ◆ ◆ ◆ ◆ ◆ ◆ ◆ ◆ ◆ ◆ ◆

The facilities that produce a recorded macro result in a single sequence program structure. There can be no alternation or repetition in a recorded macro. The procedures created by recording may include many operations, but they are always sequences. Multiple sequences may be produced by recording more than one macro.

A macro procedure is a program, even if it was created by recording. It can be simple or complex, short or long. An entire macro could be created by writing statements in a macro programming language. However, doing so requires understanding many details of the syntax of the macro language. An alternative approach to writing macros that include decision logic is to develop the sequence structures by recording and then edit the result to insert dialog, and alternation and repetition structures.

There are three major benefits from using this approach in developing complex macros:

1. The programmer need not be familiar with all of the instructions of the macro language in order to record sequences of operations. (Therefore, the focus can be on the set of instructions to implement control structures or insert dialog.)

2. Errors made while recording can be ignored. (When a recording error is made, it can be noted for later modification or deletion and recording can proceed.)

3. Users can learn by doing.

The following steps outline the method used to create a complex macro, starting with a recorded macro:

1. Record the keystrokes or mouse actions to be performed (prior to any alternation choices or repetition) in the order in which they will be performed.

2. When there are two or more possible sequences from which to choose, record performance of the first set of actions followed by the second set of actions. The two sequences will follow one after the other, but with no alternation structure to select between them.

3. When there are actions to be repeated, perform the instructions to be repeated. The sequence will appear once, but there will be no instructions to specify repetition.

4. If the preceding steps are too complicated to perform in one macro recording sequence, record them in two or more separate macros.

Once you have recorded the instructions to be executed without dialogs or alternation and repetition structures, enter the macro editing facilities of the software package to edit your macro.

Adding Alternation Structures

To edit your macro, do the following:

1. Identify the beginning and ending statements in the set of instructions to be conditionally executed.

2. Using the editing function, insert an **if-then** statement with the appropriate condition before the first statement.

3. Locate the set of instructions to be executed if a condition is false.

4. Using editing, insert an **else** statement before the first statement.

5. Locate the end of the set of instructions under control of the condition.

6. Using editing, insert the **end if** statement after the last statement to terminate the alternation control structure.

After inserting the instructions, the sequence is changed to the following alternation structure:

if conditional expression **then**
    Instructions from recorded macro if condition is true
else
    Instructions from recorded macro if condition is false
end if

More complex alternation structures such as a **case** structure that selects one from a set of alternatives may be inserted in the same way when needed.

Adding Repetition Structures

The process of adding repetition structures is similar to the approach for the alternation structures. The instructions to be repeated are produced by performing them once as part of the macro recording process. Having recorded the set of instructions to be included in the loop, the programmer uses the editing facilities to add repetition.

After locating the first and last instructions in the set of instructions that are to be repeated, the programmer inserts the statements for the control structure. A critical decision in selecting the repetition structure statements is whether the sequence within the repetition may be bypassed if the repetition condition is false (**do-while**) or must always be performed at least once (**repeat-until**). If the sequence is executed a predetermined number of times (indexed repetition), use a **for loop**. Insert the appropriate structure: **do-while**, **repeat-until**, or **for to-end for**. Specify the governing condition and check that the condition is in the appropriate positive or negative form. The specific commands for these structures will depend on the language being used.

Example
Table 10-1 lists the three repetition instructions in Microsoft Visual Basic™. ◆

Adding Dialog and User Input

When a recorded macro is run, it does not stop to allow user input, nor does it provide messages about outputs, inputs, or other actions. Messages can be added to a recorded macro by editing. Input boxes or text boxes (or other methods of coding dialogs) can be inserted in the recorded macro.

Table 10-1 Three Repetition Instructions in Microsoft Visual Basic™	
Repetition Structure	*Visual Basic*
do-while (skip if condition is false)	**Do while condition** statements **Loop**
repeat-until (execute at least once)	**Do** statements **Loop until** condition

for to-end for
 	
(indexed repetition)
	For counter variable=initial value **To**
	    ending value **Step** increment value
	
	    statements
	
	Next

The process involves recording the macro and then editing it by inserting dialog and user input instructions. For a spreadsheet macro, the macro can be recorded with an input for a cell. On editing, the cell input can be replaced with an input box that requests an input. The instruction is written to place the value from the input box in the designated spreadsheet cell. Message instructions can be inserted in the macro code to display messages.

Achieving Modularity in Designing Macros

As the size and functionality of a macro increases, its complexity also increases. Also, because control structures interact combinatorially, complexity increases geometrically. At some point, such as five to seven control structures, a macro will become so complex that it is likely to contain errors.

Modular structure is one of the important tools for dealing with the problems of complexity. The key to achieving modularity, therefore, is to plan ahead. Whenever a macro must evaluate multiple conditions and repeat operations, it should be designed as a set of modules, using the following three step process:

1. Organize functions into modules.

2. Define the control structures for each module.

3. Separately record the sequences of operations to be included within each of the control structures and edit in the appropriate control structures and modules.

Example

The "envelope" macro distributed with WordPerfect 5.2 for Windows illustrates modules in a complex macro. This macro allows its user to select from many options including return address formats, fonts, and envelope sizes. The macro consists of 17 modules. A listing of the complete macro is 25 pages long! The fact that it is provided as a macro makes two important points: (1) macro programming languages are real programming languages, not limited or constrained subsets, and (2) professional programmers (such as the authors of this "envelope" macro) use modular designs and carefully planned control structures.   ◆

Macro Programs Without Recorded Macros

Using recorded macros as a building block for a macro and adding dialogs and control structures has significant advantages. However, there may be many situations when the macro must perform operating system or other functions that are difficult to include in recording mode. With increased proficiency, a knowledge worker may wish to develop macros directly. When this is done, they should be structured into modules as appropriate and should employ carefully designed control structures within each module.

$\mathcal{S}$ummary

◊ ◊ ◊ ◊ ◊ ◊ ◊ ◊ ◊ ◊ ◊ ◊ ◊ ◊ ◊ ◊ ◊ ◊ ◊ ◊

◊ Some opportunities for productivity enhancements involve knowledge of programming. This knowledge may be applied in the development of macros that have more functionality than can be achieved with simple recording or to write simple application programs.

◊ Computer programs are complex artifacts, and even simple programs require the strategies and techniques developed to deal with complexity. Program design occurs at three different levels: (1) program architecture, (2) organization of a program into modules, and (3) internal design of modules.

◊ The top level of program design is program architecture. The three architecture approaches are hierarchical procedure design (often called structured design or traditional design), event-driven design, and object-oriented design. The next level of design is the organization of a program into program modules. The lowest level of design is the internal structure of the module design units. A module consists of program statements that define sequences of actions plus statements that specify decision or control logic.

◊ A limited set of carefully assembled control structures helps make programs understandable to humans.

◊ In order to begin writing more complex macros or simple application programs, a user must understand the conventions for coding operations, naming variables, and coding simple input from a computer screen. The user must also understand how to design and code program control structures.

◊ The three major control structures are sequence, alternation, and repetition. These control structures can be nested to produce more complex structures.

◊ The combination of macro recording and macro editing maximizes the benefits of macros. This is especially useful for knowledge workers who are not professional programmers, since macro recording reduces the need to learn the details of a programming language.

◊ Editing can be used to insert dialogs with user instructions and actions. Editing control structures into recorded macros supports the development of rather complex programs.

◊ As macro programs become more complex, careful design becomes very important.

EXERCISES

1. The purpose of this exercise is to test your ability to read and explain a set of program language statements. In using the **HELP** facilities, there are often examples of language statements that can be used in learning about a feature. They can also be used as a template for using the feature. The code can be copied and then altered to fit user needs. The following examples are from Microsoft Visual Basic, but other visual programming languages have similar facilities. Note that the same capabilities can be obtained within the Visual Basic portions of Microsoft Excel 5.0 (such as Help, Visual Basic, and functions).

   Explain, for the two routines, what the routine does and explain each statement.

   a. InputBox example from Microsoft Visual Basic Help example for InputBox:

   ```
   Sub Form_Click ( )
      Dim Answer, DefVal, Msg, Title ' Declare variables.
      Msg = "Enter a value from 1 to 3." ' Set prompt.
      Title = "InputBox Demo" ' Set title.
      DefVal = "1" ' Set default return value.
      Do
         Answer = InputBox(Msg, Title, DefVal) ' Get input.
      Loop Until Answer >= 1 And Answer <= 3
      MsgBox "You entered" & Answer ' Display message.
   End Sub
   ```

   b. If ... Then ... Else statement example from Microsoft Visual Basic Help for IF ... (the last If ... Then was not indented in the example.):

   ```
   Sub Form_Click ( )
      Dim X, Y ' Declare variables.
      X = InputBox("Enter a number greater than 0 and less
                                          than 1000.")
      If X < 10 Then
         Y = 1 ' 1 digit.
      ElseIf X < 100 Then
         Y = 2 ' 2 digits.
      Else
         Y = 3 ' 3 digits.
      End If
      If Y > 1 Then Unit = " digits." Else Unit = " digit."
      MsgBox "The number you entered has " & Y & Unit
   End Sub
   ```

2. Prepare a spreadsheet using macro recording. Edit it with an InputBox that enters the date. Print the macro and print the result of using the macro.

3. In Chapter 9, Exercise 6, you were asked to produce a list of checks for a bank deposit based on a macro recording with a spreadsheet. The macro created a heading and a format for the spreadsheet, and set a date. Using the macro facilities of the spreadsheet package, make one or more of the following additions to the recorded macro. (This exercise uses terminology for Visual Basic, but other software may be used.)

   a. Add an InputBox to obtain the date. Be sure the message to the user indicates the date format.

   b. Record a second macro that prints two copies of the deposit check listing with no grid lines. Edit it to add some comments in the macro that describe its function, your name, the date it was recorded, and so forth. Execute the macro to make sure it works.

   c. Create a new module to manage the previous two modules. Write the new module so that it executes the heading and date module and then obtains the check amount inputs. After the last input, return control to the spreadsheet (see "d"). Manually enter a line of dashes under the last amount and use the sum function to get a total. Finally, execute the **print** macro to print the spreadsheet.

   d. The following lines of code illustrate the instructions to obtain the check amounts. Before writing your statements, be sure you understand what each statement does. Why does the program test for "End"? Each cell in the spreadsheet has an index number, so the repetition structure employs that to identify the cell in which to store the result. To store a variable named "Stuff" in a cell 2,3 (row 2, column 3), the instruction is: Cells(2,3).**Value** = **Stuff**

```
Sub CheckInput ( )
   I = 8
   Do
      I = I + 1
      CheckAmount = InputBox("Enter Check Amount and ENTER;
      When No More Checks, Enter the word End and ENTER",
      "Check Entry Box")
      Cells(I, 1).Value = CheckAmount
   Loop Until CheckAmount = "End"
End Sub
```

   e. As an additional assignment, you can add features:

      (1) Change the test of condition to include **END** or end. For example, Do until CheckAmount = "End" or CheckAmount = "end" etc. (You could use the **Ucase** function to convert any reply to uppercase

so the only test needed is for uppercase **END**.) Use Visual Basic **Help** (within Excel) to look up **Ucase** function information.

(2) Test for check amount greater than 1000. If found, display an error message and request correct input. Reset the cell index so that the erroneous amount is replaced.

(3) Automate all of the processes including the sum function and printing within the same procedure. (Note that this makes the macro both much more complex and easier to use.)

4. Record two printout macros—one to print two copies with grid lines and one to print one copy without grid lines and without header. Record a small spreadsheet. Edit the spreadsheet recorded macro to ask you what option you would like (1 or 2) and then select one of the printout macros. Run the macro to remove errors. Print the macro and the results of both selections.

5. Record a macro to set up a spreadsheet and print it. Write statements to accept input data and place in cells (1,1) through (10,1). Write a **do while** control structure to sum all cells where the amount in the cell is less than 100. Place the result in cell (1,11). Continue with another loop, but using a **do until** structure. Store the result in cell (1,12). Continue to print the spreadsheet. Make sure you are using the equivalent structure as specified for the language you are using. Run the macro with different inputs (e.g., 110 as the fifth input and 110 as the first input). Note the differences in outputs for the two structures.

6. Design a spreadsheet application that is useful to you that can be accomplished by macro recording plus adding input or dialog and control structures. Present simple documentation of problem description, program description macro listing, and sample outputs (including a screen capture of input box or message box use).

Designing and Implementing a User Interface

◊　　◊　　◊　　◊　　◊　　◊　　◊　　◊

OBJECTIVES

After completing this chapter, you should be able to:

◆ Describe some of the design criteria that impact effective user interface design.

◆ Explain the impact of user interface design on various types of system users.

◆ Describe the various types of user interfaces.

◆ Describe the process of creating and using graphical user interfaces (GUIs).

◆ Describe the relationships between software development environments and their potential users.

◆ Describe the use of the following screen objects used to access information: option

button, check box, list box, combo box, and scroll bar.

◆ Explain the use of Help facilities, icons, and hypertext links in accessing and using information.

◆ Explain the difference between software testing and debugging.

◆ Write a simple event-oriented program.

◆ Build a prototype of a simple application program.

KEY TERMS AND CONCEPTS

This chapter introduces the following key terms and concepts, listed in the order in which they appear:

user interface	power user	user interface design tool
screen events	command-based interface	code development tool
user mental model	menu-selection interface	testing
system image	direct-manipulation interface	debugging
user interface design	data input interface	version control systems
novice user	help facilities	
knowledgeable user	toolbox	

An interface is the connection between two systems. The user interface—which normally employs graphics with icons, menus, buttons, instructions, input forms, and report layouts—is what the user sees and interacts with when using a program or software package. This type of interface is termed a graphical user interface or GUI (pronounced "gooey"). User interface design is critical to productivity. A poor interface requires more time, both for learning and using the features and functions of an application and for error correction. A good interface facilitates correct use with labels, instructions, and messages that guide the user.

User design and implementation of application interfaces applies to both macro programs within software packages and user-developed programs. Many software packages (such as spreadsheet processors, database systems, and word processors) enable users to write macros that incorporate user-developed interfaces to facilitate applications within the package framework.

When a desired application cannot be built within the framework of a software package, it must be written as an independent application. The application may employ some existing components or be built entirely new. The programs to be designed and implemented usually involve user interaction with a graphical interface. Programs frequently need to retrieve or store data. Therefore, it is useful to separate program design and implementation into three parts: (1) the user interface, (2) the processing performed in response to user interface inputs, and (3) database access. This chapter explains the characteristics of a user interface and the kinds of tools that facilitate interface design and development, describes various elements and alternatives in the user interface, and surveys the interface design and development process.

The chapter is both conceptual and practical. It explains concepts and principles, but also describes methods used in practice. It also explains interface design principles and major methods for accessing and selecting program choices and describes principles of form and report design. Since a GUI is the most common approach to user interface with desktop computer systems, it is emphasized in this chapter. The exercises provide experience in using the interface design tools of an application development environment to develop simple user interfaces.

User Interface Design Objectives

◆ ◆ ◆ ◆ ◆ ◆ ◆ ◆ ◆ ◆ ◆ ◆ ◆ ◆ ◆ ◆ ◆ ◆ ◆ ◆

The **user interface** consists of input and output screens (and other media such as printed reports) presented by a software package, application, or program. The interface displays alternatives; accepts choices, requests, and data; and displays results and informative messages. High-quality interfaces are important to every knowledge worker using software packages and custom applications. A well-constructed interface fits the user's conceptual model, and its use is intuitively clear from the on-screen layout and instructions. Consequently, users seldom need to consult instructions, since they are guided to make effective use of the software facilities. The interface assists productivity by reducing user time and effort and minimizing lost time from errors and misunderstandings. A poor user interface leads to errors, omissions, and incorrect use because it is not intuitive and does not fit the user's mental model.

This leads to productivity losses from error corrections and additional time required to repeat operations because of misunderstandings. Time to input data or respond to system instructions is greater than with a well-designed interface.

The user interfaces emphasized in this chapter are associated with applications in which the user interacts with the program through a display device and enters commands and data via keystrokes and mouse pointer movements or clicks (see Figure 11-1). Such applications are characterized as event-driven because the program responds to **screen events**, such as a selection via a keystroke, pointer movement, a button click, or an input from the keyboard. Choices are presented on the screen by screen objects such as menus and icons. Screen events determine the actions to be taken by the program, which might be to generate messages, process data, request inputs, or display outputs. Program messages can direct user actions, display alternatives for selection, describe errors, or explain what the program is doing.

The following user interface design quality objectives must be met by the design of the screen interface plus the design of user help facilities:

1. *User understanding of alternatives and choices.* The interface should help users understand available alternatives and the meaning of the choices presented. The user interface should fit the way users think about the

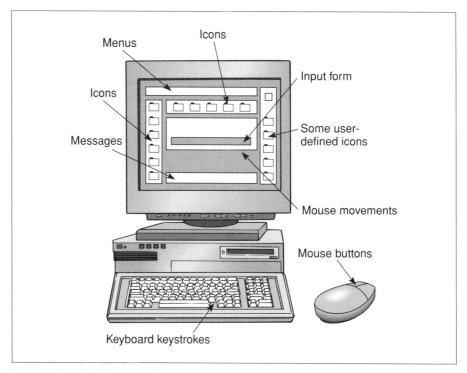

FIGURE 11-1   *User interfaces*

problem and fit with existing user expertise. The set of alternatives and choices should be complete.

2. *User understanding of input requirements and output content.* The interface should clarify the form and content of any inputs. The output screens should be understandable, with formats that include headings, labels, and names that identify screen content.

3. *User error prevention, reduction, and recovery.* The user interface should prevent or reduce user errors due to misunderstanding or mistakes and help users correct errors and recover from mistakes.

4. *Efficient system use.* The user interface design should present a logical and natural flow of operations and instructions. It should minimize time for user inputs by supporting fast methods such as keystrokes and by anticipating inputs.

User Interface Design

◆ ◆

A design principle presented earlier emphasized simplifying application design by dividing or partitioning the design task into several smaller tasks. Given current technology, the design task consists of dividing the system into three design components: the user interface, programmed procedures, and the database. Design and implementation support tools reflect this division: there are user interface design tools, procedural programming tools, and database management systems. This partitioning into three separate design tasks does not work for every problem. However, it does apply to the majority of information systems, and especially to small systems for individuals or groups. This chapter concentrates on user interface design and development.

The user interface design task is simplified by the division of tasks into user interface, programmed procedures, and database management because interface designers are able to make assumptions about the products of the other design tasks. For example, they can assume that a database design exists and that major processes have been defined elsewhere. This enables them to focus on the direct and specific interactions between the system and its users.

There are numerous guidelines for user interface design. In order to understand the context for the use of these guidelines, it is helpful to understand the interaction between the developer's mental model of the system that will be produced and the user's mental model of the system. The term "user" has been employed as if all users were the same. However, in practice, there are three major types of users: beginners, experts, and intermittent users. The user interface should reflect the needs of all three types of users.

User Interface and the System User Mental Model

The user interface is the visible portion of a system. To the user, it *is* the system. Conceptually, the idea of a user interface includes every aspect of the system that can be perceived. For software, that means the user interface can be extended beyond the screen and manipulation devices to documentation and training. However, this chapter concentrates on the screen interface.

The user of a system develops or constructs a mental model of that system. The **user mental model** is a result of the different aspects perceived by the user, including accumulated experience with the system. The user model or image of a system guides behavior. To the extent that the user model is inconsistent with system behavior, use will lead to problems, errors, and frustrations. A principle of user interface design, therefore, is to understand the user mental model and to design in such a way that the image produced by the computer system is consistent with it.

The designer of a system also has a mental model of the system. In the ideal situation, the designer's mental model and the user's mental model will be congruent or identical. The designer's task is to learn the user's requirements in order to construct the system. The impressions the completed system produces on its users should generate a user mental model of the system consistent with user requirements. Figure 11-2 illustrates this concept. The user image of a system is developed entirely from the user interface and this image guides subsequent user behavior. "Behind the screen interface," the designer writes procedures to produce the results. The design goals of the designer reflected in the designer mental model of the system are broader than the user interface, but these designer goals result in an implementation that produces the **system image** perceived by the user. This notion of multiple mental models is important in design and in user/designer communication.

User Interface Design Guidelines

Ben Shneiderman, a noted researcher in human-computer interaction, defined eight "golden rules" for **user interface design** (see Figure 11-3). These rules are general and cover a broad range of user interfaces. The following discussion applies these rules to the GUI common to personal computer use.

1. *Strive for consistency.* User interface layouts should be consistent in terms of terminology, syntax, and actions. Adherence to this rule is evident in Microsoft Windows™, which has established a high level of consistency for software that runs under its Presentation format. For example, the **EXIT** command is in the same position in all menus (at the bottom of

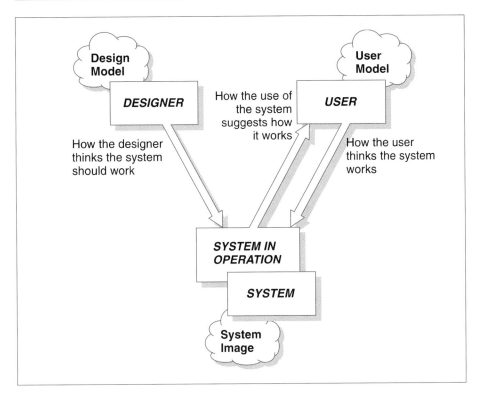

FIGURE 11-2   *The designer model, user model, and system image*

Source: Adapted from Donald A. Norman, *The Psychology of Everyday Things,* New York: Basic Books, 1988.

the **FILE** menu). The **EXIT** command is used the same way in all applications. Terminology should be consistent across menus, input prompts, messages, and help screens.

2. *Enable frequent users to use shortcuts.* Occasional users may find that going through a set of menus is the best way to establish a sequence of required actions; experienced users may like to use keystrokes as a shortcut. (The issue of different interfaces for different types of users is discussed in the next section.)

3. *Offer informative feedback.* The user interface should give feedback for both successful and unsuccessful operations. For example, an hourglass may appear on the screen to indicate that an operation is in process. A message indicating operation failure should indicate the reason for the failure.

4. *Design dialogs to yield closure.* The user should understand the beginning of a set of actions, the sequence of actions, and the ending of the sequence. The user interface should guide the user through the sequence and define the end of the actions.

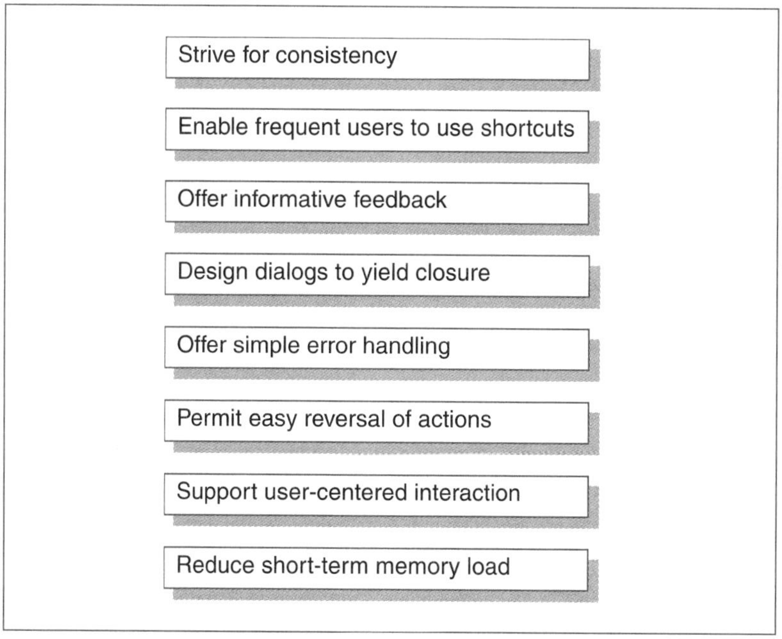

FIGURE 11-3 *Shneiderman's golden rules for user interface design*

Source: B. Shneiderman, *Designing the User Interface,* Reading, MA: Addison-Wesley, 1987.

5. *Offer simple error handling.* Error messages should indicate the nature of the error and what the user must do to correct it.

6. *Permit easy reversal of actions.* When possible, the interface should let users reverse an action or group of actions.

7. *Support user-centered interaction.* The interface should be designed so that the user can focus on the task rather than on directing computer actions. The user has control of the way the task is to be performed.

8. *Reduce short-term memory load.* A user should not be required to remember things that can be provided by the system. The system should list options and provide assistance and examples to refresh user recall of what needs to be done.

The essence of Shneiderman's rules is to keep users in control and provide support so that they can focus on the task to be performed instead of the details of instructing the computer. The interface rules are consistent with the "dual processing effect" described in Chapter 4. If the user must concentrate on both the task and the computer commands, there will be a loss of productivity. A good user interface is easy to use. Once learned, it supports the user's task so that each step is clear and obvious.

Different Interface Designs for Different Users

Shneiderman's second rule suggests interfaces should be different for frequent (power) users. Research suggests that users can be classified into types based on their knowledge of a system and their patterns of use. Three types of users that are usually contrasted are novice or new users, knowledgeable but intermittent users, and frequent or power users.

1. *The novice or new system user.* **Novice users** may have a poor or incomplete understanding of the task to be completed. They may have poorly-formed mental models of the system that are often incomplete and erroneous. To support the novice user, a system should provide the following:

    a. *A small set of alternatives or choices for each action.* The novice needs to be protected from the effects of unintended actions and mistakes. The design should present only the necessary subset of choices or should structure the interface so that the simpler alternatives are presented first or made easier to choose. An incorrect choice should be easily reversible.

    b. *Easily accessible help.* The novice user should be able to access an explanation of any feature at any point. The implications of every choice should be clearly presented.

    c. *Built-in training and tutorials.* The novice user should be allowed to suspend operation at any point and switch to a learning mode. This allows novice users to perform work they understand and to add knowledge they do not already possess while they are working (another example of using "just-in-time" learning). Reversible actions aid in this learning process.

2. *The knowledgeable intermittent user.* **Knowledgeable users** understand the task at hand and have a well-formed mental model of the computer application. However, if they do not use the software often, they may not remember the specific operations and sequences of actions. This category of users should be supported in ways such as the following that assist in recall of operations:

    a. *Present choices in a "recognition" mode.* Menus can be used to present alternatives, and icons or symbols may be used to prompt recognition of functions. An intermittent user with a clear understanding of task objectives can be expected to select from the available alternatives with few false starts.

    b. *Provide accessible but condensed help.* Intermittent users need support to recall what to do rather than a complete explanation. Overviews and short explanations are more important than complete reference support.

c. *Protect the user from "dangerous" activities.* Lack of immediate familiarity with a program or system, coupled with an outcome rather than a learning orientation, may lead to dangerous activities or destructive actions. This user needs to be able to reverse the effects of choices and short sequences of choices that may appear to have been impulsive. When actions (such as record or file deletion) are irreversible, the user should be warned of the result before the action is completed.

3. *The frequent or "power" user.* **Power users** can be expected to have clear mental models of both the task and the software application. The interface design for the frequent user should be oriented toward efficiency. A power user can be expected to have committed many operations and task sequences to memory. To assist power users, the system should provide the following:

a. *Limited feedback.* Users should be able to carry out commands completely and be furnished with only simple confirmations in return. Excessive feedback and the delays it causes are frustrating to this type of user.

b. *Frequent shortcuts.* Users should be able to execute sequences with a single command or keystroke. They should not be forced to deal with a list of alternatives, but be enabled to go directly to the action to be performed.

Because software packages may be employed by users from novice to power, many packages explicitly support each of them. They provide a menu hierarchy that lists all actions that may be taken, and they offer ways to specify the actions more directly. Some packages allow the user to specify their level of expertise and then present an interface that fits the choice.

Understanding the different types of users and the differences in user interface design can assist individual users in making choices. When an individual or small group designs a macro or other application, the design should reflect the various types of users.

Types of User Interfaces

♦ ♦

There are several different types of user interfaces, based on different technologies and, to some extent, upon user needs. The six most common types are command-based interfaces, menu interfaces, direct manipulation interfaces, data input forms, reports, and help facilities. The dominant user interface for user-developed systems is the direct manipulation allowed by graphical user interfaces. This chapter reviews all six types of interfaces, but focuses on direct manipulation interfaces.

It may be difficult for a user doing development to deal with the entire range of user interface options. The design can, however, evolve as the application is used and refined. For example, a user might construct an application based on a task currently performed. As a new design is created, the steps of the user task also change, necessitating revisions to the initial task model. For this reason, a prototyping process is usually an integral part of user interface design. Working from an initial model of data, outputs, and user task, a prototype design is constructed. The objective of the initial prototyping cycle is to build an interface that the user can work with in a live setting. It should handle fundamental data and the most common process sequences. As the system is used, it affects the work being performed and new requirements emerge. This necessitates a revision of the system. The evaluation-revision cycle may be repeated to implement the changes needed to meet user needs.

Command-based Interface

In **command-based interfaces**, the user enters specific commands, usually by typing full command words or abbreviations, plus necessary parameters or specifications that belong to the commands (see Figure 11-4). An example is the command "**PRINT** file." A command-based interface is typically not appropriate for a novice user and is usually not satisfactory for a knowledgeable intermittent user because effective use of a command-based interface requires the user to memorize the commands. Command-based interfaces are most

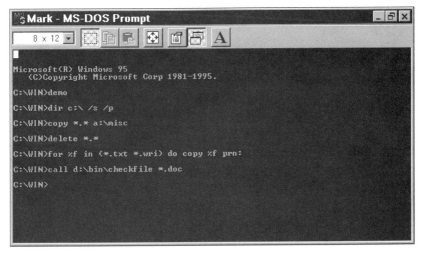

FIGURE 11-4   *Example of box on screen for entry of command and sample of commands*

appropriate for expert users, although they can be an option for others. Following are some principles of command-based interface design:

◆ *Use commands as alternative shortcuts for menu and direct manipulation interfaces.* Reminder menus should be available as backup with limited help.

◆ *Limit the set of commands.* Even experts have limits to the number and variety of commands they can effectively memorize and retrieve.

◆ *Select command names that fit the task and the user's mental model.* Use natural names and abbreviations, and accept alternative names and spellings. Use a consistent pattern for commands and command parameters, and prompt for parameters upon request. For example, if the command is "END," the program might be written to accept "Quit" or "Exit" as well.

Menu Selection Interface

In **menu-selection interfaces**, a list of alternatives is presented to the user. Menus may be organized into hierarchies, so that a menu choice at the top-level menu may bring up a second-level menu with choices that follow from the top-level choice. As illustrated in Figure 11-5, there are several variations on the concept of menu selection, based on whether there is a hierarchy of menus and how the menu is accessed.

Menu interfaces may include the following features:

◆ *A simple list or row of options.* A list is presented as choices in a column. The entire list is shown. In a menu bar, the alternatives are listed along a row.

◆ *A drop-down menu.* If the list is too long to be displayed, the box for the menu displays only the heading of the list. The details "drop down" when the heading is activated by a mouse action. This type of menu conserves screen space because the list is displayed only when requested.

FIGURE 11-5a *Different ways to present and access menus: simple list*

FIGURE 11-5b   *Menu bar*

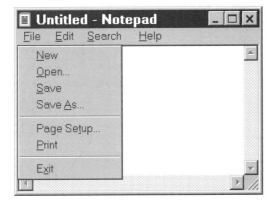

FIGURE 11-5c   *Drop-down menu*

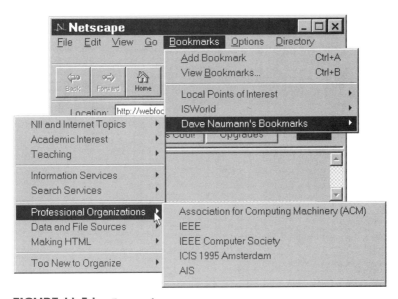

FIGURE 11-5d   *Layered menus*

◊ *A hierarchy of menus.* When there are many choices, they may be organized as a hierarchy. The top level of the hierarchy is always displayed. A pull-down or drop-down menu is used to expand the hierarchy. When a

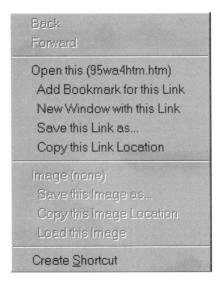

FIGURE 11-5e *Pop-up menu*

selection is made, additional options are presented in a list that appears below the original selection. The next level of the hierarchy drops down.

◆ *A layered menu.* When designing the layout for presentation of a hierarchy of menus, the menus may appear individually or in layers. With layering, all layers of a hierarchy are displayed at once.

◆ *A pop-up menu.* The menu appears ("pops up") on the screen when the user indicates that some action needs to be taken. The pop-up menu provides the alternatives from which the user can select. For example, in a word processing document, the user may mark a word and press the right mouse button. In response, a menu pops up with the alternatives that can logically be selected for processing a marked word.

A menu selection interface may support all three classes of users. Menus may be used effectively with both the older text-oriented interfaces and graphical user interfaces. Most interface design tools provide a mechanism that supports menu creation.

Menu selection is especially useful for novices because it presents the choices. Figure 11-6 illustrates various user selection objects for making choices. Help can be obtained to provide more information on any choice. Menu selection is also an appropriate interface model for the knowledgeable intermittent user because this type of user needs help to recall the appropriate set of choices at each step. Easily available explanations in a standardized form provide reference information, as needed. Menu selection is not likely to be used for frequent operations by an expert user, but menus may still be

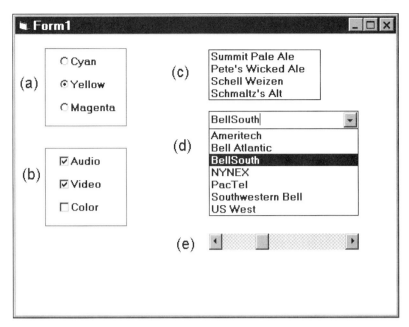

FIGURE 11-6   *Examples of screen objects making choices: option button, check box, list box, combo box, and scroll bar*

useful for those operations that are used infrequently. Following are some guidelines for the design of menu selection interfaces:

◆ *Design the semantics of the menus based on the user task and task sequences.* Simple tasks may follow a linear sequence. Most tasks include choices that are best represented by a hierarchy of menus. Complex tasks may require a hierarchy plus the ability to branch among subtrees of the hierarchy (a type of network structure).

◆ *Select among various possible alternative menu structures.* These include permanent menu locations, pull-down and layering for hierarchies, "drop-downs" for long lists, and "pop-ups" for in-context selection. The choices available depend upon the capabilities of the design tool, but each variant has positive and negative aspects that should be considered.

◆ *Design or sketch menus and review them before implementation.* Revise after trial use.

Direct Manipulation Interfaces

In **direct-manipulation interfaces**, the user manipulates a screen object (such as an icon or scroll bar) with a mouse or other pointer. The screen objects respond to direct manipulation and may even change their appearance or position while performing the function associated with them. Special keystrokes may be treated as events and processed in a way similar to mouse actions.

The graphical capabilities available on most computers used by knowledge workers support interfaces characterized by direct manipulation. The mouse is the most common method for direct manipulation. Examples of direct manipulation with a mouse are pointing and clicking or scrolling to make a selection, marking a location or text, and dragging an object across the screen.

Icons are used in personal computer systems as direct manipulation interfaces. They are used in connection with a mouse to call or invoke software actions. Icons are presented on toolbars (see Figure 11-7). Users may customize toolbars to include icons for actions they perform frequently. In some cases, icons provide an alternative to the use of menus or keystrokes. For example, a user may cause a document to be printed by using one of three methods to instruct the computer:

1. *Menus.* For example, a mouse movement on the **FILE** menu on the menu bar will cause a drop-down menu to be displayed. One of the items is **PRINT**. Selecting this menu item causes a pop-up box to be displayed that allows the user to specify certain characteristics, such as number of copies.

2. *Keystrokes.* In Microsoft Windows™, the keystroke combination **Ctrl + P** will invoke the pop-up box for printing.

3. *Icons.* Some toolbars provide an icon for printing. A mouse click on the printer icon invokes the pop-up box for printing.

FIGURE 11-7

Example of toolbar with icons. Mouse action on icon invokes icon function.

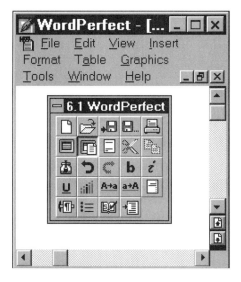

Users can place icons on a toolbar to invoke frequently used macros. This interface reduces the time needed to select and play a macro.

In a graphical user interface, keystrokes are treated as a direct manipulation. The system responds to selected keystrokes as events similar to mouse actions on an icon or menu. Keystrokes may be used to improve speed of use by experts. Keystrokes may also be assigned to user-developed macros to reduce the time needed to invoke their use.

Data Input Interfaces

Data input interfaces are input forms. Input forms provide a structure with locations for data input and instructions for use. They are similar in some respects to paper forms, but add functions such as input validation and anticipated inputs (a prior input or a partial input prompts the program to display anticipated inputs that can either be accepted by the user or replaced with different data).

Data input forms can be combined with other interface methods. For example, if data values to be input are limited to the contents of a list, the input form can present the list and enable the user to select a value. An alternative is to allow the user to input the value directly, but have the list available if the user cannot remember the value or how it is spelled or presented. For example, a data input might be the vendor of a software package. Since vendor names can be enumerated in a list, the user may refer to the list, if necessary. This combination input box thus provides for fast entry by an expert, but preserves the list of options for a novice or for recall by an expert or intermittent knowledgeable user (see Figure 11-8).

In order to reduce input time and eliminate errors, the data input program may check a list of prior inputs as the user keys in characters. If the first few characters match a prior input, that input is displayed. The user can accept the prior input or continue to enter new input. For example, an input of names of

FIGURE 11-8

Form with combo box. User can enter choice directly in box or select from list.

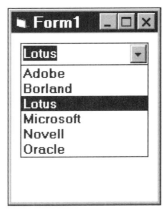

fruits and vegetables might input the letters "Wat" and the system will display "Watermelon." If this is correct, the user can stop keying and accept the input. If the user intends "Watercress," entry continues.

Forms design for input is an important part of interface design. Poor design leads to wasted effort, both in entry and in resolving errors or misunderstandings. Following are guidelines for data input form design:

◊ *Define the required data structures.* Define both the information source (if the source is a document, for example) and the data that will be the result. In this case, a data structure definition refers to the details of the contents of each field or element of data, the sequence in which elements appear, and their relationships with each other. Depending upon the complexity, the definition may be informal or employ formal data structure models or diagrams. (Refer to Chapter 7.)

◊ *Define the sequence of user activities.* Many data input activities are dependent on the sources of data for task structure. The interface should be designed to follow the sequence of user activities. For example, if a user enters data during a telephone conversation, data entry should follow the natural flow of the telephone interaction rather than the logical structure of the data to be obtained.

◊ *Identify and document all validation rules.* Depending on the data items, validation rules may be very strong or weak. But in virtually every case, there are some rules that can identify errors in input. The validation rules can help detect errors that must be corrected and can identify potential errors that should be reviewed by the user. The validation may be applied to the structure of the data being input (for example, the data must fit within a range of values, can only be one of a list of values, or must be numeric) or it may be checked by reference to other data. Checking against other values may involve checking against stored data or data entered in the same session for the same person or company. For example, the size of an order from a customer may be compared with prior orders for the same item. If the current order is for 100 cases (with 144 boxes per case) and prior orders have always been for some number of boxes fewer than a case, validation rules will highlight a possible input error. If the order entry specifies a shipping address, but there is no entry of shipping charges, this suggests an error.

◊ *Define rules for referential validation.* Since the user interface is part of a system that includes database tables, inputs that depend upon the state of existing data (such as a new order that depends on an existing credit rating) should be validated by referring to that data at the time they are entered.

◊ *Sketch the boundaries of the form and arrange the necessary input fields to match the sequence in which items are received for entry or are normally entered.* For example, last name is often used first in an entry sequence.

◊ *Add menu choices or other command elements.* These should reflect all the decisions the user might need to make.

◊ *Adopt or design a standard way of presenting messages to the user.* Document a set of messages that explain every error that can be detected by the validation rules. Plan to provide help or reference material that outlines the steps of the task and describes the valid sets of input values.

Reports

Screen reports present results in a format that supports user activities such as data analysis, decision making, and presentations. The reports can be printed or stored on other media. The most important guideline for report design is to model the behavior of the user of a report. Before designing a report, work through the task(s) and activity(ies) it is to support. Format the report with only the data needed (plus report identification data).

Three types of reports of particular significance in business systems are the detail report, the summary report, and the comparison report.

1. The detail report includes all the transaction data that supports business records. It is a reference list.

2. The summary report classifies data into meaningful categories. Such reports support high-level review (rather than review at the detailed, transaction level) and decision-making based on results in total rather than in detail.

3. The comparison report may show details or summaries. It is characterized by comparison with elements such as prior time periods, budgets, standards, other locations, or competitors. A variance report is a common comparison report showing the variance from budget or standard and providing an analysis of the reasons for the differences. Graphics are often employed to visualize the comparisons or trends.

Help Facilities

Help facilities are an important part of the user interface that allow online access to program documentation and user instructions. Help facilities can be used for reference, training, and specific problem solving. Although they may have reference manuals, most software packages include much of their tutorial and reference material in an interactive help system that is available to the user while the package is being used (see Figure 11-9). A user developing

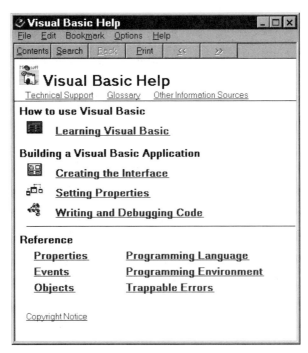

FIGURE 11-9 *Using Help facilities for documentation. Use of icons and hypertext links (in color on screen and underlined in figure)*

an application should consider at least modest use of help facilities to support the applications.

Documentation of applications is an ongoing problem for user-developed systems. Documentation is often an afterthought, if it is done at all. It is best done as a byproduct of good systems development. Because of the value of adequate online help, there is software that aids in converting documentation into help systems. A "help compiler" accepts specially annotated text files and converts them to a help format that is standardized within an operating system (for example, Apple's Finder or Microsoft Windows). The designer of help documentation must specify indexes and mark terms to be indexed and references to be used as hypertext links.

Following are some general guidelines that can be applied to facilitate use:

◇ *Provide user or usage-oriented indexes.* An index of the commands of a language is not useful to the person who needs to know what command to use for a particular task. An index that classifies commands according to their functions is much more appropriate to the typical user of a help system. A single index or method of access to documentation is never enough. The documentation designer must consider the types of users and anticipate the problems they are likely to be trying to solve by searching in the help facility.

◊ *Match the help system's capabilities to the intended users.*   If a user is building a personal system, it is important to think about how the system will be used in the future. Efficiency in documentation is not nearly as important as preserving vital data. The documentation should, as a minimum, explain why the application was created, describe the problems it was intended to solve, and outline potential modifications.

◊ *Employ help construction software if available.*   Documentation should be written using a text or word processor. Indexes and hyperlinks that provide access can be added with the aid of a help compiler.

Creating Graphical User Interfaces

◆ ◆

User interfaces on older applications often employ character or text interfaces; interfaces on personal computers and workstations are almost always based on graphical or direct manipulation of screen objects. Direct manipulation fits the event-driven model of a computer application.

The Event-driven Object Model and User Interfaces

The event-driven object model explained in Chapter 10 applies to the design of a direct manipulation interface. In this model, each visible element of the interface on the screen is an object and every object has a set of properties controlling its appearance and functions. Screen objects may be connected or linked to data and may have sets of behaviors or methods that respond to user actions. In other words, the user receives information from screen objects (such as boxes containing messages) and causes a system response by manipulating an object on the screen. The manipulation may involve placing data in a box, clicking with the mouse on a button or menu, selecting an option or item from a list, moving a scroll bar, or entering keystrokes. Figure 11-10 identifies specific objects on a computer screen.

While screen objects are not exactly the same as objects in the object-oriented programming paradigm, they do have many of the same characteristics. Understanding screen objects is necessary to use the event-driven paradigm. It is also a very useful introduction to the object-oriented model.

A graphical user interface consists of screen objects organized on one or more forms. In this context, a form is the design version of a window. That

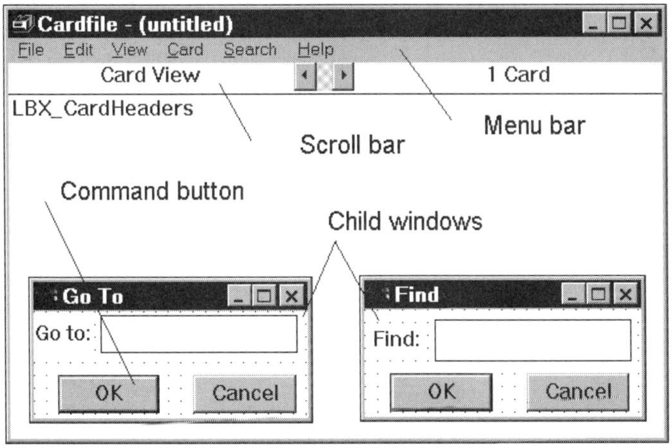

FIGURE 11-10 *Application screen with objects identified*

means it is the smallest entity recognized separately by the operating system. The operating system can display, move, and hide forms and windows, and can allow them to be resized and moved between foreground and background. It also supports such standard activities as scrolling and may allow a user to set such properties of a form as background color.

Direct manipulation of a form means that the user is able to perform standard actions on any form that follows the interface capabilities provided by the operating system, including mouse or keyboard selection; window positioning and scrolling; and switching among full-screen, window, and iconic representations.

The object model states that objects are encapsulated data and procedures. In the context of GUI design, an object is a *screen object* that has an appearance and a user interface function to perform. In this model, every component of the interface is a screen object, so that each form and each of their contents are objects. Every form is an object that has a screen representation with properties that dictate its appearance, and there is a set of events that may "happen" to a form that will invoke specified procedures or methods. Figure 11-11 is an example of a form with some of its properties and a list of the events that may apply.

The designer of a GUI, in the event-oriented model, must implicitly decide on the appropriate values for as many as 40 or 50 properties for each screen object and must specify the appropriate behaviors for from 5 to 20 standard events. This appears formidable, but in practice most of the properties are set to default conditions and need not be set by the designer. Most standard events require no unique methods. Thus, in many cases, creating the underlying form component of a GUI is as simple as double-clicking a form icon and entering its caption.

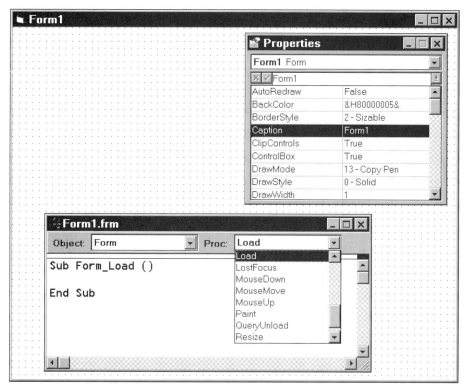

FIGURE 11-11   *A form as a screen object along with its list of properties and events in a drop-down box*

The software used to design and implement a GUI will have tools such as the following:

◊ *A "toolbox" of objects.* The user interface for a typical application is made up of several different types of screen objects that are selected from the **toolbox**.

◊ *Ways to add objects to the toolbox.* Many applications can be constructed entirely from the screen objects included in the basic toolbox. But in many cases, supplementary libraries of screen objects provide support for more complex tasks, facilitate interface construction, or both.

◊ *Object size and placement tools.* An important subset of the properties of screen objects are their dimensions and placement relative to the form that contains them. GUI design tools allow the designer to drag screen objects into position and to adjust their size with a pointer. An interface can be laid out almost entirely with the mouse or other pointing device.

◊ *Support for property setting.* Many screen object properties are chosen from a discrete set. GUI design tools often provide pop-up menus of the set of choices. Other tools may also be available. For example, in addition to a discrete set of foreground and background color choices, a color palette may be provided for custom coloring.

◆ *Linking of contents (and other properties) among objects.* All screen objects and each of their properties are identifiable by name. Within the context of a *container* of screen objects (a form may be viewed as a screen object container) an object may refer to a specified property of another object. For example, it may be useful to set a property such as a basic font in one screen object (or the container) and then reference that value in other screen objects so that they use the same font.

◆ *Linking of properties to data.* GUIs are often constructed as interfaces to other programs or to databases. The "content" or "value" property of an object may be linked to a database field by setting the names of the database table and field as the value of the object's data source property.

◆ *Support for method creation.* As Figure 11-11 shows for the case of the screen object "form1," screen objects have a list of potential events they can recognize. When a designer decides that a method is needed, GUI tools provide a link to tools to specify the details of a method. For example, the tool may present a code template in its code editor. When a method has been defined, the GUI tool establishes the appropriate links so that occurrence of the event triggers execution.

The Event-driven Design Process

A key element in successful GUI design is to plan before designing. For complex designs, the hierarchy of menus and the purposes of each form and its contents should be carefully planned and reviewed with the users. Portions of the design that include data entry and/or reports should follow the guidelines presented in the preceding section. A set of documentation or user help should be planned and integrated into the design. The structure of the interface should be grounded in knowledge of the details of the user task.

For small, single-user applications, it is still important to plan before building. It is deceptively easy to create a form and add screen objects to it. It can also appear very easy to set the properties and "write some code" for the events. The risk is that the very ease of construction tempts the builder to move to construction without adequate planning. The following guidelines may be useful in designing a simple application, especially one that is based on a single form:

◆ *Decide on the set of screen objects that will accept the inputs, present the choices, and display the results.* Make a list of these objects.

◆ *For each screen object in the list, decide what properties should differ from the default settings.* Note these properties and the desired values for each object on the list.

◆ *Make a separate list of events that each object must respond to (screen object events).*

◆ *Define in pseudocode form the actions or procedures the computer should perform in response to each screen object event.* Where the required action appears to be complex, first try to find a simpler way. If complexity is unavoidable, use the techniques of structured design to specify a module structure and detailed control structures. Write these in pseudocode.

◆ *Lay out the screen.* Review it with respect to the steps of the user task. Modify the design as needed. The review step is an important one. When possible, and especially for beginners, review the design with another person and then modify it. As part of the review, step through the user task, "playing computer." Make sure the specification is consistent with the expectations derived from your knowledge of the task.

After having carefully worked through these design steps, implement an initial prototype and proceed with the prototyping process.

Software Development Environments

◆ ◆

Writing computer application software is knowledge work. The user is expected to have knowledge of how to perform the work and manage the resources used in the work. As with all knowledge work, there are ways the computer can be used to reduce repetitive or routine effort, improve individual performance on cognitively difficult tasks, and support documentation activities. The set of software tools to support programming is termed a *software development environment*. These tools are more than just individual applications; they fit together to support the programmer in proceeding from the beginning to the end of the software development process. The following sections describe five tools or facilities of a software development environment that support interface design, code development, program libraries, testing and debugging, and documentation.

User Interface Design Tools

Preparing a screen for a graphical user interface to an application would be an impossibly time-consuming task if the programmer had to code all the instructions in some procedural programming language. There are, however, many repetitive, almost clerical activities involved in implementing a user interface. Both of these conditions suggest the value of a tool to automate much of the design and coding of a user interface. Such a tool for user interface design is sometimes called a screen painter. The metaphor suggests a process of interface creation by painting or drawing the screen image. Such tools are available with or included in programming environments that support software development for screen-based applications. These applications include event-oriented programs on personal computers and workstations.

Every GUI makes use of one or more windows on a display screen. A window occupies part or all of the screen. It may even be larger than a single display screen. The designer of a graphical user interface must recognize which aspects of the interface may be unique to an application and which are the responsibility of the underlying operating system. Window position and size, for example, are often managed by the operating system, while the contents of a particular window (or form) are defined by the application designer.

The application designer must decide what windows (forms) are to be part of an application and define the size, position, and other properties of all objects on each form. An interface design tool provides a set of tools for drawing boxes, buttons, and other screen objects, for creating menus, and for placing labels, texts, and graphics on a form. It also assists the user in defining such properties of objects as fonts, borders, colors, and shading. A **user interface design tool** relies on direct manipulation of screen objects, such as placement and size. Figure 11-12 lists the contents of the toolbox provided with a development environment for event-oriented programs.

Code Development Tools

Although many parts of an application can be generated by using such tools as user interface design aids, significant parts of an application must often be written directly in the chosen programming language. A **code development tool** within a software development environment aids in reducing routine, repetitive coding effort, assists in detecting coding errors and writing instructions in structured form, and prompts the programmer to be complete in coding control structures. A code development tool might be termed an "intelligent editor" for creating statements in the programming language it supports. Following are some typical features that illustrate the power and usefulness of code development tools for programming tasks:

◇ *Create structure for a program module.* All program modules have some characteristics in common. When a programmer indicates a certain type of module is to be developed, the code development tool creates a skeleton for it. The code skeleton is assigned a name that follows appropriate naming conventions. The tool also specifies required parameters and needed language statements.

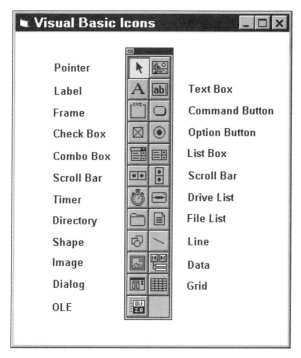

FIGURE 11-12 *Icons for functions in application development toolbox (Microsoft Visual Basic)*

◊ *Create skeleton program structures.* When a programmer begins an **if-then-else-end if** statement (by typing the word **if** at the beginning of a line), a code development tool recognizes the beginning of an alternation structure. It can immediately create properly aligned **then**, **else**, and **end if** terms, and position the cursor to enter the conditional expression. This simple feature reduces coding effort, helps maintain proper program structuring, and eliminates errors of omission such as forgetting to complete the control structure with an **end if**. Similar support is supplied for other program structures.

◊ *Detect syntax errors "on the fly."* If a programmer uses a variable name that has not been defined for the module or program, the editor detects the error and alerts the programmer. Syntax checking while statements are being entered applies to command words and other predictable elements of program code.

◊ *Provide menus and help with commands and functions to use in the program.* A programmer may not remember a command or function. A code development tool provides an efficient search mechanism. Help facilities assist in checking the meaning and usage of language statements.

◇ *Provide templates and examples showing usage and supporting copying of commonly used code structures.* Many programming problems have worked-out solutions. An effective development system helps find and insert these.

Program Libraries

Another method to increase productivity in programming is to incorporate previously written subprograms, functions, or objects selected from a library. Library contents may be supplied by the vendor of the software development environment, purchased from a third-party vendor, written by others in the organization, or written by the current user of the environment. Several different mechanisms exist to manage and support such libraries. In the event-driven and object-oriented paradigms, object libraries that contain specialized sets of objects may be developed or acquired. New objects are then used in the same way as existing or built-in objects.

Another frequently used mechanism is to provide compiled functions that may be linked into a program when it is compiled or executed. This is especially useful for standard but complex calculations such as mathematical functions. A third approach is to provide source code that may be copied and tailored as part of the program development process. In each case, program libraries must provide tools and procedures to enable developers to find appropriate library resources based upon descriptions, appropriate names, and other characteristics.

Testing and Debugging Support Tools

Two of the most significant activities in programming are testing and debugging. The purpose of **testing** is to detect errors in the behavior or results of a program. **Debugging** is locating and correcting the faults that cause the erroneous behaviors. (Although testing and debugging are very different activities, they are often coupled and sometimes mistakenly confused for a single process.)

In testing programs and applications, sets of test data are used to produce the symptoms of errors. Each set of test data is designed to exercise a program function and try to locate a point of failure or error. In large and complex programs, the generation and management of test cases is a major undertaking. Test data generators reduce the problem of developing test data by generating test cases from specifications. The result of executing a large number of tests requires significant analysis to locate faults. Testing tools provide for test data generation, test results analysis, and test data management.

In program testing, it is necessary to develop and apply test data, but the number of tests for individual systems is usually small enough to be generated, managed, and analyzed without special tools. For this reason, software development environments for individual system applications tend not to have extensive testing support tools.

Debugging to locate and repair the cause of defects uncovered during testing is similar for both large and small applications. Various debugging tools assist in replicating errors and locating their causes. Following are some of the debugging mechanisms provided in development environments.

◊   *Immediate execution.* In some software development environments, instructions may be executed immediately after constructing a program statement or module. Many errors are detected by such immediate testing. The advantage of an immediate execution environment is that errors may be detected and corrected and the corrections immediately tested.

◊   *Monitoring.* Debugging tools allow the programmer to track changes in specified variables as the program executes. This monitoring allows the programmer to identify unexpected changes. Monitoring can also help in locating the causes of subtle errors.

◊   *Breakpoints.* A programmer may establish points in the program at which the value of all specified variables will be displayed, and/or execution temporarily halted. This helps to isolate errors to specific parts of a program.

◊   *Step execution.* Debugging tools allow the programmer to execute source instructions one at a time (or one module at a time) while observing changes in the values of variables. This is especially useful after an error has been localized to a module or part of a module. The debugging tool may provide a window that displays the instructions being executed and another window that simultaneously displays corresponding variables and their values.

Version Control and Documentation Support Facilities

Most software systems are subject to a nearly continual process of revision and improvement. In a large or complex system with many components there are certain to be several versions of some components such as modules or chapters of documentation. In most cases, only one version is in "production mode" or is approved for operational use. Other versions are in various stages of development and test. Again, a combinatorial problem arises: if there are a large number of components, there is a much larger number of possible complete configurations. **Version control systems** are tracking and inventory systems that maintain a history of changes to each component, subassembly, and complete system. Most provide a set of checkpoints so that components under development cannot be included in the operational version without proper authorizations.

The version control system provides more than administrative control, however. Even moderate or small systems consist of numerous components that must be managed. A version control system can relieve the programmer of this responsibility by keeping track of every component, keeping a record of changes so that it is possible to return to earlier versions, and assembling a complete configuration of the operational system on demand.

A major portion of a computer program or system is documentation. While individual systems do not need to meet the documentation standards of program products, some documentation is usually desirable. In addition to configuration management, documentation support tools help by assembling, cataloging, and indexing documentation, and providing a uniform interface for user access.

Summary

◊ A user interface is critical to an application. A good user interface facilitates correct and complete application use. A poor interface may interfere with correct use and lead to user errors. The best user interface design is one in which the system corresponds to the user model of how the system is operating. A set of simple guidelines is very useful to design a good user interface. The interface designer needs to consider the user. Users may be novices, knowledgeable intermittent users, or experienced, "power" users.

◊ User interfaces may be command-based, menu selection, direct manipulation, data input, report, or help systems. The graphical user interface (GUI) is most common on personal computers. The GUI is especially applicable to event-driven application design in which a user action on a screen object causes processing to take place.

◊ Software development needs support tools. A software development environment is an integrated collection of software development tools. Tools include an interface designer or "screen painter," code creation tools, program libraries, testing and debugging tools, version controls, and support for documentation preparation.

EXERCISES

1. Go through the **Help** tutorial for the development environment you are using.

2. Select one or more examples in the **Help** tutorial. Then do the following:

a. Copy the examples.

b. Make your own program using the example code.

c. Make simple modifications.

d. Run the program.

3. Write a simple event-oriented program to display a screen image that reflects your mood.

   a. Review and walk through the steps in doing a simple program in the development environment you are using. Find the instructions to do the following:

      (1) Select **new project**. (Set the name when you save it.)

      (2) Select **new form** (you can change size if you want). Set **caption** for the caption you want to appear on the form and name property for program reference purposes.

      (3) Draw an object on the form.

      (4) Size and position the object.

      (5) Set the object properties.

      (6) Write the code.

      (7) Test the code.

   b. Write a simple program. The purpose of the program is to display three option buttons to allow a user to specify one of three personal moods (happy, OK, or sad). When an option is selected, an image of an appropriate face appears. Print the form and all program statements as evidence of your program.

4. Build a first prototype of an application that computes compound interest and uses a scroll bar for input of interest rate. The screen objects should allow the user to vary the interest rate and see the results immediately. The input screens should display the following:

   a. A scroll bar for interest rate input from 0 to 25 percent.

   b. Input boxes for initial investment and years of accumulation.

   The output screen should display the following:

   a. Rate used.

   b. Interest earned.

   c. Value of investment.

   To design the application, define the form and objects; define the properties; and list the events and define the "methods" that respond to them. Use **Help** to get information on programming features.

5. Try out the prototype developed in Exercise 4. Use yourself and at least one other person to test it. Write a list of deficiencies and difficulties. Be sure to look for user misunderstanding of inputs or outputs, failure to detect errors in input, and difficulties in making corrections, rerunning the program with new data, and exiting the program.

6. Prepare a prototype of an application for exploring monthly savings options. There are four factors in the final output:
   a. Yearly interest rate (but compounding monthly)
   b. Number of monthly payments
   c. Amount of each monthly payment
   d. Accumulated amount at end of payments

   The program should accept inputs for any three of the four figures and compute the fourth.

   Test the prototype as explained in Exercise 5 and write a short deficiency and difficulty analysis.

7. Exchange your program and deficiency and difficulty analysis with another student. Evaluate and comment on the analysis. Modify the program you have received to correct the problem presented to you and any others you found.

8. Define a need you have for a simple event-oriented program. Define your requirements and build a prototype. Test the result. Provide simple documentation including a screen image of your design, inputs, and outputs.

Developing Solutions Using Database Software

◊　◊　◊　◊　◊　◊　◊　◊

OBJECTIVES

After completing this chapter, you should be able to:

◆ Define and explain basic database concepts.

◆ Describe the difference between a flat file and a relational database.

◆ Explain how to define data tables and relations.

◆ Describe the four common ways to place data into the tables of a relational database.

◆ Describe the three functions involved in database application output (selection, organization, and presentation).

◆ Explain the concept behind Query by Example (QBE) software facilities.

◆ Explain the use of Structured Query Language (SQL) in the output selection process.

◆ Describe the impact of database macros and custom programs on knowledge work productivity.

◆ Describe the steps involved in the database development process.

◆ Design and develop a simple database application program.

KEY TERMS AND CONCEPTS

This chapter presents the following key terms and concepts, listed in the order in which they appear:

flat file
relational database
foreign key
Structured Query Language
   (SQL)

Query by Example (QBE)
detail reports
summary reports
external documents
exception reports

analytic reports
one-to-one (relationship)
one-to-many (relationship)
many-to-many (relationship)
associative entity

Many knowledge work tasks involve data management. This is the last of three chapters that explains how individuals can use the data management facilities of information technology. Chapter 7 focused on how to access data maintained in organizational databases. Chapter 8 focused on sources and methods of accessing external data. This chapter deals with managing data maintained by individuals.

A significant portion of the data employed in knowledge work tasks is the responsibility of individuals or workgroups. Therefore, knowledge workers in the information age should be able to manage their own data. In practice, this means they should be able to make use of database software for personal computers. The focus of this chapter is on managing individual databases using personal computer database software or other packaged database software.

Responsibilities include defining, building, maintaining, and using data stored in individual databases.

This chapter also explains important concepts and methods for developing individual solutions using database software. It surveys the functions necessary for database management and relates these to the functionality typically found in database software packages. It explains how to define data tables and relations, how to develop individual database user interfaces, and how to program supplementary procedures for database applications.

Database Software and Personal Productivity

◆ ◆

As outlined in the following paragraphs, there are three major reasons why a knowledge of database software can help individuals achieve greater productivity in managing data:

1. *Database package knowledge applies to a wide range of software applications.* Many specialized software packages have a database at their core, although it is generally concealed from the package user. Examples are personal information managers, personal finance packages, and inventory packages. For most individual and many workgroup data management problems and opportunities, such specialized software is more appropriate and cost-effective than custom applications of database packages. Even though a user who needs to store and retrieve data should consider a software package as an alternative to custom development, knowledge of a database package will aid in making such a decision. If a specialized package is indicated, this knowledge helps users select an appropriate one (The "make or buy" decision is discussed in the next section).

2. *Database package knowledge helps users understand the procedures used to access organizational and external data.* Database package experience adds useful general knowledge because the basic principles of database construction and use are very similar across different packages and applications. Databases for large-scale systems or external databases employ concepts, methods, terminology, and access procedures quite similar to personal computer database packages. For example, relational tables are used in most structured databases. SQL (Structured Query Language), a database query language, is the basis for most structured query languages in both mainframe and personal computer software. Therefore, learning a personal computer software package and applying

it to individual databases will improve individual skills in accessing data in organizational databases.

3. *Database package knowledge can be applied to building and managing individual files and databases.* Two categories of applications are based on database structures:

   a. *Structured databases with two or more tables.* These databases are well supported and benefit from the full range of database software functions. The tables may be built from individual input, or they may be subsets of organizational or external data that have been copied into an individual database.

   b. *Single-table lists of records.* These databases consist of a simple file (or list) of records, rather than a relational table. The "flat file" collections of data can be managed easily with almost any data management software. They do not need all of the facilities of a complete database package. On the other hand, there are productivity advantages in using one database package for both relational tables and simple lists. Users need to learn only one set of commands, since simple flat file management employs a subset of the commands used with more complex database structures.

Example

A researcher prepares a list of dissertations in information systems over a twenty-year period. Each record in the list contains an identification number, the first and last name of the person doing the dissertation, the dissertation title, the year accepted, and the school. The list is not connected to any other tables. Such a simple flat file can be constructed and managed with almost any data management facilities. For instance, the list can be built and simple operations performed on the data using the data management facilities in a spreadsheet processor. Managing the list within a database package provides some added functionality. If the database package is being used for another purpose, personal productivity is achieved by using the same set of commands for this application. ◆

The "Make or Buy" Decision for Database Applications

◆ ◆ ◆ ◆ ◆ ◆ ◆ ◆ ◆ ◆ ◆ ◆ ◆ ◆ ◆ ◆ ◆ ◆ ◆ ◆

A database management software package is more than a data storage and retrieval tool. The package—which provides a complete set of software resources to build personal application systems—contains the following components:

◊ *Facilities for defining database tables, relationships, and data fields.*

◊ *Mechanisms for storing and retrieving data.*

◊ *Input and data processing facilities.* (This component supports input forms, data validation rules, and some data processing capabilities.)

◊ *Output facilities.* (This component includes query processing to select data, and provisions for defining and producing output screens and printed reports.)

Figure 12-1 depicts the components of the typical database management system (DBMS). A similar model can be used to depict a computer application that defines the databases to be employed and performs input, data storage and management, and output procedures. In other words, the basic flow of processing in custom applications developed using a database package is the same as many specialized software application packages that have data management as a core activity.

This discussion leads to the conclusion that specialized packages should always be considered as alternatives to custom development with database package facilities. A custom solution may have some advantages, but the lower cost, lower risk, and immediate availability of the specialized package tend to offset them. There are numerous specialized packages that illustrate this concept. Table 12-1 illustrates a variety of database applications and specialized software packages that are constructed around database functions.

These applications illustrate the use of database management as a core component. A PIM application, for example, typically supports a personal calendar, phone directory, notes and "To-Do" lists, plus records of personal contacts. A simple PIM—which includes various inputs for appointments, tasks, and contacts—could be organized around several files. A complete PIM will explicitly recognize the relationships among the entities of interest: appointments involve people, contacts are related to a calendar, individual entries relate to points in time and types of business contacts, and so forth.

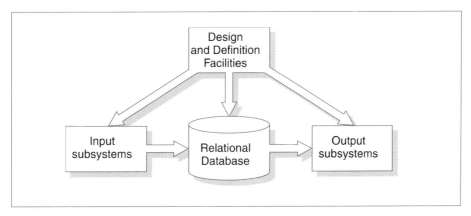

FIGURE 12-1 *The architecture of a typical database management software package*

Table 12-1 Personal Database Applications and Solution Approaches	
Application Area Using Database	*Solution Approach*
Keep track of business contacts	PIM (Personal Information Manager)
Track documents, books, and other references	Bibliography package
Keep family records and photos	Genealogy package
Maintain personal financial records	Personal Financial package
Track personal property inventory	Personal Inventory Manager package
Provide accounting services for a small business	Accounting package

As a second example, operating a small business may entail accounting, order processing, payroll, and inventory records. For a new business, a low-cost accounting application package manages basic databases. Transaction records, accounting journals and ledgers, inventory records, vendor files, and customer records are built in, along with appropriate relationships. Such an application package will include generalized input forms and output reports that the new business can customize (with company name, logo, etc.).

An established small business with existing forms and reports may not wish to replace these with a package solution. Rather, it may decide to develop a custom solution. In that case, a generalized DBMS package is an important resource in building the customized system. The customized solution will be similar in architecture to the package solution (relational database with input screens and forms, output screens, documents, and reports) but it will fit more closely to the existing system.

Review of Database Concepts and Definitions

◆ ◆

An information management application developed with the standard database design features and default options of a database package has three primary operational components: (1) the relational database, (2) input forms and processing interface, and (3) output queries and reports. A database application based on standard facilities and default options can be very useful, and it can be built easily with very little development effort. However, this approach may be insufficient for many database applications. The standard features may need to be altered or extended; the user interface may need to reflect the specific characteristics of the problem, the inputs, and the users; and the various operations may need to be tied together to reduce effort and operational errors.

A database package includes facilities to alter and extend the features of the application and improve the operational flow. To accomplish these modifications and extensions, the database package provides customizing and programming facilities. These are an extension of the macro-building and user interface development facilities covered in previous chapters. In other words, a database application is developed by using the standard database package features and extending them. The extensions apply macro programs and specialized user interfaces (such as special screen forms for input and tailored output designs). Before explaining input, output, and customizing, the concept of a relational database will be summarized and the definitions reviewed.

The Relational Database

Any database application (standard or customized) includes a database organized as tables. When accessing organizational databases, users do not need to be concerned with defining and building them, since database developers or administrators have already defined the relational tables, maintained the data with updates and corrections, and specified user access privileges.

However, when a database is created and maintained by a knowledge worker, these activities must be performed by that individual. A database management software package includes facilities that assist in the design and definition of a relational database. Design activities include definition of entities and relationships and specification of attributes and identifiers. The application designer also defines input forms, input processes, and outputs.

Relational databases are based on a mathematical formulation known as relational calculus. This demonstrates that the most desirable data organization is a "fully normalized" structure. A formal examination of the characteristics of a fully normalized structure is beyond the scope of this text. Broadly speaking, it means that normalized data is simplified and has minimum redundancy. This is desirable because it reduces data errors and conflicting data values. It has other advantages as well. Normalized data is the most flexible form possible. It provides for both anticipated and unanticipated output queries, reports, and analyses. A database is normalized if it meets the requirements for *third normal form*. Although third normal form can be stated formally, an individual user can achieve it by following some simple rules explained later in this chapter. Must a database be normalized? For a database that must meet both stated and unknown uses, the effort to achieve a normalized form is justified. For single-use data (such as downloaded data for a report), considerations of normal form are not applicable.

It is useful to distinguish between a database containing only a single table or list (a flat file) and a database containing two or more related tables. A **flat file** is used to store and retrieve information about a single topic or subject. Examples might be a "To-Do" list, a list of contacts, or a reference list for a report. A single topic list that does not have relationships to other data can be maintained without using any of the rules that apply to relational tables. However, data tends to be related to other data. Ignoring these relationships when establishing a flat file database may mean that the database must be re-designed in the future. Since a **relational database** approach can be used with a flat file, the user can employ a relational database management system for both flat files and relational tables. Given that flexibility, the remainder of this chapter will focus on building a relational database.

Review of Database Terminology

Database terminology was introduced in Chapter 7. Since the following terms are key to understanding relational databases, they are repeated here, along with short definitions.

Term	*Definition*
Database	A collection of related data records or tables.
Entity	A class of things about which to maintain data, represented in table format.
Entity instance	An individual occurrence of the thing about which data items are stored. An entity instance (also referred to as a record) is represented by a table row.
Attribute	An individual data item. Each row in a table contains the attributes of the instance. Each column contains data items for a single attribute.
Key attribute	A data item (or set of data items) that uniquely identifies an instance and differentiates it from all other rows in the table.
Relationship	A correspondence or association between entities. The degree of a relationship is characterized by the numbers of instances associated.
Foreign key	A key attribute of one table stored as an attribute in another table. (A **foreign key** implements a relationship between two tables. When a foreign key in one table corresponds with a key attribute in another table, the table rows can be joined in a query.)

Using these definitions, the criteria for the normalized relational data model can be stated fairly simply. A data model is in fully normalized form when it meets the following criteria:

◊ *Each entity (table) is named and has one or more attributes (columns) that uniquely identify each entity instance (row).* For example, each employee (an entity instance for the **EMPLOYEES** entity) has an employee number, a social security number, or some other attribute that uniquely identifies the person.

◊ *Each entity (table) has all relevant attributes defined, and no attribute has more than one value for an entity instance.*

◊ *One-to-one or one-to-many relationships associate pairs of entities.* When two tables are joined, a row in the first table may be joined to one or more rows in the second table. For example, a salesperson may have one or more customers (one-to-many). Information about an individual salesperson in a table of **SALESPERSONS** may be joined to a table of **CUSTOMERS** by using the salesperson-unique identifier in the **SALESPERSONS** table stored as a foreign key in the **CUSTOMERS** table.

◊ *Many-to-many relationships exist among entities of interest.* They are not implemented directly. Instead, a table that acts as an intermediate or intersection entity between them must be designed and implemented. (An example is presented later in this chapter.)

Although these conditions are complicated, they can be achieved in simple databases quite easily. Relational database software packages facilitate implementations consistent with the relational data.

The Input Interface

◆ ◆ ◆ ◆ ◆ ◆ ◆ ◆ ◆ ◆ ◆ ◆ ◆ ◆ ◆ ◆ ◆ ◆ ◆

When the tables in a database have been defined, data must be input. There are four common ways to input data: (1) importing data from an existing source, (2) entering data directly, (3) entering data in single-record form, and (4) entering data in multiple-record form.

Importing Data

If the data to be placed in one or more tables in the relational database already exists, it may be possible to import the records using the **convert** or **import** facility found in most database packages. **Import** and **convert** facilities cover a range of conversions. One conversion imports one or more tables in an existing database (perhaps a different vendor's software package) into tables in the importing database package. Databases maintained using columns in a spreadsheet are also easily imported to a database.

Another importing option converts text files into database tables. This is useful when records have been maintained using word processors or other packages that can produce fixed-field or comma-delimited fields for data items. Fixed field format means each attribute or field is assigned a fixed number of character positions. In that case, text fields are "padded" with as many space characters as needed to fill the field, and numeric attributes are stored with leading zeros to fill the field. This fits the **tab** or **column** features used to enter a list in word processing. These fields use a specified number of positions for each data item. For example, the following word processed text separated by tabs can be imported to five attributes in a database:

Ralph P. Johnson   4218 Burton Street   St Paul   MN   55198

In a comma-delimited format, every attribute value is separated by a comma, including attributes with null values. The preceding record with items defined by number of spaces allowed would be entered in comma-delimited format as follows:

Ralph P. Johnson,4218 Burton Street,St Paul,MN,55198

Because these data formats are different, the **convert** facility may recognize the type of each field from its contents and set database table attribute types automatically. In some cases, **convert** facilities require additional parameters to be entered before they can translate data.

Entering Data Directly into Tables

When data does not already exist or when new records must be entered into a database, the database package provides a user interface for data entry. Data input and maintenance facilities can take a variety of forms. Three common methods are direct entry into a table, use of a single-table input form, and use of a multiple-table input form.

Since data items are stored in a table, it is possible to enter new data items or make modifications directly in the table. The database package presents the user with a view of the table and allows entries and corrections. Figure 12-2 is an example of a table view in Microsoft Access™. The representation of tables is similar in other DBMS packages. A user can select a row or a single field and alter contents. A complete new row can be added to the table. Typically,

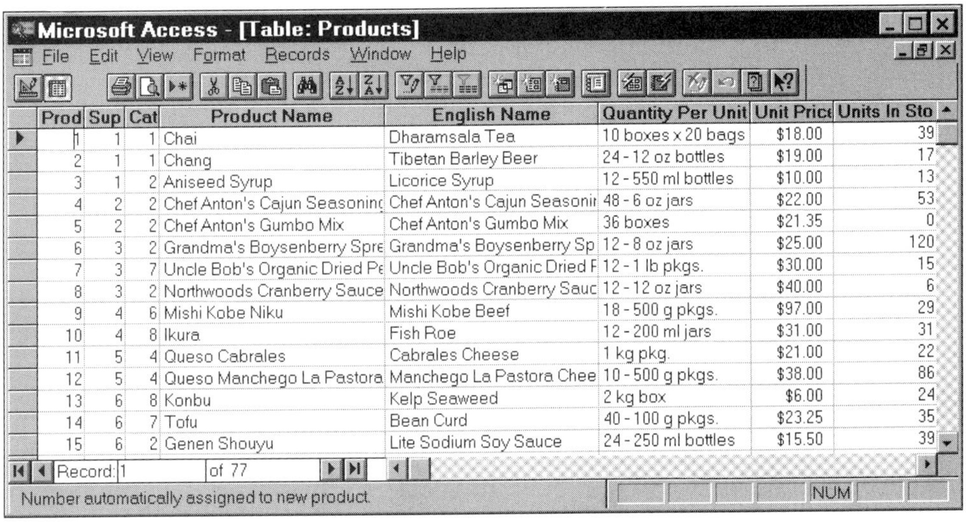

	Prod	Sup	Cat	Product Name	English Name	Quantity Per Unit	Unit Pric	Units In Sto
▶	1	1	1	Chai	Dharamsala Tea	10 boxes x 20 bags	$18.00	39
	2	1	1	Chang	Tibetan Barley Beer	24 - 12 oz bottles	$19.00	17
	3	1	2	Aniseed Syrup	Licorice Syrup	12 - 550 ml bottles	$10.00	13
	4	2	2	Chef Anton's Cajun Seasoninç	Chef Anton's Cajun Seasonii	48 - 6 oz jars	$22.00	53
	5	2	2	Chef Anton's Gumbo Mix	Chef Anton's Gumbo Mix	36 boxes	$21.35	0
	6	3	2	Grandma's Boysenberry Spre	Grandma's Boysenberry Sp	12 - 8 oz jars	$25.00	120
	7	3	7	Uncle Bob's Organic Dried Pe	Uncle Bob's Organic Dried F	12 - 1 lb pkgs.	$30.00	15
	8	3	2	Northwoods Cranberry Sauce	Northwoods Cranberry Sauc	12 - 12 oz jars	$40.00	6
	9	4	6	Mishi Kobe Niku	Mishi Kobe Beef	18 - 500 g pkgs.	$97.00	29
	10	4	8	Ikura	Fish Roe	12 - 200 ml jars	$31.00	31
	11	5	4	Queso Cabrales	Cabrales Cheese	1 kg pkg.	$21.00	22
	12	5	4	Queso Manchego La Pastora	Manchego La Pastora Chee	10 - 500 g pkgs.	$38.00	86
	13	6	8	Konbu	Kelp Seaweed	2 kg box	$6.00	24
	14	6	7	Tofu	Bean Curd	40 - 100 g pkgs.	$23.25	35
	15	6	2	Genen Shouyu	Lite Sodium Soy Sauce	24 - 250 ml bottles	$15.50	39

FIGURE 12-2 *Table view of a data table*

the underlying stored table's values are changed as entered (and as shown on the screen) with little or no processing or error-checking.

The table representation is simple and direct. It requires no effort to design or produce, since the user sees the contents of the underlying table. However, there are two significant deficiencies in the direct table entry method:

1. *There is little or no error-checking.* It is quite easy to accidentally replace or delete valuable data with this form of input. Although a database package may check for some errors, the user is responsible for entering data correctly with very little assistance from the system.
2. *The view represents a single database table.* A single-table view may be inconsistent with the user's way of performing tasks and activities that require use of multiple tables. For example, in an order processing application, a single order might require changes to customer, order, line item, and product tables. If this must be done for each individual table, it is difficult to process a single order without making a serious error.

Entering Data in Single-record Form

Figure 12-3 is an example of a form that provides for input for each field of a single table. Filling in the form results in data entry for one row of the table. The user can use a control on the form to step from one row to another. The contents of each selected row are displayed. Corrections to these existing rows are made using the form. This display is easier to work with than the tabular view, since it helps focus attention on one entity instance at a time and the data to be entered, modified, or deleted. Most database packages provide

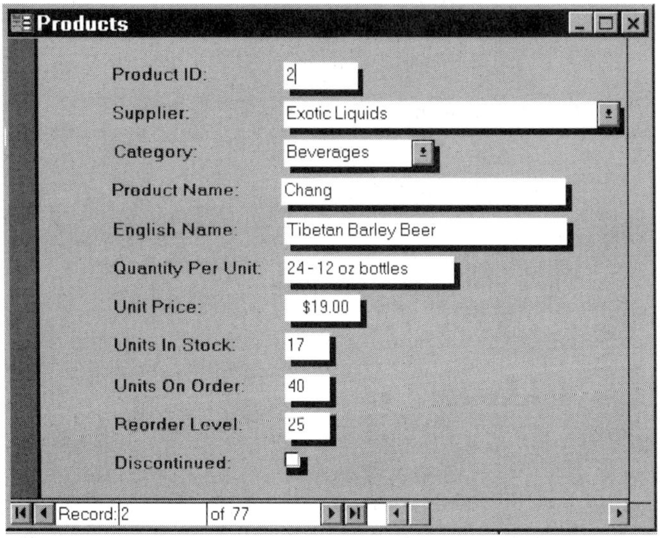

FIGURE 12-3 *Example of record input form from Microsoft Access*™

assistance in generating such input forms. Limited error-preventing features are often included in this input support mechanism. However, the contents of only one table can be displayed on one form. Tasks and activities requiring input into several tables are not supported by a single-table entry form.

Entering Data in Multiple-table Form

Data input for several tables may be input using a single form. Figure 12-4 is an example of a form designed to resemble a paper customer order form. It contains data from multiple tables and updates those tables when data items are entered. Significant design and implementation work are necessary to produce such a multiple-table form. However, the form has advantages because it reduces the probability of errors and omissions in input by matching the form design and flow of work to the user task of creating a new order. In addition, the form can be designed to display stored data to a user during input. When this individual enters a customer name or number, the form retrieves and displays other information, such as address, salesperson, and "ship to" address. This not only reduces input requirements, but also allows the user to confirm the validity of input by inspecting the retrieved values. For example, the product code can be checked by inspecting the product name provided by the form. The form can also be used for entering corrections to existing records in more than one table.

More complex input forms may be implemented by basing them on the result of a database query, since a form can contain one or more queries.

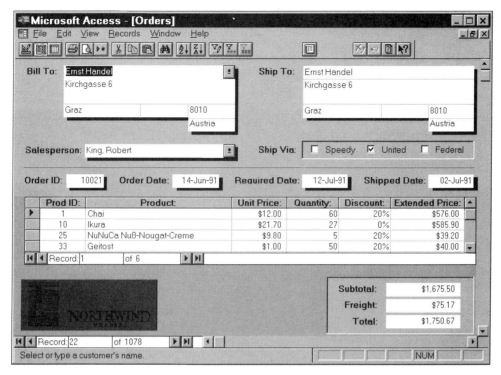

FIGURE 12-4 *A multiple-table input form*

Input forms may also be implemented by linking to data maintained by other database software. An external table that has been linked may be accessed and, in some cases, even updated as though it were part of the current database application. This capability means that an individual may be able to access all or part of a department or organizational database as though it were local. Not all implementations of database software support this form of access.

Database Application Output

◆ ◆ ◆ ◆ ◆ ◆ ◆ ◆ ◆ ◆ ◆ ◆ ◆ ◆ ◆ ◆ ◆ ◆ ◆ ◆

This section describes database software package output in terms of three separate functions: selection, organization, and presentation. This section is, in part, a review of the query and output discussion in Chapter 7. A database typically contains more data than users want at any one time. Selection specifies the criteria that determine the table rows and columns to be extracted for presentation. Selected data may be displayed in tabular form without further processing (often the default mode of presentation). However, the results of selection must usually be organized by ordering and grouping operations. Additional functions may be applied to convert the selected data into the display or report that supports the user task/activity. Database software packages usually have auxiliary utility facilities to export query results or entire tables for use in other applications.

Output Selection

Underlying the query facility in a relational database software package is the **Structured Query Language (SQL)**, a complete and powerful database language that supports all of the data access and manipulation necessary with a database. However, SQL is designed for data processing professionals. Therefore, most major database software packages include alternate, user-oriented methods for specifying or prototyping queries. Figures 12-5, 12-6, and 12-7 show three different perspectives of the same complex query. Figure 12-5 illustrates a query design screen that applies the concept of query by example. Figure 12-6 is the same query in the Structured Query Language. Figure 12-7 demonstrates a table result from the query.

The concept of a database query is to select the desired attributes of the pertinent rows of one or more tables. There may be several reasons for the selections made by queries. For example, users may want to select data for presentation, to select rows and change the values of specified attributes, or to create new tables from existing tables. This section focuses on selection for presentation or other output purposes.

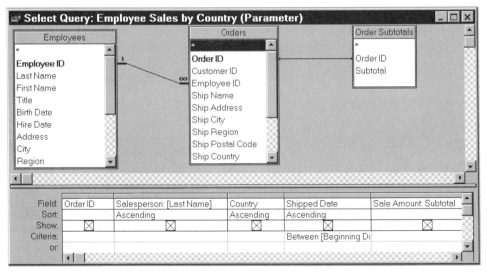

FIGURE 12-5 *A multiple table query formulation in Microsoft Access™ QBE*

```
Select Query: Employee Sales by Country (Parameter)
PARAMETERS [Beginning Date] DateTime, [Ending Date] DateTime;
SELECT Orders.[Order ID], [Last Name] & ", " & [First Name] AS Salesperson,
Employees.Country, Orders.[Shipped Date], [Order Subtotals].Subtotal AS [Sale Amount]
FROM Employees INNER JOIN (Orders INNER JOIN [Order Subtotals] ON Orders.[Order ID]
= [Order Subtotals].[Order ID]) ON Employees.[Employee ID] = Orders.[Employee ID]
WHERE ((Orders.[Shipped Date] Between [Beginning Date] And [Ending Date]))
ORDER BY [Last Name] & ", " & [First Name], Employees.Country, Orders.[Shipped Date];
```

FIGURE 12-6 *A multiple table query in Microsoft Access™ SQL*

Order ID	Salesperson	Country	Shipped Date	Sale Amo
11043	Buchanan, Steven	UK	23-Mar-94	$210.00
11034	Callahan, Laura	USA	21-Mar-94	$539.40
11056	Callahan, Laura	USA	25-Mar-94	$3,740.00
11050	Callahan, Laura	USA	29-Mar-94	$810.00
11038	Davolio, Nancy	USA	24-Mar-94	$732.60
11064	Davolio, Nancy	USA	28-Mar-94	$4,330.40
11067	Davolio, Nancy	USA	30-Mar-94	$86.85
11069	Davolio, Nancy	USA	30-Mar-94	$360.00
11022	Dodsworth, Anne	UK	28-Mar-94	$1,402.00
11053	Fuller, Andrew	USA	23-Mar-94	$3,055.00
11042	Fuller, Andrew	USA	25-Mar-94	$405.75
11060	Fuller, Andrew	USA	28-Mar-94	$266.00
11030	King, Robert	UK	21-Mar-94	$12,615.05
11037	King, Robert	UK	21-Mar-94	$60.00
11048	King, Robert	UK	24-Mar-94	$525.00
11047	King, Robert	UK	25-Mar-94	$817.88
11066	King, Robert	UK	28-Mar-94	$928.75
11055	King, Robert	UK	29-Mar-94	$1,727.50
11041	Leverling, Janet	USA	22-Mar-94	$1,773.00
11052	Leverling, Janet	USA	25-Mar-94	$1,332.00
11057	Leverling, Janet	USA	25-Mar-94	$45.00
11049	Leverling, Janet	USA	28-Mar-94	$273.60

Record: 1 of 26

FIGURE 12-7 *Multiple table query results*

Even though the computer may not physically store the results of a query, the user can visualize the results of a query as a table. From a practical standpoint, a table exists for user purposes. (It is often referred to as a "virtual table" because it only appears to exist.) The user may manipulate the virtual table as though it were physically stored as a table. Queries may be stored and recalled. A stored query may be referenced in another query, resulting in a nested query.

Output Organization

Every set of data has some order. In databases, the default order is the order of the underlying table. In many cases, database table order is not meaningful. For example, new customers may be assigned Customer ID numbers as they are added to the database. Therefore, the order of the underlying Customer table is essentially random with respect to any analysis other than length of time as a customer. Information about customers will most often need to be ordered by name, location, amount of purchases, or some other specific criterion. Ordering and grouping operations are applied to the results of selection before those results are arranged in a display or report. Operationally, both ordering and grouping are part of the query specification.

The specification to order or sort the results of a query contains the attribute(s) that determine the sort sequence and whether it is to be ascending or descending. In SQL, an **ORDER BY** clause is attached to the query sentence along with the list of one or more fields that determine the sequence of the output. The query design facilities of a **Query by Example (QBE)** method will include facilities to specify sequence. More than one field may be used to establish sequence. Multiple ordering fields are listed in an importance sequence. (The first sort field is used for the first (major) sort and the second sort field sequences items grouped together by the first sort.) This can be continued with several fields. Figure 12-8 is an example of an SQL query that specifies an order.

Grouping is a method of organizing groups of records under an attribute that differentiates the groups. The query outputs the attribute only once for the group. In other words, the **GROUP BY** organization retrieves and presents the attribute for a group of records that belong to the group. Figure 12-8 illustrates the specification of grouping as an organizing feature. The SQL **GROUP BY** clause in the example directs the query to output only one row per country, including a count of customers in that country. QBE facilities also provide for grouping. The grouping function is very useful in data analysis and is a fundamental part of reporting and presentation.

Output Presentation

There are three alternative output presentations for queries: tables, input forms, and reports.

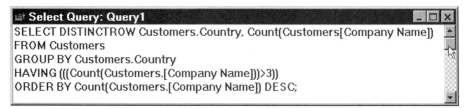

FIGURE 12-8 *Example of SQL instructions to list the number of customers by country in countries with more than three customers*

1. *Tables.* Tables are the default results of a database query. They may be presented in tabular form or exported to another application as tables.

2. *Forms.* Forms are often used to display relevant outputs as part of an input function. An example of such a function is updating via a query in which the contents of a selection are displayed on a form in order to identify fields to be changed.

3. *Reports.* There are five categories of reports that present selected and organized information to support knowledge work and decision making:

   a. *Detail reports.* **Detail reports** list each of the entity instances relevant to the topic of the report along with the relevant attributes. A list of customers is a detail report. A list of sales for each customer and a list of sales transactions for the day are other examples. Detail reports may be ordered and grouped. Their distinguishing feature is that the lowest level of detail is always included.

   b. *Summary reports.* **Summary reports** present totals for groups of data records. A summary report includes the totals, but not the details of the items that were summed. Financial statements are summary reports because they give the total for all of the transactions in a classification, but include no details. Summary reports are often combined with detailed listings. The total is presented, followed by a list of the items included in the total. Both detail and summary reports can be presented as comparisons with prior periods.

   c. *External documents.* **External documents** include documents such as sales invoices produced as the result of a transaction. They may be considered a form of report. The invoice, for example, is a report to a customer. External documents (external reports and transaction documents) project the image of the organization. They must also be self-contained in terms of elements such as labels and descriptive comments.

   d. *Exception or variance reports.* **Exception reports** are designed to present records that identify potential problems. An exception report applies selection criteria to identify the records for events or conditions that fall outside acceptable limits. A list of overdue accounts is an example. A report showing variances from budget presents data in a way that allows the user to identify problems.

   e. *Analytic or statistical reports.* **Analytic reports** may be presented in an analytical form or with statistical analysis. Examples are reports that categorize customers by size of order, reports that analyze customer profitability, and reports of inventory analyzed by how long each stock keeping unit will last at normal usage.

Macros and Custom Programs

◆ ◆

Macros or custom program code in applications developed using a database software package are created to achieve unique functionality or improve ease of use. When a database application can benefit from additional capabilities not provided in the package, the added functionality may be purchased from vendors or developed by the organization. The market for added functions often provides the capabilities needed. Custom in-house development is an option, but complex development is nearly always too costly for a single user. Modest development efforts can sometimes be justified if they can be implemented using the macro and customizing features of a database software package.

Macros and custom code can also be used to improve ease of use for the sets of tables, forms, queries, and reports that make up a database application. As more and more functions are added to a database application, it can become very complex. Customizing features in the database software package allow a user to organize forms, queries, and reports around menus, so using the application involves a selection from a small set of choices at each step rather than requiring detailed instructions. Such customization is useful in long-lived individual applications and may be very desirable when complex applications are used by workgroup members. The details of such customization of database applications are beyond the scope of this chapter.

The Database Application Development Process

◆ ◆

Database application development is a moderately complex process that benefits from a systematic approach. Costs are always incurred in software systems development efforts when changes must be made. The cost of changes increases as application development progresses. Once a database has been designed and data has been entered, making design corrections can become difficult and costly. Therefore, getting the design correct or close to correct the first time is worth the extra effort required up front. The recommended design process is prototyping, in which the user-developer decides enough about needs to build an initial version that is close to correct and complete. This prototype is used or tested to identify omissions and design deficiencies.

The prototype is altered to correct problems and reflect a deeper understanding of the needs. The prototyping approach works very well for personal database applications.

As illustrated in Figure 12-9, developing a database application consists of four parts: (1) defining the initial requirements, (2) designing and developing database tables, (3) designing inputs, and (4) designing reports and other outputs. These four parts are included in a process flow description that consists of nine steps, ranging from defining the purpose of the application to developing each query and report. These steps are described in the following sections.

Define Purpose of Application

Requirements analysis was discussed in Chapter 9. Requirements analysis for a database application focuses on defining the uses for the data by asking questions such as the following:

◊   Why is the application needed?

◊   What problems will it address, or what questions will it answer?

◊   How will data be obtained to respond to the problems or questions?

◊   What kinds of analysis will be performed with the data?

◊   What are the documents and reports to be produced?

In addition to the usage requirements, it is important to examine some characteristics of the database. Questions such as the following explore the maintenance of the database, duplication of effort, its relationship to other databases, and its future:

◊   How long will the database remain current and useful?

◊   How will the data be kept current and useful?

◊   Does (or is it likely that) the data needed already exists elsewhere (in workgroup, departmental, organizational or external databases)?

◊   Will the contents of this database need to be coordinated with another database?

◊   Is it likely that the content of this database will be extended in the future?

The documentation of requirements need not be extensive. Some notes that cover these essential issues and requirements are sufficient.

Determine Tables in the Database

This step makes use of the list of outputs identified in the previous step. The next step involves identifying the subjects or entities about which data must be stored. (Each entity will become a separate table.) Questions such as the

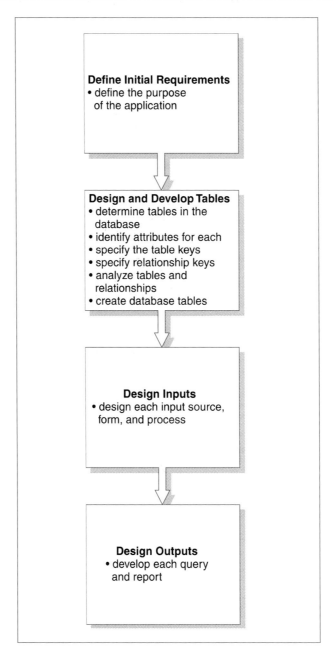

FIGURE 12-9 *The prototyping process used to develop an individual database application*

following will assist in the identification process (Iterate through the questions using the words "person," "abstract concept," or "event" in addition to the word "thing."):

◊ What are the things about which I need information in order to perform activities in my tasks?

◊ What are the things about which I will make decisions or analyses?

◊ What are the things that I need to track or monitor?

◊ What are the things about which I need information in order to author or persuade?

The list of entities (things, persons, abstract concepts, or events) is a tentative list of tables for the database. Subsequent steps may cause the list to be revised.

Identify Attributes for Each Table

Define and name the attributes associated with each entity instance. Use the following questions to help identify the existence of attributes:

◊ *What facts about the entity are important to activities?* Each fact about an entity is represented by an attribute. For example, "number of dependents" is a fact about an employee. If it is important, define the "dependent" attribute.

◊ *What attributes are needed for analysis, explanation, or presentation?* For example, "title" (such as professor, doctor, congresswoman) may be an important attribute in an address book table.

◊ *Is this attribute related directly to the entity?* For example, customer name is directly related to the customer table, but product purchased is probably not. (Perhaps there should be another table that "product purchased" can be related to?)

◊ *Can this attribute be calculated from other data?* If so, it should not be stored at all.

The processes of defining tables and defining attributes interact. As attributes are defined, a need may emerge for additional tables. Some tables may be better defined as attributes in other tables. The process of analyzing needs, defining tables, and defining attributes continues until the tables appear to be complete.

Specify Table Keys

For each table, select and specify the key attribute that uniquely identifies each instance. Examples of a key attribute are social security number, employee number, customer number, customer order number, and textbook ISBN. Each of these examples uniquely identifies an entity instance and distinguishes one entity instance from another.

In some cases, an attribute proposed as a key is not appropriate because it is not unique for every instance. The name of a person or company is usually not a good key attribute since people, companies, and other entities may not have unique names. For example, there are 18 Dale Ericksons in the Minneapolis telephone book (and four of them have the same middle initial). The solution is either to create a new unique attribute or to define a compound key. A new unique attribute is usually a number that can be arbitrarily assigned to each new instance, such as customer number or order number. Occasionally, a single attribute is not sufficient by itself to be a primary key. For example, if the entity instances are customer purchase orders, the customer-assigned purchase order (P.O.) number might not be unique across customers. A solution is to use the compound (or composite or concatenated) key of customer number and customer P.O. number.

The lack of an attribute that uniquely identifies each instance may also mean that the proposed table does not really represent an entity. For example, customer address may be proposed as a table since many customers seem to have more than one address: a bill-to address (such as the purchasing office) and a ship-to address (where goods are to be sent). In looking for a unique identifier, customer number might be examined as a unique attribute to identify customer address for an address table. However, a further investigation will disclose that since different customers do not have the same address, there is no need for an address table, and the customer addresses should be included as attributes in the customer table.

Specify Keys for Table Relationships

A logical or conceptual relationship exists between tables if the entities are related in some way so that it makes sense to join one table with another to produce one or more of the needed outputs. To join two tables, both must have a common key attribute. In other words, one column of each table must have the same attribute (even though the attributes may have different names). Since the key for a table may be different than the attribute that allows it to be joined with another table, the key attribute that associates it with the other table is a foreign key. A foreign key that is included in one table of a relationship must be the key of the other table. A table may be part of multiple relationships and, therefore, include several foreign keys.

A user will find it useful to prepare a graphical representation of tables and their relationships. The tables should be depicted with their attributes. Lines should connect keys with corresponding foreign keys. These lines identify valid relationships that allow tables to be joined. No line between two tables means the tables cannot be joined (and this may be appropriate). The graphical diagram for the database is useful in analysis to make sure foreign keys are included when needed. It is also useful in formulating queries to join tables. The database software may provide such a graphic to identify the connections between tables (see Figure 12-5 for an example).

The graphic showing the relationships among tables can also show the connectivities of each relationship. These are one or many, shown in Figure 12-5 by 1 and ∞ at each end of the connection. The relationship can be **one-to-one** or **one-to-many**. A **many-to-many relationship** is not allowed. Handling this is discussed in the next section.

Analyze Tables and Table Relationships

Examine each table for attributes that violate the conditions of the relational model. Evaluate each attribute (each column) as a fact about the entity. Each fact should be elementary; that is, it should say something about just one instance of the attribute or represented entity. It is functionally dependent on the key, meaning the attribute does not depend on any other attribute or instance or entity to specify its value. For example, **employee name** is dependent on **employee number** (the key), so **employee name** is a suitable attribute for **employee**. However, the name of the employee's supervisor is not dependent on the employee number (the key) because a change in the supervisor is not dependent on the employee.

When an attribute is not dependent on the key of the table, this suggests it belongs in another table. In the case of the employee supervisor, a table for department (with department key) might contain the department supervisor name (or employee number) because that position is dependent on the department (department key).

Following are appropriate questions for attribute analysis:

◊ *Is the attribute a fact that is of interest only for this entity (this table) or is it of interest beyond this entity?* If it is of interest beyond the current entity, it probably belongs in a different table and can be associated with the current entity by a relationship. For example, assume a user has a table for **Textbooks**. Each entity instance has attributes that describe a book. One of the attributes can be **publisher**. If the publisher is of interest only as an attribute of **textbook**, then it is an appropriate attribute in the **textbook** table. If, however, the user is also interested in other information about the publisher (such as editor, address, and royalty rates) a separate table should be established for **publisher** that contains the added information. The publisher name (or other identifier) becomes a foreign key attribute in the **textbook** table to point to the **publisher** table (see Figure 12-10).

◊ *Can the attribute for an entity instance have multiple (repeating) values?* This is termed a one-to-many situation. For example, a customer may have

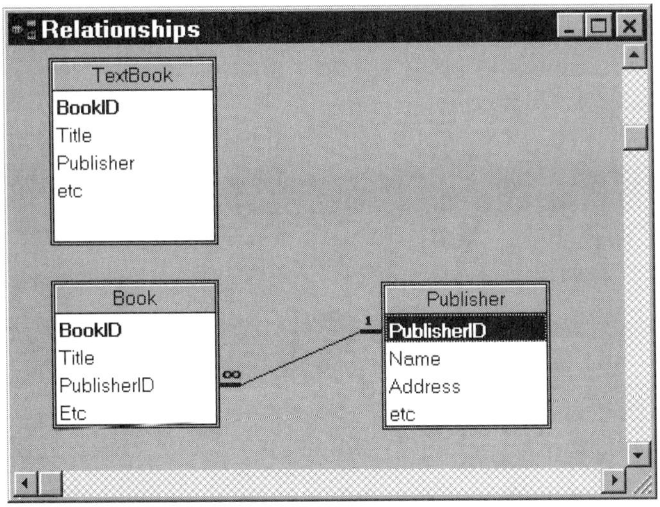

FIGURE 12-10 *One table versus two related tables*

placed many orders, so there is a one-to-many relationship between customer and orders. Since an attribute can contain only one value, a separate table is needed for customer orders. Its key will be **order number** and it will contain **customer number** as a foreign key. This satisfies the condition of the attributes being dependent on the keys. The attributes of **customer** are dependent on (change with) **customer number** and the attributes of **order** depend on **order number**. The contents of a specific customer order can be retrieved by joining the tables to obtain information on the customer and orders identified with the customer. Figure 12-11 depicts this relationship.

Relationships that have a many-to-many connectivity are a special case in database design. Such relationships cannot be directly implemented. Instead, a special type of entity called an **associative entity** must be inserted to represent the many-to-many relationship as a combination of a one-to-many and a many-to-one relationship.

The relationship between the customer order entity and the product entity is a classic example of a many-to-many relationship. That is, a specific customer order is often for more than one product, and a popular product is likely to appear on more than one order. Analysis of the many-to-many relationship leads to the new associative relationship ordered product (see Order Details in Figure 12-11). In some cases, the only attributes of an associative entity are the keys of the tables to which it relates. In the ordered product example, the attributes of unit price, quantity, and discount are dependent on this entity, not on either of the entities it relates. That is, they depend on a specific order for a particular product.

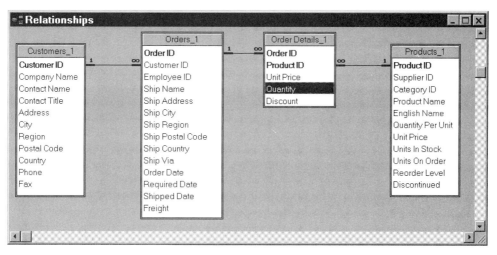

FIGURE 12-11   *An example of database relationships*

Create the Database Tables

Using the database package software enables users to enter the definition into a new database. Following are suggestions and guidelines for completing this process:

◆ *Plan names for tables and attributes.* Names are fundamental and may be difficult to revise once they have been referenced in queries, reports, and forms. Follow the rules for naming provided by the database software package being used. Use names that are complete, expressive, and unambiguous.

◆ *Define each attribute.* In most packages, a user will be presented with choices of data types, field sizes, and other properties for each attribute. These characteristics are usually possible to revise later on. A good guideline is to treat every item as text unless it will be part of some calculation. This is often the default selection.

◆ *Try out the newly defined database by entering a very small number of entity instances that illustrate the types of data expected in the database.* This test data can be saved and used to test queries, reports, and forms, or to modify the database design.

Design Input Forms and Procedures

The design of input procedures should consider both the initial input of data to establish the database and subsequent entries and corrections. The initial data to set up the database may come from external sources, corporate databases, or other computer files. If so, it may be necessary to define processes, queries, and/or tables that are used only during the initial creation process. If the data being extracted from an existing source is significantly different from the database being created, it may be efficient to use the import facility of the database software package to create a temporary table or tables that contain the new data with its original organization. Queries can then be developed to migrate the attributes and instances into the new database.

In designing input procedures for ongoing use of the database, two factors should guide the design: (1) the risk associated with errors and (2) the frequency of a given type of input. Where the effect of errors is low and a particular input occurs infrequently, the default approach of modifying a table directly is appropriate. This approach might be used, for example, in updating a customer list if changes in customer data are relatively infrequent.

Where error detection during input is important or there will be a significant amount of data entry, an input form is appropriate. In many cases, the default form provided or generated by the package will be adequate. It is usually possible to add validation criteria to either the underlying tables or to specified fields of a form. Validation criteria are automatically executed when entering data, together with messages and explanations when the conditions defined are not met. Although it is unlikely to be necessary in an individual or workgroup database application, special validation procedures may be written in the macro programming language of the package.

Design Queries and Reports

Report design benefits from careful planning in all but the simplest cases. The starting point for report design is clarity of purpose, plus a layout or sketch. The sketch should be a rough but correct visualization of the output. The simplest report is a listing of details from a single table or query. Many database application packages provide facilities to automatically lay out such a simple, straightforward report design based on the user's responses to a few questions.

Summary and exception reports are more complex because the user must define each level of grouping, plus headings and totals for each group. Database application packages include report design facilities that help a user specify ordering and grouping criteria and associated heading and footing layouts. The design that results from such tools can be modified by the user. Such additional modifications include adding graphic items and modifying the properties of selected fields such as their positions, captions, formats, colors, and fonts.

Designing an external document is much like designing a form. There is an emphasis on appearance and clarity for external users. An example of such a document is shown in Figure 12-12.

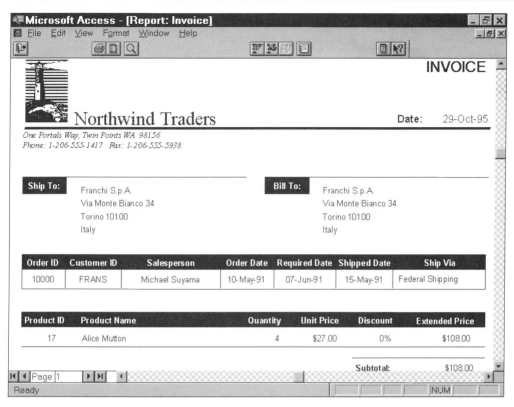

FIGURE 12-12 *Invoice from the Microsoft Access™ sample applications*

Summary

◆ ◆ ◆ ◆ ◆ ◆ ◆ ◆ ◆ ◆ ◆ ◆ ◆ ◆ ◆ ◆ ◆ ◆ ◆ ◆

◇ A database management software package is a complete application building resource. Database software package capabilities are the core of many
   specialized software packages. A database application includes a relational
   database, input forms and input processing procedures, and output queries
   and reports. With many database software packages, it is possible to build
   a complete application with little or no procedural programming or customizing. Simple "flat file" applications can be efficiently implemented using relational database software packages.

◊ The relational database component provides a database that is flexible and non-redundant. The relational model of personal computer database software packages is the same model employed by departmental and organizational databases. The default input interface provided in database software packages presents a tabular view of data consistent with the relational model. The software also provides a mechanism for defining a custom input form. Some packages generate input forms automatically. These forms can be tailored to fit the user. Complex forms may be used to implement complete transactions such as orders. Such forms may include error checking and may update multiple database tables. Input facilities include provisions for importing or converting data from other databases and files.

◊ The output functions of database software packages include provisions to select the desired data from one or more tables. Selection results may be presented in default tabular formats or organized by ordering and grouping. Presentation facilities help develop output displays and reports. Output reports include detail reports, summary reports, external documents, exception or variance reports, and analytic or statistical reports. Database software packages provide interactive report specification tools to help design outputs and include extensive support to customize the content and appearance of the outputs. The packages also contain macro and other customizing facilities.

◊ Developing a database application benefits from a prototyping approach that starts with simple requirements determination and focuses on the design of database tables. Every entity of interest has a corresponding table with the necessary attributes. Entities are linked by relationships implemented by storing the key attribute as a foreign key in the related table. A diagram of tables, attributes, keys and relationships is an important database application design tool.

◊ Default tables and input forms are appropriate for many inputs. The risk associated with errors and the frequency of use of a given input are important factors in deciding how much customizing is needed for input design. Output design and implementation effort is guided by the intended use of the display or form. Defaults are often adequate for personal, workgroup, and some organizational use. Customizing facilities may often be used for external documents.

EXERCISES

1. Use a database package to design a "flat-file" database for personal use. A simple address book works well. Create an input form and use it to add

15 to 20 rows to your table. Be sure to modify your design if you encounter any problems with this prototype. Design and implement an output report that presents your address data in a usable format. Optionally, design an output report that has the same form as your current personal address book. Print out a sample input form, the definition of your database, and a sample of the output(s) you can produce.

2. Many individual records in an address book have multiple phone numbers, such as home, home fax, office, office fax, cellular, and pager. You could add a column for each different type of phone number. Instead, consider phone number and phone number type to be a separate table with some number of rows related to each individual in the address book. Revise your design from Exercise 1 to reflect this relational implementation. Produce the outputs that correspond to those from Exercise 1. Add a graphical model for the tables in the database. Is the telephone table useful or necessary? Explain.

3. You have decided to operate your own consulting business. You need to develop a database application to keep track of clients and work applied to each client. The input should be simple and easy to use. The primary output will be a summary report that includes the details of each task with totals by type of work. You will use this report as the detail part of a monthly letter to bill each client. Prototype your application and modify it until you are satisfied that it is adequate to support you during your first year of business. Print out a graphical model of your database along with sample inputs and outputs. (Remember to keep it simple!)

4. Select one of the following problems. Then design a database with at least three tables. Enter sample data. Print the tables. Define and do queries that join pairs of tables and one that joins all tables.

   a. A database will be used to store information about major running marathons in the United States. The database will contain information about specific races and about the people who run them. A **Races** table will contain records describing the marathons themselves: race name, location, and course description. A **Runners** table will have information about specific runners: name, home town and state, birth date, and favorite pre-race snack. A **Winners** table is an intersection table used to keep track of the top three male and female finishers for each race.

   b. A small database will be used to keep records on a personal music library. An **Artists** table will have name, date of birth, place of birth, and nationality. A compact disk (CD) database will have CD name, artist, year, style of music (because an artist can have different styles in different CDs), storage format, and number of songs. A **Songs** table will include the name of the song, the artist, the CD, and the length of the song (in minutes and seconds).

    c. A database will be used to track employee health benefit utilization. The first table will be an employee listing with first and last name, middle initial, gender, employee number, phone number, location, and medical plan. The second table will be a list of clinics covered by the company medical plan with attributes of clinic name, health plan coverage, and city. The third table will be a list of insurance claims made by employees with employee ID, claim amount, service provided, and date of service as attributes.

    d. A database will be used by the president's office to track guest lists for social events. The tables are **social function**, **invitation/attendance**, and **people**. Each social event has people invited from the list of potential invitees.

5. List four databases you might find worthwhile in your personal life. Explain the characteristics of each. Explain the value (if it exists) of having multiple tables instead of a flat file.

6. Describe requirements for a genealogy family history database. Identify a set of tables and a set of queries (including tables used). Compare these requirements and tables with database features in a commercial PC genealogy database program such as Family Treemaker™.

Evaluating, Refining, and Integrating Applications

◈ ◈ ◈ ◈ ◈ ◈ ◈ ◈ ◈

OBJECTIVES

After completing this chapter, you should be able to do the following:

◆ Describe the process of evaluating system requirements.

◆ Explain the concept of robustness in terms of application design.

◆ Explain the concept of usability in terms of application design.

◆ Describe the goals and methods in risk analysis.

◆ List and explain the alternatives available to system developers assessing the results of application evaluations.

◆ Describe the differences between testing and debugging.

◆ Describe the processes of refining inputs and outputs.

◆ Describe the process of refining data integrity.

◆ Describe the role of access control and backup in enhancing data integrity.

◆ Describe the role of application integration in the system development process.

◆ Explain the importance of standardization in application usability.

KEY TERMS AND CONCEPTS

This chapter introduces the following key terms and concepts, listed in the order in which they appear:

application risk
requisite variety
robustness
usability
task/technology fit

risk analysis
prototype evaluation
testing
input interface refinement
output interface refinement

referential integrity
access control and backup
  refinement
application integration

Previous chapters emphasized the prototyping approach to applications development. Prototyping is appropriate in both customizing and custom development. Through repeated cycles of use and revision, an application is improved until desired functionality is obtained. The prototyping approach allows functional requirements to emerge during system development, rather than being specified in advance. Some basic requirements are needed to start the process, but many useful requirements are discovered as part of the creative process of building and using a prototype.

Prototyping produces a solution with the desired functionality, but does it produce a solution suitable for everyday use? What has been left out of the prototype? Is it possible that the application will be used by others who did not participate in its development? This chapter suggests a process for evaluating an application. Beyond the basic functionality of a prototype is its ability to deal with exceptions and unusual situations, its appropriateness for use by others, and the risks involved in its use. Risk analysis is useful in evaluating whether the application design is consistent with the probability of failure and the exposure associated with its use.

The results from risk analysis and evaluation can be used to refine the prototype. Refinement frequently involves adding error-detection and control features to the data input interface. Outputs may be improved so that they communicate more effectively. Data integrity refinements can help assure that data is neither lost nor corrupted.

As noted in earlier chapters, integrating solutions such as templates and macros is one approach to improving efficiency in knowledge work because it reduces user effort and time. Custom applications should also be evaluated in terms of their integration with other applications. The steps involved in application integration include standardization, command interface development, application linking, and the use of add-on tools to supplement generalized software packages.

Risk from Individual Applications

◆ ◆

The preceding chapters emphasized making individual use of information technology more productive by applying one of three approaches:

1. Customizing packages by selecting options that improve task productivity
2. Developing new functions using the macro facilities of software packages
3. Developing complete custom applications using the development facilities in software packages or in separate development software

Two of these approaches add new functionality, but with added functionality comes added risk. In terms of error potential, a computer system allows a user to make both observed and unobserved errors more quickly than by manual processing. It is, therefore, critical to understand and address the **application risks** associated with productivity tools.

Risk implies exposure to hazard or loss that can be costly to the individual or organization. Since the hazard or loss will not always occur, probability of occurrence is a significant factor in assessing risk. The risk from individual applications is expected loss. It is the product of error probability and error cost: *application risk = p(error) × cost(error)*. In other words, error omissions and losses have a probability of occurrence. Each expected error results in costs.

The total cost of the expected errors is the risk. (See Figure 13-1.) This section focuses on the concept of risk as it applies to personal use of information technology in carrying out organizational tasks.

There are two entities that bear risk in this context: the organization and the individual. The organization incurs the following risks:

◊ Faulty decisions made as a result of erroneous information. An individual system may produce faulty results because it was not developed properly.

◊ Additional time required to correct erroneous information. This may include the time required to correct errors and the time lost processing erroneous information.

◊ Productivity lost due to personal systems development. Time used by an individual in customizing or developing applications is time not devoted to assigned tasks. If the results are not useful, the organization has wasted resources.

The individual who uses information technology tools to customize or build applications incurs the following risks:

◊ Errors introduced due to lack of error control. Technology enhances productivity, but makes it possible to make more errors more quickly. Lack of error control is a serious deficiency with many user-developed systems.

◊ Data lost due to mistakes that destroy data files. In some cases, the lost data is irretrievable, causing faulty results. In other cases data must be recreated, resulting in lost productivity.

◊ Time lost due to use of poor tools. Features and applications consume more resources than they save and result in recurring lost time and productivity.

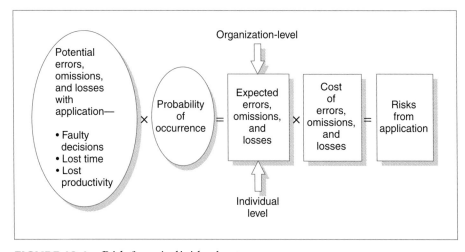

FIGURE 13-1 *Risk from individual systems*

Each application should be evaluated relative to probability and cost of errors, and risks should be recognized and realistically assessed. Because of the rapid change in technology, risks may change. New technology features may reduce some risks and introduce others.

Some organizations have a policy that prohibits individuals from enhancing their systems. These organizations believe the development costs are too high and the risks too great. However, changes in operating systems and packages have reduced both costs and risks. An organization with a "no enhancements" policy may be stifling significant productivity improvement and process innovation. However, risks do exist, and it is a good policy at both individual and organizational levels to explicitly recognize and evaluate risks with each application.

◆pplication Evaluation

A prototype demonstrates that an application works, but a prototype is not a complete application. Usually a prototype is developed only to a needed level of functionality at the expense of properties such as flexibility, accuracy, and reliability. Therefore, it may not be very robust: errors may be easy to make and hard to detect or rectify, and functions may not adequately support intended tasks and activities. This section explains how to evaluate a prototyped application in terms of several important properties: evaluating fit with real requirements, evaluating robustness and usability, evaluating appropriateness and suitability for the task, and analyzing risks.

Evaluating Fit with Real Requirements

One of the advantages of individual application development is the reduced time needed to identify requirements. The individual arrives at the requirements without having to schedule meetings and spend time explaining the requirements to an outside analyst, since the prototyping process itself forces exploration of requirements and identification of missing elements.

As explained in Chapter 2, eliminating the second party in the requirements determination process reduces the time required and eliminates mistakes due to miscommunication between the user and analyst; however, some advantages of the analysis process are lost, which may affect the completeness of requirements. User-analyst dialog has some positive effects on the following types of requirements; in the absence of the dialog, the same issues should be explored by the user alone (see Figure 13-2):

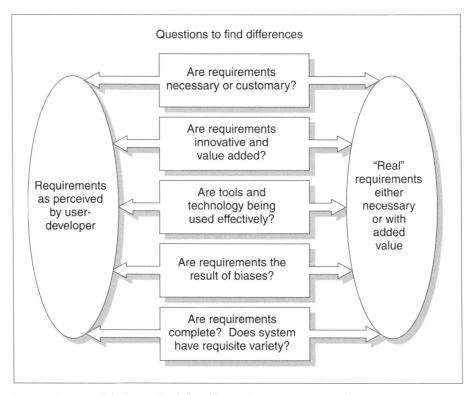

FIGURE 13-2 *Dialog to find "real" requirements compared to user-perceived requirements*

◊ *Identifying unnecessary (although customary) requirements.* The analyst may challenge the user and recommend reevaluating requirements that the user assumes to be necessary.

◊ *Identifying innovative requirements that add value.* An outsider may think about needs differently and suggest new ideas about information and its use.

◊ *Using the full potential of tools.* Expertise in databases, spreadsheets, or other development platforms will improve the development process and aid in asking the right questions. A professional developer is likely to have experience with the intended resource.

◊ *Compensating for biases.* A professional analyst will usually employ an established fact-gathering process to elicit requirements. Requirements determination processes have been designed to elicit complete and correct sets of requirements and to overcome biases such as the following:

   ♦ *Recency bias.* An individual focuses unduly on recent events. If there was a recent need for a particular type of information, it may be included as a requirement even though it was an unusual event.

- *Concreteness bias.* Concrete data (based on physical counts or physical measurements) tends to be given more weight than "soft data." The concreteness bias may be incorporated in the data collected and used.

- *Availability bias.* Information that is easily available is favored in system design. Searching for more data may be eliminated in favor of available data. Users designing their own applications may demonstrate this bias by focusing on data readily available rather than establishing new data capture processes.

- *Small sample bias.* A user may be unduly influenced by events that occur infrequently. The result may be data analysis and decision procedures that do not explicitly recognize the data as small sample data. For example, complaints, errors, exceptions, and similar events that occur with a low frequency may be incorporated in reports and analyses without an analysis that reflects the low occurrence.

◆ *Evaluating completeness of application requirements.* An application is a system, and one characteristic of a well-designed system is that it has **requisite variety**. This means that the system will be able to make an appropriate response to any type of input or input value. For example, a database that records customer information may have a field for fax number. The two most logical input actions are entry of a fax number or a null entry indicating that there is no fax number. However, some customers may have more than one fax number. Requisite variety in the application means that the system (or its user) will be able to make the appropriate response in this case too. The appropriate response may be to have a data field for a second fax, to record only the fax number that is usually used (ignore the second fax), or to include the second fax number in a "remarks" or "comments" field. The appropriate action depends on the application requirements.

Since no system can deal with all possible conditions, requisite variety usually requires that the user (or a supervisor) deal with conditions not anticipated. How to achieve completeness (i.e., what to include in the system and what to leave to the user) is an important requirements consideration.

Evaluating the application should focus on requirements that are often deficient in user-developed applications. The user should examine the application using questions such as the following:

◆ *Are all the requirements necessary?* Have they been included because of custom rather than necessity?

◆ *Does the application reflect innovation regarding the function to be performed?*

◆ *Do the requirements take into account the capabilities of the chosen development platform?*

◊ *Do they take advantage of the strengths of the hardware and software they will operate on?*

◊ *Does the application reflect biased behavior with respect to recency of events, concreteness of data (bias to hard data versus soft data), and availability of data?*

◊ *Does the analysis and presentation of low occurrence data aid the user in overcoming small sample bias?*

◊ *Does the application have requisite variety?* Is there a proper division between system responses incorporated in the application and responses (to unusual conditions) that are left to the user?

Evaluating Robustness and Usability

Robustness is defined as the behavior of the application when a mistake is made or a fault occurs. Mistakes usually happen when a user performs some operation that was not anticipated in the design, or inputs some data not expected and not covered by the logic of the application. Faults include hardware and software failures as well as occurrences such as accidental file deletion. A robust application will deal with the unexpected by preventing or rejecting it and by assisting user recovery. A robust application will not fail and give non-meaningful messages. It will not run to completion with nonsense results, but a robust application will provide for unanticipated actions, data, and other faults (see Figure 13-3).

In developing for robustness, the designer must anticipate potential errors and provide appropriate responses. Error detection is often very important in individual systems that perform complete tasks, because data checks that might be imposed when data is handed off to another person in a manual system are absent. This is even more important when others are to use an application or the application is to be used infrequently. The cost of robustness can be significant. A professional developer's guideline is that two-thirds or more of the effort in developing an application system are for error detection and error handling or other exceptions.

Usability is defined as the behavior of the application with respect to the user. It is associated with a "user friendly" application. The person using the application must be able to understand how to input data, how to deal with error conditions, and how to interpret messages and outputs. An individual may be able, with effort, to cope with cryptic messages, but a usable, robust system will provide complete explanations and suggestions for the correction of any problem that it can detect.

Evaluating robustness and usability involves analyzing the context of intended use. As illustrated in Figure 13-4 and outlined in the following paragraphs, different users require different levels of robustness.

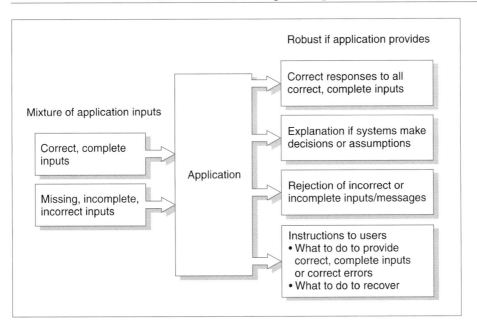

FIGURE 13-3   *Characteristics of a robust application*

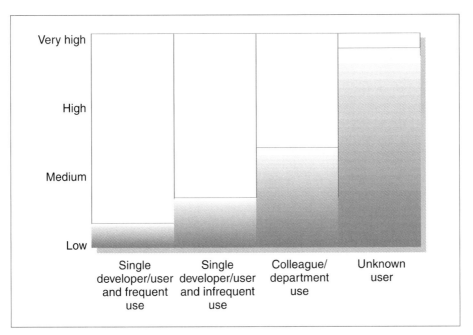

FIGURE 13-4   *Level of robustness required under different conditions of use*

◊   *Single developer/user and frequent use.* An application used only by the developer can have a lower level of robustness and usability because the developer/user understands the limits of the application and how to deal with error conditions.

◇ *Single developer/user and infrequent use.* An individual may well lose track of features that seemed logical and obvious at the time an application was designed. A person can easily forget the details of an application that is used once per month or infrequently. For example, in most organizations, software to evaluate an acquisition will be used infrequently.

◇ *Workgroup or departmental use.* The requirements for robustness and usability increase, but the presence of the developer and shared understanding of the application domain mean that the users are likely to be able to use an application effectively, even though it lacks robustness and usability features. However, more features providing for robustness and usability are needed.

◇ *Unknown users.* An application that will be used broadly by unknown users (within the same organization or in other organizations) probably needs to be redesigned for that audience. The robustness and usability features must be increased significantly. This adds to development cost. A software developer's rule of thumb is that the cost to develop an application for unknown users is ten times the cost of the same application for an individual. This heuristic strongly suggests a different design approach to build in the necessary robustness and usability.

An application by an individual developer should, therefore, be evaluated in terms of own use or use within a workgroup or department. Colleagues will be familiar with the domain of use and the way the application fits into their work. If the application is to be used beyond this scope, it should receive additional attention from professional developers.

The following questions can be used to evaluate robustness and usability:

◇ Given the intended use of the application, does the user understand the nature of the application, the inputs, and the use of the outputs? Does the user have sufficient knowledge to interpret the application instructions and outputs?

◇ Is documentation satisfactory for persons using the application, especially in understanding the nature of the application, the inputs, outputs, and error handling?

◇ Does the application present a clear and consistent image that is relatively easy to learn, use, and remember?

◇ Given the intended use of the application, will the user be able to understand the behavior of the application if mistakes are made in using it?

◊   Given the intended use, will there be an appropriate and well-defined means of correcting for the effects of data and system errors?

Evaluating Appropriateness and Suitability for the Task

Appropriateness and suitability can be evaluated only in terms of the task to be accomplished. The technology and design of the application should, therefore, fit the task in four major areas: (1) technology employed, (2) user interface, (3) organizational culture, and (4) responsiveness to changing task needs. This is termed **task/technology fit**.

Technology may not perform adequately for the application. One reason may be that an application may be designed to use the software the developer knows rather than using the software most appropriate to the task.

E•xample
An individual user with significant experience in using a spreadsheet may employ the spreadsheet for writing memoranda. Although it is possible to do word processing with spreadsheet software, it is not a good technology fit. ◆

A second reason for lack of technology suitability may be performance in the task environment. If the task depends on a fast response, the technology should match the expectations. Hardware and software must be matched as well. Software packages with extended application development facilities usually require larger, faster hardware platforms to perform effectively.

User interface design should fit the task environment and user knowledge. If an application is designed for online use, such as recording data during a telephone interview, the design of the data collection form should reflect the capabilities of the persons doing the input and facilitate the specific interviewing topic and process flow. The user interface should facilitate a range of expert and novice users if these are likely.

The application should not violate the norms and culture of the organization except in cases where the application is specifically designed to bring about change in these characteristics. If the organization expects all budget and financial data to be based on the current official finance system, a separately maintained individual or departmental financial database would be such a violation.

Most applications that are useful will have to be changed over time. There are many causes of change in the organization, its environment, and the task environment, such as planned changes and improvements in technology. Most often, use of an application will lead to new insights and task innovation. Changes are costly and must always be justified. If an application does not change to fit its changing environment, its value decreases. Changeability is an important attribute of an application. One of the very positive aspects of generalized software packages (compared to custom software) is the relative ease of change they provide.

In evaluating the appropriateness and suitability of the application, users should ask questions framed in terms of the tasks to be accomplished. For example:

◊ Does the application employ appropriate technology—hardware and software?

◊ Is the user interface suitable for all users (novice, expert, etc.) of the application?

◊ Does the application violate organizational norms or culture?

◊ What changes can be anticipated and how feasible will it be to make them?

Analyzing Risks

Risk should be evaluated for every application. The appropriate point for risk analysis in individual application development is when a prototype application is completed. Up to that point, developer thought and effort have been primarily devoted to achieving the necessary functionality to support the intended task. At the stage where the desired functionality has been achieved, the prototype is likely to be missing many properties that control or minimize risk. At this point of development, prior to operational use, the effects of problems or errors have not been observed. As soon as operational use commences, the individual and the organization will be exposed to loss. Risk analysis is an attempt to identify and evaluate that exposure and to manage application use. There should be two results from risk analysis: (1) a determination of what to do with the application prototype (discarding it and starting over, using it "as is," or making modifications) and (2) a specification of required modifications. Assuming that risk can be managed by adding to or changing the prototype, the developer must determine the necessary improvements.

Risk analysis is an analysis of the effect of errors in the application or its use. There are three classes of errors or problems to investigate: (1) financial loss from incorrect or incomplete output, (2) loss of data, and (3) loss of time. The most complex of these is the use of incorrect or incomplete output, and the majority of risk analysis and corrective modifications are oriented toward this risk. The issue of data loss is especially significant with personal systems because the individual must take special steps to preserve data, although such backup procedures are the exception in practice rather than the rule. Loss of time is significant for a similar reason. An application may cause the individual to spend an excessive amount of time due to its failure to fully meet needs, be robust, or fit the task.

To evaluate the financial risk associated with an application, assess the following:

◇ The potential loss with each use of the application, if the application is in error and leads to faulty decisions or actions. Make rough estimates. If the risk is not immediate loss, but potential loss resulting from issues such as damaged customer relations, make a rough estimate of the dollar cost.

◇ The expected number of uses (decisions or actions) per year.

◇ The total exposure per year (loss per use times uses per year).

◇ The estimated probability of error with use (decision or action).

◇ The computed financial risk (the product of exposure times error probability.)

To evaluate the risk of data loss, estimate the following:

◇ The value of the outputs to the decisions or actions it supports. In some cases no decisions or actions can be taken if the outputs are not available. In most cases, decisions or actions can proceed with lower quality results. Estimate a dollar cost of the effect of having no application output (no data) for a single decision.

◇ The per period (yearly) exposure based on the potential loss per use and the number of uses.

◇ The probability of partial or complete loss of data.

◇ The financial risk of data loss (the product of exposure times loss probability).

The risk of lost time due to application design requires an estimate of the time loss because the actual time required for application design must be compared to the ideal time. Loss exposure due to the risk of lost time requires a different analysis. The only risk issue is reduced productivity due to the deficiencies of an application that was intended to improve productivity. To evaluate the risk of lost time for an application, estimate the following:

◇ The extra time required to repeat inputs or correct data and produce correct outputs compared to an ideal design. Estimates should include cases where data must be re-input or database tables modified after outputs have been produced.

◇ The proportion of application uses where time is lost due to design flaws.

◇ Lost time per period (year). This can be expressed as follows:
number of uses per year × time required for product correction
× proportion of uses where time is lost

The risk to the organization is also a function of the number of application users. If an individual application is used only by the individual who developed it, potential losses are reduced. The user/developer is likely to make fewer mistakes caused by poor input design, and any productivity loss is limited to only one individual.

When an application is used throughout a workgroup or other organizational unit, risk increases in two ways: (1) exposure increases because there are more uses, and (2) probability of error increases because there are additional users. Increases in the probability of error with additional users beyond the developer is non-linear, because the second and subsequent users do not share the developer's problem knowledge and solution details.

Using the Results of Application Evaluation

A range of alternatives is available once an application prototype has been evaluated. The appropriate choice depends upon the **prototype evaluation** and level of risk associated with its use. The range of alternatives is illustrated in Figure 13-5 and described in the following paragraphs:

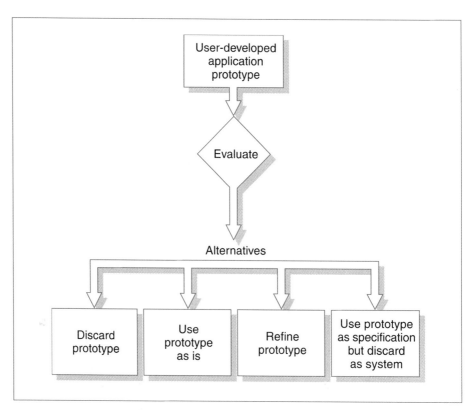

FIGURE 13-5 *Results of prototype evaluation*

◆ *Discard prototype.* A prototype application may have been completed, but may not be appropriate for use. The various risks of loss may be too high, relative to other alternatives. For example, after developing an application, a specialized package that delivers the needed functionality may become available and be a better solution.

◆ *Use prototype as is.* When the prototype delivers the desired functionality, meets the requirements, is reasonably robust and usable, and its risk of use is not great, additional investment may not be warranted. This is often the case with simple applications that are well within the ability of the individuals who developed them.

◆ *Refine prototype.* One of the most likely outcomes of evaluation is the recognition that some deficiencies can be remedied, or that the risk of application use is moderate. In both cases, the application should be used only after additional investment of time and effort.

◆ *Use prototype as specification, but discard as system.* An application prototype may provide most of the desired functionality, but may need additional development or revision that is beyond the capabilities of the individual developer. The application may be of high value, but the risk of loss may be so great that a departmental or organizational development effort is justified. In this case, the prototype defines the task as a complete definition of user requirements, database, and user interface design. Professional application developers can use the prototype to produce an application that delivers its functionality with a decreased risk.

The outcome of evaluation is a choice among these alternatives. Testing can be used to change application risks. An adequate testing program can provide some assurance that the probability of failure is in an acceptable range. At any level of these alternatives, the costs and results of testing should be included in the decision about the application.

Testing is an attempt to find errors. To the extent that an application is tested without failure, the expectation of future failures is lower than that of an untested application. In other words, testing provides evidence of the quality of the application. Paradoxically, if many errors are detected, there are likely to be many more errors, since error detection is like a statistical sampling process. Not all errors can be detected by testing. The responsibility for fixing the errors is separate from testing, since the focus of repair is different (see Figure 13-6).

Testing of an individually developed application is generally done by that individual based on their understanding of the way the application will be used and the characteristics of the application design. However, there are limits to the ability of individuals to adequately test their own applications. The

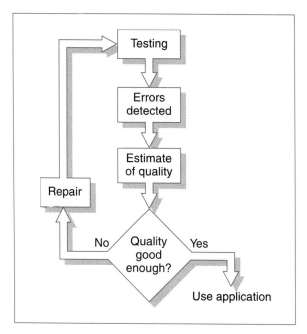

FIGURE 13-6 *Relationship of testing and repair*

reasons are the overconfidence that is associated with one's own work and also the fact that people often cannot see their own errors (as in proofreading). The test plan should reflect this risk; the participation of others should be connected to the organizational risk.

The following guidelines can be used to determine the required level of testing:

◊ If the risk is relatively small, as when the results of the application are to be used only for one person, the testing can be done by the user/developer.

◊ If the risk is medium, either because the application is to be used by others in the workgroup or department, or because of the degree of financial exposure, testing should involve others in the workgroup or department.

◊ If the risk is relatively high, testing should be done by the professional application testing group, and/or by personnel from the systems group and the internal audit staff (for certain applications).

Most individual applications will fall into the first two categories. The testing decision is, therefore, whether to perform testing individually or to involve others in the workgroup or department.

Completion of testing calls for a final selection from the preceding alternatives. If testing reveals failures, they may be repaired. After failures have been repaired, retesting and reevaluation may be performed. For most individual applications, an informal reevaluation may be enough.

Refining the Application

◆ ◆ ◆ ◆ ◆ ◆ ◆ ◆ ◆ ◆ ◆ ◆ ◆ ◆ ◆ ◆ ◆ ◆ ◆ ◆

After an application has been evaluated, the prototype version can be refined to correct the deficiencies identified in the evaluation. Unnecessary features may be eliminated, new features may be added to reflect innovation, and features may be modified to compensate for bias inadvertently introduced in the prototype. To improve the robustness and usability of the application, and to reduce errors, the input and output are refined. To further improve the application, enhancements can be made that help assure data integrity.

Refining the Input Interface

Input validation must be added to detect and handle values that are incorrect, in a process referred to as **input interface refinement**. Many software packages have facilities to detect incorrect values and provide appropriate user messages. For example, the data definition facility of a database software package may allow definition of minimum and maximum values and specification of acceptable input data types for each data field. Such packages may enforce reference to another table when a particular value is required, or limit selection to a predefined set of values. Each detected input error may be associated with a user message. A good interface provides an explanation of the error and the requirements for a correct entry. In the refinement stage, the developer should take advantage of the input validation features of the software. Even an application for personal use will benefit from this refinement if the software is to be used over an extended period.

The user interface should be further refined to remove ambiguity, clarify instructions, and make sure that all elements of the interface are correctly labeled to reduce the chance for errors. Refinement to remove input ambiguity and incompleteness includes use instructions and help messages. The input instructions should be reviewed to make sure they are clear and unambiguous.

Refinement to improve error control may add features that reduce the likelihood of undetected input errors, as illustrated in the following examples:

◊   If a stored record is referenced, display its values for visual validation that it is the correct record.

◊   Display the meaning of codes when they are input.

◊   When there is a computation involving several factors, show the factors used (make both actions and results visible).

◊   Display warning messages if a data item appears to be out of the normal range.

◊   Display a count of input items entered and a control total for numeric data. (A control total may be a meaningful total such as total receipts or a hash total from summing numbers not used to calculate, such as order number.)

◊   Provide data for reconciling input data with other control information.

Refining the Output Interface

Refining the output (**output interface refinement**) involves removing semantic ambiguity, i.e., ambiguity about meaning. Additional output fields or values can be useful in detecting errors and evaluating correctness or suitability of outputs. Removing ambiguity in outputs is accomplished by improving headings and labels. Ambiguity can also be reduced by including elements such as dates and times, versions, counts and summaries of records, and ranges of dates and account numbers.

The output should provide ways for the user to assess its correctness. Refinements respond to the question of what a user must do to assess correctness and completeness and also to detect errors. It should also consider the additional task efficiencies the application can define. Examples that can help improve productivity include counts of items, counts of items in classifications, subtotals, totals, crossfooting (in a table, the row totals are summed separately from the column totals and the two are compared), and tallies of zero and missing items, if relevant.

Refining Data Integrity

An application constructed using the facilities of a database software package relies upon the validity of the data contained in the database. By refining the user interface inputs, the developer helps assure that the application accepts only correct and valid data. But even if input data is valid, changes in stored data may lead to data loss. For example, a table row referenced from another table may be deleted erroneously, causing the referencing table to lose a vital connection. In another instance, a customer record may be deleted when there are records that refer to that customer in the order table. In that case, errors are likely in any output that relies on the relationship between customer and customer order. The kind of problem this issue refers to is called referential integrity. As illustrated in Figure 13-7, **referential integrity** is the need for referenced records to be present in the database. There are two possible

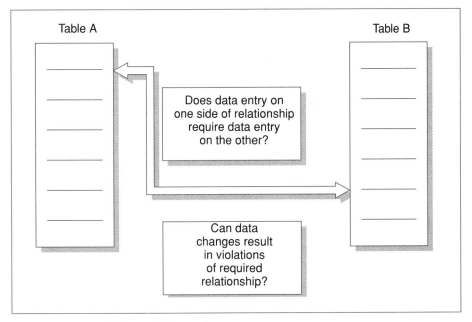

FIGURE 13-7 *Referential integrity*

violations: (1) deleting a referenced record, and (2) inserting a record that refers to a non-existent record. Most database software packages provide built-in functions that can be used to assure referential integrity.

In this stage of refinement, the developer should ascertain, for every relationship, whether a reference is required. Where references are required, the referential integrity features should be set up to check each time a change is made to the data. Use the following steps to evaluate each relationship defined in the database:

1. For each direction of the relationship, evaluate whether a data entry on one side of the relationship requires a data entry on the other side. For example, generally an order should not exist without a customer, but a customer might be part of the database even though no order has been recorded.

2. Where entries are required on both sides, apply the relationship definition facility of the database software package to specify enforcement of referential integrity for this relationship.

3. Consider additional referential integrity options. For example, a database package may offer features that help define relationships, such as "cascade changes" which apply when changing the key value of a referenced record. Cascaded changes automatically update foreign key values of the referencing records. "Cascading deletes" automatically delete referencing records when a referenced record is deleted.

The relationships enhanced by referential integrity specifications will help avoid output errors related to "orphan" dependent records.

Access Control and Backup

Additional steps that enhance data integrity are **access control and backup refinement**. Special provisions for access control are unnecessary when an application is used only by an individual on a personal computer that is physically inaccessible to others. It is also generally unnecessary when the individual has taken steps such as "keyboard lockout" to prohibit others from accessing a personal system. When unauthorized, accidental, or malicious data access is not otherwise prevented, the application developer may need to employ the security features of the database software package. Two basic features are user authentication and encryption.

User authentication features may be set to require a log-in identifier and password. As the owner of a database, an individual can allow certain types of access and forbid other types. For example, an individual can assign workgroup members authority to read a subset of the tables in a database, but prohibit them from making changes and prevent them from even reading other tables in the database.

Even when authentication features have been specified, database tables might be readable in raw form by word processing packages and text editors. If this is a threat, encryption can be used. When the database is encrypted, only authenticated users have access, and the data is stored in encrypted mode.

Backup provisions are another critical aspect of refinement to assure data integrity. To the extent that the data in an individual application has value, there is always an exposure to data loss. Such exposure can be minimized by backup provisions, as explained in Chapter 6.

One approach to refinement is automating backup for a database application. This involves creating a macro that saves a copy of the data each time a database application is executed. Such a provision need not rely on human memory or macros outside the database software package. A second approach is to backup using the operating system facilities so that files are backed up when the application is opened. For example, a simple batch file can be set up to copy the database before it starts the application. Making the batch file or other operating system command the only way to start the application will assure that files are copied.

As explained in Chapter 6, depending on the risk involved, it may be desirable to store copies at another location. Since many personal systems are networked, a critical database may be duplicated on a network drive. Many network managers provide off-line and even off-site backup of data stored on network drives. Other networks may provide automatic backup of specified files stored on user drives. The refinement task is to identify and take advantage of the most effective features available consistent with the risks involved.

◆Application Integration

◆ ◆ ◆ ◆ ◆ ◆ ◆ ◆ ◆ ◆ ◆ ◆ ◆ ◆ ◆ ◆ ◆ ◆ ◆

As an application is developed, components and features are added to satisfy needs that were part of the original requirements or were discovered during development. Enhancing and refining steps modify existing programs or other components and create new ones. The result for even a simple application may be a larger accumulation of components than can be easily managed without errors.

Application integration is one process for simplification. The purpose of this process is to make correct and error-free use of the application's features more likely and to reduce the effort required for such use. Most software packages that can be extensively customized or extended also include facilities that can be used to help integrate application components. Application integration may involve several different types of enhancements:

◆ *Standardization.* This is one of the simplest integrating enhancements. Standardization assures consistency both within and across applications.

◆ *Command interface integration.* This involves the use of features such as menus, macros, icons, and toolbars to organize the components of an application into an integrated whole.

◆ *Linking or embedding applications or application components.* This enhancement connects the capabilities of multiple packages or programs to present the appearance of a single software package.

◆ *"Add-on" products.* These are vendor add-ons or independent products that may be used to extend the features of software packages. Add-ons include custom controls, mini-applications, and supporting applications such as graphics editors.

Application integration should take place throughout application development. Ideally, features such as custom controls, menus, and linking and embedding capabilities should be planned and built into the application from the beginning. Sometimes they are simply overlooked, but in other cases including these "extras" from the start would reduce the ability of the user/developer to evolve a successful prototype. Therefore, after application evaluation, it is appropriate to consider what can be done to make the transition from an operational prototype to a useful, permanent application.

Application integration can be costly. Adding extra features can be more expensive than developing the basic functionality. Any integration steps should be justified by the value of the application and its intended use.

Standardization

A number of simple steps can be used to reduce usage effort and improve the usability of an application by standardizing its look and feel to be consistent. An example is naming. During development, it is easy to name each object created without regard to the names of other objects. Often, a default name is used in order to concentrate on the development objective. The problem is that when development is completed, names such as "query1," "table6," or "report12" are meaningless. Names such as "**customerquery**" and "**salesreport**" are better, but are still likely to be unusable without additional information. During the final stages of development, when all or nearly all application features and components have been defined, organization and simplification by naming can be applied.

Software packages differ in their support of name changing. In some cases, it is possible to change the name of an object and have all of its references updated automatically. In other cases, changing the name of a data item, a table, or a query requires a manual search for references. In the latter case, standardization may not be justifiable for most individual applications. Where it is feasible, standardization guidelines suggest the following:

◊ List all component names that must be understood to use the application in its normal operation.

◊ Organize components according to external user (rather than developer) related concepts. For example, group all the functions dealing with "customers," rather than using developer-oriented categories such as "updates" and "deletions."

◊ Assign meaningful names to all listed objects in a consistent pattern. If the software package permits, use multiple words such as **Customer Update**, **Customer Delete**, **Customer List**, and **Customer Volume Ranking**. If abbreviations must be used, follow a similar pattern. Since spaces are frequently not permitted in names, use capitalization to show the beginning of words (such as **CustomerList**).

◊ Rename the objects and test to make sure functionality has not been lost or errors introduced.

Standardization should extend to the layout of input and output interface components. Input is easier to standardize when components are first created, but this may not have been done. Examine related forms and reports, and modify them where feasible. Consider such items as consistent headers and footers; fonts and font properties such as size, bold, and italics; and graphic objects such as lines. Where graphic controls such as text, list, combo boxes, or command buttons have been added, check to see that they have been used consistently across forms and reports.

Command Interface

An important aspect of application integration is to organize the user interface into coherent parts. Such organization and simplification can be extended to specializing the interface of the underlying software package to more directly support the functions of the application. Menus, menus containing macros, and graphics such as icons or command buttons added to toolbars are some of the resources available to tailor the interface of a custom application.

To construct a command interface, proceed as follows:

1. *List the possible user actions and organize them to match the user functions provided by the application.* Interface organization is hierarchical. A good tool is a simple outline.

2. *Design the user Command Interface using the outline of user actions and application functions.* Depending upon the effort to be expended on this step and the capabilities of the underlying software package, a straightforward single- or a multi-level menu may be used. Alternatively, graphic images may be used if they are more consistent with the intended use of the application.

3. *Use the features of the software package to implement the specified menu or graphical command interface.*

Figure 13-8 is an example of a user menu created in Microsoft Access™. In the example, the top-level menu is always visible, while succeeding layers are displayed in drop-down boxes when they are selected.

Graphic command interfaces require more effort and are generally more difficult to justify for an application developed and used by an individual. After organizing user functions, background graphics or bitmaps are selected or designed and artwork or icons created to identify selections. Implementation of a graphic menu may also require more effort. While the menu-building function may be automated in a software package, macros may be necessary to display and link graphics and icons. Figure 13-9 is a graphic menu from the Northwind Sample application included with Microsoft Access.

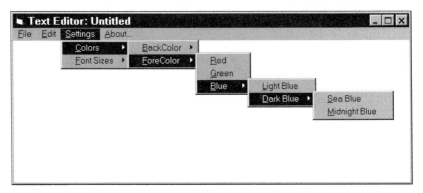

FIGURE 13-8 *Example of user menu (created in Microsoft Access)*

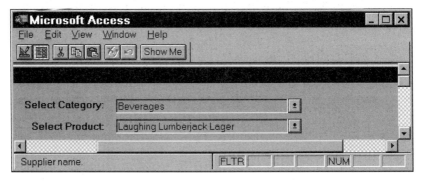

FIGURE 13-9 *Example of graphic menu (from Microsoft Access)*

The command interface can be integrated with security features using macro facilities. By starting an application with a macro that displays a menu and coupling user access to the macro, an application developer can assure that access to data is limited to menu functions. This step is probably not justifiable for a single-user application, but as use of an application is extended to members of a workgroup or beyond, such capabilities become more valuable.

Linking Other Applications

Applications are usually developed using the facilities of a single, powerful application package. Because generalized packages like spreadsheets, word processors, and databases contain many features, one package is often sufficient. In some cases, however, the features of a different generalized package—or of a specialized package—are useful in developing or refining an application. Linking was explained in Chapter 6. In the context of integration, a table and chart might be embedded or linked into a report. An embedded object is independent from its original file, but can be edited or modified in place by its creating application. A linked object remains part of its original file, and is updated whenever its source changes.

To the application builder, this means the most appropriate tool can be used for each function, even though it was not part of the original software package. A common and appropriate use of this form of package integration is including analytic or graphic information in a document or report. In many knowledge work tasks, the results of analysis in the form of tables, graphs, and charts are included as exhibits and illustrations in reports. Especially when the production of such reports is a repetitive task, application integration can increase productivity and product quality, and reduce production time and cost. For example, a "Product Life Cycle Analysis Report" may extract sales data from an organizational database, match it to summary data preserved in a local database, process selected products through a spreadsheet analysis resulting in tables and charts, and include the results in an analytical report. The knowledge worker responsible for producing this report can evolve the application toward an advanced level of integration. It may be feasible to link the data acquisition, selection, analysis and charting, and some of the reporting into one application rather than three or four separate ones.

Third-party Add-ons

A wide range of products is available to extend generalized software packages to support specific tasks or provide generally useful features that were not part of the original package. One type of product provides development tools or add-ons to application development software. A second provides collections of custom objects available to support both general development and more specific classes of applications.

An example of add-on software for development is software that provides linkage to existing databases. Such tools make it feasible for the developer of a new application to include graphical representations of tables, forms, and queries using database software that does not provide a graphical user interface.

Custom functions provide capabilities that may be added to applications. An example is a function that makes it possible for the application user to directly manipulate screen objects. In an application constructed with such a function, the user can, for example, draw flowcharts as part of an analysis or document.

Object linking and embedding and related tools and techniques are part of a package vendor movement or trend toward package and component integration. Some forecasters expect generalized software packages to move toward becoming collections of components to be assembled by each user to form a well-integrated custom package. Some vendors have developed and are delivering software objects to create and maintain portions of documents inside other documents. An example is a package that adds a drawing and charting capability to word processing packages. It does not stand alone, but integrates the added functionality into the original package.

Summary

◇ ◆

◇ User-developed applications improve task performance, but also increase the risk of loss to individuals and organizations. Therefore, it is important to evaluate every finished prototype for risks and make decisions about it. The first step involves determining whether the prototype meets the "real" requirements. The second is to evaluate the application's robustness and usability.

◇ Robustness is the behavior of the application when something goes wrong. Errors will happen, but must not be allowed to cause data loss or produce invalid results. The intended use of an application is a primary criterion in deciding how much time and effort should be devoted to improving robustness and usability. Part of the evaluation process involves determining whether the completed application properly fits the intended task and to analyze potential risks.

◇ Risks can be reduced in various ways. Risk evaluation considers both failure probability and exposure to loss. The result suggests alternative uses of a prototype, depending upon risk. High risk suggests the prototype should be discarded or used only as a specification for subsequent development. Low risk suggests the prototype may be used "as is," while moderate risk suggests additional refinement.

◇ Refinement for the input interface means checking the values of input data and providing assistance to the user in making sure inputs are correct. Output interface refinement involves making sure the outputs are clear and logically presented to support the intended uses.

◇ Data integrity is an additional refinement. Using built-in data integrity features helps avoid acceptance of invalid and incorrect data. Adding data backup and user authentication are relatively simple steps that can reduce risk by lowering the probability of data loss.

◇ Prototype development is directed toward achieving functionality. The tools of individual application development support application integration. The concepts of application integration may be applied both during development and after a prototype has been developed. Modifications to assure consistency of interfaces and modifications to organize application commands help complete the prototype and fit it into the context of its use. Integrating the features of multiple software packages and package components is made feasible by current technology. Such integration is properly done during application design. However, effective integration technology should be considered as an application evolves, and even after it is completed.

EXERCISES

1. Evaluate an application you developed in connection with a previous chapter. How robust is it? In hindsight, how appropriate to the task is it? Itemize the likely points of failure. What is the risk associated with the application? What should be done with the prototype as a result of your evaluation?

2. For the application evaluated in Exercise 1, list the refinements that could be made to the input and output interfaces and to ensure data integrity. Which are feasible? Which are not feasible? Explain.

3. For an application you have developed or used, make a list of integration features that would make the application easier to use, or that would make its user more productive. Comment on the feasibility of each feature. For each feature, would the feasibility change if the application were to be used by a department rather than one individual? Explain.

4. Select one software package you use frequently and one you use infrequently. Perform a range of input, process, output, and error correction operations. Use Help facilities. For each, evaluate robustness, usability, appropriateness, and suitability for your tasks, and analyze potential risks. Based on your analysis, list the most robust features and the most serious deficiencies.

5. Select an application software package you use. Then select one or more user input screens and outputs for evaluation. Evaluate the user input interface for error control and the output for ease of error detection. List both good and bad features.

6. Explore and test the low-level access control (password) features of your word processor, spreadsheet processor, and database package. Test password protection for a document, spreadsheet or database. Remove all unnecessary passwords. When you have finished, write a short description of the results of your test.

7. Explore and test higher level password protection for access to:
   a. Your system
   b. An application package
   c. A directory

Write a short description of the results of the test.

8. Prepare a spreadsheet to do a budget or financial forecast (or use a copy of an existing one). Evaluate the robustness of the application relative to errors, using suggestions such as the following:

    a. Separate inputs, calculations, and outputs.

    b. Organize relatively constant data in a different area than data that changes frequently.

    c. Give input data cells range names with descriptive words.

    d. Print inputs as well as outputs so the reader can examine input data.

    e. Print version number, date, and time.

    f. Include tests for out-of-limit data or results.

    g. Provide a crossfooting test (check that column totals are equal to row totals) for tables.

    For further discussion, refer to "How to Make Spreadsheets Error-Proof," David Freeman, *Journal of Accountancy*, May 1996, pp. 75-77.

9. For the following situation, show the added program statements to make the application more resistant to errors. Explain the need for them. The prototype statements accept user input of 1 or 2 to select one of two processing alternatives:

```
Accept user input for processing method
IF UserInput is 1 THEN
   Perform ProcessOne
ELSE
   Perform ProcessTwo
END IF
```

10. Database design facilities for database tables generally allow user-defined data validation procedures. Input forms can also be designed with some validation rules. The validation rules are not required during initial prototyping, but may be added during refinement. As an exercise in refinement, use the table design features to evaluate opportunities for more complete validation of data item fields. For example, using Microsoft Access, build a table with the following fields: EmployeeID, LastName, FirstName, BirthDate, HireDate, SalaryClass, AnnualSalary, and Dependents. Using the Design View of the table, for each data field, explain the possible use, form of use, and value for error control of the data type specification and the properties for format, input mask, default value, validation rule, validation text, required entry, allow zero length for entry, and indexed value.

Information Technology Infrastructures

◇ ◇ ◇ ◇ ◇ ◇ ◇ ◇ ◇ ◇ ◇ ◇ ◇

The emphasis of this text is on individual productivity and how information technology may be used to enhance it. The first part of the book (Chapters 1 through 4) stressed an understanding of productivity, examined the role of information management in productivity, and analyzed individual tasks and activities in knowledge work and requirements related to collaborative work and knowledge work management. Part 2 (Chapters 5 through 8) focused on data and communication requirements and how to attain them. Part 3 (Chapters 9 through 13) explained how to design and implement productivity solutions using methods and tools appropriate to individual systems. This section addresses two issues: developing an information technology infrastructure for individuals and working with the infrastructure of systems and information management at the organizational level.

Chapter 14, Anticipating Core Information Technology This chapter discusses core information technology and provides an information technology review based on seven core technologies: digital encoding, digital circuits, digital storage devices, digital communications, human-machine interfaces, software, and information technology standards. This chapter is optional and may be introduced at varying points in the sequence, depending on the user's background. For example, it may be introduced earlier to improve technology understanding, it can be used as background before considering individual technology infrastructures, or it may be omitted.

Chapter 15, Analyzing an Individual Information Technology Infrastructure This chapter examines issues and alternatives in developing an individual information technology infrastructure. This may be fairly simple because of the packaging of personal computer systems. However, knowledge of

important considerations can aid in the design and selection process.

Chapter 16, Cooperating with the Information Management Function This summary chapter examines the link between the information system function and individual information management. The information system function is responsible for the corporate information management infrastructure, corporate information system applications, and organizational databases. It is also responsible for creating policies to promote compatible information technology systems in the organization and for providing technical support to individuals and departmental systems. In working with information system specialists, it is helpful for individual users to understand their perspective.

The principles and methods applied in building small, individual systems are useful in understanding large system methods, but there are significant changes when development methods are scaled up to more complex systems. The information system function is responsible for supporting individuals who develop and use personal systems; this role introduces a tension between a support function with a broad view of systems and individuals with a pragmatic view based on their individual capabilities. Understanding the basis for this tension can help individual users and specialists work together. Working together may involve users being part of large corporate application development teams. Knowledge of good practice with individual systems plus an appreciation of large system differences can aid users in being effective team members. At the same time, an information systems specialist can be more effective by having a good understanding of individual system development and use dynamics. Specialists can benefit from experience in assisting individuals in developing and implementing personal systems. The work can be part of a process of career development.

Anticipating Core Information Technology

◊   ◊   ◊   ◊   ◊   ◊   ◊   ◊   ◊

OBJECTIVES

After completing this chapter, you should be able to:

◆ Explain the core approach to information technology in terms of the seven core technologies: digital encoding, digital circuits, digital storage devices, digital communications, software, human-machine interfaces, and information technology standards.

◆ Explain the difference between analog and digital representation and coding.

◆ Explain digital coding of characters, pictures, and graphs; voice and sound; and video with motion.

◆ Explain compression of data.

◆ Describe improvements in digital circuits, how these have been used, and the potential for further improvement.

◆ Describe a hierarchy of storage devices in terms of cost and access speeds.

◆ Explain the difference between magnetic disk storage, magnetic tape storage, and optical storage.

◆ Explain the use of busses and channels in data transmission.

◆ Describe the role of protocols in electronic communications.

◆ Explain the difference between system software, development software, and application software.

◆ Describe the impact of operating systems on application programs and computer hardware.

◆ Describe the impact of Fourth-Generation Languages (4GLs) on application development.

◆ Explain some of the challenges involved in enhancing human-machine interfaces for data entry and data presentation.

◆ Describe the differences between *de facto* and *de jure* technology standards.

◆ Explain the impact of change drivers and change inhibitors on information technology.

KEY TERMS AND CONCEPTS

This chapter introduces the following key terms and concepts, listed in the order in which they appear:

digital encoding
digital circuits
digital storage devices
digital communications
human-machine interfaces
data compression
byte
pixels
space suppression
Lempel-Ziv algorithm

Moore's Law
channel
analog signal
digital signal
modem
bus
bandwidth
multiplexing
protocols
communications architectures

system software
development software
application software
operating system
multi-programming
4GLs (Fourth-Generation Languages)
de facto standards
de jure standards

lthough knowledge workers cannot be expected to be experts in information technology, they *can* be expected to be aware of major technology trends. A general knowledge of information technology is useful in specifying the major components of an individual information technology infrastructure and in working with vendors and specialists in making choices. This chapter may be optional reading, depending on the reader's prior background knowledge. It is designed to provide perspective for those without depth grounding in information technology.

The chapter focuses on seven core technologies, providing an overview of each technology, a short explanation of its importance, general expectations about future developments, and the effect of potential changes on personal information technology systems. The following overview provides brief definitions of these seven technologies, along with short statements concerning the expected changes in each field.

1. *Digital encoding.* **Digital encoding** extends the scope of information processing, because whatever can be digitized can be stored, processed, and communicated by information technology.

2. *Digital circuits.* **Digital circuits** are the basic building blocks of information and communication hardware. They continue to decline dramatically in price and increase in speed and capacity, thereby enabling greater use of digital communications, better human/machine interfaces, new applications, and greater use of digital storage.

3. *Digital storage devices.* Data stored in digital form on hard drives, CD-ROMs, and other media **(digital storage devices)** is essential to most knowledge work application. Increased storage capacity and reduced costs support access to voice, picture, graphics, and video data.

4. *Digital communications.* **Digital communications** employing digital networks provide increased communications capabilities. Higher speeds and reduced costs of local area networks make feasible new applications, new ways of working, and new interpersonal interactions.

5. *Human-machine interfaces.* **Human-machine interfaces** (the interactions between humans and computers) are bottlenecks in information processing. Enhanced machine capabilities in both hardware and software support interface designs increase the speed and reduce the effort required for humans to input data and instructions and use outputs.

6. *Software tools.* Improved hardware capabilities cannot be used effectively without improved software tools. New tools, techniques, and methods

for developing software produce more reliable software with greater functionality at reduced cost and make it easier for users to develop their own applications.

7. *Information technology standards.* Common standards (such as standards for hardware and software interfaces) increase the number of alternatives in the marketplace and reduce the cost of technology and user training.

The relationship among these seven core information technologies is diagrammed in Figure 14-1. Information technology appears to be in constant change. This chapter examines some of the factors that encourage or inhibit this change.

◢◆ Core Approach to Information Technology

This chapter applies a core technologies or fundamental characteristics approach to building, maintaining, and refreshing information technology understanding. The approach reflects the dynamics of technology change and

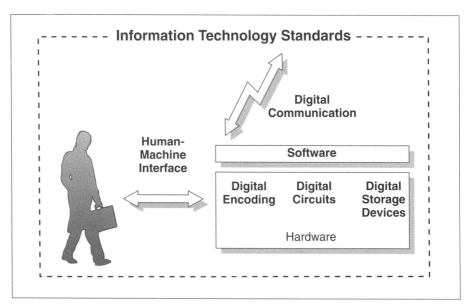

FIGURE 14-1 *Relationship of seven foundation information technologies*

provides a practical approach to fundamentals the knowledge worker needs to know. It is based on the premise that, in the information age, knowledge workers must have a core of information technology knowledge, but most need not be experts.

Prior to making decisions about an individual information infrastructure, a knowledge worker must have an up-to-date awareness of information technology and an appreciation of what is likely to happen in the near future. It is risky to rely on experience with information technology of just a few years before. In designing a personal system, attention should be directed to innovative and creative ways to employ information technology. Old ideas may constrain thinking and creativity. For example, a person who is acquainted only with keyboard input and printed output may not be able to design systems that effectively use multimedia capabilities.

Given the need for fundamental knowledge and continuous learning, how should a knowledge worker deal with the dynamics of information technology change? Keeping up with detailed information technology features and performance characteristics is generally not feasible. These features change rapidly, so knowledge of current features and latest characteristics has a very high rate of obsolescence. Examples of characteristics that quickly become obsolete are disk access speeds and sizes, computer memory sizes, and computer processing speeds. Scanning trade and technology publications can quickly result in a mass of conflicting details that are difficult for even technical specialists to assimilate.

Keeping up with changes in products and product technology is useful but incomplete. The trade press generally reports current technology as represented by new product announcements and reports. Any person or organization selecting technology for a particular application can benefit by scanning or monitoring such information sources. However, researching new product announcements does not provide much insight into trends or emerging capabilities.

A more useful approach for keeping current with technology knowledge is to learn the basic characteristics of the core technologies, plus the drivers and inhibitors of change. These provide a framework for tracking technology at a survey or awareness level. They are also useful in guiding in-depth investigation, if necessary.

Seven core technologies form the basis for understanding and tracking changes in information technology. In this fundamental characteristics approach to information technology, there is no distinction between information processing technology and communications technology. In the past, the development of computers and communication technologies were separate, but they are now clearly unified into the single domain of information technology.

Core Technology: Digital Encoding

◆ ◆

Digital encoding is a core technology because data in natural form (such as data on documents, the documents themselves, voice, pictures, and diagrams) is not ready for computer storage or processing. The data in its various forms must be encoded in a representation using binary digits. For output, the process is reversed: digital codes are converted to representations such as printed characters, diagrams, pictures, and voice. Even though inputs and outputs take many forms, the concepts of coding data digitally are similar. Closely related to digital coding is **data compression.** Coding may be efficient for input but not efficient for storage or transmission. Most data has redundancy and most coding methods result in significant redundancy. Compression methods reduce redundancy, thereby reducing both storage and transmission requirements.

Digital encoding is a core technology because the range of data types to be stored and processed has expanded. Understanding the concept of digital encoding is, therefore, useful in understanding the use of computers for storing and processing a wide range of data (such as numbers, text, documents, diagrams, pictures, voice, and motion video). The following two sections focus on two key aspects of coding. The first section on coding of alphanumeric characters reviews basic coding concepts and methods. The second section applies these concepts to the coding of pictures, sound, and motion, and explains the concepts and techniques of data compression.

Analog versus Digital Representation

Information can be represented in either analog or digital form. Analog coding is done with continuous signals or wave forms; digital coding is done with discrete, binary digits. Although human processing of voice, sound, image, and motion is analog, computer information processing is based entirely on digital equivalents. This means that anything a computer is to process must be converted from analog inputs to digital coding. For output, it must be converted from internal digital coding back to analog for presentation to humans.

Analog methods are still in use in some voice communication, entertainment distribution, and telephone technology. In human speech communication, sounds are continuous wave forms that are produced by vocal cords, sent through the air, and received and interpreted by the ears of the recipient. When microphones and speakers are used, they also employ analog electromagnetic wave forms. Until fairly recently, methods for storing sound were based on storing analog wave forms on the magnetic surface of a disk or tape.

Similarly, most video is broadcast in analog signal form, moves via cable as analog signals, and is stored on magnetic tape as analog signals.

In contrast to continuous analog signals, a digital signal can represent only two states. Digital codes that represent analog signals include information to reconstruct the original analog signal if there is need for an analog output.

Since analog representation is used in human communications, why are computers digital? Why do newer data transport facilities, recordings, telephone communications, and other systems employ digital devices and digital coding? There are basically two reasons for the dominance of digital devices and digital coding in modern electronics: (1) the simplicity (and low cost) of electronic components based on two states, and (2) the significant increase in quality gained by using digital error detection and correction methods. In other words, digital devices are superior because of simplicity and because they virtually eliminate noise and errors in processing, storing, and transporting information.

Coding of Alphanumeric Characters

If computers processed only numeric digits, the coding scheme could be quite simple. As illustrated in Table 14-1, encoding the 10 numeric digits from 0 to 9 requires a code with a set of four binary digits (bits), each with a value of 0 or 1. In other words, the digital code for 4 is 0100 and the code for 9 is 1001.

There is a logic to the coding, but what is important is the fundamental concept that a unique combination of a set of four bits can encode the numeric digits from 0 to 9.

Since computers need to represent not only the 10 digits but also alphabetic and special characters, the size of the code needs to increase. The basic coding and storage unit for personal computers consists of the set of 8 bits called a **byte.** An 8-bit code can encode 256 different input characters. A byte is sufficient to code both upper and lowercase letters plus a large number of special characters. However, one byte is not sufficient when different non-Roman

Table 14-1 Coding Scheme for 10 Numeric Digits from 0 to 9			
Numeric Value	*Digital Code*	*Numeric Value*	*Digital Code*
0	0000	5	0101
1	0001	6	0110
2	0010	7	0111
3	0011	8	1000
4	0100	9	1001

language characters such as Hebrew, Cyrillic, or Greek are included. The coding method must expand to use two bytes (that can encode 65,536 symbols). The fundamental principle is that the code size must increase as more characters are represented.

Various coding schemes have implications for data processing and communication. The specific binary codes assigned will affect the way data items are ordered. For example, if uppercase letters are given a smaller binary value than lowercase letters, the three words "Alpha, Beta, Gamma" will be sorted by the computer in that order; however, if the words were "Alpha, beta, Gamma," they would be ordered as "Alpha, Gamma, beta." There are work-arounds to deal with this problem, but the underlying concept is that character encoding has implications for processing.

Example

The United States developed a code for English language coding called ASCII (American Standard Code for Information Interchange). ASCII works fine for English, but what about other languages? An international extension provides some graphic characters and the special characters of European languages within the one-byte unit. In this standard, the Danish letter ø is coded as 11111000. Other codes can be used for math and science symbols. In order to include characters from languages that do not use Roman characters, a 2-byte (16 bit) international code standard, Unicode, has been established. This standard provides specific codes for most alphabets including Cyrillic, Japanese Kanji characters, Arabic, Hindi, Farsi, and other alphabets, and even for a large subset of Chinese ideograms. ◆

Coding of Pictures and Graphics

The screens used for computer output display alphanumeric data, graphics, pictures, and video. If the screen needed to display only alphanumeric characters, data, and simple line drawings, the display device could encode these as combinations of lines. However, the full use of a graphical interface means that a different method is used. The screen consists of thousands of tiny dots, each of which can have a picture value of white, black, or a specified color. These individual picture elements are called **pixels** (sometimes pels). A digitized picture is composed of a large number of pixels. The number of pixels represented can vary with different implementations of the technology. For example, the widely used VGA (Video Graphics Array) display standard for personal computers is 640 pixels across by 480 pixels high. The number of dots to be encoded per unit of area determines the size of each pixel and also the texture of the result. Display resolution is independent of the physical size of the screen. A fairly small number of pixels gives a rough picture in which the individual dots are clearly visible. A large number of picture elements per unit of screen (such as per inch) makes the picture smooth and sharp, so that individual pixels cannot be identified by the viewer. The practical implication is that there is a tradeoff in which higher resolution requires more pixels per unit of screen than lower resolution (Figure 14-2).

The size of the digital code for a pixel depends on the variations that must be encoded. For example:

◆ If a pixel is either black or white, then the code for a pixel can be a single bit with 0 representing white and 1 representing black. If a pixel can represent only a few basic colors, a half-byte of four bits can encode 16 different colors. Limiting displays to black and white or the basic colors is considered too restrictive for most personal computer displays.

◆ If one pixel can represent 256 different colors, one byte is needed for each pixel. This is currently sufficient for many high-resolution personal computer displays.

◆ If a pixel needs to represent more colors and shades of colors, a three-byte (24 bit) coding is used to represent 256 levels for each of the three primary colors. With 24 bits, over 16 million variations of color can be coded to represent the full range distinguishable by the human eye.

If there were no way to reduce the stored representations of the pixel codes, a one-byte pixel code would require 307,200 bytes to store one standard PC color display screen with 640 x 480 pixels. A high resolution (1024 x 768 pixels) 24-bit photo-quality display requires 2.4 million bytes to represent an

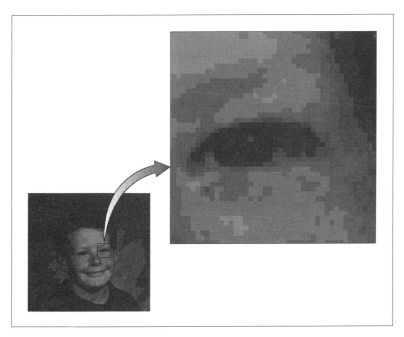

FIGURE 14-2 *Coding of a picture using pixels*

entire screen at that resolution. Figure 14-3 is a graph showing the increase in bits required to encode a screen moving from simple black and white standard VGA resolution to high resolution 24-bit color.

Coding of Voice and Sound

A sound is captured by a microphone or reproduced by a speaker as a continuous wave form. The analog method for coding voice and sound is to capture and store the wave form. With digital technology, however, analog wave forms are encoded with digital codes in such a way that they can eventually be reconverted to analog.

Analog to digital conversion is performed by measuring the analog signal at frequent intervals and encoding the measurement as a digital value (see Figure 14-4). In telephony, for example, the analog voice signal is measured or sampled 8,000 times per second. Each measurement is encoded as one of 256 voltage levels using 8 bits. This means a voice telephone message requires 64,000 bits per second, or 480,000 8-bit bytes per minute. To reproduce the sound for humans, a digital-to-analog conversion process recreates the analog signal for a speaker output by generating each of the appropriate voltages from the digital codes. This same principle is used for other sound encoding,

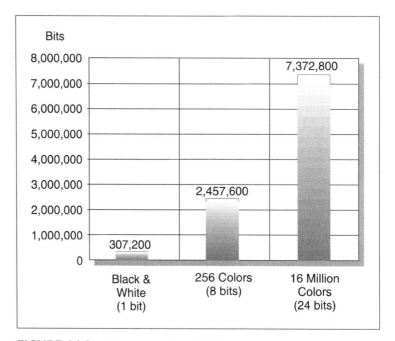

FIGURE 14-3 *Bits to encode a VGA screen*

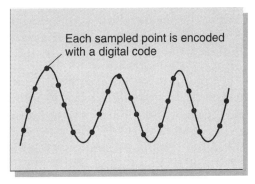

Each sampled point is encoded with a digital code

FIGURE 14-4   *Sampling wave form to obtain digital description*

such as music compact disks. A sampling rate of 22,100 per second for each stereo channel is needed to capture the properties important to human ears.

Coding of Video with Motion

Motion video consists of a sequence of separate pictures that replace each other rapidly. As each new image is displayed, the human vision system blends the changing images into continuous motion. This phenomenon begins to occur when a picture is completely redrawn about 15 times per second. For comparison, the USA standard for broadcast TV, NTSC (National Television Systems Committee) video, has about 480 rows of 440 pixels repeated 30 times per second. When analog NTCS video is digitized at 30 frames per second, it requires one billion bytes of storage (one gigabyte) for one minute of video.

Compression

The need for compression is based on four factors: (1) storage costs, (2) communication costs, (3) limits of storage devices, and (4) convenience.

1. *Storage costs.* Compression reduces storage requirements. For example, software packages are compressed to reduce the number of diskettes that must be distributed. The program to decompress the data is included in the installation program.

2. *Communication costs.* Information transmission is often a significant cost. Compression reduces redundant information and speeds transmission.

3. *Limits of storage devices.* The costs of storage devices continue to decrease, but the architecture of most systems places limits on available storage capacity.

4. *Convenience.* When copying data files, compression makes the operation more convenient because it reduces the volume of media and the time required.

There are many different procedures or algorithms for data compression. The simplest example of data compression is called **space suppression**. Space suppression takes advantage of the presence of frequently occurring strings of the space character. Strings of spaces are significant in the transmission of computer generated reports to remote printers. In space suppression, each string of spaces is replaced at the transmitter by a special code called a flag character and a count of the number of spaces. The receiver then replaces the flag code and count with the specified number of spaces. A similar scheme is used by facsimile transmission, which replaces strings of black or white pixels with encoded string length characters.

For data compression, variations on an algorithm by Lempel and Ziv are very common. Data files are compressed for storage or transmission, or both, often to less than half of their original size. The LZ approach is related to space suppression, but is able to substitute short codes for virtually every string that repeats once or more in a file. **Lempel-Ziv algorithms** are built into high-speed modems. They are also the basis for many software products that effectively double the capacity of disk storage. (For additional information, see J. Ziv and A. Lempel, "A Universal Algorithm for Sequential Data Compression," IEEE Transactions on Information Theory, May 1977.)

These approaches to compression are called "loss-less" since the exact bit-pattern of the original is always completely restored. Loss-less compression is often not necessary in communicating sound, graphics, and motion images. By carefully developing compression algorithms that remove just those aspects of an image that are not noticeable (or barely noticeable) to humans, very high compression ratios have been defined. For example, the JPEG (Joint Photographic Experts Group) standard for images provides loss-less compression of about 3:1, but reaches ratios of more than 50:1 with some loss of the original signal. A color photo scanned into 3 million bytes may appear very close to the original when viewed after JPEG compression to 60,000 bytes (one fiftieth of the original).

Motion video compression can rely on all of these techniques, and some additional characteristic of both the human vision system and motion pictures. Most of the time, only a small part of the video image changes from one frame to the next. By encoding only the changes over time, very high-quality compressed video can have compression ratios of more than 200:1. For example, the MPEG-2 (Moving Picture Experts Group) standard for High Definition TV will compress from an original picture digital coding of 1.2 billion bits per second to less than 6 million.

Core Technology: Digital Circuits

◆ ◆

The first, primitive computers in the late 1940s and early 1950s used vacuum tubes to represent the two states in the circuits that performed arithmetic, logic, and comparisons. They generated significant heat and were subject to high failure rates. A breakthrough in computing was the late 1950s use of solid state transistors instead of vacuum tubes. Smaller size and lower power consumption allowed transistors to be packed much closer together. Much higher reliability meant that computer users could expect several hours of operation between hardware failures. The next major change was the combining of transistors and connecting circuitry on an integrated circuit. Integrated circuits continued the process of lower power consumption and increasing density, allowing higher speeds and better reliability. The microprocessor is an integrated circuit that contains transistors, gates, and supporting circuitry on a single silicon chip.

A semiconductor chip or microprocessor is built on a substrate of crystalline material, usually silicon, that is grown for that purpose. The crystal is cut into thin wafers some 3 to 5 inches in diameter. On each wafer are etched tiny transistors, logic gates, and the connections among them. The process uses repeated photo-etching of many thinly deposited layers of materials to produce complete circuits and elements. The advantages of the high density are low cost, high speed, and reduced power consumption and heat from the circuits. The first microprocessor in 1971 had 2,300 transistors and performed 60,000 instructions per second. In 1996 microprocessors contained over 10 million transistors and performed 300 million instructions per second. Gordon Moore is one of the co-founders of Intel, one of the dominant microprocessor manufacturers. His 1965 prediction, sometimes referred to as **Moore's Law**, was that transistor densities on chips would double approximately every eighteen to twenty-four months. This is illustrated in Figure 14-5.

Figure 14-5 uses a logarithmic scale on the X-axis. This means that each interval goes up by a factor of 10. This gives rather remarkable results. Intel's Pentium microprocessor of the early 1990s has about 3 million transistors. Moore's law projects that by the year 2000 a microprocessor will have about 30 million transistors, ten times more than the Pentium. The high-speed microprocessors of the year 2000 will be able to execute 2,000 MIPS (Millions of Operations Per Second), compared to about 400 MIPS for 1996's fastest.

There have been imposing changes in the number of circuits on a single chip. The price drop has been equally dramatic. It has been said that if progress

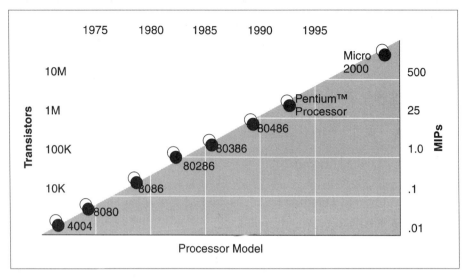

FIGURE 14-5 *Moore's Law for transistor density in microprocessor chips. Intel chips are illustrated.*

Source: http://www.intel.com/product/tech-briefs/man_bnch.htm

in automobile technology had kept pace with computer technology, a Rolls Royce would cost $5 and get 75,000 miles per gallon! An important question is the ability to make productive use of the dramatically increasing computing power. During the same period of outstanding increases in density of chips and reductions in prices, there were many significant developments that made use of the improvements, such as the following:

◊ *Increases in processing activities using graphical user interfaces.* Producing graphical displays and managing the interface requires substantial storage and processing power.

◊ *Increases in the size and complexity of all major software packages.* Features and requirements expanded as the speed of chips increased and cost decreased. Major software packages for spreadsheets and word processing have increased from 10 to 100 times in size in less than 20 years.

◊ *Changes in the operating system software.* This allows more than one application to run concurrently.

◊ *Coding, storage, and processing of pictures, voice, and video that require large amounts of computer storage and processing capabilities.*

◊ *Increases in the processing requirements for output.* Printed output became more complex with more fonts and features. Graphical output and multimedia output increased the need for processing power and speed.

◊ *New forms of input.* These include voice input and handwriting recognition, which require high-speed processing and large storage capacity.

Did the demand for these uses cause the changes in performance and price to meet the demand, or did the availability of hardware at low cost enable software changes to be implemented? Unquestionably, both forces interacted to result in the current computing environment.

Is there a need for these continual significant increases in performance? The issue of demand is related to the question about whether demand caused availability or availability generated demand. Most current chip technology innovations that increase performance and reduce cost generate new applications because there remain many opportunities to supplement or enhance human performance with information technology. The demand for performance appears to rise to meet the supply of capabilities.

Are there limits to the improvements in density, speed, and cost of semiconductor chips? There are physical constraints on the improvements that can be achieved with current chip technology. These limit the number of transistors on a single chip. Mid-1990s circuit lithography (etching technology) is limited to about .35 micron (millionth of a meter) for the smallest conductor on an integrated circuit. This limits practical microprocessor designs to about 10 million transistors. Scientists know that there is a limit to the minimum size that can be achieved, even though there is no consensus about the limit. New lithography methods achieve .18 micron size allowing up to 40 million transfers per chip.

Example:

Sandia National and AT&T Bell Laboratories have developed an experimental system that uses "extreme ultraviolet light" to etch circuit lines as small as 0.1 micron wide on computer chips—one-third to one-fifth the width of the lines on today's best chips. The technique could be used to handle 16- and perhaps even 64-gigabit memory chips. (*Business Week,* 3/20/95, p. 103) ◆

Even assuming some ultimate limits to density, however, there remain many opportunities for improvement in performance not associated with density or switching speed. These are the design of circuits and the way these are reflected in software. For example, a chip design may be based on a complex instruction set (CISC). This may simplify some software, but may also impose restrictions on instruction timing such that performance may be lower than that of a comparable reduced instruction set (RISC) chip. One approach may be superior for certain problems or methods; the other may be superior for others. Bus design (to be discussed later) and other methods for transport of data may also affect chip performance. On the other hand, smaller, cheaper chips may be economically used in multiple sets, further increasing computing power.

Core Technology: Digital Storage Devices

◆ ◆

There is a broad range of storage media and storage devices which differ in technology, cost, and retrieval time. There is an inverse relationship between cost and retrieval time: faster retrieval times are associated with higher cost storage. This suggests that the largest volume of storage will be on the lowest cost, highest access time media. Data needing faster access will be stored on higher cost media. In terms of volume and cost, storage can be represented as a pyramid (see Figure 14-6).

The fastest and most expensive storage medium is semiconductor memory—memory chips. Semiconductor memory prices in the mid-1990s have dropped below $5 per megabyte. Near the base of the pyramid in Figure 14-6 are optical disks that store 640 megabytes and can be priced below $5—less than $0.01 per megabyte. Magnetic tapes can store 8 gigabytes on a $20 cassette—$0.0025 per megabyte. A wide variety of electronic, electromechanical,

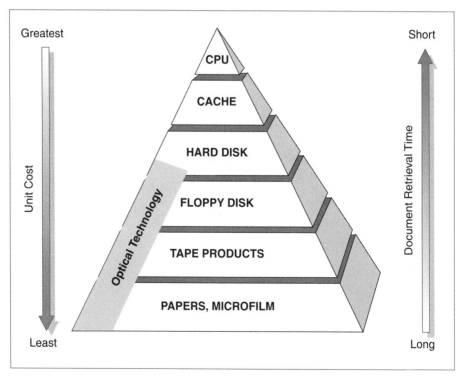

FIGURE 14-6 *Hierarchy of storage*

and electro-optical devices provide capacities and prices between these extremes. In terms of retrieval time, the most expensive semiconductor memory can provide access to a randomly selected unit of storage (32, 64, or even 128 bits) in less than 50 nanoseconds (50 billionths of a second). At the other extreme, access to CD-ROM or magnetic tape is usually assumed to require media mounting, either by a robot or a human, and can take from several seconds to several minutes for random access.

Another important characteristic of storage devices is "writeability." ROM (Read Only Memory) is the term used for a broad range of storage devices and media that can record data only once, but can be read many times. This category includes ROM chips. These semiconductor memory devices are used to store programs that will never be changed, such as the inner kernels of operating systems and programs for peripheral control devices. At the other extremes of capacity and cost, CD-ROMs are machine-stamped from inexpensive plastic. Copies contain exactly the data encoded on the master.

Most storage is read and write storage. Read and write storage includes internal chip memory (RAM), permanently installed large-capacity internal disk (hard disk), disks and diskettes, rewritable optical disks, and magnetic tape. The primary difference between memory chips and other means of read and write storage is that chips are entirely electronic rather than partially mechanical.

Magnetic Disk Storage

Magnetic read/write storage employs both electronic and mechanical methods. Physical motion, usually rotating, is used to pass the storage medium close to very sensitive read-write heads. Magnetic disks store data on concentric tracks. Read-write heads are mounted on mechanical arms that move them from one track to another. Storage capacity is determined primarily by the density of bits on each track (the space between polarized spots that can be set to represent a 0 or 1 value for a bit) and the space between tracks. The performance of rotating memory devices such as magnetic disks is determined by two factors: rotational delay and positioning delay. Rotational delay or latency refers to the average time expected for a given bit to move under the stationary read-write head. Various techniques including faster rotation and multiple heads per track are used to reduce latency. Positioning delay is an average defined as the time it takes the mechanical arm to move one-half the distance across the recorded surface of the disk. Many improvements in positioning have come from reducing the mass of the movable arm and read-write heads and reducing the distance to be traveled.

Storage densities for magnetic devices are described in terms of bits per square inch. In the mid 1990s, recording densities of 100 million bits per square inch are available. Because area is involved, as in integrated circuit technology, a small reduction in the space needed for a bit results in a large increase in storage density.

There are physical limits to magnetic disk density. However, the limits have not been reached. Magnetic disks are relatively mature technology. Capacity per unit cost can be expected to continue to double every three years, as it has over the past twenty-five. A one gigabyte hard drive costs less than $200 in 1996, so a three-gigabyte drive should be available for that price by 1999.

Magnetic Tape Storage

Magnetic tape storage is similar to disk storage in the use of multiple tracks and magnetic areas that can be polarized in one of two directions. It differs from disk storage because tape must be moved from its current position to the position of the data sought, a process that usually requires minutes. Magnetic tape storage is too slow to support real-time human activity, but its very low-cost and large capacity make it useful for archival and backup storage. Magnetic tape was the first high-capacity computer storage medium. As a result, many different tape formats, specifications, and mechanisms have been developed. Because it is a removable medium, cost can be lower than $0.0025 per megabyte of storage.

Optical Storage

Optical storage devices are available in all three storage modes: read-only, write-once, and read and write (rewritable). The read-only optical disk has emerged as the preferred low-cost approach to distributing large files (of various types). It is represented by a data disk (compact disk or CD-ROM) that follows an audio recording format. Data is stored on a CD-ROM by means of microscopic pits molded into the disk surface. A laser beam focused and aimed by a system of movable mirrors reads the pits. The advantages of CD-ROM are high capacity, high permanence, and very low reproduction cost. The disks do not wear out because there is no physical contact during the reading operation. Most CD-ROMs are prepared by a specialized vendor. A master is recorded and duplicated by a low-cost stamping operation. During the early 1990s, many vendors began distributing software such as operating systems on CD-ROM rather than on diskette. Convenience, not just cost, has motivated this change: current software systems may occupy 30 or more high-density diskettes. One CD-ROM has the equivalent capacity of 450 diskettes and can, therefore, contain not only the software, but also documentation that might otherwise require a foot or more of shelf space. A significant limitation of the CD-ROM format standard is that it is based on audio technology: data bits are recorded on a single spiral track rather than on the concentric tracks of magnetic disks. While this helps make CD-ROMs inexpensive, it limits flexibility. A *de facto* standard, the Kodak Photo-CD, provides a way to add to the recorded data. But this standard does not overcome the limits to access time and transfer speed.

Write-once optical disk (often referred to as WORM—Write Once, Read Many) technology is closely related to CD-ROM. The difference is that write-once optical disks are written by the user, and information can be added until the disk is full. The information format is concentric tracks as used in magnetic disk storage. (This, however, makes WORM disks and drives incompatible with CD-ROM.) In the write-once mode, a write operation creates a permanent variation in the layer on the disk for each bit; the laser beam reads by detecting the difference in reflection. For example, one technology "burns" a hole into a layer of the disk.

A variant of CD-ROM is CD-recordable, or CD-R. In this medium, instead of stamped microscopic pits, a layer of dye is permanently changed by a write laser. CD-R disks can be read by all CD-ROM drives. In 1996, CD-R recorders dropped below the $1,000 price barrier, leading many to predict widespread use as a replacement for magnetic tape.

Rewritable optical disk storage is similar in concept to magnetic storage, but is expected eventually to allow higher density and reliability. In writing to a rewritable optical storage, a laser beam applies enough heat to each storage spot to reverse polarity, but not to change the surface. The recorded data can be read by a laser beam and can be erased or altered by writing new data at the same location. Order of magnitude improvements in speed and capacity can be anticipated for optical storage.

Core Technology: Digital Communications

◆ ◆ ◆ ◆ ◆ ◆ ◆ ◆ ◆ ◆ ◆ ◆ ◆ ◆ ◆ ◆ ◆ ◆ ◆ ◆

A large proportion of the work of information processing is moving digital data (including instructions or programs). Data movement may be within a chip, within microprocessor circuits, between the processor and input/output devices, within a local work environment such as a department or workgroup, or over long distances within one organization or among organizations. The movement of data employs a **channel** of communication, i.e., a pathway for transmission. Its implementation may be different for the two types of transmission (analog and digital), but the basic idea is the same. The speed of transmission is affected by the technology used. Channel capacity and speed must match the speed of the agents involved, whether processors or humans.

If a channel is too slow, it will be a bottleneck; if it is too fast, there will be unused capacity.

Signals for Transporting Data

Data may be transported using either analog or digital signals (see Figure 14-7). An **analog signal** is a continuously varying electromagnetic wave. A **digital signal** is a discrete sequence of voltage pulses (either two voltage levels or a somewhat more complex digital signal code). There are four methods of representation for transporting data important to information processing:

1. *Digital data is represented by digital signals.* A personal computer connects to a printer via a short cable and digital signals are transmitted to the printer.

2. *Digital data is represented with analog signals.* A **modem** (modulator/demodulator) converts digital data from the computer to an analog representation for transmission over voice telephone lines; the receiving modem reverses the procedure.

3. *Analog data is represented by digital signals.* Voice telephone data is digitally encoded for switching at a central telephone office using a codec (coder-decoder). The original analog signal is represented by sets of bits that describe the shape of the continuous electromagnetic signal. The wave form is sampled, so that many digital codes are required to represent the shape of the wave form. The digital codes are used to reconstruct the analog wave form at the receiving end of the transmission.

4. *Analog data is represented by analog signals.* A portable telephone broadcasts analog voice information using an analog radio carrier signal.

Since the early 1970s, the trend has been toward digital communication, representing digital or analog data with digital signals. One reason has to do with signal loss and noise. All electrical signals become weaker over distance and must be strengthened. In the case of continuous analog signals, the only

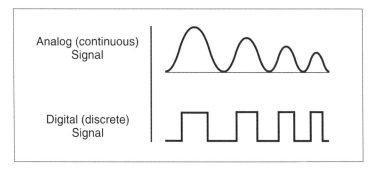

FIGURE 14-7 *Difference between analog and digital signals*

method of strengthening a signal is amplification. But signal amplification also amplifies any noise that is present in the signal, so the signal becomes distorted. Noise accumulates with repeated amplification, until eventually part or all of the original information is lost or becomes unintelligible. Digital signals also weaken over distance, but instead of amplifying digital signals, the original signal can be decoded, re-created, and sent on at full power. During the decoding process, errors may be detected and corrected so that the repeated signal is free of both errors and noise.

There are several additional reasons for the dominance of digital transmission. Because of the technology of digital circuit manufacture, digital repeater circuits cost less than analog amplifiers. Digital circuits can be physically much smaller and consume less electrical power. Finally, digital signals may be processed by microcomputers and circuits in many ingenious ways to increase transmission capacity and improve reliability.

Digital data transmission speed is defined in terms of bits per second (bps or b/s). Speeds range from current modem standards of 14,400 bps, 28,800 bps, and 33,600 bps to high speed fiber optic cables carrying more than 10 gigabits/second. A rough estimate of what these speeds mean for the transfer of character data may be obtained by using 8 bits for a character, 6 characters per word, and 500 words per page of text. This results in an expected transfer rate of about 10 seconds per page at 2,400 bps, 3 seconds per page at 9,600 bps, and less than one second at 28,800. These speed differences become quite significant when large amounts of data are being transferred, such as graphics. At gigabit speeds (10G bps is over 400,000 pages per second), the contents of an encyclopedia or even of an entire library can be transmitted in seconds.

Busses and Channels

The core technology characteristic for data transmission is the pathway for moving data. The pathway must handle traffic at speeds consistent with the speed of data processing, or it will be a bottleneck. An extremely complex problem of data movement is communication within the processing unit and internal computer storage. If every possible path for data within a processing and storage unit were made with direct wiring, there would be little room for computing or memory. The technology commonly employed to simplify internal data movement is a pathway called a "bus." A **bus** is a common data pathway shared by a group of related devices. Data items needed are sent on the pathway and picked up by the intended receiving unit. A single conductor pathway has proven to be much too slow. A parallel bus that also supports two-way traffic achieves much higher speeds.

This discussion of bus architecture illustrates the concept that the capacity of a communications channel is a combination of channel width (in terms of the number of bits that can move in parallel—similar to lanes in a highway) and the speed at which bits move along the channel.

External to the microprocessor is the connection between the processor bus and peripheral devices. One of the most widely-used peripheral busses is a 16-bit wide data path. This bus design dates to the early 1980s, but newer microcomputers still conform to this industry standard, so peripherals of different vendors may connect to the system. For many peripherals such as printers and modems, this relatively slow bus is still adequate. In the 1990s, however, the extensive use of applications with graphics and the development of higher speed storage devices have created a need for faster peripheral busses (with, for example, a 32-bit data path to match the processor). Newer microcomputers include a local bus that operates at processor speed to support the movement and display of screen images and to exchange data with high-speed disk drives and other peripherals. New, wider, and faster bus designs are characteristic of new generations of computers.

Bandwidth

An important concept of signaling in the world of analog communications is bandwidth. **Bandwidth** defines a range of frequencies. In analog signaling, a communications channel is bounded by an upper frequency, representing the maximum signal rate that can be transported, and a lower frequency that represents the minimum. The difference between these upper and lower frequencies is the bandwidth, a measure of the capacity of a channel. In telephony, for example, the upper limit chosen for human voice signals is 3,400 Hertz (Hz), while the lower is 300 Hz. The bandwidth of an analog telephone channel is, therefore, 3,400 minus 300, or 3,100 Hz. This bandwidth excludes some tonal qualities of the human voice, but does not hinder understanding of message contents.

The term "bandwidth" is applied to communications channels, where it describes capacity. It is also, somewhat confusingly, applied to information in terms of transport requirements. For example, a broadcast or cable television signal may be described as needing a bandwidth of 6 MegaHertz (MHz), meaning that a channel with a bandwidth of at least 6,000,000 Hz is required to transmit a television signal without loss. The term is used loosely to describe both the capacity of digital channels and the requirements of digital signals. Saying the bandwidth of an Ethernet LAN is 10 MHz is equivalent to saying it has a capacity of 10 million bits per second. (While technically incorrect, such usage has become common.)

It is useful to conceptualize a transmission medium as providing a large capacity that can be divided into multiple channels of varying bandwidth. Bandwidth is an important characteristic in the purchase of communication services from common carriers (vendors of communications). There are various methods for dividing a large capacity channel into two or more channels, so that two or more transmissions can share the use of one medium. The technology of dividing and sharing media is known as **multiplexing**. In general, analog signals may be multiplexed only by reserving a specific frequency for each. In contrast, digital signals may be multiplexed by allocating time slices to each separate signal, a more flexible approach.

Protocols

For communications to take place, the sender of information must speak the same language as the receiver. This is clearly true in natural language. English makes no sense at all to someone who understands only Tagalog and vice versa. Like natural language grammar and vocabulary, data communications can be extremely complex. To deal with this complexity, **protocols**—clearly defined agreements on all of the details of communications—have been established. The most widely known of the many different communications protocols is the ITU's (International Transport Union) OSI (Open Systems Interconnect) Reference Model, sometimes called the "seven-layer model." In this model, separate sets of rules (protocols) are defined for different communication conditions and needs.

There are other models or collections of protocols. These models are also called **communications architectures**. Examples include IBM's SNA (Systems Network Architecture) and the rapidly expanding Internet communications architecture called TCP/IP (an acronym for Transmission Control Protocol and Internet Protocol, two key elements of the protocol architecture). Communication on networks using a single protocol architecture is simpler and more efficient than communication involving multiple architectures. While no single collection of protocols is dominant at this time, TCP/IP as the basis of the Internet is rapidly displacing other architectures. Since there are significant advantages for communications using one protocol, it is likely that one will finally dominate.

Wireless Communications

A major innovation in communications is the opening of broadcast frequencies to wireless communications. Wireless telephones are one result. Another is the availability of communications through portable computers. With a modem, transceiver, and antenna on a laptop computer, the computer can communicate with a home office, send and receive fax messages, and send and receive e-mail.

The use of wireless communications can begin in an office using line-of-sight transmission of signals from one computer to another via an infrared beam, and can be extended to wireless LANs. Wireless communications can expand a shared network without a requirement for installing wiring. Workers who travel in their jobs can keep in contact and send and receive data about customers and deliveries without the need to find and connect to a phone.

The Effect of Distance on Data Transport

Different protocols are used for local area networks (LANs) that operate over limited distances than for wide area networks (WANs). Within a work environment, a single building, and even adjacent buildings (like a campus), a LAN is likely to be used. A LAN uses a transmission medium such as twisted pair wire, coaxial cable, or optical fiber. LAN signals are digital rather than analog. Over the relatively short distances involved, the inefficiencies of digital signaling are an acceptable tradeoff for their simplicity and economy.

WAN transmission over a longer distance uses a wider variety of transmission media such as optical fiber, copper wire and coaxial cable, microwave radio, and satellite microwave radio. The cost of long-distance channels has decreased rapidly as fiber optic cables have been deployed to replace wire and microwave channels. Long-distance signaling usually employs some form of analog technology (although the analog signals carry encoded digital information).

When information is transported beyond the boundaries of the computer and its peripherals, the delays caused by distance become more significant. Electrical signals travel at or close to the speed of light in the air or in space, and at about 2/3 the speed of light in a conductor such as copper wire. Light travels at 300 million meters per second (186,000 miles per second). In most communication between humans over terrestrial distances, this delay is not significant: a signal can travel completely around the earth in less than 2/10 second. But a communications satellite in geosynchronous orbit is 40,000 kilometers above the earth. For a signal moving at the speed of light, the round-trip travel time of about 1/4 second is noticeable and disconcerting to humans. Satellites are often not used for voice telephone for this reason.

At data communications speeds, transmission delay is even more significant, and transmission time known as "propagation delay" affects most data communications systems. For example, consider a high-speed communication channel between Minneapolis, Minnesota, and San Diego, California. The distance between the two cities is about 3,000 kilometers. A signal in an optical fiber cable requires 1/100 of a second to travel from one to the other. If communications were to take place at the common LAN speed of 10 Mbps (megabits per second), 100,000 bits could be in transit on the fiber cable at any one time! If smaller message units had to be sent and acknowledged, both stations might spend most of their time waiting. Much of the complexity of communications protocols is due to the effect of propagation delay on communications between parties. The protocol processor at each end in this example must buffer (temporarily hold) and manage the data in transit so that users are not held back and channel capacity is not wasted.

Constraints on Data Transmission

There are several limits to the availability of increased bandwidth. They include technological, economic, and social/political issues. On the technical side, during the past decade, fiber optic cables have provided an increase in long-distance capacity of 100 to 1,000 times. Current technology, however, requires that optical signals be converted back to relatively slow electronic signals for any processing, including repeating, multiplexing/demultiplexing, and switching. This constraint severely limits the ability to economically use all of the potential capacity of optical fiber. High-speed switching protocols such as ATM (Asynchronous Transmission Mode) partially compensate. ATM is considered an important data transmission method because it provides for efficient use of the bandwidth in transmitting messages requiring different bandwidths. The development of high-speed optical processing and switching is anticipated over the next decade. This development will facilitate another speed increase of 100 or more times.

The economic issue is a problem of scale. Communications systems are very large. One figure used to show the scale of communications systems is an estimate of $100,000,000 as the cost of developing the software for a new type of central telephone office switch. This number is so large that there are perhaps only three communications companies in the world large enough to be central office switch manufacturers.

In order to realize desired returns with a reasonable degree of certainty, service providers must anticipate that new products will gain significant use very rapidly. Numerous experiments involving communications systems are being implemented during the 1990s. Many involve data transmission for entertainment, since that is seen as a mass market with much greater potential than business data communications. If or when some of these experiments prove to be economically viable, there will be significant increases in available bandwidth and large economies of scale for the providers. That, in turn, is likely to result in more economical bandwidth for data. Estimates are for reduction factors of 10, 100, or 1,000 in cost and comparable increases in performance.

Telecommunications systems have social implications. American Telephone and Telegraph Company (AT&T) gained its USA monopoly at least partly on the promise of "universal service." Some concept of universal service is built into the legal, political, and social structure of all developed countries. Under this concept, low-cost access to the communication system is subsidized by higher bandwidth users. The optical fiber and integrated circuit revolutions in technology have re-opened the definition of universal service and called into question the relationship between the industry and society. These changes and challenges to existing communications services and prices will continue until the technology stabilizes.

Core Technology: Software

◆   ◆   ◆   ◆   ◆   ◆   ◆   ◆   ◆   ◆   ◆   ◆   ◆   ◆   ◆   ◆   ◆   ◆   ◆   ◆

Software can be classified into the categories of system software, development software, and application software. The most important and visible **system software** is the operating system. Other system software tends to be close to specific hardware devices and relatively invisible to users. **Development software** influences the processes and costs of creating applications and the capabilities of those applications. The availability of packaged **application software** to solve business problems depends in part on the capabilities of development tools used by application vendors. Custom applications—whether developed by users, IS professional staff, or contractors—likewise depend on the features and capabilities of software development tools.

Operating Systems

An **operating system** is software that manages and coordinates the computer's resources in support of application programs. Users of the computer and application programs interact with computer hardware only through the interfaces provided by the operating system. Operating systems began as supplements to proprietary hardware architectures and systems. Each hardware vendor sold or leased an operating system with every computer. Application software had to be developed to operate on a specific combination of hardware and operating system. Applications developed for one operating system could not be executed on a different one without revisions.

Although the choice of hardware and operating systems will involve some constraints, there is a trend toward open systems that allow more flexibility. On the hardware side, a single operating system design is able to control computers of different hardware architecture, presenting a uniform interface to the application systems designed for it. On the application side, layers of "middleware" between operating system and application program allow execution of an application on different operating systems. The trend is strongly toward interoperability, whereby applications can be developed to operate on more than one platform, providing flexibility for the user.

Operating systems manage the resources of the computer system. Typically this management includes allocating processor cycles among programs or tasks, assigning main memory space, cataloging stored data, accounting for resource usage, and supporting various peripheral devices such as displays, printers, disk drives, and tape drives. On a single-user system such as a PC or workstation, operating system functions such as accounting and resource-sharing may be omitted or be very simple. The trend (even on personal computers) is toward **multi-programming** (executing more than one program in a way that appears to the user to be simultaneous). Multi-programming requires sophisticated process and resource management by the operating system.

The most visible feature of operating systems is the user interface. Operating systems tend to be characterized in terms of their basic user interface. However, differences among user interfaces are decreasing. An important implication for the knowledge worker is that time and effort spent developing skills with any modern operating system user interface is a long-term investment that will continue to pay off.

Operating systems are responsible for managing shared resources for mainframes, minicomputers, and network servers. These functions are recognized as part of the network operating system (NOS). Hardware and operating system platforms continue to be specialized at this (server) level, even while the services they provide appear to converge. They provide file access and support multiple users of a single copy of data. The NOS provides the underlying mechanisms that permit workgroup computing, electronic mail, network transaction processing, and many other applications that involve multiple users.

Application Development Software

Nearly every computer program is written in some "high-level language." There are hundreds of specialized programming languages, but only a few are important to the individual user. The most widely-used business application language is COBOL. Engineering and scientific applications have predominantly been developed in FORTRAN. Systems software and much microcomputer software and packages have been developed in the C programming language or its variants. All of these programming languages are designed for expert programmers. Languages designed for persons with less training are exemplified by the Basic language and its many variants.

Another category of application development tools that can be used by both specialists and non-specialists is the **4GLs** or **Fourth-Generation Languages**. Fourth generation languages began as simplified tools to select, format, and print information from database management systems, but have evolved into complete programming languages. They speed the development of relatively simple applications and make it possible for non-specialists to access and process organizational data.

The collections of tools for application development have evolved into application development systems. A development system may be based on and include a particular programming language. It will also include either a database management system (DBMS) or tools that facilitate access to DBMSs. Tools to develop user interfaces are also part of application development systems, as are documentation systems and programs and procedures to manage the components of a project. These development support components include data and database definitions, modules of program code, and interface screen and report definitions. Development systems can support both professional and occasional software developers. The trend is toward seamless integration of development tools with high levels of automated support for both programmers and nonspecialists.

Connectivity of Package Solutions

Packages have traditionally been designed as stand-alone applications. The spreadsheet processor output was not in a form that could be used by a word processor. But users often want to connect package solutions and combine them. Data from an accounting package may be needed in a spreadsheet processor, and the results of a spreadsheet may need to be incorporated into a document being prepared by a word processor.

There is a strong trend toward package connectivity. Most major packages have export and import instructions that facilitate connectivity. Graphical user interface systems facilitate capturing data from one application and pasting it into another application. This is useful, but primitive compared to the strong connectivity needed by some users. The trend is to make different packages operate together in a seamless way (i.e., without special handling or manual processing). This trend is likely to continue and is an important issue for ease of use when several packages are employed.

Core Technology: Human-Machine Interfaces

◊ ◊

Humans are very fast and effective at some processing operations; for other operations, humans are very slow and error-prone. For example, a human can read and remember a picture or graphic image very quickly (even compared to computer scanning and storage). But humans can read text output relatively slowly. Even a slow laser printer can print four pages per minute, which is more than twice as fast as the average human can read. However, keyboard entry of data is slower than humans formulating ideas and other text. Even a reasonably fast keying speed (more than 60 words per minute) is probably only one-fourth or one-fifth the speed at which humans can convert ideas into sentences.

The limits of human performance at the interface with computers suggest that improving the human-machine interface will be a major, continuing challenge. In order to think about the issue and the potential for technology-based solutions, the following discussion examines data entry and data presentation.

Data Entry

There are many alternatives to keyboard entry. This section presents five methods, discussed in terms of their potential for improving productivity: (1) selecting from a set of options, (2) coding input on original documents, (3) handwriting recognition, (4) limited voice input, and (5) full text voice recognition.

1. *Selecting from a set of options.* If a full set of options is known, selection reduces input time and errors. If the frequency of selection is known, options may be ordered in terms of their use, thereby further reducing selection time. For example, limited keyboards are used in fast food outlets with each key representing a different product. A display may present a limited list of options on a menu from which the human selects with a mouse, keystroke, or by touching a screen.

2. *Coding input on original documents.* If data items can be encoded in a machine-readable form on an original document, it may be read by machine instead of having a human key the data. Examples are bar-coded documents, documents that can be scanned for computer input, and magnetic encoding on credit cards.

   a. *Bar coding.* The most common use is bar coding of product codes for supermarket checkout. A second common application is tracking inventory. However, bar coding may be used to identify any item that must be counted or inventoried. Bar codes are read by handheld scanners or by units such as those used in supermarkets, where the product is moved over a scanner beam.

   b. *Document scanning with Optical Character Recognition (OCR).* Why isn't everything that is printed scanned and input rather than entered by using a keyboard? Currently, input document scanning requires some human processing to eliminate ambiguous results. For some poor quality documents, manually fixing errors may take more time than keyboard entry. However, the quality of character recognition software continues to improve.

   c. *Magnetic stripe encoding.* Rather than keying in account information for obtaining cash from an automatic teller machine, the user inserts a plastic card with the information. Limited input cards use a magnetic stripe; more information is provided with a "smart card." The smart card not only holds more data, but can also be programmed.

3. *Handwriting recognition.* Hand printing has long been used for input; the newer development is recognition of cursive handwriting. Some primitive handheld devices are on the market, but the full potential will require greater processing power.

4. *Limited voice input.* Speech recognition technology has been available since the mid-1980s, but applications have been limited and expensive. They are generally applied to situations in which a worker's hands are being used and the data to be recognized consists of a small set of words or numerals. For example, an inspector can give a voice command specifying one of ten quality classes. Currently available computer software can recognize voice input of operating system commands (such as **Close, Copy,** etc.).

5. *Full text voice recognition.* Full text voice recognition is difficult because of the large number of variations in speech, differences in clarity of diction, lack of pauses between words, and the large number of words that sound alike or somewhat similar. Homonyms (words that sound the same, but have different spellings and meanings, such as "two," "to," and "too") present a problem. Human recognition of speech is based on a complex process of recognizing words in context, so lack of pauses between words or differences in diction or accent do not prevent understanding. For example, a person may say "youbetchyourlife" with no pauses between words. The listener knows the colloquial expression and interprets the meaning as "you bet your life."

In 1997, personal computer voice recognition systems are available for dictation of words, text, and numbers into cells in a spreadsheet. The software requires a period of training to adjust to the diction of the individual user. The user must employ discrete speech with distinct pauses between words. Background noise must be minimal. When the software has difficulty in recognition, alternative words are displayed for the user to select. Over time, such software can refine its recognition algorithms to select words the user is likely to use. For ordinary dictation with a variety of words in different contexts, current voice recognition software may misread 5 to 10 percent of words. The time required for correcting the errors means ordinary keyboard entry is still more productive. However, with a limited vocabulary and use of mainly present tense, such as in professional notes or memoranda, the rate of correct speech recognition may rise to a satisfactory level. Applications that appear to be successful include simple memoranda or notes in business and dictation of notes by professionals such as lawyers, pathologists, physicians, and psychologists.

Improvements in voice recognition will require significant processing speed and a large amount of disk storage. Improved voice recognition will depend on increasingly complex algorithms for recognizing words in context and phrases that are often spoken quickly without pauses. The processing speed and storage capabilities will certainly be available. More complex algorithms will be developed. Larger vocabularies will be available. Background noise filters will improve. The prognosis is, therefore, for voice recognition as an alternative to keyboard entry for a broad spectrum of users. However, it is not likely that full text voice recognition of complex text will, in the near future, surpass the entry speed of a skilled person with medium to high keying speed and low error rate.

Data Presentation

Computer systems provide outputs in printed form, as graphs and pictures, with sound, and in full-motion video. These can all be calibrated to the reading or comprehension speed of human recipients. Output systems must be designed to reduce the possibility of errors caused by failures in human comprehension or human variations in attention.

Fonts and formatting add to text output quality and help readers understand and remember the content. Examples include bold, italics, different typefaces, boxes, underlining, and similar formatting. Color also has a significant impact on comprehensibility, especially in images.

There are very few emerging technologies for output that will change the dynamics of output to humans. However, some existing technologies such as the following are being used to reduce errors in comprehension and to compensate for human variations in attention:

◊ *Results may be output redundantly in more than one form.* Text and data tables may be supplemented by graphs, drawings, and pictures and enhanced by both text and voice, or sound. For example, an instruction may appear on the screen and also be given as a voice output.

◊ *Compensation for variations in levels of attention may be achieved by use of sound.* The division of labor between computers and humans may also be designed to require humans to perform tasks that reestablish attention, for example, by responding to sounds, pop-up menus and messages, and flashing or blinking icons.

Core Technology: Information Technology Standards

◆ ◆

During the early development of information technology products, each provider established unique designs, often crafted to prevent interoperability with competitive products and services. While such practices tend to lock in customers, they inhibit innovation as well as user choice. One solution was the development of standards. These may be *de facto* (by fact) or *de jure* (by law). *De facto* **standards** may exist because the industry adapts to a standard set by a single dominant vendor. (The DOS operating system from Microsoft is an example.) De facto standards may also emerge because they are recognized in the marketplace. (The icon-based user interface that originated with the Apple Macintosh is one such standard.)

De jure **standards** are promulgated by official standards-making organizations at the national and international levels. In information technology, the most pervasive standards are those for telecommunications, since all telecommunications systems must be able to interoperate globally. Telecommunications standards are defined by the International Telecommunications Union (ITU), a treaty organization of the United Nations. The function of the ITU is to ensure that all telecommunications systems interoperate without regard to political boundaries. The ITU has committees that operate on a four-year cycle to draft, study, and promulgate standards.

The International Standards Organization (ISO) is a voluntary, non-treaty international agency for a broad range of standards. Its members are the designated standards bodies of participating countries. The ISO addresses a much broader range of issues than information technology. (For example, the ISO 9000 series concerns standards for quality management and quality assurance.) One of its IT standards is the Open Systems Interconnection (OSI) reference model that links telecommunications and computing functions.

As an example of a member organization in ISO, the designated USA member body of ISO is the American National Standards Institute (ANSI). ANSI is a governmentally sanctioned voluntary federation of standards-making and user organizations. ANSI's function is to certify standards developed by member groups. When standards are proposed to ANSI, its function is to solicit comments and reviews. When a consensus is reached, ANSI certification makes the proposal an official American National Standard. For example, one of the most widely used computer and communication standards is the 7-bit American Standard Code for Information Interchange (ASCII).

One of the members of ANSI is the Institute of Electrical and Electronic Engineers (IEEE). IEEE committees and task forces develop standards which may be presented for consideration by ANSI and ISO. For example, Local Area Network standards are known as IEEE 802 standards after the 802 Working Group. Other ANSI member groups develop and submit standards as well.

Standards have had a very positive influence in information technology. Both *de facto* and *de jure* standards have allowed equipment and software from many vendors to be used together in a system. This capability has fostered competition and lowered costs. In some cases, anticipatory standards have been established to foster development. Standards also reduce the buyer's risk of rapid obsolescence. Examples of standards are LAN standards, the Open Database Connectivity (ODBC) standard, the Common User Interface (CUI) standard for keyboard and screen functions, and hardware interface standards such as the parallel port for printer connections.

The negative aspects of standards are twofold: (1) Standards may emerge prematurely. If standards are set too soon, innovation may be stifled and more effective and efficient solutions will be inhibited. (2) A *de facto* standard may concentrate economic power in the manufacturer that developed it so as to inhibit alternatives. Microsoft's dominance in the PC operating system field has been claimed by some to inhibit development and use of alternatives.

The Fundamental Forces for Change in Information Technology

◆ ◆

Why should information technology change so rapidly? This section identifies a few very significant drivers that cause change and inhibitors that delay or prevent change.

An unanswerable question is whether the information technology marketplace is pulled by customer demand or if customer demand is pushed by new technology developments. If demand pull is most important, then users identify needs and ask developers to innovate the technology to meet the needs. If technology push is most important, then technology developers will keep innovating without regard to demand with the hope that users will see the value of what is made available. In computing technology, both pull and push are present, with some innovations being influenced most by the pull factor and others by the push. Often, technology developments are motivated by the system imbalance caused by innovating in one part of the computer system without making changes in the other. For example, initial graphical user interfaces were user friendly, but slow in execution and required much memory. This created a strong demand for faster processing and more low-cost storage. The discussion of drivers and inhibitors does not seek to answer the question of demand pull or technology push. One or both may be present for a given change.

Change Drivers

The most significant drivers for change have been integrated circuit technology, magnetic and optical storage technology, and the existence of dominant *de facto* standards for operating systems, graphical user interfaces, and communication services.

Telecommunication has recently emerged as a major driver of change, both because of better, lower-cost communication services, but also because of an increase in the use of e-mail services, online databases, and other services. Facsimile transmission, commercial e-mail, public data networks, and information service providers have improved access and availability of data at reasonable cost. The Internet and World Wide Web have reduced the cost of making information widely available and the cost of access to global data networks. The changes in communications speeds has not yet been as dramatic as chip speed changes, but for most applications, there has been at least an order of magnitude improvement, with much more expected.

Change Inhibitors

The installed base of hardware and software is always an inhibitor of change. However, in the personal computer market, this effect has been reduced by the rapid reduction in cost and increase in performance, so replacement of obsolete hardware and software is fairly easily justified, especially at the individual level. Another factor that reduces the negative impact of the existing base of hardware and software on change is a gradual approach to innovation for the operating systems and interface standards. Users see a more gradual evolution of technology, even though there may be fairly dramatic changes in chip performance and significant new capabilities.

A major inhibitor of change to the operating systems and user interface software has been the time it takes for vendors to produce new software. A hardware innovation may be implemented without new software, but the benefits of the hardware change are reduced by old software or bug-filled new software. To train analysts and programmers to take advantage of new features and create new-version software is a major investment and market risk.

Training and retraining of users are also inhibitors to change. Software vendors have dealt with this primarily by making versions upward compatible, or providing new software that can be operated using the same instructions as the old. This adds to the complexity of the software, but reduces the user cost of migrating to new software. Most major packages also allow files and program specifications to be imported from competitor packages. For example,

WordPerfect can process documents prepared using all versions of Microsoft Word, and vice versa.

The lesson from this section is that the installed hardware base is a relatively low inhibitor of change. The installed operating systems, user interface software, and application packages are a medium inhibitor of change, but developers have somewhat adjusted for these inhibitors. The training of developers and the time to develop new application software to take advantage of new hardware and software innovations is the most significant inhibitor of change. The inhibiting effect of training of users in new software versions is moderated by features in new versions that preserve the ability of users to use the software with the old set of instructions.

Summary

◆ ◆ ◆ ◆ ◆ ◆ ◆ ◆ ◆ ◆ ◆ ◆ ◆ ◆ ◆ ◆ ◆ ◆ ◆ ◆

- ◇ The chapter surveys core technologies for information processing. The objective of the chapter is to provide a basis for individual scanning of technology developments and periodic updating of technology knowledge prior to a major system update or replacement.

- ◇ Seven core technologies form the basis for understanding and tracking changes in information technologies: (1) digital encoding, (2) digital circuits, (3) digital storage devices, (4) digital communications, (5) human-machine interfaces, (6) software, and (7) information technology standards. The core technologies approach makes no distinction between technology for information processing and technology for communications.

- ◇ The characteristics of information technology can be used to form scenarios for creative thinking and planning. Technology planning can benefit from a consideration of the forces for change in computer systems, both drivers of change and inhibitors of change.

EXERCISES

The objective of these exercises is to explore technology developments as a way of understanding how information technology is changing, as well as gaining experience in using sources of information that are useful in updating knowledge.

1. Select an information technology hardware, software, or communications component. Research its past, present, and five-year future.

2. Research two standards (one a *de facto* and the other a *de jure* standard) used in information processing. Compare the rate of adoption and forecast adoption for the next five years.

3. Identify a current or recent legal issue such as an antitrust action or a governmental constraint. Document the relevant facts and evaluate the effects of possible outcomes on information technology for knowledge workers.

4. Locate a specific technology forecast from five to ten years in the past. Document its content and evaluate how and why the outcome is consistent with or different from the forecast.

5. Define an "ideal" information technology for you as an individual. Specify performance capabilities. Describe hardware and software improvements or innovations required to support your ideal system.

6. Choose a recent technology announcement and analyze it in terms of the core technologies it depends on. Is the announcement a real advance or just hype? Forecast its five-year future.

Analyzing an Individual Information Technology Infrastructure

◊　　◊　　◊　　◊　　◊　　◊　　◊　　◊

OBJECTIVES

After completing this chapter, you should be able to:

◆ Survey the role of an individual information technology infrastructure and its relationship to workgroups, departments, and organizational infrastructures.

◆ Explain a process to identify information technology components to support tasks and activities.

◆ Explain how to organize requirements into an individual IT architecture of components.

◆ Explain how to evaluate alternative sources of technology.

◆ Provide guidelines for technology acquisition.

KEY TERMS AND CONCEPTS

This chapter introduces the following key terms and concepts, listed in the order in which they appear:

infrastructure
information technology
   infrastructure
data infrastructure

application software
   infrastructure
configuration specifications
benchmarking

pricing structures
maintenance pricing

This chapter focuses on one of the three individual information management infrastructures defined in Chapter 2, namely, the information technology infrastructure. An *individual information technology infrastructure* consists of technical components directly supporting the individual. These components include a computer, communications technology, peripheral devices, system software, and support software. The infrastructure provides individuals with the tools to perform their work.

Determining and maintaining an individual information technology infrastructure involves numerous choices. The infrastructure should support the knowledge worker's tasks and activities and address other important factors including workgroup, departmental, and organizational requirements and constraints; personal characteristics; and the rapidly evolving technology. Individuals are usually able either to make critical decisions or influence decisions relative to their technology infrastructure. Using the simple process outlined in this chapter can help individuals make effective technology decisions.

Designing an Individual Information Management Infrastructure

◆ ◆ ◆ ◆ ◆ ◆ ◆ ◆ ◆ ◆ ◆ ◆ ◆ ◆ ◆ ◆ ◆ ◆ ◆ ◆

The definition of an information infrastructure is somewhat intuitive, but may be ambiguous. This chapter focuses on individual system infrastructures, but individual systems exist within the framework of the organization and its technical information management infrastructure. An individual infrastructure may also depend on individual work habits and ability.

Definition of Infrastructure

The term **infrastructure** usually refers to facilities, equipment, and services that provide an organization with the capability to perform its work. Chapter 2 identified four infrastructures for information management in an organization: (1) information technology, (2) data resources, (3) core applications, and (4) information systems personnel. An infrastructure provides general capabilities needed by an organization, but these capabilities must be made effective for the specific tasks and activities performed. As explained in Chapter 2, one of these (IS personnel) is not applicable to individual systems. Therefore, a conceptual framework for an individual information management system infrastructure consists of an information technology infrastructure, a data resources infrastructure, and individual application software infrastructures. All three are defined, although the chapter focuses only on technology.

The **information technology infrastructure** for an individual consists of the technical components (computer, communications, peripheral devices, system software, and support software) in a system directly supporting the individual. The system is usually under the individual's control and operation. The individual technical infrastructure can stand alone or be interconnected and interrelated to the larger information technology architecture of the department and the overall organization. It also supports collaborative work.

The **data infrastructure** for an individual consists of the files and databases that must be accessed by an individual. The data resources in the data infrastructure are based on the tasks and activities performed by the individual. The infrastructure consists of individual databases and access mechanisms and authority for databases maintained by others. The data resources may be maintained by the individual, a department, the organization, customers or suppliers, or external data suppliers.

The **application software infrastructure** consists of software applications necessary for the work of an individual. These applications may have been provided by the organization or developed by the individual, or they may be packaged software. The architecture of the application software infrastructure describes the structure of packages and custom applications and how they relate to individual work and the tasks to be performed.

Effects of Organizational and Departmental Infrastructures on Individual Systems

The three types of infrastructures defined in the preceding paragraphs emphasize the fact that individual information infrastructures (technology, data, and application software) are designed for the work of an individual, but fit within two broader sets of infrastructures for departments and organizations. The individual system should conform to all three architectures. For example, the individual may share data and application programs or packages with others in the department, or a local area network may provide shared access. With respect to the shared parts of the infrastructure, individual infrastructures must conform to the higher-level infrastructures of departments and organizations.

Since organizational infrastructures incorporate standards and policies, they may constrain the individual system. For example, the procurement policies set by the information systems function may constrain individual hardware and software choices. A decision by the organization to support a particular software package for spreadsheets provides strong rationale for the same package to be used for the individual system. A decision at the corporate level to adopt certain technology standards constrains the choices for the individual system. There are many strong reasons for these organizational constraints, including communications, advisory support, and cost.

Recognition of the cost involved to support personal computing infrastructures is leading many organizations toward more standardization. For example, estimates are that average annual organizational support costs for individual computers are equal to or exceed the average purchase price of their hardware and software.

In addition to technical standards, the organization has expectations and group norms that define desired and acceptable behavior. A corporate culture of cooperation will encourage adherence to standards; a culture of individual entrepreneurship may discourage standard solutions. The organization provides a context for deciding the extent to which a knowledge worker can innovate with an individual system. Some organizations encourage creativity and innovation; others emphasize adherence to standard procedures, even at the risk of inhibiting creativity.

Influence of Infrastructures on Individual Work Habits and Ability

With organizational infrastructures, the designs are generalized, and systems are designed to fit the organization's mission. There is usually no attempt to design for the differing needs of individuals since organizational infrastructures must persist through changes in staffing. An individual system is designed for and tailored to fit an individual. If that individual moves to another job or another organization, a new or revised system may be needed at the new position.

An important influence on the design of the infrastructure is, therefore, the locus of work and connectivity with other individuals or groups. If the tasks require sharing and interaction, the system should support connectivity and collaborative work. The mix of tasks and the events or conditions that define interrupts will influence the design of the system with respect to concurrent tasks and dealing with interrupts.

Individual abilities and aptitudes relative to technology will also influence the individual system. Some people have a high aptitude for technology and are eager to adopt new technologies; others find technology difficult and do not want to adopt new technology even after it is well proven.

Concepts Guiding Technology Evaluation and Selection

In some areas of product evaluation and selection, requirements can be very explicit and can be matched to technology with precision. In the case of the information technology infrastructure, requirements can be specified with only moderate completeness, and requirements can be matched to technology with only low to moderate precision.

Is it worthwhile to proceed with an explicit, step-by-step evaluation and selection process? Why not just make an overall judgment? The basis for an explicit process is the observed phenomenon that humans do not tend to do well in making intuitive judgments when a large number of somewhat ambiguous factors are present. An explicit process reduces the variations observed in intuitive overall assessment. The evaluation reveals important considerations and allows difficult issues to be addressed directly rather than being submerged in a fuzzy overall conclusion. The premise of the following process is that explicit processes, even with many hard-to-estimate elements, will yield better results than nonexplicit, intuitive conclusions. However, the process should be designed to keep the time and effort low enough to be consistent with the modest level of confidence and precision that can be expected in the results.

Identifying Information Technology Components

◆ ◆ ◆ ◆ ◆ ◆ ◆ ◆ ◆ ◆ ◆ ◆ ◆ ◆ ◆ ◆ ◆ ◆ ◆ ◆

An information management technology infrastructure provides the basis for a variety of different activities. The architecture should fit together both technically and economically. The following discussion examines individual components relative to needs and then combines these components into an architecture.

The approach is presented as a sequence of six steps:

1. Specify generalized software packages.
2. Define specialized software package support.
3. Specify need for development software to prepare custom applications.
4. Analyze communications software and hardware needs.
5. Analyze system software and system management software needs.
6. Analyze hardware needs.

However, as illustrated in Figure 15-1, the analysis may need to iterate back at any step to modify a previous analysis. For example, when analyzing hardware, it may be necessary to iterate back to generalized software packages to consider the effect of tentative hardware decisions on software packages.

Specify Generalized Software Packages to Support Activities

Task/activity analysis (Chapter 3) identifies the activities that should be supported by the information management infrastructure. Without specifying the details of features that will be important, the activities suggest the need for software packages that provide the functionality usually required for the activities.

The idea of an infrastructure indicates some generality of support, so that the system will respond to variations within the same general category of needs. Generalized software packages provide a broad range of capabilities for the knowledge work activities already identified and for responding to new needs as they arise. For personal computer systems, generalized packages are very cost effective.

The mapping of needs from task/activity analysis to generalized packages is straightforward. Although software packages are most economically available in package suites sold as a unit, a first cut analysis should treat each software function separately. The results of an individual generalized software package

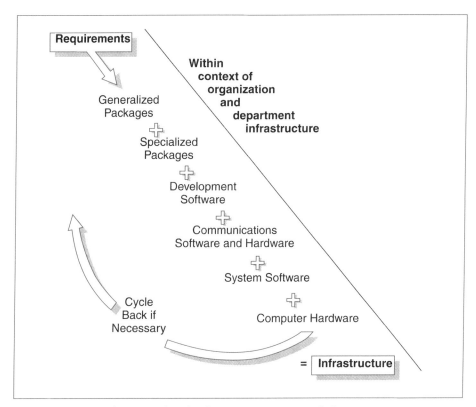

FIGURE 15-1 *Flow of individual infrastructure analysis*

analysis is a list of the generalized software packages needed. The analysis is by individual function rather than as packages that combine more than one major function.

Define Specialized Software Packages for Tasks

Generalized software packages provide broad support, but they may not meet specific needs. As illustrated in the following examples, many specialized packages are designed for knowledge work tasks or classes of tasks.

Examples
An individual needs to input graphs, pictures, and text not available on computer media. In addition to scanning hardware, specialized software to control the scanner, manipulate graphics, and convert text into machine-readable form may be part of the requirement. ◆

An individual needs to keep track of a stock portfolio. This could be done with a spreadsheet, a generalized software package. However, specialized software for keeping track of investments is available. Such software is easier to use and provides more advanced capabilities. To illustrate the extended, specialized capabilities, several financial management packages support automatic retrieval of specified stock prices via the Internet. ◆

Individual and business tax returns can be prepared using spreadsheets or word processors. However, there are specialized tax packages that support data input, output, computations, and rules to simplify this task. ◆

Accounting and billing for a small professional practice can be done with generalized software. However, practice management software is available for many professions. As an illustration, a professional software package for a psychologist will include client record keeping, billing, and insurance reports. ◆

The process of analysis involves examining each task and its activities to identify needs that are not met or are poorly met by generalized packages and then listing known specialized packages. If no specialized packages are known, but there is a reasonable expectation that a specialized package exists, the requirement should be listed for later search. The result of the analysis is a list of needs and known specialized software packages (or notes to search for specialized packages likely to be available).

Specify Need for Custom Software Development Tools

A clear definition of tasks and activities that are candidates for custom software development is needed at this time. A discussion of the reasoning that led to these candidates is also important. A list of generalized and specialized software considered for this task/activity and the reasons these are inadequate should be sufficient.

Custom software may be developed or prototyped by an individual using development software tools. (These tools assist a developer in designing and programming an application.) At this stage of planning for technology components, noting the need for development software and the type of potential custom software is sufficient.

Analyze Communications Hardware and Software Needs

Communications hardware and software needs are considered together because communications software is closely coupled to the communications hardware.

Software must be able to interact with existing networks supported by the organization. The corporate systems group will normally take care of any local area network that connects an individual to a workgroup, a department, or the organization. The corporate group may also provide and support a wide area network connecting individuals, plants, and sales locations within the organization (an intranet). The group may also provide individuals with software for managing interactions with these networks, and with connections to the Internet or to another external network, usually through the local area network.

Telephony services are rapidly being combined with data communications facilities and computing equipment via technology such as voice mail and computer dialing. For the communications components analysis, list any specific software that is needed to use company local and wide area networks and any other computer communication or telephony services.

Hardware and software must also be able to support independent communications outside the company networks. This may include fax, e-mail, access to commercial data services, the Internet or similar external network access, and telephony services. Internet software may also be required. This may include Web browser software, file transfer software, and other utility functions.

Some tasks and activities might require information dissemination, either on an intranet or the Internet. Information dissemination requires packages in the information server category and may impose both hardware and systems software requirements.

Communications outside the organization will require connectivity with local networks or communication carrier services for wide area access. The carriers provide a wide range of services from long-distance calls to high-speed data channels. At this step, list the major communications service requirements that are not part of the current organizational infrastructure, as well as the hardware and software needed to support expected independent communications requirements.

Analyze System and System Management Software Needs

The operating system is an important part of an individual system, but individual choices may be limited. Organizational policies and standards will often specify a set of options together with selection criteria. Maintaining compatibility with colleagues, departments, and the company, plus complying with software standards will constrain the choice even further. The selection of an operating system or even a particular version of an operating system has a far-reaching, long term impact. Most operating systems facilitate data exchange with other combinations of hardware and system software. However, there is always a cost in terms of increased time and effort or increased risk of error or failure when more than one operating environment is used. In this step, list the operating system selection that meets organizational policies, plus any other group compatibility considerations.

Operating systems are designed to include system management features. However, many desirable system management capabilities are provided only by additional software. The trend is to bundle many desirable features into future releases of the operating system. For example, data compression tools came into general acceptance as add-on software packages, but they are now included in many operating systems. Systems management includes features such as backup and recovery, virus checking, and hard drive analysis. For this step, also list requirements for any system management software not included in the operating system.

Analyze Hardware Needs

The hardware components for an individual system can be thought of as a standard configuration plus additions. Analysis can be divided into peripherals, memory size, and processor speed. The peripherals reflect needs based on tasks and activities. Memory size and processor speeds reflect judgment about performance (and costs/availability). Consider the locus of work. If all of a person's work is performed in one location, a desktop system offers performance advantages. If work can or must be performed in multiple locations, consider various alternatives that provide portable computing.

The following peripherals must be considered in specifying hardware components:

◊ Monitor screen size, resolution, and color capabilities (based on amount of usage, task switching requirements, and vision requirements of the user)

◊ CD-ROM drive to support need for relatively static materials

◊ Speakers and sound board for sound output

◊ Printer, including speed, color, and font capabilities

◊ Hard drive capacity and speed

◊ Internal or external fax modem

◊ Scanner to digitize text, pictures, and graphs

◊ Diskette drives

◊ Tape or other drive for backup

◊ Local area network interface

Memory requirements are dependent upon the operating system and the packaged software that will be used. While memory chips are relatively inexpensive, modern software packages require large amounts of memory. Graphic interface systems also require ever-increasing amounts of memory. The preferred approach to estimating memory requirements is to be sure to support the most demanding application software that will be used. Especially when a high degree of task switching is to be supported, estimate conservatively (that is, on the high side).

There are several important factors to consider in estimating disk storage requirements. For many knowledge workers, the software itself (such as word processors and spreadsheets) will use several times as much disk storage as working data and files. An exception is when multimedia must be supported. Many forms of multimedia make high demands on disk storage. If multimedia is not involved, a practical guideline is to total the storage requirements of all the software needed, and then double that number. However, note that in many networked (LAN) environments, software is accessed from a central server and does not consume local disk storage.

Processor speed requirements cannot be estimated precisely. Software that operates primarily on text can be supported at the low end of currently available speeds. A high proportion of graphics generally requires hardware near the upper end of the speed range. Certain tasks, such as mathematical modeling or processing very large spreadsheets, may require hardware at the upper end of the performance spectrum.

The need for concurrency increases performance requirements. Like humans, computers waste resources when switching tasks. From 10 percent to 50 percent of a processor's capacity may be used by an operating system and ancillary software supporting a user who must have several applications active at the same time.

Specifying an Architecture of Components

◆ ◆

Specifying an architecture for an individual computer system without detailed specifications is like specifying the layout of a house without detailed blueprints. Only the rooms, utilities, and site constraints are shown. Likewise, an architecture of components brings the specifications together in a tentative system. Matching a proposed system architecture with requirements allows an evaluation of the proposed system. Two critical issues must be considered: sufficient room for expansion and balancing of the system.

Room for Expansion

One issue in specifying an architecture of components is making sure there is sufficient expansion for the replacement time horizon. A reasonable replacement horizon is two to three years for active users, but as much as four or five years for users who anticipate little change in their tasks and activities. Feasible expansion includes additional peripheral devices, additional memory, and increased disk storage. There should be no technical constraints on add-ons to double available memory and disk storage. Where doubling memory or storage capacity may be a problem (as it is in portable computers), an investment in excess capacity that extends the useful life may be justified.

Balancing of System

Balancing of the system involves examining the different components for bottlenecks and for peripherals that do not fit the speed and performance of the rest of the system. A slow printer with a high-performance system or a fast color printer with a low-performance system are examples of unbalanced systems. There are many complex balancing issues that require expert advice. One important problem area is support for graphics displays. A matching combination of graphics monitor, high-speed processor bus, video processing logic, and video memory is necessary to obtain a specified level of performance.

After listing components and tentative specifications for each, examine each component in terms of expansion and balance. Then compare this configuration with those offered by vendors as a check against errors in configuring the system. This comparison may reveal features and specifications that had not been considered. You may also want to consider other resources, such as evaluations and comparisons published in the trade press or provided on the Internet. The final result is a specification for hardware, communications, and software.

An Example of Configuration Specifications

The configuration analysis in this section was performed by the supervisor of a group that prepares databases for legal research. The requirements for hardware are based on software requirements. These are in turn based on tasks and activities. The manager has documented the need for the **configuration specifications** by following the six-step analysis.

1. *Generalized software packages.* The supervisor's requirements for generalized software suggest the following packages:
   a. Word processor
   b. Spreadsheet
   c. Database
   d. E-mail, desk-top productivity, and PIM (personal information manager)
   e. Connectivity (mainframe terminal emulation software)
   f. Connectivity (Unix connection)
   The first three software packages represent core tools necessary for reporting and analysis. Spreadsheet and database packages are used by the

supervisor for querying, analyzing, and charting staff salary information, project labor hours, and schedule management. An e-mail and PIM system are important for intra- and inter-department communication, such as meeting scheduling. The two connectivity packages are for tracking the progress of work being run on the mainframe and Unix systems. They also provide utilities for uploading and downloading. As a supervisor, he uses software for his processing tasks and to access the task software of employees for training, mentoring, and troubleshooting project difficulties.

2. *Specialized software packages.* The supervisor of the group preparing databases for legal research has requirements for the following specialized software:

   a. User interfaces to the company's information products
   b. Research software
   c. Employee evaluation software

   The company has created specialized software for accessing and searching information databases and researching CD-ROMs. The company has also built research products in off-the-shelf specialty software. These are used for product testing and troubleshooting for the work being done by the group. Employee evaluation software is needed for generating and customizing employee evaluations. This software allows the supervisor to concentrate on employee evaluation and standardizes the evaluation process.

3. *Custom software development tools.* In addition to generalized and specialized software, the supervisor and the workgroup require the following custom software development tools:

   a. Macro additions for word processing and spreadsheet package
   b. Internally developed publications systems

   The group is responsible for data conversion and maintains several hundred macros representing thousands of lines of code. These turn an off-the-shelf word processor into interactive mark-up software. Most of the mainframe publication management systems are internally created. They have been developed specifically for the tasks and modified to suit the group's needs.

4. *Communications hardware and software.* The supervisor and database preparation group have requirements for the following communications hardware and software:

   a. Internally developed data acquisition software
   b. Communications software
   c. Modem access (network modem pool)
   d. Connection to local servers, printers, and mainframe (token ring adapter connection)
   e. Voice mail

Access to the networks is important because relatively little data is stored on stand-alone equipment. Almost all software, including the operating software, is housed on the networks to simplify software management and upgrading. When network connections are unavailable, so are most of the software tools necessary to perform jobs. Voice mail access is imperative. Employees must be able to retrieve messages from remote locations. Message forwarding capability is also critical.

5. *Operating system and system management software.* The operating system requirements include the following:
   a. DOS
   b. Windows
   c. Mainframe job control utility

   DOS is needed to run applications that are not Windows applications. Windows helps increase the ability to multitask. A typical set of tasks that are performed concurrently require four to five general software packages to be open. Much of the data processing is done in a mainframe environment. Mainframe time share software is used to manage resources and job submittal.

6. *Hardware configuration.* The following hardware requirements are defined by the supervisor based on tasks, activities, and software requirements (they are fairly standard, provide for growth, and are balanced):
   a. PC with sufficient RAM and processor speed (120 MHz Pentium with 16M RAM)
   b. External CD-ROM drive
   c. Locally connected laser printer
   d. LAN access to four network servers and high-speed networked laser printer
   e. 15-inch monitor
   f. 3.25-inch disk drive
   g. Minimal hard disk space (1 GB)
   h. Telephone

   As the number of concurrent tasks increases, memory and memory management become increasingly important. Working with extremely large spreadsheet and database tables requires an ever-increasing amount of RAM. Since the group's product is a CD-ROM, the drive is imperative for testing. Data is stored on several different networks with ready access. Because of the sensitive nature of some of the supervisor's work (such as disciplinary documentation and salary increase proposals), he has a printer attached locally. This is to avoid embarrassment and legal implications of someone picking up a sensitive printout at a network printer and reading it. However, access to a high-capacity laser printer on the network is needed for printing out large documents.

Evaluating Sources of Technology

◆ ◆

This section discusses general factors to consider in selecting among alternative technologies and vendors. Topics include single-source versus multiple-source technology acquisition, the implications of an operating environment, stability of technology, stability of vendor, reliability of products and services, and compatibility of vendor products (see Figure 15-2).

Single-source versus Multiple-source Technology Acquisition

The issue of single-source versus multiple-source for information technology is similar to the issue for other technology. Multiple sources offer greater opportunity for cost savings and improvements in performance of individual

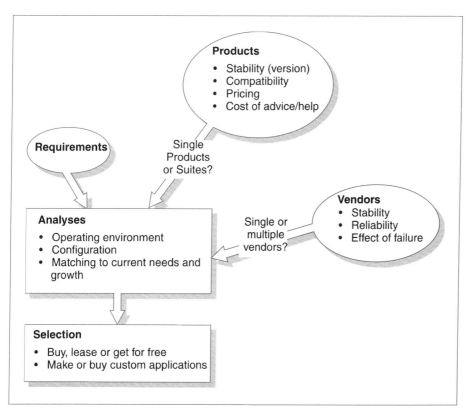

FIGURE 15-2 *The selection process for information technology*

components. However, the risk is that the technology from multiple vendors may not fit together in a system. A single source provides significant assurance that the components are compatible.

Personal computers have become relatively standard. Therefore, it is technically quite feasible to acquire components from multiple sources and successfully assemble a system at virtually any desired level of performance. This is the case with external devices such as printers and monitors. It can also be true for internal devices such as disk drives and plug-in boards.

Significant savings from multiple sources for internal components may not be achieved since the total cost of separate components may exceed assembled system prices. Additionally, warranty protection may be lost or reduced. In spite of standards, there is some risk that assembly from components can introduce problems. Therefore, a single source is usually preferred for all internal components. External peripherals do not present the same problem, but economies for external peripherals are often available when complete systems are acquired.

Implications of the Operating System

The operating system significantly affects the capabilities of computers. There are only a few different personal computer operating systems, so analysis can be limited. The operating system also has an effect on the availability of hardware and software for a given architecture. Both software vendors and after-market hardware component vendors must meet specifications related to the operating system. This has resulted in a much greater variety of software available for the leading architecture.

Most personal computers use Microsoft Windows, either version 3 or Windows 95. A minority use IBM's OS/2, while another minority still use some form of DOS. Some professions, such as the graphic arts, are dominated by the Apple Macintosh™ with its proprietary operating system. Another important category is the technical workstation, the platform of choice in many design professions such as engineering. The majority of technical workstations run the vendor's proprietary version of the Unix operating system. Microsoft's NT operating system is rapidly gaining acceptance at the low end of the technical and business workstation market.

Comparative performance is rarely a deciding issue in the selection of a personal computer operating system. Three other factors dominate the selection:

1. Personnel training and experience
2. Availability of both generalized and specialized software packages
3. Workgroup compatibility

The cost of learning an unfamiliar operating system can be very high, perhaps as much as several work-months of lost time. Software package availability is critical. Competition within an operating system domain results in increased package availability. The workgroup compatibility issue is larger than just data exchange. Shared terminology and concepts resulting from the same operating system are often of significant value.

Additional information about the capability and performance of operating systems is widely available in the trade press and in research reports. Where performance (speed and capacity) is a significant criterion, statistics from tests conducted by computer publications and labs may be useful, but such comparisons are only weak substitutes for **benchmarking** (running systems with a mix of typical applications to obtain a measure of performance under operating conditions). However, the cost of benchmarking is prohibitive in all but a few special cases.

Stability of Technology

New technology tends to be less stable and have more problems than mature technology. However, new technology may have more desirable features and improved capabilities. Vendors often issue "beta test" versions to selected customers who are willing to try the new technology and provide feedback in return for being on the leading edge of change.

Individuals who are innovators in the use of technology may find it useful to try technology that has not yet proven stable. However, most knowledge workers are not in the innovator category with respect to technology. Therefore, they should not adopt technology that is so new that it does not yet have a record of stability in performance. The adage, "If it isn't broken, don't fix it," applies very well to early adoption of computer technology: if the current system is working, don't "fix" it with unproven new technology. Another adage, "Never use the 'point zero' version of anything," counsels waiting for the relatively problem-free second version of any software.

Stability of Vendor

It is relatively easy for a vendor to enter the market for hardware and software components for personal computer systems. The desirable results of the low barriers to entry are high competition, high innovation, and low prices. The undesirable effects are a large number of vendors without a proven history of performance and a high failure rate.

If a hardware or software component is from a relatively new and, therefore, unstable vendor, a useful analysis is to estimate the effects of vendor failure and compare this with the benefits from using the products. For example, a specialized software package may provide excellent capabilities, but if the vendor fails, the software will not be updated. If the product is very good and has a reasonable life expectancy, acquisition may still be a good decision.

Given the dynamic quality of the information technology industry, a person designing a system should be open to new vendors. However, analysis prior to acquisition of a product from such a vendor should explicitly consider the consequences of vendor failure.

Reliability of Products and Services

For individual users, who generally find it difficult to deal with defective products, the reliability of vendor products is a primary concern. The reliability issue applies not just to the products themselves, but also to ease of setup and ability to obtain technical support to deal with problems. Some vendors have excellent reputations for quality products and prompt responses to problems; others have poor records. When the vendor has supplied hardware, but not the operating system, it may be difficult to sort out the sources of the problem.

◊xamples

An individual user of a personal computer system purchased it from a mail-order vendor. At installation, she could not find the connecting wires for the speakers. A call to the vendor handled the request promptly—the wires were contained within the speakers themselves. About two years later (but within the warranty period), the color on the monitor failed. It took six calls and significant time on hold to reach the right technical support person. When the vendor representative heard the symptoms, he indicated a diagnosis of monitor failure or color board failure. Both components were sent with instructions to try the new monitor first. If the new monitor did not correct the problem, she was to install the new color board. The monitor worked and the old monitor and the unused color board were returned to the vendor. ◆

An individual user had his system ordered by the organization's computer services department, which ordered installation of Windows 3.1 instead of the newer Windows 95. Windows 95 was installed after the system was received. When the CD-ROM drive failed to work (even though a diagnostic routine pronounced it as working), the company was called. The diagnosis was confused because the company had delivered a different operating system with the computer. However, the company technical representative, on the phone with the user, performed a number of diagnostic steps. The drive was found to be working, but there was a problem with the operating system. The technical analyst thought it was a virus. A virus detection program was used and found the virus. The problem was not hardware or operating system, but a virus that destroyed the driver software for the CD-ROM. ◆

Compatibility of Vendor Products

Products must be compatible with the operating environment. Standard interfaces provide significant assurance of compatibility. However, many features of operating environments are not standardized. This can lead to incompatibilities as the versions of software for the different vendors are placed in service. For example, a vendor of an application software package must have an interface with parts of the operating environment. Much of the interface is specified by the operating system vendor, but other features may be left to the application vendor. A new operating system may change the interfaces with respect to these optional features.

The second issue of compatibility is upward and downward compatibility of package software versions. Does version 2.0 accept the files and input from version 1.0? Can version 1.0 read and process data for and from version 2.0? This upward and downward compatibility can be very significant for applications. Incompatibility leads to high cost for installation and use of new versions.

A third issue of compatibility is data exchange among a group of packages. Users of word processing often wish to insert spreadsheets into documents. Users of spreadsheet software may need to incorporate data from databases maintained on database software. If this is an important requirement, the compatibility of products should be tested.

The issue of compatibility across application software packages has been addressed by vendors. They offer a suite of application packages that are lower in cost (on a per application basis), are simpler to install, and are compatible across applications. Although no suite is perfect on all dimensions, desired goals may be met better with suites than with individual applications from different vendors (see Table 15-1). However, there may be a loss of functionality because the products in the suite may not be the best in all categories.

Technology Acquisition

◆ ◆

Although the technology acquisition process follows proven principles of asset acquisition, there are some unique features of information technology to consider. For example, the process needs to consider not only traditional buy or lease but also obtaining "freeware" or "shareware." The technology acquisition process should consider not only traditional "make or buy analysis," but also **pricing structures** for original purchase and maintenance.

Buy, Lease, or Get for Free

Outright purchase is generally the most cost-effective approach for low-priced technology that cannot support the extra cost of dealing with leases. Vendors usually have a site or volume license pricing scheme that significantly reduces software costs when there are many users in an organization. Leasing is used to reduce technology uncertainty. With a lease, the person or organization acquiring the technology has a fixed price and reduced technology obsolescence risk.

Table 15-1 Eight Desired Goals of a Compatible Suite of Software	
Desired Goal of Suite	*Comments on Goal*
1. Inexpensive	Low cost per application in suite.
2. Well integrated	Shared tools for common operations and data exchange without difficulties.
3. Economical in use	Reasonable in use of disk space and system resources.
4. Easy to learn and use	Interactive tutorials and context-sensitive help.
5. Easy to customize	Consistent methods for altering menus, toolbars, dialog boxes, and other customization.
6. Simple to do collaborative work	Simple to import, export, collaborate on documents, do version control, etc.
7. Easy to install and uninstall	Install complete, custom, or minimal installation. Uninstall facilities.
8. Good assistance	Clear documentation and readily available technical support by telephone.

Source: George Campbell and John Walkenbach, "Are Suites Worth It?" *PC World*, May 1994, pp. 112–138.

Unlike many other areas of technology, information technology has low-cost or free software available. This "freeware" or "shareware" may be completely without cost, or it may be on an honor system in which a voluntary payment is made if the software proves to be useful. Some of the share- and freeware packages are excellent and dominate utility software categories such as file compression. The corporate information systems function has historically resisted the use of software in this category on the theory that "you get what you pay for" and because of concern for viruses.

Getting software free does not include unauthorized use of commercial software purchased for use by another. Such "pirating" is both illegal and unethical. Apart from the ethical arguments, economic incentives for piracy tend to be small because of the low cost of most packaged software. Companies that have encouraged (or not prevented) software piracy have been heavily penalized when taken to court.

Make or Buy Custom Applications

The "make or buy issue" is simple if software packages are available. The rule is to use the existing package even if it isn't perfect. The question is how to proceed when there is no existing software to purchase. Should the software be developed by an individual, an outside vendor, or a professional developer in the corporate information management function?

Developing a custom application has some real benefits and some significant costs. If an individual develops it, the software will fit individual needs. The individual as developer can make corrections easily without cumbersome interactions with outsiders. The costs are individual time and effort (which may involve substantial learning time) and the costs of failure from a poor job of design, construction, testing, and documentation. An individual application may work well for the developer, but it may be difficult to transfer to a colleague or a successor in the job position.

The benefits of contracting to an outsider are the use of a professional developer who can be instructed to include controls, adequate testing, and documentation. The outsider may also be able to suggest solutions not considered by someone "too close to the problem." The direct cost will most certainly be higher for an external developer, but indirect costs of do-it-yourself systems are often underreported.

Pricing Structures in the Industry

The pricing structure in the personal computer software industry is to price very low in anticipation of high-volume sales. Once the market leader prices this way, competitors are obliged to price in the same way.

Six significant price reductions that are routinely available: (1) introductory, (2) upgrade, (3) competitive upgrade, (4) bundled prices, (5) site license, and (6) selected discounts.

1. *Introductory.* A low price is given at the introduction of a new product. Early adopters are rewarded for their willingness to buy a new product. Once a customer has adopted a product, there is a strong incentive to stay with the same vendor in subsequent versions. For example, two new vendors of personal tax software virtually gave away the software the first year in order to obtain customers for subsequent years.

2. *Upgrade.* There is often a price reduction for existing customers who upgrade to a new version. For example, a version 2.0 may be priced to owners of version 1.0 at one-third the price for new adopters of the software. This preserves the customer base.

3. *Competitive upgrade.* In an attempt to increase market share, vendors offer deep discounts (often the same as upgrade discounts) to anyone who indicates ownership of a competitor's product.

4. *Bundled prices.* There may be an effective price reduction when software is bundled with other software (from either the same vendor or another

cooperating vendor). For example, a vendor of a new spreadsheet processor package may offer it in a bundle with a well-known word processing package at very little or no extra cost. The objective is to establish a customer base of users. A variation of this is the packaging of a suite of software packages at a much lower aggregate price than the individual packages.

5. *Site license.* This comes in two variations. One allows unlimited use of the software at a single site (such as a network) for a fee based on the expected number of users. The second method is to price for only a certain number of users at the same time. In other words, there is a limited number of users of the package at any one time.

6. *Selected users.* Vendors often reduce prices for a selected population of new users. The most prominent example is the educational discount offered by most software vendors to students and faculty. These prices are usually available only through the college bookstore or other restricted outlet.

Maintenance Pricing

Maintenance pricing relates to the cost of upgraded versions and to the cost of advice when problems are encountered. The cost of upgrading was mentioned previously. Unlike large software systems for mainframes, where maintenance is a large ongoing expense, version updating costs for microcomputers are relatively low. In fact, upgrade prices are often so low that the relevant issue is not the cost of the upgrade, but the time and effort required to install the new version and adapt to the changes. In other words, the most significant cost the user may incur is the cost of learning new features and procedures and using them until they become automatic.

Support for software has proven to be very costly for software vendors. Consequently, the software industry has moved to limit free support. In many cases, free support is limited to 30 or 90 days from purchase. Many vendors charge for support only on a "per call" or "per minute" basis. For multi-user site licenses, software vendors provide a menu of support choices and costs, often based on fixed annual fees.

Summary

◊ ◊ ◊ ◊ ◊ ◊ ◊ ◊ ◊ ◊ ◊ ◊ ◊ ◊ ◊ ◊ ◊ ◊ ◊ ◊

◊ The individual information management infrastructure is constrained by the organization and departmental infrastructures. Within those infrastructures, the individual system supports task and activity requirements. It can be tailored to individual aptitudes and abilities as long as it supports these requirements and provides needed connectivity.

◊ The approach to selecting information technology components for an individual infrastructure consists of a sequence of steps: (1) specify generalized software packages, (2) define specialized software package support, (3) specify need for development software to prepare custom applications, (4) analyze communications software and hardware needs, (5) analyze system software and system management software needs, and (6) analyze hardware needs. An architecture of components meets these specifications and considers expansion potential and system balancing.

◊ Decisions must be made relative to sources of technology, operating system, stability of technology and vendor, and compatibility. Software may be purchased, leased, or obtained free.

◊ Custom software may be developed by the individual user or contracted with outside developers.

◊ Pricing structures for software packages are designed to obtain first-time users for a package and to retain or expand the customer base for the supplier. A factor in the selection process is the cost of upgrading and the cost of obtaining advice or help. A policy of upgrading only to proven, reasonably mature software is usually best for an individual.

EXERCISES

1. Specify a personal information infrastructure of hardware, software, and communications. Base your requirements on a task/activity analysis you completed in Chapter 3. Make the specifications in six parts, with each element justified by one or two sentences: generalized software packages, specialized software packages, custom software, communications hardware and software, communications services, operating system and system management software, and hardware configuration. Follow the pattern of the example in this chapter.

2. Analyze your present personal information infrastructure (home or office, or both) and define changes. Assign priorities to these changes.

3. Choose a particular generalized or specialized software category based on your activity analysis. Locate one or more evaluations of this category, either in the trade press or on the Web. Recommend and justify a selection based on the data you found.

4. Interview one or more knowledge workers. Determine the selection process employed for their current infrastructure and assess their satisfaction/dissatisfaction with it.

5. Add to the preceding exercise a task and activity analysis for the knowledge worker. Prepare a personal information technology infrastructure specification for the worker and compare it with the existing technology infrastructure.

6. Select a software suite and evaluate it using the eight goals in Table 15-1.

Cooperating with the Information Management Function

◊ ◊ ◊ ◊ ◊ ◊ ◊ ◊ ◊ ◊ ◊ ◊ ◊ ◊ ◊ ◊ ◊ ◊ ◊

OBJECTIVES

After completing this chapter, you should be able to:

◆ Explain organizational productivity objectives for products and services and business process improvement.

◆ Explain the differences between small and large systems development.

◆ Explain the standard-setting role of the information systems function.

◆ List and explain problems that could result from user-developed systems.

◆ Explain the benefits of small-system development knowledge for careers in functional areas of business.

◆ Explain the benefits of small-system development knowledge for careers in information systems.

◆ Describe the functions of the following information systems support personnel: user support specialist, systems analyst, programmer/analyst, programmer.

KEY TERMS AND CONCEPTS

This chapter introduces the following key terms and concepts, listed in the order in which they appear:

process entropy
small system development

private systems
public (or formal) systems

information center
Help Desk

Previous chapters explained how to apply information technology to the tasks and activities of knowledge workers working alone or in collaboration with others. This chapter returns to the theme of productivity introduced in Chapter 1 and explains how personal productivity objectives fit with organizational productivity. The idea of a small system development process explained in Chapter 2 is reviewed and its relationship to methods for developing multiuser or complex, large organization applications is explained. The chapter concludes with a discussion on making the transition from building personal systems to cooperating with the information systems function.

Additional Organizational Productivity Objectives

Productivity is a fundamental objective in virtually all organizations. Productivity in production of goods is achieved if there is an increase in the quantity of outputs for a given set of inputs. For example, productivity in production of potatoes can be computed easily. Potatoes are a well-defined product without significant change over the years. The costs of production can be compared to the quantities produced. If outputs are increased or costs are reduced, there has been an increase in productivity. If a new fertilizer increases yields, the productivity effect (after factoring in the cost of the fertilizer application) can be computed.

As explained in Chapter 1, this simple approach to defining productivity works well for physical outputs that do not change over time, but it does not work as well with knowledge work outputs. In the traditional approach to productivity analysis, investment in information technology should reduce the number of clerical and knowledge workers. This reduction in employment costs would show up as an increase in productivity from information technology. The expected reduction in employment for clerical workers has often, but not always, occurred. When information technology is applied to knowledge work, a reduction in employment has seldom occurred.

The primary reason for the lack of knowledge worker staff reductions is that the savings are used for more effective work. These savings can be used for effectiveness by extending the scope of work and increasing work quality. Analyses can be performed with more assumptions and with more sophisticated methods not feasible without computers. Consequently, work can be more complete and timely, and coordination and communication can be improved. In other words, information technology investment tends to reduce time per unit of knowledge work, but the technology increases the quality and scope of the work. The productivity effect comes in the form of better decision and planning processes. In most cases, it does not reduce knowledge work employment (see Figure 16-1).

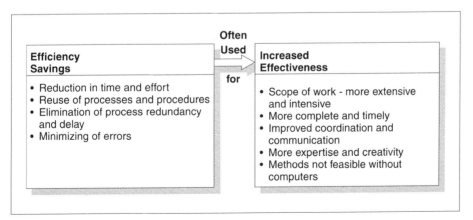

FIGURE 16-1   *Why information technology efficiencies don't reduce knowledge work employment*

Organizations have other uses for information technology. Business products, services, processes and service levels associated with them can improve significantly through the use of information technology. Through information technology, both clerical and knowledge workers have more information about products, suppliers, product availability, customers, and customer needs. This additional information makes possible personalized, more responsive services. In other words, information technology investment can be used for improved, more effective processes leading to better customer service and better decisions in responding to customers. There may be no reduction in employment related to the products and services.

The danger relative to productivity is that organizations will not use information technology effectively. Processes for analysis and decision-making will not be improved, and products, services, and activities will not be redesigned. This suggests three areas of productivity emphasis relative to investments in information technology: (1) knowledge work, (2) products and services, and (3) business processes (see Figure 16-2).

These three areas of productivity emphasis contain two levels of responsibility: an individual's responsibility to apply information technology to improve performance and productivity in individual and collaborative activities, and the individual's responsibility to participate in organizational efforts to achieve new or improved products and services, and implement improved business processes. Experience in applying information technology with small, individual and collaborative work systems will assist an individual in suggesting creative solutions for products, services, and business processes. Preceding chapters emphasized individual knowledge work improvement. This chapter focuses on productivity objectives at the organizational level and surveys use of information technology for improving products, services, and business processes.

Improvements in Products and Services

Chapter 5 analyzed individual work requirements and examined knowledge worker involvement in products and services, and how information technology might improve individual activities relative to them. An organizational level of analysis looks at the use of information technology for the design and delivery of products and services across all the functions of the organization. As illustrated in the following paragraphs, information technology can be applied in one of three ways: (1) as an integral part of the decision process to acquire products and services, (2) incorporated in the product or service itself, or (3) as a part of ongoing service or replacement.

1. *Part of the decision process to acquire products and services.* Information technology may assist customers by providing information processing

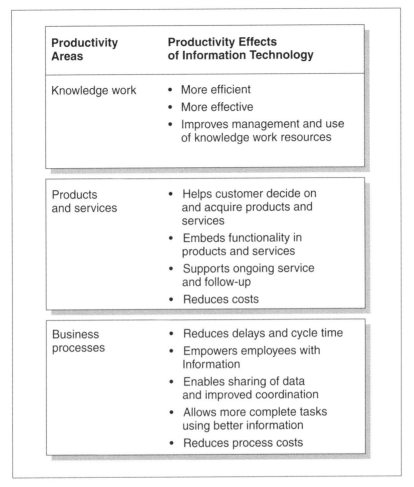

Productivity Areas	Productivity Effects of Information Technology
Knowledge work	• More efficient • More effective • Improves management and use of knowledge work resources
Products and services	• Helps customer decide on and acquire products and services • Embeds functionality in products and services • Supports ongoing service and follow-up • Reduces costs
Business processes	• Reduces delays and cycle time • Empowers employees with Information • Enables sharing of data and improved coordination • Allows more complete tasks using better information • Reduces process costs

FIGURE 16-2 *Productivity areas and productivity effects of information technology*

functions that will analyze customer requirements, suggest solutions, and provide scheduling, financing, and installation information. For example, an insurance sales representative may employ a software package to analyze customer requirements, suggest insurance plans, and provide information on costs for each year in the future.

2. *Incorporated in the product or service.* Information technology may be embedded in the product or service. An example is an automated teller machine that accepts deposits and provides account balance information. Many devices such as automobiles, VCRs, and cameras include information technology in the controls and functions of the products. A financial management package consists of software to maintain records and access financial information such as stock prices.

3. *Part of ongoing service or replacement.* Tracking products sold and following up with add-ons, product recalls, and replacement or service suggestions is made feasible with information technology.

This list of ways in which information technology is incorporated into products and services can guide individuals in being creative in suggesting applications of the technology.

Business Process Improvement

Business processes are the activities involved in tasks such as selling and servicing customers, obtaining or producing products, hiring and training employees, and billing and collecting amounts due. These processes can be improved with information technology. Cycle time may be significantly reduced, inventory may be reduced, and service made more prompt, complete, and reliable. In Chapter 5, individual analysis of requirements included examining a knowledge worker's involvement in business processes and analyzing how information technology might improve associated activities. An organizational level of analysis looks at redesign of business processes across all functions and activities. Information technology is typically a significant part of the redesign. Process change and improvement is indicated when:

1. There is a process that has degenerated, so that re-engineering it can produce significant improvement.
2. There are forces for organizational change in response to the environment of competition and regulation. The forces suggest broad changes involving business strategy, organizational design, and process redesign.

Processes represent an opportunity for change or improvement because there is a natural tendency for business processes to decay and become disorganized. This might be termed process "entropy." In physical systems, entropy is visible in physical decay or "falling apart." In business processes, entropy is represented by a disorganization into unnecessary activities. The ultimate disorganization or highest entropy is when everyone involved in the process is busy, but there is no useful result or no business purpose is being achieved. In other words, there is an inevitable and reoccurring opportunity to reengineer. The opportunity is not manifest by processes that don't work, but rather by processes that appear to work but have grown into a mixture of necessary and unnecessary activities with significant unnecessary delays and useless or unused information processing.

The decay—or **process entropy**—can be observed in characteristics such as:

◆ Undue delays in providing products or services
◆ Collection and storage of information that is never used

◆ Useful information that is not collected or stored

◆ Inflexible systems that lack requisite variety (a response of "because that is the policy" when a question cannot be answered)

◆ An accumulation of rules to cover situations that happened only once

◆ Evidence of unwillingness to empower people to make independent decisions.

Changes in the environment—such as changes in customer expectation, the actions of competitors, or new government regulations—frequently demand that the organizations make changes to:

◆ Revise objectives and strategies

◆ Restructure business processes across organizational boundaries

◆ Remove organizational barriers to communication

◆ Reduce process cycle time.

Indications of need to change or opportunities to benefit from changes include:

◆ Confusion and lack of shared meaning about process objectives

◆ Failure to agree about competitive and service strategies

◆ Functional boundaries that partition processes and restrict cooperation

◆ Multiple queues, delays, and inventories that ignore the purpose of the organization.

Organizational process change objectives include more flexibility, rapid response to changing demands, and reduced product and service cycle time. Achieving these objectives involves extensive use of information technology. The goals and objectives drive the application of information technology to:

◆ Improve coordination to reduce cycle time, delays, and queues of pending tasks

◆ Allow more effective communication with customers and suppliers by providing more information and more complete decision support

◆ Empower employees by providing them with more information about organizational objectives and more complete ability to see the process and decisions in context

◆ Capture and share data to improve understanding and coordination and reduce delays in processes

A knowledge worker who has evaluated individual systems and applied information technology for individual process improvement will be able to "scale up" to assist in larger organizational process and reengineering efforts.

Learning from Small System Application Development Principles

◆ ◆

Previous chapters pointed out that the process used to develop individual applications (small systems) is a simplified version of the large system development process. Some steps are eliminated or minimized, while others are reduced in scope. This section reviews two aspects that illustrate similarities and differences between the development of small systems and the development of applications that are large, either in size or in number of users. These two aspects are prototyping and the use of formal development methods.

Prototyping Methodology

Prototyping as a method in analysis, design, and implementation dominates in the development of individual applications. The tools and the programming environments for small applications provide excellent facilities for rapid prototyping. The following advantages were observed in the small system environment; in general, they also apply to large system development.

◆ *Prototyping assists in defining functional requirements.* The user/developer can establish an initial set of requirements, include them in the prototype, and use the results to prompt more requirements.

◆ *Prototyping assists in refinement.* Functional requirements can be tested and verified. They can be observed in the prototype and evaluated for robustness in use, usability, and error risk. The user/developer can approach refinement for these three issues in terms of an existing input and output prototype. The prototype allows other potential users in the area or department to try the application under actual working conditions and identify ambiguities and omissions in screens and operating instructions.

◆ *Prototyping assists in testing.* The existence of a physical representation of the way the application will operate provides a user/developer with a basis for testing inputs, logic, and outputs.

There are three important differences between prototyping in **small system development** and large system development: (1) the development environments, (2) the number of stakeholders, and (3) the robustness requirements.

1. *The development environments.* Small system development environments reduce the complexity of application development by reducing the options available to a developer. Most options have a default setting so a

developer can concentrate on the few options that make a difference to the application. The high proportion of default option settings means that the small system development environment allows rapid prototyping using the defaults. It also reduces the complexity of the logic that must be tested. Large system development environments are designed for professional developers; therefore, there are more development options and less use of defaults.

2. *The number of stakeholders.* The number of stakeholders affects the prototyping process. Since prototyping must begin with an initial solution, this should reflect the views of the important stakeholders. For example, an application used by both accounting and finance personnel should reflect both their needs. The number of different stakeholders increases the coordination that must take place during development. Each change in the prototype must be examined and approved by key stakeholders or stakeholder representatives.

3. *The robustness requirements.* The requirements for a robust application that will minimize user errors and help users recover from mistakes or system errors is increased with multiple users. A single-user application can take advantage of the knowledge of the user and eliminate many requirements. For example, a single user may be knowledgeable about inputs and aware of errors; the application need not be complete in handling all input conditions and errors. When an application must meet the needs of a wide range of diverse users, it must include many more controls, Help screen instructions, and clear and complete error messages. These requirements can easily double or triple the size of an application.

Formal Development Methods

Development of large, complex applications usually involves a system development methodology that defines the procedures and methods to be employed, the phases of the process, and deliverables at each phase. The requirements analysis phase of the methodology may include analyzing the existing system and eliciting and analyzing new system requirements. The analysis may involve a study group consisting of representatives of the major stakeholders (those affected by the new system) and system development personnel.

Many of the methods of large system development are designed to deal with complexity. Small system analysis can omit some of those methods, but they are still often useful if the small application increases in size (although it may remain small by professional developer standards). Large system analysis emphasizes formal modeling and representation for procedures and processes, data, and user interfaces. In the small system process, an informal verbal description may be sufficient to document analysis. The analysis itself may focus on an understanding of how the computer application will aid the knowledge work task, rather than on a formal analysis of processes and data.

Some system methodologies emphasize two levels of design: general and detailed. General design focuses on the overall flow and behavior of the application. Detailed design focuses on procedures, databases, and user interfaces (individual screens and printed outputs, such as reports). The need for formal design methods is less important in small applications because of less complex systems, but also because of the use of prototyping tools. The prototype (with some documentation notes) provides a method for design using a "trial and error" approach. Prototyping tools allow a general design to be established based on default settings. As the prototyping process proceeds, some of the default settings may be replaced with tailored features. The natural iterations of prototyping produce the detailed design products: screens, reports, and documents.

A large, complex application includes methods and tools to document the application and its programs and to keep track of the names and descriptions of processes and data items. Application program structure is diagrammed by methods such as program structure charts. A repository of data about the application will include names and descriptions for all data items (identified in the data model) and processes (identified in the process model). Small application implementation does not need such formal methods and tools, and documentation of small systems can employ simplified methods.

In a large, complex application, the logic and structure of program components may be defined by a pseudocode approach. In this method, the logic and structure are written in English-like statements that are complete enough to be understandable and structured like the program to be written. The conversion from pseudocode to computer language statements is essentially a mapping from the explanation to the program statements. The pseudocode establishes the structure of the program; the code follows this structure. In small system modules, the pseudocode approach may not be necessary. However, even simple modules often benefit from the discipline of being designed in pseudocode and then written in program code.

In large, complex system development, testing is a separate activity from design and coding of application programs. Separate staff may be used to develop test plans and data. Testing of modules is followed by testing of the entire application. In other words, modules (after being tested as independent modules) are tested in the context of the rest of the application. In small system implementation, the user/developer often does all testing, although it may be desirable to bring in others to assist.

During implementation and during maintenance, large systems undergo an evaluation, refinement, and integration process similar to the process prescribed for small systems. However, the methods are more formal and there is more emphasis on integration. Small system evaluation, refinement, and integration is done on a limited scale with fewer participants. In some cases, the user/developer is the only evaluator, but it is often prudent to involve other evaluators, especially the developer's colleagues.

Additional Concerns for User-developed Applications

The issue of risk with individual systems was discussed in Chapters 2 and 13. In Chapter 2, four concerns were explained relating to the risks introduced by eliminating the separation between developer and user. The user has a good understanding of requirements as they appear at the time; the developer has broader experience with systems and a higher level of development expertise and technical skill. Because of the lack of a dialog between a user and a professional developer, there is some likelihood that users may not identify complete and correct requirements, select the best methods and technology to use, test appropriately, and build in features to make the application robust and resistant to errors. Whereas Chapter 2 identified general risks of systems to be built, Chapter 13 emphasized the evaluation of a completed application. Since the system was assumed to be completed, the evaluation did not deal with testing, but focused on evaluating results with respect to three key issues: (1) fit of the completed system with real requirements, (2) robustness of the completed system in use, and (3) appropriate use of technology in the completed system.

The information systems organization has to develop large, complex applications used by many diverse users. Their requirements methods, development methods, robustness requirements, and testing reflect the characteristics of the systems they must build. The information systems organization may also have advisory and standards responsibility for individual systems and may assist in building small applications. In advising individuals developing systems for their own use, the information systems organization focuses on the concerns described earlier: requirements, methods and technology use, testing, and robustness. However, the context within which the information systems personnel operate is broader than that of an individual. This broader organizational context means that the information systems organization has three additional concerns relative to individual systems: the introduction of private systems, training support, and incompatible systems. (See Figure 16-3.)

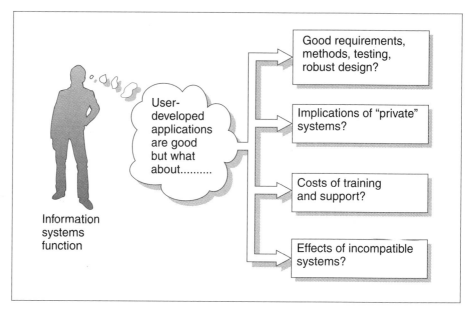

FIGURE 16-3 *Concerns of information systems function about user-developed systems*

Concern for Individual (Private) Systems

There have always been individual, **private systems** of information in organizations. Individual salespersons have their own notes and "black books." The contents of this important, private system may not be passed on to their successor. One of the trends in information systems has been to convert private information systems into **public (or formal) systems** that remain with the position when there is a change of personnel. These systems represent part of the "information assets" of the organization.

The development of systems by individual users tends to result in many private systems that may not be transferred to the subsequent office holder. The most common reason for failure to transfer a user-developed application to the next office holder is inadequate documentation (system documentation and user documentation). There are several reasons for this. One is that individual users tend to develop systems they understand. They do not need the documentation, structure, and quality required by an outside maintenance person. Another reason may be that the development effort to convert a private, individual system into a formal system is likely to exceed the original cost of development of the private system. There is a high cost associated with system conversions. On the other hand, the hidden costs of developing private systems instead of public systems may be very high. Benefits from private systems will not be passed on, or the systems may have to be redone by the next officeholder.

Concern for Training and Support

Earlier in the text, the cost of training and retraining was emphasized. Intuitive estimates of these costs tend to be too low, since individual developers frequently underestimate the time and effort they have spent learning. This underestimation has been noted in the case of software packages or new versions of packages. It does not take very long to learn a few basic instructions or the fundamental features of the package; however, it takes much longer to be an effective user and make the package the preferred mode of operation. If a software package is used infrequently, there is a relearning cost each time there is a delay between uses. For example, an accountant may use a graphics package only once a quarter to prepare graphs and charts for the board of directors meeting. Consequently, there is probably a relearning cost associated with each use.

Users may develop individual applications, but this does not eliminate the need for training and support. The user may not understand certain features and uses and may request information system training support. If the application is provided to another person, this may also create a need for training. If the user-developed application does not follow standards for elements such as application design, user interface, and error handling, developing a training program can be costly.

Concern for Incompatible Systems

The information systems function is responsible for planning and implementing the organization's information systems infrastructure. This includes ensuring that hardware, software, and systems are compatible and often involves establishing standards for hardware and software. Systems are designed to minimize incompatibilities. For example, the output of one system may be input to another application. The planning of the application structure includes such considerations.

In its advisory and support services for individuals, the information system function strives for a limited number of different hardware and software configurations in order to reduce the problems in providing help. Some organizations have strong rules against the use of unapproved software. The information systems function employs mechanisms to enforce version control for approved software.

An individual user developer may use approved, standard software but still employ nonstandard methods. This creates difficulties for the function if they are called upon for advice or help. It also presents problems relative to any data transfer or other interaction with organizational systems.

The Information Center in Support of Users

◆ ◆ ◆ ◆ ◆ ◆ ◆ ◆ ◆ ◆ ◆ ◆ ◆ ◆ ◆ ◆ ◆ ◆ ◆ ◆

In many organizations, the large number of users of personal computers and workstations has created a need for training, advising, installation and setup, and problem-solving services. These services may be provided as part of the organization's information management function, or the company may out-source the provision of these services to a specialized user-support provider. In both cases, the services are similar. The centrally located area in a large organization where users can come to receive training and access these services is often referred to as an **information center**.

The training services provided can range from formal courses on major software systems used by the organization to topical courses on how to use features of software packages. If the company acquires specialized software, the information center provides instruction (or works with the vendor in providing training).

The advisory services of the information center consist of evaluating and recommending hardware and software for individual systems and recommending training options. If the organization contracts with suppliers to provide items on the recommended list, the center will provide training and support services for this hardware and software. The information center does not routinely provide support services for hardware or software not on the list.

Although many personal computer systems come with much pre-installed software, there are still a number of installation and setup activities. Since an individual user seldom performs these activities, it is more efficient for an expert to assist in preparing the new installation for individual use. The installation process may include transferring files from an old system to a new one and selecting options that reflect both organizational standards and individual preferences.

Many information center services are provided by a **Help Desk** staffed by personnel who accept telephone inquiries or walk-in questions about hardware, software, and communications. Questions may range from simple queries about how to exit a certain program, to difficult questions related to advanced spreadsheet functions. If the Help Desk personnel do not know the answers, they know how to access experts on the software vendor staff. Some complex problems may require on-site visits. When Help Desk personnel work with a user's system and make changes, they are responsible for explaining the changes and testing the results.

Examples

A user unknowingly destroyed the directory of files on a diskette. A call to the Help Desk revealed the existence of a specialized program to recover files from a diskette. The user delivered the diskette to the information center for this service.   ◆

A user had a troublesome virus. The steps to locate and remove the virus required specialized skills. A Help Desk staff member "walked through" the steps with the user over the telephone.   ◆

Working with the Information Systems Function

◆ ◆ ◆ ◆ ◆ ◆ ◆ ◆ ◆ ◆ ◆ ◆ ◆ ◆ ◆ ◆ ◆ ◆ ◆ ◆

A knowledge worker who has applied the principles and methods explained in this text is in a position to work with the information systems function in connection with organization-wide applications and organizational infrastructures for information processing. Two roles in this connection are application development team member and steering committee member for information systems planning. The experience and knowledge developed during individual system development can also be used as preparation for a career as an information systems specialist (see Figure 16-4).

Working as a User Member of an Information Management Team

A knowledge worker who employs information technology effectively with individual systems can apply this knowledge as a member of teams doing large application system development and system planning. Members of an application development team have dual responsibilities for representing the requirements of their function and the overall interests of the organization. The role is manifest in both technical and social design choices. In other words, any application reflects a mixture of choices about the technology and how it is applied (technical design) and the way the technology will be applied by people (social design). A team member from a functional area can represent the views of the people who will use the system or be affected by it. The various combinations of technical and social design choices can be evaluated in terms

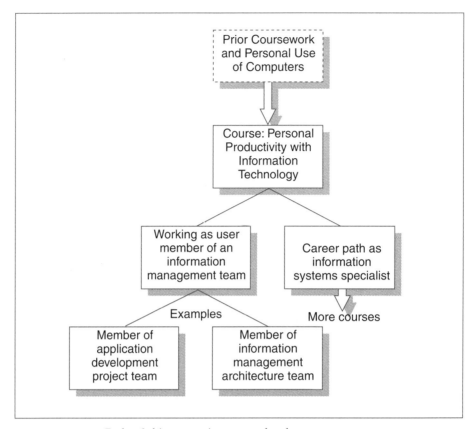

FIGURE 16-4 *Role of this course in career development*

of the user community. Given that systems often cross organizational boundaries or require some redesign of the organization, members of the application development team should be able to take an organizational view as well as representing their respective areas.

Some of the principles observed in individual systems may be important in making decisions about organization-wide systems. For example, the principle that packaged systems should always be evaluated as the first contender for an application can also be applied to organizational applications. The value of prototyping and well-designed user interfaces are well supported by experience with individual systems.

Knowledge workers experienced in managing an individual system are in position to contribute to the planning effort for the organization's information architecture. These individuals will have had experience in accessing organizational databases and using facilities provided by the organization and in accessing external data. They will have firsthand knowledge of the current hardware and software infrastructure and can, therefore, be effective team members. Personal experience can also be applied to issues of standards, departmental systems, and support for individual systems.

Career Development for Information Systems Specialists

For many, the knowledge of personal productivity with information technology fills a direct need, since they can be more effective in managing their information resources. For example, they can work in areas such as finance, marketing, human resources, or accounting, and they will be more effective and efficient in applying the powerful technologies available for knowledge work.

Individuals planning careers as information systems specialists will be able to use knowledge and experience with individual systems as a step in career development. The scope of work in individual systems allows broad experience, yet each part of the experience can be related to the work of information systems specialists. Three broad classes of specialists illustrate the concept of individual systems experience in career development: (1) user support, (2) systems analyst, and (3) programmer.

1. *User support specialist.* User support requires a lower level of technical knowledge than development, but the support person benefits from knowledge of the domains being supported. User support specialists for accounting will be more effective if they have accounting experience. The methods presented in this text for helping knowledge workers improve their productivity are applicable to a broad range of knowledge workers. The technology and methods for developing solutions reflect the quality and scope of available software and the cost/benefit from using it.

2. *Systems analyst.* "Systems analyst" is a common job title. It is sometimes combined with "programmer" to create the job title "programmer/ analyst." A systems analyst does requirements analysis and develops application designs. There is an emphasis on understanding the business and the requirements of application users. The resulting design should reflect both technical and organizational (social) knowledge. The interface design should reflect principles of human-machine interaction. Experience with individual systems provides a good introduction to the business considerations that motivate applications, the development of requirements, and the design of user interfaces.

3. *Programmer.* A programmer takes the specifications prepared by the systems analyst and writes and tests programs to meet the requirements. The programmer requires more detailed technical knowledge of program design, coding, and testing than a systems analyst. (This text provides

only a modest background for programming, including a short discussion of program structures, some exercises on programming, and some insight into the process of programming and testing.)

Consequently, the experience obtained in applying information technology to individual knowledge work needs (development in the small) provides a basis for more detailed study of programming, analysis, and application for large, complex systems.

Summary

◇ ◇

◇ Productivity is the theme of this text. It is also a common objective in society and in organizations. Knowledge workers are an interesting example of productivity improvement with information technology, because the improvements have generally been applied to increase work effectiveness, rather than decrease the number of employees. Although this text has focused on improving individual knowledge worker productivity, organizations are also concerned that investments in information technology will result in improved products, services, and business processes.

◇ A small system application development process is the basic approach to development and can be expanded to include the processes for development of larger, more complex multiuser applications. Prototyping is a key method for small systems, but it is also useful for large systems. Large application development methods are more formal and tools are more comprehensive.

◇ In working with the information systems function, it is helpful if the user/developer understands the concerns of specialists who recognize the value of user-developed systems, but are also aware of development process limitations. They have concerns related to the effects of individual systems, training and support problems, and the difficulties presented by incompatible systems.

◇ Those not intending to be information systems specialists will find that the perspectives and experiences of improving productivity with individual systems will aid them in being development team members in organizational projects and will help with information systems planning in their organizational function. For those who intend to become information systems specialists, the introduction to systems development processes provided by learning to develop individual systems is a natural entry point for further learning, leading to positions in user support, systems analysis, or programming.

EXERCISES

1. Identify the productivity effects of information technology as applied to a product, service, or business process with which you are familiar. How did the investment in information technology affect employment? How did it affect the product, service, employees, etc.?

2. Examine business processes with which you interact.
   a. Identify how information technology might change your part of the process. Explain how it would improve productivity or work quality.
   b. Look at the entire business process. Explain how information technology could change the process. Explain what changes would be necessary in the organization, the division of work, the information provided, and employee empowerment.

3. Examine a user-developed application. Then evaluate the following:
   a. The adequacy of the documentation for training and support.
   b. The likelihood that the application could be used by the successor in the position.
   c. Incompatibilities with organizational systems.

4. Make a personal career development plan as if you planned to be an information systems specialist. Define the type of specialists within information systems. Complete four columns:

Type of specialist	*Technical/process knowledge and experience needed*	*Current knowledge and experience*	*Need to do to meet needs*

5. Identify several critical incidents (good or bad) in your dealings with the information center (or other help) in your organization. Evaluate the fit of the help organization and the services available to meet your needs.

INDEX